BOMBER HARRIS

BOMBER HARRIS

Sir Arthur Harris' Despatch on War Operations 1942-1945

Introduced and compiled by
Martin Mace and John Grehan
With additional research by
Sara Mitchell

Pen & Sword
AVIATION

First published in Great Britain in 2014 by
Pen & Sword Aviation
an imprint of
Pen & Sword Books Ltd
47 Church Street
Barnsley
South Yorkshire
S70 2AS

ISBN 978 1 78303 298 3

Printed and bound in England
By CPI Group (UK) Ltd, Croydon, CR0 4YY

Pen & Sword Books Ltd incorporates the Imprints of
Pen & Sword Aviation, Pen & Sword Family History,
Pen & Sword Maritime, Pen & Sword Military, Pen & Sword Discovery,
Pen & Sword Politics, Pen & Sword Atlas, Pen & Sword Archaeology,
Wharncliffe Local History, Wharncliffe True Crime, Wharncliffe Transport,
Pen & Sword Select, Pen & Sword Military Classics, Leo Cooper,
The Praetorian Press, Claymore Press, Remember When,
Seaforth Publishing and Frontline Publishing.

For a complete list of Pen & Sword titles please contact:
PEN & SWORD BOOKS LIMITED
47 Church Street, Barnsley, South Yorkshire, S70 2AS, England
E-mail: enquiries@pen-and-sword.co.uk
Website: www.pen-and-sword.co.uk

CONTENTS

PREFACE

In this book two figures come together as they did in the Second World War, when the relationship was far from an easy one – Air Chief Marshal Harris and Group Captain Bufton.

If Arthur Harris was a towering wartime commander, the impact on the Bomber Offensive of Sidney Bufton, an acting Air Commodore at the end of the war, was substantial, but mostly achieved from a desk at the Air Ministry. He served there as Deputy Director of Bomber Operations from November 1941, being moved up to Director in March 1943 and retaining that post until 1945.

Bufton was an articulate and analytical ideas man and somebody who got things done. Whoever had been at the Air Ministry would have incurred the frequent displeasure of Harris – his personality and the situation he was in would have made sure of that – and there were others in London who came together with Bufton in the AOC-in-C's contemptuous references to "junior staff officers". However, the relationship between Harris and Bufton is perhaps particularly interesting.

Harris was capable of hyperbole and some may have crept in to the letter he wrote to "Peter" Portal, CAS, on 14 April 1944, in which he remarked that ideas from Bufton, "have been and still are rammed down our throats [at Bomber Command] whether we like them or not. I have personally considerable regard for his ability and honesty of purpose. … In practice he has been a thorn in our side and the personification of all that is un-understanding and unhelpful in our relations with the Air Staff … his name has become anathema to me and my senior staff."

Other passages in the letter might be argued to be insubordinate towards CAS. The idea of removing Harris did come to Portal from time to time, but he always saw the value of putting up with the difficulties, as well as recognising that such a plan would not be acceptable to the Prime Minister. Portal also highly valued "Sid" Bufton and, according to Denis Richards in *Portal of Hungerford*, even consulted him on whether to keep Harris in post. Bufton proved firmly in favour of the status quo.

At the time that "Bert" Harris wrote the letter, the main point of issue was the Pathfinder Force, something on which the clash between Harris and Bufton had previously been fundamental.

In his biography, *Bomber Harris his Life and Times*, Henry Probert wrote that Harris first heard of the proposal for such a force shortly after he had arrived at Bomber Command. Portal passed to him a letter from Lord Cherwell, close adviser to the Prime Minister, suggesting that one bomber group should be specifically given the task of target finding.

Portal seems to have been surprised by the determination of the opposition Harris mounted to the suggestion. For one thing Harris considered that if the cream of crews were skimmed for the chosen group from across the Command, as they would surely have to be, then the effect on the morale of the rest would be highly detrimental.

Bufton was a "convinced and courageous champion" (*The Strategic Air Offensive Against Germany,* Webster and Frankland) of such a force and would be credited by Portal with being its main architect at the Air Ministry.

Faced with Harris's opposition and that of his senior team (albeit expressed in the presence of Harris) Bufton made a move which would probably have riled a more placid Commander-in-Chief than Harris. Without telling Harris in advance, Bufton wrote to a significant number of his service contacts, plenty of them in Bomber Command, explaining his ideas on the subject of target marking and enclosing a questionnaire. He then showed the replies, endorsing specialised target marking, to Harris.

One of Bufton's reasons for taking this bold step (though the response from Harris was restrained) was his operational background in Bomber Command and his belief (not entirely fairly or logically held) that Harris and most of his close subordinates suffered in their decision-making because they lacked such recent experience.

Bufton had commanded 10 Squadron, flying nineteen operations in Whitleys, before moving to 76 Squadron, the second to fly the Halifax operationally, and commanding RAF Pocklington. He was awarded the DFC. His youngest brother, John, had been lost in a Hampden of 49 Squadron.

At a much higher level than Bufton, Harris lost the argument over what became the Pathfinders. However, as was often the case with him, he accepted the new situation with some grace, though certainly not enthusiasm.

On the first occasion that the new force operated Harris sent a message to Donald Bennett, whom he had selected to be its leader, rather than Basil Embry whose name had been put forward. Harris had served with them both, with Embry in Iraq and with Bennett amongst the flying boats at Pembroke Dock.

In part the message to Bennett read, "All the crews of Bomber Command now look to the Pathfinders for a lead to their future objectives which will ensure the maximum infliction of damage on the enemy with the greatest economy of force. They will I know not be disappointed. Good luck and good hunting."

Any situation involving two or more men or women needs to be considered against the background of their previous relationships. Sidney Bufton's comments in this book are, I suggest, the more interesting for knowing something of his previous dealings with Arthur Harris.

Today papers that belonged to Air Chief Marshal Sir Arthur Harris rest in the RAF Museum, Hendon, while a collection of Air Vice Marshal Bufton's papers and photographs, particularly relating to Bomber Command, can be found at the Churchill Archives Centre, Churchill College, Cambridge.

Geoff Simpson

LIST OF ILLUSTRATIONS

1   A portrait of Air Chief Marshal Sir Arthur Harris, Commander-in-Chief of Royal Air Force Bomber Command, seated at his desk at Bomber Command HQ, High Wycombe, 24 April 1944. (HMP)

2   A painting of Air Marshal Sir Arthur Harris that was completed circa 1943 at the instigation of the Ministry of Information. (The National Archives)

3   Aircrew under training in 1939 as part of the expansion of Bomber Command. At the start of the Second World War, Bomber Command faced four problems. The first was lack of size; Bomber Command was not large enough to effectively attack the enemy as a pure, stand-alone strategic force. The second was rules of engagement; at the start of the war, the targets allocated to Bomber Command were not wide enough in scope. The third problem was the Command's lack of technology; specifically radio or radar derived navigational aids to allow accurate target location at night or through cloud. The fourth problem was the limited accuracy of bombing, especially from high level, even when the target could be clearly located by the bomb aimer. (HMP)

4   Ground crew work on a pair of mines in front of 300 (Masovian) Squadron's Vickers Wellington Mk.X, HF598 'BH-E', at RAF Ingham, Lincolnshire. Note the Polish checkerboard on the nose and the fact that the left hand mine has the message "From Polish Airmen" chalked on it. Of the 48,060 air-dropped mines laid off the northern and western coasts of Europe, 47,152 had been laid by Bomber Command – these were termed as *Gardening* sorties. For the loss of around 500 aircraft, these mines sank over 700 enemy-controlled ships (nearly 700,000 tons) and damaged over 550 more. This amounted to some 40% of all German-controlled shipping, more than twice the figure lost to Royal Navy surface and submarine forces (ww2images)

5   A line-up of 408 Squadron Handley Page Hampdens about to be loaded with Mk.I Air Deployable Anti-Ship mines, November 1942. The aircraft in the background of this picture, taken at RAF Leeming, North Yorkshire, is P1166, KE-Q. By the end of the war, Bomber Command had run up an impressive tally

through its mine-laying work. Indeed, this could be considered one of the most successful campaigns of the Second World War. Every large, expensive enemy ship lost to mines cost the RAF 0.55 bombers. Compare this to the more well-known Coastal Command strike wings, which suffered 5.28 aircraft lost to every ship sunk while accounting for a smaller figure of 20% of German-controlled shipping losses. (ww2images)

6   A remarkable piece of wartime history, Avro Lancaster B Mk.VII NX611, *Just Jane*, is pictured being "bombed-up" at the Lincolnshire Aviation Heritage Centre at East Kirkby. Part of a batch of 150 B Mk VII Avro Lancasters destined to take part in the war against Japan as part of the RAF's Tiger Force in the Far East, Avro Lancaster B Mk VII NX611 was built by Austin Motors at Longbridge near Birmingham, in April 1945. (Courtesy of Gaz West)

7   Taken on 2 June 1944, by a photo-reconnaissance aircraft from No.106 (PR) Group, this image shows a small part of Bomber Command's contribution to the D-Day landings. It reveals the severely damaged railway yards and junction (top right) at Saumur, France, after an attack by fifty-eight Avro Lancasters of No.5 Group on the night of 1/2 June 1944. Seven days later, aircraft of 617 Squadron attacked a nearby railway tunnel, dropping the first 12,000lb Tallboy bombs that had been developed by Barnes Wallis. (HMP)

8   Members of RAF ground crew prepare a Short Stirling for its next mission. Designed and built by Short Brothers to an Air Ministry specification from 1936, the Stirling entered service in 1941. It was the first British four-engine heavy bomber of the Second World War. The Stirling had a relatively brief front line operational career as a bomber, being relegated to second line duties from 1943 onwards when other four-engine bombers, such as the Halifax and Lancaster, began being delivered. However, the Stirling provided vital service as a glider tug and resupply aircraft during the D-Day landings and subsequent Allied operations in Europe during 1944-1945. (HMP)

9   Ground crew loading containers filled with propaganda leaflets – "Nickels" – into the bomb bay of a Vickers Wellington. The Nickeling effort reached its peak in August 1942, when some 72,500,000 leaflets were dropped in just four weeks. The increasing strength of Bomber Command was one factor, another was that the leaflets were by then being dropped from containers in bomb bays, making the task much easier. Two months later, Operational Training Units began to supply aircraft for Nickeling, providing crews with valuable operational experience (HMP)

10   One of many. This photograph shows the wreckage of an RAF bomber that was shot down near Hanover, though the exact date, location, and identity of the aircraft and crew is unknown. The picture was received in the UK on 26 August 1940 via the US Clipper news service, having been released for publication a few days earlier by the Germans. (HMP)

of Holland. By the end of the war in Europe large sections of the Dutch population, particularly in the big cities, were starving. By April 1945, for many the daily ration was just "two potatoes (often bad), three slices of bread, a small quantity of meat substitute and a slice of skimmed milk cheese" – barely enough to survive on. This image shows a 150 Squadron Lancaster, 'IQ-Y' (JB613), flying low over the flooded Dutch countryside en route to deliver food aid. (ww2images)

17 Huge quantities of water pour through the breach in the Möhne Dam a few hours after the Dams Raid – an image which clearly shows the depth of water which was lost following the attack. As a result of this breach some 335 million tons of water flooded the West Ruhr valleys. In its path, this flood destroyed 125 factories, made some 3,000 hectares of arable land useless, demolished twenty-five bridges and badly damaged twenty-one more. The attack on the Ruhr dams, Operation *Chastise*, is arguably one of Bomber Command's best known missions of the war. (HMP)

18 This vivid night photograph shows a Handley Page Halifax of No.4 Group RAF Bomber Command silhouetted against the glare of more incendiary fires, releasing its bomb load through cloud during a successful night raid on Leipzig on 3/4 December 1943. (HMP)

19 Avro Lancaster ED749 pictured during a War Savings Campaign in Manchester during early August 1945. ED749 was one of the last production batch of 620 aircraft completing the final part of contract No.B69247, and was one of 135 Mk.Is from this batch – the remainder were delivered as Mk.IIIs. The first examples reached the RAF in November 1942, the order completed in June 1943 with an average production rate of twenty-five aircraft per week. (HMP)

20 During a raid on Hamburg on the night of 30/31 January 1943, the Pathfinder crews of Nos. 7 and 35 squadrons, from No.8 Group Bomber Command, carried out the first operational use of H2S, the airborne, ground scanning radar system, using the new device to mark the target. Although H2S would later become a more effective device, its use was not successful during this attack, despite the fact that Hamburg, situated by the coast and on a prominent river, was considered an ideal H2S target. Bombing was scattered over a wide area, with most of the bombs falling in the River Elbe or in the surrounding marshes. The image seen here depicts one of the 135 Lancasters involved over the target. The original caption states that the "silhouette of the aircraft was formed by a photographic flash, but owing to prolonged exposure light tracks caused by fires (A) and light flak (B) were superimposed on the detail photographed by the flash". The pilot of the photographing aircraft, Lancaster 'ZN-Y' of 106 Squadron, was Flight Lieutenant D.J. Shannon who, as a member of 617 Squadron, took part in Operation *Chastise* (the "Dams Raid") the following May.

21 A bomb-damaged street in Hamburg, May 1945. The Battle of Hamburg, *Operation Gomorrah*, was a campaign of air raids that began on 24 July 1943,

and lasted for eight days and seven nights. It was at the time the heaviest assault in the history of aerial warfare. The first attack on Hamburg included the first use of *Window*, small metallised strips, like tin foil, which when dropped from RAF bombers produced a gently drifting cloud of metallic strips that created confusing signals on German radar screens and concealed the position of the actual bombers. The results were dramatic. The entire German radar system was disrupted; British crews reported searchlights waving aimlessly, that the anti-aircraft fire was hesitant, and that the night-fighters were unusually ineffective. (HMP)

22   The successes of Bomber Command were purchased at terrible cost. Of every 100 airmen who joined Bomber Command, forty-five were killed, six were seriously wounded, eight became prisoners of war, and only forty-one escaped unscathed (at least physically). Of the 120,000 who served, 55,573 were killed. Of those who were flying at the beginning of the war, only ten percent survived to see the final victory. This telegram represents the death of one of the many aircrew who made the ultimate sacrifice: Lancaster navigator Flying Officer Donald Arthur Colombo. Donald was killed on 25 March 1944, whilst serving with 12 Squadron. The son of Frederick Alfred and Gertrude Louisa Colombo, of Ickenham, Uxbridge, Middlesex, he is buried in Berlin 1939-1945 War Cemetery. (HMP)

23   The city of Nuremberg was severely damaged by Allied bombing between 1943 and 1945. On 2 January 1945, the medieval city centre was systematically bombed by the RAF and USAAF, and about ninety percent of it was destroyed in only one hour. The attacks killed 1,800 residents and roughly 100,000 were displaced. In February 1945, additional attacks followed. In total, about 6,000 Nuremberg residents are estimated to have been killed in air raids. (NARA)

24   The devastated German city of Wesel pictured in May 1945, its centre completely destroyed by Allied bombing. Particularly because of the town's strategic position with bridges on the Rhine, Wesel soon found itself a target of the RAF and USAAF. The former, for example, undertook several attacks in February and March 1945. It was reported that 97% of the town was destroyed before it was finally taken by Allied troops and the population had fallen from almost 25,000 in 1939 to 1,900 in May 1945. Following the capture of Wesel, Field Marshal Montgomery stated that "the bombing of Wesel was a masterpiece, and was a decisive factor in making possible our entry into the town before midnight." (HMP)

25   The most controversial attack undertaken by Bomber Command during the war was that on Dresden. In four raids between 13 and 15 February 1945, 722 RAF and 527 USAAF bombers dropped more than 3,900 tons of bombs on the city, which at the time was the seventh largest in Germany and the largest un-bombed built-up area left. The resulting firestorm destroyed fifteen square miles of the city centre; between 22,000 and 25,000 people were killed (an investigation

conducted in 2010 on behalf of the Dresden city council stated that a maximum of 25,000 people were killed, of which 20,100 are known by name). Post-war debate of whether or not the attacks were justified has led to the bombing becoming one of the moral *cause célèbres* of the war. (Courtesy of Deutsche Fotothek)

26 A low-level oblique aerial photograph showing the damage caused to Frankfurt during the Second World War. By the time of the German surrender, the once famous medieval city centre (seen here with the Cathedral in the foreground), then the largest in Germany, had been destroyed. After the war, the official assessment of the damage caused to this city by the RAF and USAAF stated that between one and two thousand acres had been devastated. (HMP)

27 Pictured on 11 April 1945, RAF officers inspect an unfinished siege gun in a wrecked building of the Krupps armaments works at Essen, Germany, a principal target for Bomber Command throughout the war. The Krupps AG works at Essen, Germany, was seriously damaged by Bomber Command in 1943, and further wrecked in the daylight raid of 11 March 1945. (HMP)

28 A memorial dedicated to the men of 158 Squadron was unveiled in the village of Lissett, Yorkshire, on 17 May 2009. It depicts a life-size seven-man crew of a Halifax Bomber and has been cast in the same metal as the Angel of the North. The memorial carries the name of each of the 851 men from the squadron who were killed in operations during the Second World War. The squadron, which operated Halifaxes in Bomber Command for most of the war, was stationed at the No.4 Group airfield at Lisset between 28 February 1943 and 17 August 1945. (HMP)

29 The memorial to Marshal of the Royal Air Force Sir Arthur Harris BT, GCB, OBE, AFC, which is located in the Strand, London, outside St Clement Danes, the Central Church of the RAF. It was unveiled in 1992 by the Queen. (HMP)

30 Thousands of Bomber Command veterans and their relatives together with twelve members of the Royal family were present as Her Majesty the Queen unveiled the Bomber Command Memorial in London's Green Park on 28 June 2012. Made from Portland stone, the Memorial, a model of which is seen here, was designed by architect Liam O'Connor.

31 The central bronze sculpture, created by Philip Jackson, which, depicting seven airmen, lies at the heart of the Bomber Command Memorial in Green Park. Above them a small section of the Memorial is open to the sky, allowing light to fall directly on the aircrew. For Bomber Command the deaths in action began with the loss of Wellingtons and Blenheims on the night of 3/4 September 1939, and ceased more than five and a half years later, after two Halifaxes from 199 Squadron at North Creake and a Mosquito from 169 Squadron at Great Massingham failed to return on the night of 2/3 May 1945. (www.shutterstock.com)

LIST OF GRAPHS

Authors' Notes

The objective of this book is to reproduce Sir Arthur Harris' despatch on Bomber Command's war operations between 1942 and 1945, as well as supporting documents by Group Captain S.O. Bufton and others, as they appeared when presented to the Air Ministry almost seventy years ago. Consequently, they have not been modified, edited or interpreted in any way.

Harris' despatch is therefore his original and unique words of how he perceived the bombing campaign following his appointment. In order to retain the authenticity of the documents that follow, any grammatical or spelling errors have been left uncorrected. The only concession that we have made relates to the footnotes. Where Harris' despatch, in its final form, used symbols, we have introduced numbers.

Finally, as was common practice at the time, Harris (and others) used numerous abbreviations in his despatch, some of which may not be immediately obvious to the reader. We have, therefore, included a full explanation of these.

SECTION 1

INTRODUCTION

At the end of the Second World War, the detailed summaries of the wartime operations from senior officers of every major military, naval and air force command were published as Despatches in *The London Gazette*. There was, however, one despatch that was conspicuous by its absence – that of Bomber Command. No-one could deny that Bomber Command had made a major contribution to the defeat of Germany, yet the words of its leader, Air Chief Marshal Sir Arthur Harris, were never officially laid before the British people.

Harris did in fact produce a despatch, as had the other service chiefs. This covered the period from February 1942 through to May 1945, though some of the views he put forward he had held consistently throughout, and even before, his time at Bomber Command. However, even the question of whether a despatch needed to be published was a difficult one.

"The general Air Council line about the publication of Service despatches is that they are something of an anachronism and that the most suitable way of making public official accounts of the recent war would be to wait for the 'preliminary' war histories which should be ready within the next year or two," explained Sir Arthur Tedder, Chief of the Air Staff, on 5 October 1947. "We were, however, committed by a statement made by the Prime Minister in reply to a Parliamentary Question in August, 1945, to the publication of despatches of general interest."

"Apart from Lord Dowding's despatch on the Battle of Britain," he continued, "we have so far confined ourselves to publishing despatches required to balance those published by the other two Service Departments ... The Bomber Command despatch is not required to balance any individual despatches by other Services. It might, however, be argued that in the broader sense it balances despatches on many other campaigns and that, since so many other Service despatches are being published, the absence of any dealing with Bomber Command operations would be most noticeable."

By this stage, of course, Harris had already written his despatch – "In conformity with Kings Regulations and Air Council Instructions, paragraph 47b, I have the honour to submit my Despatch on the War Operations undertaken by Bomber Command from the 23rd February, 1942, when I assumed command, to the 8th May, 1945, when warlike operations were concluded," he wrote in his covering letter on 18 December 1945.

After the completion of this monumental report in October 1945, which amounted to more than 150,000 words, 100 copies had been reproduced and bound by His Majesty's Stationery Office. Of this number, it was reported on 13 March 1946, five had been forwarded to the Air Ministry and five allocated to H.Q. Bomber Command. The remaining ninety copies were circulated among a selection of Air Ministry officials and senior RAF officers for their comments. They rapidly drew a response.

For the researcher, much of the communication that resulted from the distribution of these copies provides a fascinating insight into Harris' despatch and the wartime service of Bomber Command. Thankfully, many of the letters and reports that resulted from the consultation survive and can be found in one file, which has the reference AIR 2/9726, at The National Archives at Kew.

One of the first objections to Harris' despatch was that the "Mosquito Force", as it was referred to, was not mentioned in the main body of the text, only in the appendices. One correspondent, the Assistant Chief of the Air Staff Air Vice-Marshal Thomas Williams, bluntly pointed out on 4 February 1947, that the "despatch itself does scant justice to the Mosquito Bombing Force".

Williams substantiated his remark by adding the following: "This force of 8 squadrons operated in almost all weather conditions, a sustained effort far in excess of that of the Heavy Squadrons; it maintained the bombing of Germany (chiefly Berlin) during the long period when the Heavy effort was diverted to OVERLORD. One of the squadrons carried out 136 raids on Berlin, and at one period Berlin was attacked on 36 consecutive nights. This sustained, though relatively small scale, effort of attack must have done much to break the spirit and sleep of the Berliners. The Mosquito Bombing Force also carried out a most successful low-level mining attack on the Kiel Canal causing a congestion of shipping at Kiel for several weeks, at a period when the enemy transportation system was heavily overloaded."

Elsewhere in his despatch, Harris wrote that there was insufficient provision of airfields and that the Works Directorate suffered "from lack of experience and supervisory personnel". Another of his criticisms was that he believed his aircraft were constantly being diverted from their main job of destroying the enemy's will and capacity to resist in favour of "targets of secondary importance which are causing annoyance to one or other Government Department".

In his despatch Harris also complained about armament design for his aircraft which "showed throughout a standard of incompetence which had the most serious repercussions on the efficiency and effectiveness of the Bomber Offensive". He then recommended "the most drastic overhaul of the design personnel concerned and the organisation responsible". Having read and digested his copy, this caused the Director General Armaments to object, writing that "this sweeping attack is ill-founded and entirely unjustified when it is examined in detail".

In his criticisms, Harris devoted considerable space to his complaints about "loose talk" concerning planned flying. This meant, Harris explained, "organised flying", and its aim was to produce a given number of serviceable aircraft at any specified time by staggering the servicing of aircraft in relation to the maximum capacity of the service personnel. This would seem to make sense, allowing consistent effort against the enemy. Harris saw this quite differently.

"The general application of planned flying, to the Main Force Squadrons, would have meant nothing less than an artificial restriction of effort, since the opportunities provided by the weather, both at base and en route to the target, was for a long time the most important factor in heavy bomber operations. The ultimate effect of 'planned flying' if applied to Bomber Command as a whole might have been a somewhat accelerated expansion, but this would have increased the shortage of airfields, etc., and have certainly been accompanied by a considerable reduction in the weight of bombs dropped on the enemy. This, in turn, would have led to a prolongation of the War."

There were also problems with some of the figures and numbers used by Harris which did not tally with the official records. This was, in particular, regarding the success of Area Bombing. Harris devoutly believed in such tactics when many opposed it on both moral grounds and in terms of its effectiveness. The debate over the effectiveness of Area Bombing was to continue long after the war. Indeed, it does to this day.

Fighter Command also complained that Harris had given little credit to the support the fighters gave the bombers or indeed to the intruder missions Fighter Command undertook into Europe. Air Chief Marshal Sir Roderic Hill wrote that Bomber Command "could never have been waged as a war winning factor without the fighter defence which kept its bases surprisingly secure, which practically eliminated enemy reconnaissance, which made such an important contribution in the form of intruders to frustrating the enemy defences at night, and which later escorted the bombers to their objectives during their daylight operations".

Hill was just as upset in that Harris' despatch implied that Bomber Command alone planned the operations into Germany, which Hill pointed out were jointly arranged. He declared that the only reason it was thought that Bomber Command were given the credit for planning the raids was because they had "the better propaganda machine".

As a result of such opposition, the Vice Chief of the Air Staff considered it "undesirable" that the despatch should be circulated outside the Air Ministry until these and other issues that Harris had raised in the document were resolved.

Amongst the other issues raised was the question of security. A very considerable proportion of the despatch concerned technical matters relating to the use and development of a strategic bombing force. These were all contained within the appendices which amount to around two-thirds of the entire despatch. So specific was Harris' information it was believed that it would be of great assistance to an enemy country in developing a strategic bomber force. By this time the enemy was the Soviet Union and the shivery blast of the Cold War was being felt across Europe.

The consequences of publishing Harris' despatch, the Chief of the Air Staff, Sir Arthur Tedder, wrote in October 1947, would be that: "Our ability to counter Russia's weight of numbers by our greater technical skill would be thereby reduced."

Tedder went on to explain this at length: "During the war the Russian long-range bomber force was employed almost exclusively in a tactical role. On the few occasions when an attempt was made to use it in a strategic role, the results were extremely poor owing to a lack of technical aids, the low state of training of crews and a lack of strategic vision on the part of the controlling authorities."

The only way that Russia could threaten the UK was through aerial attack and, as Tedder pointed out, the Soviets had made "strong efforts" to build up their strategic bomber force, particularly displaying "extraordinary progress" in constructing heavy bombers. "The publication of the Harris Despatch in its entirety would be to hand them on a plate much of the fruits of our own experience," continued Tedder. "Close attention to the lessons of the Despatch would save the Russians from making a number of mistakes in the organisation and training of their Strategic Air Force, and this would save them an incalculable amount of time."

Whilst this was eminently sensible at the time – as the Soviet threat was considered to be real as the Cold War was developing – there was also a public clamour for a despatch on Bomber Command as there had been for the other services. There was already considerable disquiet over the apparent lack of recognition of Bomber Command's contribution to the war. In particular, the attention given to those of Fighter Command who had flown in the brief period of the Battle of Britain compared with the seemingly official disregard of the prolonged effort of those in Bomber Command was already the subject of much anger. Not to publish a despatch on Bomber Command might create even more resentment.

It was widely believed that Harris' Area Bombing tactics, which had inevitably resulted in heavy civilian casualties, were the reason for this apparent official disapprobation. Though, as Harris points out at the start of his despatch, his remit (under General Directive No.5 (S.46368/111. D.C.A.S) when he was appointed to Bomber Command was, "to focus attacks on the morale of the enemy civil population, and, in particular, of the industrial workers". The objectives set for Harris were, as he wrote, quiet clear:

"The ultimate aim of the attack on a town area is to break the morale of the population which occupies it. To ensure this we must achieve two things; first, we must make the town physically uninhabitable and, secondly, we must make the people conscious of constant personal danger. The immediate aim is, therefore, twofold, namely, to produce (i) destruction, and (ii) the fear of death."

Against such a background, Harris had done what had been asked, indeed ordered of him. His crime, if there was one, in the eyes of some, was that he had been too successful in his destruction of German towns and cities. As is well known, after the destruction of Hamburg in July 1943, Albert Speer told Hitler that a repetition of such an attack upon another six cities would bring about a rapid end to the war. Times though had changed, and such tactics were the cause of some embarrassment to politicians seeking reconciliation across Europe, and who, no doubt, sought the moral high ground in their relations with former Axis countries.

The Air Ministry responded in the form of an Air Staff Memorandum, and circulated it to those officials that had already been sent a copy of the despatch. This was, in reality, nothing more than a rebuttal of most of Harris' criticisms. Whilst acknowledging that the despatch was "a lengthy, interesting, and valuable record of the achievements of and methods adopted by Bomber Command", it noted that it included a large number of Harris' personal opinions, which the Air Ministry felt were incorrect.

Predictably, the first comments refer to Harris' above claim that his instructions were to bomb the enemy's civilian population. As this was no longer politically acceptable the Air Ministry sought to deny responsibility.

"Air Ministry intention was always to return to the bombing of precise targets as quickly as the tactical capabilities of the bomber force, and the improvement of night bombing techniques, would permit," ran the wording of the Memorandum. "The earlier directives to Bomber Command were, in fact, based on the attack of precise targets, but precise bombing in 1940 and 1941, owing to the development of enemy defences, became increasingly ineffective."

The authors of the memorandum then went on to explain that from as early as 1941 the Air Ministry had been pressing Bomber Command to improve its accuracy by developing the Pathfinder Force that Harris persistently tried to resist, delaying its introduction by six months. The authors also point out that in the Area Bombing Directive certain targets were specified in order of priority. These targets included industrial areas, dockyards and aircraft factories. Such targets would, of course, be considered legitimate and morally justifiable. Harris makes no mention of these targets, merely emphasising the aspects of the Directive he felt supported his policies. The Air Ministry concluded: "The point of these comments is to stress the fact that while the Air Staff had accepted, temporarily, the need to concentrate efforts on area targets, it hoped later ... to be able to revert to the attack of precise targets." The implication is that Harris exceeded his orders. Harris does in fact list the Directives he was issued in Appendix L of his despatch, though, as we shall shortly learn, not quite in their entirety. The Air Staff Memorandum, which is reproduced in full, can be found in the second section of this book before the full transcript of Harris' despatch (the third section).

Not all of those who read the despatch when it was circulated were opposed to Harris' despatch. Amongst those that supported its publication was Air Vice-Marshal J.W. Baker (who had finished the war as Air Officer Commanding No.12 Group before, in 1946, he became Director-General of Personnel).

"The Marshal was never one to mince matters," Baker wrote on 10 September 1946, "and I am sure his Despatch would lose much of its historical value and interest if we watered down too far the forthright language he has used throughout. We must, of course, check facts and qualify statements where these are incorrect; but it is easy to be wise after the event and in would be the greatest pity if we failed to give the C-in-C full credit for the immense personal contribution he made in building up the bomber offensive in the face of such immense difficulties. However unpalatable some of the Marshal's opinions may be, they deserve a niche in history."

Baker does make one important point regarding Harris' choice of targets. He points out that in Harris' citing of Directive S.46368/111, he does not include the instructions regarding "transportation and morale". This, Baker believed, "was regarded as the long term basis for the offensive whenever we could concentrate the Command on its main task". He also uses Harris' own statistics to show that the big fall in German production took place from July 1944 onwards when the words "Communication attacks" were included in the resumption of the offensive on German industry after the support for the D-Day landings had ceased.

Equally, Air Marshal the Honourable Sir Ralph Cochrane, who at the time was Air Officer Commanding at RAF Transport Command, believed that the despatch "provides a very fair summing up of the situation". To this he added, "subject to the deletion of one or two matters of domestic concern only, I should have thought it entirely suited for publication".

Cochrane was also highly supportive of Harris' tactics: "It was not until air power was brought to bear in full strength in 1944, that the power of destruction decisively overtook the enemy's power of reconstruction. The collapse quickly followed and preceded the invasion of German territory. I cannot therefore see that the concluding paragraphs of the Bomber Command despatch can be seriously gainsaid, or that it is unreasonable to think that had bombardment on this scale started a year earlier, a result similar to that in Japan [surrender without the need for a ground invasion] would have been achieved."

In direct contrast to Baker's (and others') opinion that attacks on communications proved more effective than area targets, Cochrane wrote the following: "At a later stage we were able to turn to transportation, in its broadest sense. From this, of course, people are apt to argue that transportation should have been the aim throughout the war, but in doing so they neglect firstly, our inability to hit targets, and secondly, the tremendous resources of the enemy for the repair of damage ... and it seems obvious that with the forces available [to Bomber Command] in the first four years of the war, a position would soon have been reached when he could have repaired the damage as quickly as we could have inflicted it, and we should have got nowhere."

The most detailed analysis of the despatch, however, was undertaken by Group Captain S.C. Bufton, who, like Baker, was a Director of Bomber Operations under Harris. In his report, dated 28 December 1946, Bufton described the despatch as being "well presented, comprehensive, and supported by a wealth of statistics and technical information". He accepted that it was written from a Bomber Command perspective and therefore tended, as he put it, "to find virtue at home, and all waywardness elsewhere". What Bufton strove to achieve in his observations was "to strike the right balance." His report, amounting to fifty-nine paragraphs, is considered of such value that it can be found here in its entirety in the fourth section of this book.

All of the arguments for and against public publication of the despatch were considered by Tedder. In his report of 5 October 1947, he stated that "as reasons for not publishing it has been argued a) that the Harris despatch is erroneous in a number of respects; and b) that it contains strongly expressed criticism of the Air Ministry.

"As regards a)," he continued, "it has always been recognised that a despatch represents the personal views of the Commander-in-Chief in the light of the information available to him at the time it was written; and statements now known to erroneous can, if necessary, be dealt with in footnotes. As regards b), the body of the despatch contains little to which exception need be taken, and I feel that there is no reason why Sir Arthur Harris should not agree to any minor deletions for which we might ask.

"The really controversial matter is contained in Appendix C. In paragraph 8 of the main report, Sir Arthur Harris states that: 'A study of these appendices is essential to a proper understanding of the course of operations summarised in this respect.' The procedure governing the publication of despatches, which was agreed by the Prime Minister and promulgated by the Cabinet Office in January 1946, lays down that appendices to despatches will not normally be published.

"I do not consider that the appendices would be needed in any published version of this despatch, and in any case I consider that there would be insuperable security objections to making these appendices public." The appendices, therefore, had become, for a number of reasons, a major stumbling block to the publication of Harris' despatch.

That said, Tedder's report went to on to summarise other issues. "The story of Bomber Command throughout the war is a single story; no despatches have been written for the period before February 1942, and it would be wrong to single out for publication the story of the last three years only – even though they were the three years in which the power of Bomber Command was really felt."

The Chief of the Air Staff even considered whether the general public needed any more information. "I consider that the public will receive sufficient information about Bomber Command's share in the war from the following sources: a) Harris's own book 'Bomber Offensive'; b) Mr Trevor Roper's popular version of the Report of the British Bombing Survey Unit analysing the results of our bombing. This should be available within the next few months; c) The Air volumes of the Preliminary Official Service Histories of the War, which may be published in a year or so."

Adding a note of caution, Tedder added that "we cannot discount the possibility that there will be some public demand for the publication of the Harris despatch. There have been suggestions in the Press that Bomber Command's contribution to victory has been insufficiently recognised by H.M.G. It is also true that past and present members of Bomber Command have expressed disappointment at the non-publication of this despatch."

Tedder drew his report to a close with this final conclusion and recommendation: "I accordingly submit for your approval that the despatch by Sir Arthur Harris should not be published."

When it had first been intimated that Harris' despatch might not be published, the Permanent Air Secretary, C.G. Caines, had made the following remarks: "I understand that it is not proposed to classify Air Chief Marshal Harris' report as a despatch for publication in *The London Gazette*, and I am sure that this is right. As, however, reports which are classified as despatches are normally published, it may avoid misunderstanding if it is described as a report rather than a despatch."

On 26 November 1947, a letter was sent to Harris via his bank in Cape Town, South Africa, concerning the "vexed" question of publication. Though it was accepted that "it is vitally important that the public really knows what airpower in general and

Bomber Command in particular did to win the last war," there remained unresolved problems.

"Briefly, the decision whether to publish your dispatch must hinge on whether it is possible to publish its appendices," Harris was told, because there were two "snags". "Firstly there is the formal difficulty that the Cabinet have decided against the publication of appendices to despatches. Secondly, even if it were possible to make an exception to that general rule in this special case, there are frankly still insurmountable security objections."

The author (who signed himself as "Tirpitz" and is believed to be Group Captain James "Tirpitz" Tait) argues that whilst it may be thought that by the time another war happens the Second World War would be only of academic interest, "I wish I felt so optimistic. As things are in the world at present I am quite sure we can't afford to take a chance or risk giving someone else a first class correspondence course in the training and conduct of strategic air warfare."

As the appendices represented such a large, and important, proportion of the despatch, Harris' view was that it was a case of all or nothing. This put the ball squarely back into the Air Ministry's court, as C.G. Caines explained: "We should, I think, be letting ourselves in for a controversy, the bitterness of which will be realised by all who know Sir Arthur Harris, if we attempt to disregard his view on this."

The debate regarding publication rumbled on until 22 December 1949, when the final decision was made. "The Air Council consider that there are insuperable security objections to the publication of the Appendices to the Despatch, and have decided that since the Appendices are essential to a proper understanding of the operations described in the Despatch, it is preferable that there should be no publication of the Despatch by itself. Marshal of the Air Force Sir Arthur Harris has been consulted and has expressed his agreement with the decision."

So, that was it. The despatches from Dowding of Fighter Command, and many of those of the admirals and generals that had led the United Kingdom's armed forces to their greatest victory, were published for all to read in *The London Gazette*. Together they formed a unique and utterly invaluable record of, and tribute to, the immense effort of the hundreds of thousands of men and women involved in the Second World War – except those of Bomber Command which made, many would consider, one of the greatest contributions of all.

The debate over the Harris despatch was, of course, conducted according to the culture of the 1940s. Coming to these matters nearly seventy years later we have been struck by the relative lack of reference to the considerable loss of life which the German civilian population suffered. There is also scant acknowledgement of the deaths (huge in proportion to the number of men deployed) that were suffered by Bomber Command. While historians must place themselves in the mindset of the period they are studying, it is safe to suggest that the human cost would loom larger in a similar debate about war in the 21st century.

Martin Mace and John Grehan
Storrington, 2013

SECTION 2

AIR STAFF MEMORANDUM ON THE DESPATCH

BY AIR CHIEF MARSHAL SIR ARTHUR HARRIS GCB. OBE. AFC ON BOMBER COMMAND'S OPERATIONS 1942-1945

GENERAL OBSERVATIONS

1. The Despatch by Air Chief Marshal Sir Arthur Harris on the operations of Bomber Command, of which a factual "digest" has already been given a limited circulation, is a lengthy, interesting, and valuable record of the achievements of and methods adopted by Bomber command during World War II. It contains, however, in addition to the narrative of the work of the Command, a number of statements, opinions, and criticisms, from the personal standpoint of the Commander-in-Chief, which call for comment.

2. Since the initial circulation of the "digest", the despatch has been examined in detail by Air Ministry Departments, also by various senior officers who were concerned with the work of the Command, and it is considered necessary for the following comments by the Air Staff, which amplify some and correct others of the statements made, to be read in conjunction with the report.

3. In the first place, it must be appreciated that the conclusions drawn by the Commander-in-Chief, and his summing-up of the effects of the bombings were necessarily based on the limited amount of evidence available in 1945, when the despatch was prepared. Since that time, the results of Bomber Command's operations have been subjected to analysis by the British Bombing Survey Unit, which does not confirm certain of the C-in-C's conclusions, and places a different complexion upon others.

4. It is not the function of this memorandum to deal in detail with this important

aspect of the subject, which is fully covered by the B.B.S.U. Report; but students of the operations should note that the despatch tends to attribute greater losses to German war production as a result of area attack on industrial cities than later investigation has disclosed. The opinions recorded in Part III of the Despatch, some of the conclusions in Part IV, and certain of the statistics and graphs in Part V must therefore be regarded with reserve, and action should not be based upon them. Graph No.9, in particular, is based on an incorrect hypothesis and must be ignored. Final Judgements on the effects of the bombing – a highly intricate subject – can only be made in the light of the British and American Bombing Survey Reports.

5. In the second place, readers of the despatch should appreciate that the drastic criticisms of certain policy decisions and other matters which appear therein give only one side of the picture, and that there are other aspects which need to be given equal prominence. The following detailed comments from the Air Staff point of view should therefore be read in conjunction with the relevant paragraphs of the despatch, which are quoted.

DETAILED COMMENTS

PART I.
INTRODUCTION

6. The C-in-C. states, in paragraph 3, that his main task was "to focus attacks on the morale of the enemy civil population, and, in particular, of the industrial workers" through the attack of certain industrial centres.

7. It will be observed that similar emphasis on the attack of industrial centres is conspicuous throughout the despatch, and it is considered that the C-in-C's brief summary of the Air Ministry directive of February 1942 tends to obscure the fact that the Air Staff intention was always to return to the bombing of precise targets as quickly as the tactical capabilities of the bomber force, and the improvement of night bombing technique, would permit. The earlier directives to Bomber Command were, in fact, based on the attack of precise targets, but precise bombing in 1940 and 1941, owing to the development of enemy defences, became increasingly ineffective.

8. From as early as 1941 (see paras. 17 to 23 hereunder) the Air Staff had been pressing Bomber Command to improve the effectiveness of night bombing by the adoption of the large scale use of flares and the formation of a target-finding force, but the Command evinced considerable reluctance to do this, and it is clear from correspondence between the Air Ministry and the C-in-C. that he had little faith in the value of attacking precise targets.

9. At the beginning of 1942, a rapid development of tactical ability was considered to be immediately practicable, and this was envisaged and implied in the wording of the directive of February 14th, 1942. With this in mind, various specific targets, in

order of priority, were also included in the Directive. No mention of this, however, is made in paras. 3, 4 or 5 of the despatch.

10. The point of these comments is to stress the fact that while the Air Staff had accepted, temporarily, the need to concentrate effort on area targets, it hoped later, when the bomber force had become large enough to achieve the requisite degree of concentration, and when night bombing technique had been sufficiently improved, to be able to revert to the attack of precise targets.

PART II.
THE COURSE OF THE CAMPAIGN – 1942/1945

Paragraph 14.

11. In this paragraph the C-in-C. comments that the Command was "expected" to destroy completely Essen and other centres within three months, but he does not explain sufficiently fully the reasons this could not be done, which are referred to at paragraphs 12 to 15 hereunder. Moreover, the word "expected" hardly conveys the intention.

12. The Air Staff, naturally, had to define the object of the attacks, which was as stated, and as to method, they sent as a guide an estimate by the Air Warfare Analysis Section of the tonnage required to do effective damage. They also advanced the principle that this estimated tonnage should be concentrated on one target before proceeding to the next. It was fully appreciated that only a proportion of the force would have "Gee", and for this reason Bomber Command was urged in the directive to develop tactical methods which would confer the benefit of the available equipment upon the force as a whole (i.e. the flare dropping and the target-finding force which they had already been pressed to adopt).

Paragraphs 15/19.

13. It was felt by the Air Staff that the "Crackers" experiment to investigate the possibilities of flare concentrations was not sufficiently exhaustive to find the right solution. Only two trials were made, one being unsuccessful owing to a "Gee" ground station failure, and in these the flares were dropped in long sticks, on a "Gee" reading. A better idea of the potentialities of the scheme might have been given if more experiments had been carried out with, for example, concentrations rather than sticks, variations in the fuse settings to find optimum burning heights, visual dropping after the first accurate illumination of the target, etc. This opinion was supported by the crews carrying out the trials, at their interrogation, which was attended by an Air Staff officer from the Air Ministry.

14. The opinion of the Air Staff was that difficulties referred to in paragraphs 16/19, at least apart from purely blind bombing, could have been overcome to a considerable extent had the following action been taken:-

(a) if the optimum employment of flares had been fully determined.

(b) if a target finding force had been formed to drop the flares on the basis of a carefully devised and developed technique relying on flares dropped by "Gee" to locate the area, visually dropped flare concentrations to illuminate the target for bombing, followed by the laying of an initial and substantial concentration of incendiaries on the target. This concentration of incendiaries would not have been so vulnerable to decoys or jettisoned loads.

15. The system adopted, nominated crews throughout the Command dropping long sticks of flares on "Gee" readings, failed to produce the required results. It should be noted, in this connection, that the principle which had been recommended from November 1941, of finding the target with selected flare dropping crews and then maintaining an effective flare concentration over it, was tried out by the Pathfinder Force in the middle of September 1942, and is referred to by C-in-C. at paragraph 20 of Appendix B. of the despatch as "a marked advance." The Air Staff considered that this principle could and should have been thoroughly tried out and adopted at the "Crackers" stage.

Paragraph 19.

16. The C-in-C., at the end of this paragraph, deprecates, by implication, the delay in the supply of marker bomb, for which he had asked in March 1942, having urged its development several years previously. It must not be assumed that the potentialities of such a weapon were not fully appreciated by the Air Ministry at the time, but all ideas on the subject had been ruled out as impracticable owing to ease of simulation or some other obvious defect. In the event, a great share of the credit for the eventual solution of the problem should go to an officer on the Air Staff at the Air Ministry who flew as an observer on the first "Gee" raid on Essen on March 8/9th 1942, and came back with the conviction that a full stick of incendiaries, if coloured, would defy effective simulation. As a result of investigations into this possible solution of the problem, it was found that, while it was not practicable to colour the 4lb. I.Bs, 250 lbs bomb cases which could tail eject pyrotechnic candles were a practicable proposition and would serve the purpose equally well if dropped in sticks. With the enthusiastic co-operation of M.A.P., this important link in the P.F.F. chain was quickly developed to the operational stage.

Paragraph 20.

17. The Air Staff cannot accept this description of the circumstances attending the

formation of the Pathfinder Force. Nor can they agree with the suggestion that a better solution would have emanated from Bomber Command if they had been given a free hand. The argument may appear plausible, but it is, in fact, misleading, as it neglects to give due weight to the time factor.

18. The Air Staff discussed with members of Bomber Command staff in November 1941, the idea of forming a special target finding force. The C-in-C. later held a conference with his Group Commanders on the subject, at which (as also at later ones) the proposal was turned down unanimously. It must be pointed out, however, that this major and purely tactical problem was discussed, and a decision made, in the absence of any person from the Command with the relevant operational experience. The only officer present with experience of night bombing was an Air Ministry Air Staff Officer who was attending as an observer, and he felt strongly that if the issue had been put fairly and squarely to a conference of experienced operational personnel, the opposite decision must have been reached. The matter was considered of such importance that, shortly afterwards, in order to confirm this opinion, the scheme was outlined, separately and individually, to some 12-16 of the most experienced operational officers in Bomber Command, who were found to be, without exception, enthusiastically in favour of it.

19. The C-in-C. states that his contention that each Group should find and maintain its own Pathfinder Force was proved infinitely the superior method when tried out in No.5 Group. It is perhaps arguable that when, towards the end of the war, some two years after the P.F.F. controversy, the tactical situation and the increased size of the bomber force made the attack of more than one target necessary, no great harm would have come of allocating portions of the P.F.F. to individual groups, as a basic technique susceptible to modification in the light of any new developments, would then have been developed. But that is a very different thing from initiating the force in that way in 1942, when no technique had as then been evolved, and the supply of the essential new equipment was limited. It is the view of the Air Staff that had the P.F.F. been split up at that time, the rapid development of technique which was achieved, and the highly effective series of attacks of 1943/1944, would not have been possible.

20. The statement that "the Commander-in-Chief was over ruled at the dictation of junior staff officers in the Air Ministry" must, of course, be refuted. The idea of a Pathfinder Force (and its accompaniment of a Bomber Development Unit) was fully discussed within the Air Staff and with Bomber Command. The arguments for and against were carefully weighed by the Air Staff, after which the Chief of the Air Staff, after full consideration and discussion with the C-in-C, finally decided in favour of the scheme. In this connection, it is interesting to note that some six months after the formation of the P.F.F. in August 1942, the C-in-C himself, in a letter to the Air Ministry dated January 6th, 1943, requested that the P.F.F. should be formed into a separate Pathfinder Group, and formal Air Ministry approval to this step was given on January 28th, 1943.

21. But for this prolonged discussion, the P.F.F. might have been formed at least six months before it was – in August 1942. Had it been, it would have had the

advantages of unjammed "Gee", and the good weather of the summer to give it a good start. Nevertheless, its formation was fully justified by results, as within four months it had brought to light many points of operational importance, and it was formed in time to enable OBOE, the marker bomb, and H2S to be immediately and effectively exploited.

22. Towards the end of paragraph 20, the C-in-C remarks that the success of the P.F.F. was limited. Presumably he means over the remainder of 1942. Some reasons for this are given in Appendix B para. 23, and it should be noted that one of the main reasons was the failure to build up the force from the best crews in the Command.

23. A reference is also made in paragraph 20 to the P.F.F. being a "corps d'elite", this term having been frequently used in arguments against its formation. It was pointed out, at the time, however, by the C.A.S., that the corps d'elite principle was only bad when all units had the same job. The Target Finding Force had a different job, and was therefore to be regarded as a specialist force, and not a "corps d'elite".

Paragraph 45.

24. The Air Staff were, in fact, strongly opposed to the proposal, (which emanated from the Admiralty) that the Biscay ports and towns containing U-boat installations should be destroyed, for the reason that such heavy destruction of French life and property could not materially affect the U-boat operations. In the end, it was decided that a controlled experiment should be made against one or two of the targets, Lorient and St. Nazaire being selected. After examination of the results, which confirmed the Air Ministry contention that U-boat activity would not be materially affected, further attacks of this kind were abandoned.

Paragraph 135.

25. It is felt that the significance of this large scale operation against enemy positions South and East of Caen is somewhat obscured by the description of one of its small tactical effects. This operation was the first of a type advocated by the Air Staff in collaboration with the War Office and adopted by 21 Army Group i.e. a combined operation in which the Army plan was made dependent upon the execution of the air plan. The basis of the air plan was the concentration of a maximum scale of heavy bomber effort on a limited and dense sector of the enemy front, as opposed to the sporadic light scale and dispersed effort which had previously been the rule. The attacks described in the preceding paragraphs 130/134 were of the then more usual type in which the army called for heavy bomber support as and when it encountered difficulties. Subsequent attacks of the new type included the American heavy bomber attack at St. Lo, which preceded the big break-through.

The Mosquito Bomber Force

26. It is felt that the Mosquito Bomber Force, which is not mentioned in the body of the despatch, deserves a somewhat fuller statement of its achievements than is provided in the brief references in Appendix B (paras 49/51) and Appendix D (paras 86/90).

27. This force of 8 squadrons operated in almost all weather, at a sustained effort far in excess of that of the Heavy Bomber Squadrons, and maintained the bombing of Germany (chiefly Berlin) during the long period when the Heavy Bomber effort was devoted to "Overlord". One of the squadrons carried out 136 raids on Berlin, and at one period Berlin was attacked on 36 consecutive nights. The Mosquito Bombing Force also carried out a highly successful low level mining attack on the Kiel Canal, causing a congestion of shipping at Kiel for several weeks at a period when the enemy transportation system was heavily overloaded.

PART III.
SUMMARY OF THE BOMBING EFFORT AND RESULTS

28. As pointed out in paragraphs 3 and 4 of these notes, final judgment in respect of the effects of the bombing must have regard to the British and American Bombing Survey Units' Reports. Paragraphs 175-194 of this part of the despatch must therefore be regarded with considerable reserve.

Leaflet Dropping

29. It is felt that no adequate account is included in the despatch of the large part played by Bomber Command in the propaganda campaign against enemy occupied Europe, during which many millions of leaflets were dropped. These operations were of considerable importance.

PART IV.
CONCLUSIONS

30. It has already been pointed out that final conclusions must take into account the results of the surveys by the British and American Bombing Survey Units; and that detailed discussion of this part of the despatch is not the function of these notes.

31. The statements made in paragraph 206, however, call for Air Staff comment. The C-in-C maintains that the experiences of the war proved that apart from a very small number of targets of special importance, the enemy's sinews of war were to be

found in his industrial cities. This is considered too drastic a statement. It is probably true that the great bulk of the enemy's armament production came from the industrial cities, (though this was not demonstrated, as stated, by the experiences of the war), but his most vulnerable sinews of war (oil and communications) were generally outside them. They were the ones which were severed and most patently brought about his collapse. It may be claimed, however, that the destruction of industrial cities, by forcing the enemy to disperse his industry, increased his dependence on communications and oil, and so rendered their ultimate destruction decisive.

32. Figures can be adduced to show that the attacks on cities failed to produce conclusive results, because, in view of the recovery factor, (the Germans' recuperative powers were remarkable) the tempo of the attacks was unavoidably too slow. A substantial increase in tempo might well have changed the picture, but such an increase was not practicable. Although from March 1943 to March 1944, Bomber Command's effort, with few major diversions, was against industrial cities, from then on, the invasion commitments had to take priority for practically the remainder of the war, though a big effort went on to cities from September 1944.

33. The C-in-C also states that the problem of selecting primary targets was never properly solved, and refers to demands for the bombers to attack "targets of secondary importance which are causing annoyance to one or other Government Department". Perfection in this respect cannot of course be claimed, and there certainly were occasions when mistakes were made on important issues. It is worthy of record, however, that the Combined Strategic Target Committee system worked sufficiently well for the Americans to adopt it, in its entirety, for the air offensive against Japan. It must be realised, however, that the work of selection must always depend heavily on intelligence sources, and it cannot be denied that there was, in Bomber Command, a reluctance to attack specific targets, born partly of operational inability and partly of an underestimate on their part of their own ability. This made it difficult to advocate for them any real target system other than industrial areas – which, as is demonstrated throughout the despatch, they wanted most to attack.

APPENDIX C.
ARMAMENT

34. The opening paragraphs of this Appendix contain very severe criticisms of the armament design organisation which, the C-in-C states "showed throughout a standard of incompetence which had the most serious repercussions".

35. There are certainly grounds for complaint in this connection, but the remaining paragraphs of this appendix show that whatever basic foundation there may be for criticism, during the period under review much valuable work on the development of various items of armament equipment was done. Incompetence, therefore, could not, as stated in the opening paragraph, have been shown "throughout the period", as

great improvements in armament matters did take place in the latter half of the war, largely owing to readjustments in M.A.P. and the Air Ministry.

36. The failings in the armament organisation were, in fact, due mainly to an incorrect outlook in the inter-war period, which resulted in a state of affairs which was too deep seated to be rectified without the most far-reaching measures, for which the resources were not then available. When the air war came, with its urgent demands for new and better equipment of all kinds, made necessary by the rapid changes in the tactical situation or by the widely varied demands upon the flexibility of the bomber force, the armament organisation was taxed beyond its limits, and could not expand and reorganise quickly enough to make up the lee-way.

37. It is quite true to say, in the C-in-C's words, that "progress was hampered by an unending series of technical difficulties and failures". The reasons for these difficulties and failures, however, should not be laid solely at the door of the Design Staffs during the war. Many were due to the deep-seated organisational imperfections which made it difficult to meet the constant (usually inevitable) changing of requirements; many to the tendency to "hang on" armament equipment to an aircraft designed purely as a good flying machine.

8. The Air Staff feel, therefore, that the circumstances which led to the state of affairs so drastically criticised by the C-in-C must be taken into consideration, as the introduction to this appendix places an undeserved stigma upon the large numbers of Service and civilian personnel who worked so hard during the war, under arduous conditions, to provide Bomber Command with the means by which it was ultimately able to achieve such successful results.

APPENDIX D.
TACTICS

39. The criticism has been made that little reference is included in the despatch to the indispensable assistance given by Fighter Command in connection with the strategic bomber offensive, and that the picture is accordingly incomplete.

40. As this despatch only purports to deal with the work of Bomber Command, it is perhaps hardly to be expected that the part played by other Commands should be dealt with at any length. It should, however, be borne in mind that the whole of the initial effectiveness of 100 Group (whose part is described in some detail in Appendix D) clearly derived from the experience of night fighting and the technique developed in Fighter Command. Fighter Command intruders also helped considerably in frustrating the enemy defences at night, and of course, later, fighter escort assisted the bombers to their objectives during their daylight operations. There is no doubt that Bomber Command's complex organisation would have been gravely impaired had it not been for the constant co-operation of the fighters.

41. The above points, which are dealt with in detail in other reports and despatches, should not be overlooked by students of the operations of Bomber Command.

APPENDIX F.
EXPANSION AND RE-EQUIPMENT

Planned Flying

42. It is considered desirable to add the following notes on the references to Planned Flying which appear in this Appendix.

43. It is stated in paragraphs 88 and 106 that "Planned Flying was unacceptable in Bomber Command as it would have reduced the overall effort" and "this in turn would have led to a prolongation of the war". The Bomber Command concept of P.F. and P.S. as defined in these paragraphs is that the daily flying effort must be artificially restricted and the total flying spread out so that the servicing personnel are kept employed to the fullest possible extent. In other words, other considerations must be subordinated to obtaining optimum employment of the servicing personnel. If this were so, there can be little doubt that Bomber Command's effort would have been considerably reduced.

44. The fact is, however, that P.F. and P.S. does not impose any such restriction on flying effort. If it is an operational requirement (as it was in Bomber Command) to despatch the maximum number of aircraft whenever the opportunity is present, P.F. and P.S. ensures the correct relative establishments of aircraft, men and other resources to do so. If it is necessary to fly every available aircraft 3 or 4 nights running, P.F. and P.S. offers no hindrance. It does, however, enable the Commander-in-Chief to know with reasonable accuracy what strength of aircraft he can expect to have available on the 2nd, 3rd and 4th nights.

45. Paragraph 106 of Appendix 'F' further states that "the ultimate effect of 'planned flying' if applied to Bomber Command as a whole might have been a somewhat accelerated expansion, but this would have increased the shortage airfields, etc". This argument is presumably based on the previous definition of "planned flying", but since the definition itself is incorrect, the argument cannot apply. In any case it would be against the principles of P.F. and P.S. to expand beyond the capacity of the airfields.

46. From information supplied by members of his staff, and also from the despatch itself (Appendix "B", paragraph 82, and Appendix "F", paragraph 100) there is little doubt that the Commander-in-Chief was actually applying most of the principles of P.F. and P.S. One thing which he apparently lacked and which P.F. and P.S. would have provided was a central progressing section which would have presented a complete and co-ordinated picture of the Command's activities so that relative costs could be immediately assessed, and which would have ensured that the working strain was being applied throughout the whole machine.

47. In conclusion, it is the opinion of the Air Staff that P.F. and P.S. if correctly

interpreted and applied, would not have reduced Bomber Command's effort. In fact it is safe to say that their effort would have been increased, or alternatively that they could have maintained their effort with reduced servicing manpower.

Work Matters

48. Certain of the figures and statements included do not tally with the records, but they are not considered sufficiently important to justify detailed comment.

49. In paragraph 22 reference is made to the shortage of airfields. This was due (as mentioned in para. 24) mainly to the handing over of completed Bomber Command airfields to the U.S.A.A.F., the arrival of which was unexpected and unprovided for.

50. In paragraph 91 the C-in-C refers to the Works Directorate "suffering from lack of experience and supervisory personnel." In this connection, it must be pointed out that the cream of the engineering profession employed by Municipal and County authorities and of certain utility undertakings volunteered for work with A.M.W.D. in such numbers that all jobs were manned effectively, and all of the volunteers were ultimately absorbed within the structure of the department. The problems which arose, and which are quoted, were largely due to the introduction of new or changed requirements during the process of construction. There was also, in some cases, failure to notify the Works Department of changes called for by increasing aircraft loads.

Air Ministry (D.S.T.).
March, 1948.
C.28933.

SECTION 3

AIR MINISTRY NOTE

Readers of this despatch will find that it contains, in addition to the operational narrative, a number of statements, opinions and criticisms, from the personal standpoint of the Commander-in-Chief, which call for comment.

An Air Staff Memorandum has therefore been prepared which amplifies some and corrects certain others of the statements made in the text, and this has been circulated to all known holders of the despatch.

Further copies of the memorandum can be obtained on application to the Air Ministry (D.S.T.) quoting the file reference C.28933.

DESPATCH
ON WAR OPERATIONS
23RD FEBRUARY, 1942, TO 8TH MAY, 1945

By
AIR CHIEF MARSHAL
SIR ARTHUR T. HARRIS, G.C.B., O.B.E., A.F.C.
AIR OFFICER COMMANDING-IN-CHIEF,
BOMBER COMMAND

October, 1945
FELDEN LODGE,
BOXMOOR,
HERTS.

18th December, 1945.

Sir,

In conformity with Kings Regulations and Air Council Instructions, paragraph 47b, I have the honour to submit my Despatch on the War Operations undertaken by Bomber Command from the 23rd February, 1942, when I assumed command, to the 8th May, 1945, when warlike operations were concluded.

2. I have not made recommendations for honours, awards or mentions in despatches in connection with these operations in this Despatch, all such recommendations having been made periodically in the past as and when requested.

3. Throughout the period of my command the Operational Research Section at Headquarters, Bomber Command, issued complete reports on every operation under the title of O.R.S. Night (and Day) Raid Reports.

4. Copies of these reports were forwarded to the Air Ministry as they were produced and none are therefore appended to this Despatch.

I have the honour to be,
Sir,
Your obedient Servant,
(signed)
ARTHUR T. HARRIS,
Air Chief Marshal.
The Under Secretary of State,
Air Ministry,
Whitehall, S.W.I.

PART I.
INTRODUCTION.

BOMBER COMMAND IN FEBRUARY, 1942

The Task allotted to the Command

The bomber force of which I assumed command on 23rd February, 1942, although at that time very small, was a potentially decisive weapon. It was, indeed, the only means at the disposal of the Allies for striking at Germany itself and, as such, stood out as the central point in Allied offensive strategy.

The German wave of success had reached its peak. In Russia the offensive was halted, British strength at home and in the Mediterranean was gradually building up in spite of everything that the U-boats could do to prevent it, while American armies and air forces were expanding and training in the West. German morale, which had been boosted by initial victories, was at its height, but showed already some anxiety and apprehension about the future.

2. The strength of the enemy defences made it impracticable to depart from the established policy of operating mainly by night. The limitations which this imposed on bombing accuracy largely controlled the choice of targets, since large industrial areas were more suitable for heavy attacks than individual factories and plants. This policy, although based on the meagre chances of direct hits on small targets except under most favourable conditions, was also supported by a study of the results of German night attacks on this country, which indicated that the quickest and most economical way of achieving the aims of the offensive was to devastate in turn the large industrial cities of Germany.

3. The main task, therefore, laid upon the Command by the Air Ministry directif letter numbered S.46368/D.C.A.S., of 14th February, 1942, was "to focus attacks on the morale of the enemy civil population, and, in particular, of the industrial workers."1 This was to be achieved by destroying, mainly by incendiary attacks, first, four large cities in the Ruhr area and, then, as opportunity offered, fourteen other industrial cities in Northern, Central and Southern Germany. The aim of attacks on town areas had already been defined in an Air Staff paper (dated 23rd September, 1941) as follows:—

> "The ultimate aim of the attack on a town area is to break the morale of the population which occupies it. To ensure this we must achieve two things; first, we must make the town physically uninhabitable and, secondly, we must make the people conscious of constant personal danger. The immediate aim, is therefore, twofold, namely, to produce (i) destruction, and (ii) the fear of death."

4. My primary authorised task was therefore clear beyond doubt: to inflict the most severe material damage on German industrial cities. This, when considered in relation to the force then available, was indeed a formidable task. Nevertheless, it was possible, but only if the force could be expanded and re-equipped as planned, and if its whole weight could be devoted to the main task with the very minimum of diversions.

5. In addition to the main task, however, the Air Ministry directif letter of 14th February, 1942, laid down that the Command should also

(i) be prepared to take on particular targets of immediate strategic importance, such as naval units, submarine building-yards and bases;

(ii) support combined operations when required;

(iii) attack specified factories in France, in order to discourage French workers from producing war equipment for the enemy.

The light bomber force of No. 2 Group was also included in my Command at that time. With the exception of night intruder activity against enemy airfields to assist the heavy and medium bombers (and also to hinder the enemy bombers) this short-range force could play no part in the main offensive against Germany. In daylight operations, executed in conjunction with offensive fighter sweeps, the chief purpose of the light bombers was to bring the enemy fighters to combat.

The Force Available

6. The foundations of the new bomber force – greatly enlarged, and re-equipped with heavies – had already been laid before I assumed command. The results of this planning were just beginning to appear; but, on 23rd February, 1942, out of a total of 378 serviceable aircraft with crews (excluding "Freshmen" not yet fit for operations) only 69 were heavy bombers.

7. This force was obliged to operate against Germany almost entirely under cover of darkness and, in consequence of the absence of effective non-visual aids to navigation and target-finding in the dark, was virtually unable to locate its targets. It is not too much to say that, owing to the small size of the force and the primitive methods then at our disposal, we could no more assail the enemy effectively by air than by land or sea. His defences were sufficient to prevent us from operating in daylight, when visual target-finding would have been possible, and by night we could not find our aiming points.

8. I confidently believed, however – and with good reason – that the Command's main task could be achieved successfully if only we could overcome the handicaps under which, so far, the bomber force had laboured in vain. These were, primarily, lack of suitable aircraft in sufficient number, absence of effective navigational aids, and a serious deficiency of trained crews. Moreover, the handicaps were not only due to lack of material and trained personnel, as there were technical and tactical problems

affecting the employment of the force which could only be surmounted by intensive research, continual experiment and unshakeable resolution. How each of these problems was eventually surmounted, stage by stage, is set forth in a series of separate appendices (A-K). A study of these appendices is essential to a proper understanding of the course of operations summarised in this report.

9. In the solution of these problems the value of scientific research has proved inestimable. Indeed, without the Operational Research Section many problems would have remained insoluble, and others would have been solved only after trials and errors extravagant not only in terms of time and effort but also in lives of our aircrews.

1 Later expanded by directif issued by Combined Chiefs of Staff on 21st January, 1943, to include the general disorganisation of German industry.

PART II
THE COURSE OF THE CAMPAIGN
1942 – 1945.

THE PRELIMINARY PHASE,
FEBRUARY, 1942 – FEBRUARY, 1943

10. As long ago as November, 1940, the Command had emphasised the need for the provision of a radar aid which would enable crews to bomb specified targets even when they could not locate them visually. When I assumed command sixteen months later this was still one of the many problems awaiting solution – perhaps the most urgent of them all. We had to wait until the beginning of 1943 before this vital need was met by the introduction of "OBOE" and "H.2.S."

11. During the intervening period many fundamental lessons had to be learned in bombing strategy, tactics and technique, and entirely new methods evolved in relation to many changing factors. Indeed, the whole course of the subsequent campaign was moulded by the developments which occurred between February, 1942, and February, 1943, amounting to a complete revolution in the employment no less than in the composition of the bomber force. Meanwhile all available effort was required for maintaining operations against Germany and Italy, although a considerable part of the force was non-operational owing to conversion from medium to heavy aircraft.

12. The size of force employed against industrial cities was generally the largest available at the time, excluding training and conversion units. Whereas in the past the tendency had been to attack a number of targets simultaneously with small forces, from 1942 onwards the bulk of the effort was normally directed against one objective on every night suitable for operations.

BOMBING TECHNIQUE
(NAVIGATIONAL AIDS)

Introduction of "GEE"

13. My assumption of command coincided with the introduction of the first radar navigational device, and the preliminary stages of the development of others. Great hopes were entertained of their performance. The use of "GEE" was expected to have a profound influence on navigation at night. It was hoped that it would enable new tactics to be employed, in particular, improved concentration and co-ordination of the individual aircraft of the attacking force. It was, also, expected by the Air Ministry that "this equipment should enable an aircraft to bomb a selected area in or through 10/10ths cloud and thus increase the average number of effective operational nights per month from, say, 3 to possibly 20 or more." (Air Ministry (D.B. Ops.) paper on "Area Attack employing 'GEE' " 16th January, 1942.) Although it was realised that the accuracy to be obtained from "GEE" in that part of Germany lying within its range (then about 400 miles from the ground stations), might not be quite as high as that obtained on service trials over this country, the provisional estimate by Air Warfare Analysis Section (upon which the Air Ministry Directif of the 14th February, 1942, was based) suggested that 47 per cent. of bombs would fall on Essen in 10/10ths cloud, and that "GEE" should therefore "be regarded as a blind-bombing device and not merely as a navigational aid."[1]

14. On this optimistic basis, the Command (with an average available force, excluding "Freshmen" crews, of some 50 light, 260 medium and 50 heavy bombers) was expected to "destroy completely" Essen, and other West German industrial cities, in the course of three months intensive operations following the introduction of "GEE." During this period only a small part of the bomber force was equipped with this instrument, and experts predicted that the useful life of "GEE" over enemy territory would be much restricted by jamming within a maximum of six months. Both the object and general method of attack for these operations was laid down by the Air Ministry.

15. To prepare for these operations and to ascertain how "GEE" could be employed to best advantage, both as an aid to routeing and concentrating aircraft, as well as to assist in hitting targets, No. 1418 Experimental Flight was established at the request of the Command (refer Appendix A); and the Operational Research Section applied itself to the many problems which arose both before and after the first "GEE"-assisted operation (Essen, 8/9th March, 1942). Two experimental exercises ("CRACKERS" and "CRACKERS II") were carried out in February, over the Isle of Man and North Wales respectively, to discover how best the small "GEE"-equipped force could lead the main (non-"GEE") force to the target. The method used was that of dropping and maintaining a concentration of flares over the aiming-point. Although valuable information concerning the use of flares was obtained, the first of these experiments was spoiled by failure of one of the ground stations; while photographs taken by

"GEE"-equipped aircraft during the second experiment suggested that the majority of aircraft would have bombed within a radius of 2 or 3 miles from the aiming-point. The use of sticks of flares to act as a beacon for attracting the main force to the area was highly successful, but their value for visual identification of the target was offset, in the opinion of most crews, by the dazzle effect produced in cloudless but slightly hazy conditions. Thus, from the outset there were some reasons for thinking that the employment of "GEE" on operations might fall far short of the theoretical standard upon which the Air Ministry directif was based. Nevertheless it was confidently expected that "GEE" would bring aircraft within visual range of their objectives, and thus unable navigator/bomb-aimers to identify the target without prolonged search.

16. For several reasons even this hope was not fulfilled on operations. It was eventually proved that "GEE" accuracy was seriously diminished in the Ruhr area. This was partly owing to a systematic error which had the effect of causing aircraft to "undershoot" the target, and partly to the difficulty of obtaining fixes with precision while aircraft were passing through a very heavily defended zone. Moreover, from the heights at which the flak obliged aircraft to operate (*e.g.,* from above 13,000 ft.), it was only in the most exceptional circumstances that it was possible at night to see and recognise particular towns in the smoke-laden atmosphere of the Ruhr.

17. Not until May, 1942, was there sufficient night-photographic evidence to assess the operational accuracy of "GEE." It was then found that the results obtained were about a third as accurate as those which No. 1418 Flight obtained over this country, the 50 per cent. zone being about 5 miles in radius. On the evidence then available[2] it appeared that only 5-10 sticks of bombs would be expected to fall within the limits of the built-up area of Essen if 100 aircraft attacked the city, relying entirely on "GEE." Only two or three sticks of bombs would fall on the area of the Krupp Works. Consequently it was evident that the Command would be unable to carry out "blind bombing" operations effectively using "GEE." Until, therefore, the arrival of "OBOE" and "H.2.S.", the bomber force remained as much as ever dependent upon visual means of finding the target, and every effort was concentrated upon improving such means (*see* Appendix B).

Continued Importance of Visual Identification

18. The multiplication of enemy decoy-fire sites in the course of 1942 greatly added to the problems of target location – as the Luftwaffe had found over here. "GEE" was not sufficiently accurate to indicate whether a promising-looking fire was one started by our own aircraft at the aiming point (or, mistakenly, in the wrong place), or was an enemy decoy some miles distant from the target. Only in clear weather conditions and with the assistance of moonlight could we have reasonable hopes of success. Even in the best possible conditions, however, industrial haze generally prevented visual recognition of Ruhr targets.

19. There was no doubt that the proportion of aircraft reaching the vicinity of the target on dark nights had been much improved as a result of the use of "GEE";

furthermore, though "GEE" was a complete failure as an aid for destroying the industrial centres of the Ruhr, rather better results were obtained at targets such as Cologne. There, the configuration of the Rhine made visual recognition of the target a practicable proposition when weather was favourable. Nevertheless, night photographs showed that the majority of crews still failed to bomb the target even when part of the force was successful. The great problem now was to ensure that the leading aircraft should be able to draw the rest to the aiming point by marking it unmistakably, not merely by fires, since realistic enemy decoys (and the jettisoning of incendiaries *en route* by aircraft which had got into difficulties) rendered that method of marking most unreliable. The necessity for navigator/bomb-aimers, especially those of the leading "GEE"-equipped aircraft, to be proficient in the difficult art of visual target-location was clearly recognised. Accordingly air bombers were introduced to relieve navigators of this part of their task, and to allow them to give full attention to their "GEE" equipment on the run-up to the target. This part of the problem was speedily handled by the Training Organisation (the principle was accepted by the Air Ministry on 29th March, 1942) but the development of a distinctive target marker took much longer. I asked[3] for such a marker as an urgent requirement in March, 1942, having urged its development many years previously, but it was not until January, 1943, that the Target Indicator Bomb was available for use on operations. Meanwhile, the use of various types of incendiaries as a substitute for the marker proved quite unsatisfactory.

The Pathfinder Force

20. "The formation of specialist squadrons to initiate raids" was recommended within the Command as early as December, 1941,[4] and the subject of special target finding units was much discussed during the first half of 1942. No one could dispute the necessity for the leading "GEE"-equipped "marker force" to be manned by thoroughly trained and experienced crews – particularly in regard to navigators and air bombers. This aim was, as far as possible, achieved in practice from the time of the introduction of "GEE." When (between April and June, 1942) the Air Ministry pressed for the establishment of an independent target-finding force of picked crews, I was entirely opposed to creaming off the best crews of all the Groups in order to create a *corps d'elite* in a special Group. This could be calculated to have a bad effect on morale in the Command as a whole, and furthermore, human nature being what it is, it would undoubtedly be difficult to extract the majority of the best crews out of the Groups, because, naturally enough, not only would the Groups want to retain their best personnel to take command of flights and squadrons, but the best personnel themselves would strongly object to leaving squadrons in which they had half-completed a tour of operations and in which they had been looked up to as the best crews, in order to be sent to another squadron and start again at the bottom as new boys. In this view I had the unanimous support of my Group Commanders who agreed with me that the best system would be to form inside each Group special

target-finding squadrons which could be used as group markers for smaller operations and, combined with those of one or more of the other Groups for bigger operations. That, in fact, was the logical development of the current tendency in all Groups to send the best crews first in order to improve the chance of the remainder being led correctly to the target. However, "Gee" had failed as an accurate bombing aid and the promise of Oboe and H2S was being continually postponed, and it was therefore obvious that urgent steps would have to be taken for improving visual finding and marking methods in the interim. The Air Ministry, however, insisted on the formation of a separate Pathfinding Force as a separate Group – yet another occasion when a Commander in the field was over-ruled at the dictation of junior staff officers in the Air Ministry. In the outcome the Pathfinder Force, although it did the most excellent work, nevertheless displayed all the handicaps and shortcomings which I had anticipated and which are referred to above, while in the latter part of the war my contention that each Group should find and maintain its own Pathfinding Force was proved infinitely the superior method when tried out in No. 5 Group. The Pathfinder Force was established on 15th August, 1942, under the command of Group Captain D.C.T. Bennett, D.S.O. During the remainder of 1942 many points of operational importance with regard to the illumination and marking of targets were brought to light as a result of the work of the Pathfinder Force. Hampered as they were by lack of special equip

ment for finding and marking (from the start, enemy interference deprived them of the use of "GEE" over Germany), their success was limited. O.R.S. investigations showed that, although bombing concentration had undoubtedly increased since the introduction of P.F.F. marking, the overall efficiency of the force showed little improvement, because the marking was frequently displaced from the aiming point. (*See* Appendix B.)

Nothing in the above should be regarded as constituting in any way a reflection on either the Commander or the members of the Pathfinder Force, who, in view of the difficulties with equipment, and the other factors to which I have referred above, in forming a *corps d'elite,* can be considered to have done wonders in the face of great handicaps, avoidable and unavoidable.

Development of "OBOE" and "H.2.S."

21. Development of both these radar devices for use in Bomber Command was under way in 1941, before "GEE" had been employed operationally. Production of radar equipment was strictly limited by lack of industrial capacity in 1941 (and long remained so), but towards the close of that year it was expected that "H.2.S." would be in use by the following autumn as an aid for navigation and, possibly, for blind bombing. Its greatest attraction lay in the fact that there was no range limitation, as there was in the case of "GEE" and "OBOE," and it was not liable to be "jammed" – as "GEE" had been and as "OBOE" might have been. After its experience with "GEE," the Command investigated the current form of "H.2.S." and pointed out[5] that

it was unsuitable for operational use, and that there was an urgent need for a clear decision as to its precise operational function, to serve as a guide for further development. As a result, its function was defined as the "blind detection of built-up areas," it being the navigator's task to determine the identity of the areas.

22. Early in July, tests by the Commander of the newly-formed Pathfinder Force showed that, while the use of the Klystron valve in "H.2.S." was unlikely to be satisfactory, the Magnetron valve gave favourable results and had more than twice the range. Many objections were raised to this proposal, on security and other grounds, but the Air Ministry agreed[6] on my recommendation, to concentrate on the production of the Magnetron version and to equip two squadrons for the P.F.F. by the end of the year. There were, in fact, 12 Stirlings and 12 Halifaxes in the Pathfinder Force equipped with "H.2.S." by December, 1942, but permission to employ them over enemy territory was not given until January, 1943.[7]

23. Meanwhile, the "OBOE"-equipped squadron of the Pathfinder Force became ready for operations in December, 1942. Owing to its dependence on ground stations, "OBOE" did not offer the tactical freedom which was one of the chief advantages of "H.2.S.", and its range was limited to some 300 miles. The small number of "OBOE" aircraft which could be handled by the ground stations during any operation also limited its use either to individual blind bombing by these few aircraft or, more profitably, target marking for the main force. Nevertheless, the potential accuracy of "OBOE" was so far in advance of anything else available that it was decided to employ it for the task which had been assigned to the Command nearly a year earlier on the introduction of "GEE," namely, the destruction of the industrial centres of the Ruhr.

24. For two months following the first use of "OBOE" against the enemy (20/21st December, 1942), small-scale experimental attacks were made, during which time the weather was generally bad, and night-photographic evidence consequently meagre. On the basis of day cover and intelligence information, O.R.S. estimated that the accuracy achieved was of the order of 650 yards, though on some occasions errors of up to 1½ miles were noted. As the weather was continuously unfavourable for ground-marking with the T.I. bomb, which was at last available,[8] the Pathfinder Force had evolved an alternative "skymarking" technique, first employed on the last night of 1942. Owing to the target priority accorded to the U-Boat bases in Western France during the first two months of 1943, it was not until March of that year that "OBOE" or "H.2.S." could be used in a serious offensive against Germany.

DEFENSIVE TACTICS

25. Towards the close of 1941 the establishment of the chain of G.C.I. radar stations from Jutland to the south-western frontier of Germany obliged the Command to work out a new system of defensive tactics. Whereas, in the past, routeing of aircraft was left to the discretion of individual crews, it became apparent that controlled enemy fighters would take a devastating toll of our bombers unless the timing and routeing

of the latter were rigorously co-ordinated. Before I took over command, the principle of concentration, both *en route* and over the target, had been accepted. Although analysis of previous operations indicated very clearly that the proportion of aircraft lost decreased with increased concentration en route and at the target, there was at first much doubt as to the practicability of higher concentrations. In the first place it was most difficult to ensure that the same route was closely adhered to by all aircraft and that they would reach the target at the planned time. Further, heavy concentration at the target necessarily led to serious congestion of landing facilities at home bases, and the risk of collision and of being struck by falling bombs in the target area had to be considered. It was not until March, 1942, that the introduction of "GEE" improved night navigation sufficiently to make concentration in time and space a practical proposition. Appendix D describes the measures taken to achieve the optimum concentration in time and space, and their effects on the loss rate.

26. A further operational advantage derived from the employment of "GEE" as a navigational aid was the possibility of attacking Germany without the assistance of moonlight. Since a concentrated bomber stream would offer easy targets for fighter interception in bright moonlight, from April, 1942 onwards it became increasingly the policy to attack targets in Germany chiefly in the non-moon period, although it was still necessary to risk increased losses in moonlight to ensure visual location of an important target (*e.g.,* Peenemünde, 18/19th August, 1943).

27. The enemy continued to develop his air defence organisation in various ways, *e.g.,* by introducing airborne radar, and our losses steadily increased during the summer of 1942. In addition to the tactical countermeasures taken by the Command in timing and routeing its aircraft, "Tinsel" and "Mandrel," the first of a series of radar countermeasures, were introduced in December, 1942. Intended to obstruct the enemy's ground to air communications and to delay his early warning, they had little effect at that time. (*See* Appendix E.)

THE STRENGTH OF THE COMMAND

28. At the beginning of 1942 it was expected that the year would see a tremendous increase in the strength of the Command. Accessions of aircraft and formed squadrons were promised from America. In the event, however, the U.S. heavy bombers eventually allocated to Britain went to Coastal Command, and practically all the light and medium bombers were sent to the Middle East and Russia.

29. Actually, Bomber Command started the year with 47 heavy and medium squadrons, and ended it with 52 – of which two heavy and one medium squadrons were on loan to Coastal Command. In all, 19 new squadrons were formed in the Command, and 13 transferred from it to other Commands and overseas theatres.

30. The average daily availability of aircraft with crews rose from 36 light, 285 medium and 42 heavy bombers in January, 1942 (total 363) to 79 light, 78 medium and 261 heavy bombers in December, 1942 (total 418). Numerical expansion, therefore, was negligible. The number of sorties made in 1942 was only 13 per cent.

above that for 1941. This would have been higher, but for the fact that many squadrons were non-operational owing to conversion to new types of aircraft. Moreover, a critical shortage of trained crews persisted throughout this period. It was not until May, 1943, that the number of trained crews exceeded 80 per cent. of crew establishment. The average daily strength of serviceable aircraft with crews during 1942 was 398.

31. On the other hand, the equipment of the force improved very considerably during the year. At its close there were 36 heavy squadrons, operational or re-equipping, as against 15 the year before, which made possible a 44 per cent. increase in the weight of bombs dropped as compared with 1941. Blenheims and Whitleys ceased operating during the summer of 1942, and Hampdens in September. Of the new types, the Manchester suffered heavy losses and had to be withdrawn from operations in June. The Lancaster, however, coming into operation for the first time on 10/11th March, 1942, soon proved immensely superior to all other types in the Command. The advantages which it enjoyed in speed, height and range enabled it to attack with success targets which other types could attempt only with serious risk or even the certainty of heavy casualties. Their high performance was a tremendous asset, but as yet their numbers were totally inadequate to deliver the concentrated attacks necessary to saturate defended objectives.

SUMMARY OF OPERATIONS

32. The force available for bombing Germany during 1942, therefore, remained inadequate for the task it was supposed to carry out. Nevertheless a number of very successful attacks were made, and many experimental operations yielded invaluable experience for the future. Of these, the "fire-raising" attack on Lübeck (28/29th March, 1942) and the "Thousand Plan" attack on Cologne (30/31st May, 1942) were outstanding examples.

Lübeck

33. Lübeck was a medium-sized town, fairly easily recognisable owing to its situation on the river Trave, reported to be inflammable, and its defences were not to be compared with those of the Ruhr. The attack was planned primarily to learn with what success the first wave of aircraft could guide the following wave by starting a conflagration at the aiming point. A total of 234 aircraft took part in this attack and dropped 144 tons of incendiaries and 160 tons of H.E., with a half-hour interval after the first wave to allow the fires to gain a firm hold before the second arrived. The raid was an unqualified success, and proved that under good weather conditions a fairly important, but not vital, German town could be at least half destroyed by a relatively small force dropping a high proportion of incendiaries. The loss of 13

aircraft (mainly along the route) on an operation of this type, involving as it did deep penetration in bright moonlight, was moderate in relation to the achievement.

Rostock

34. A month later similar attacks were made against Rostock on four consecutive nights and fully confirmed the lesson of Lübeck. The town was wrecked and considerable damage inflicted on the neighbouring Heinkel Works, which was the special aiming point for aircraft of No. 5 Group. Twelve aircraft were missing out of a total of 521 sorties.

35. Three great problems remained to be solved:—

(i) could the defences of a vital industrial area be "saturated" by a similar operation on a much larger scale;

(ii) were the high concentrations, now seen to be desirable, a practical proposition; and

(iii) how could the weather limitations on finding and marking the target be overcome?

The first of these problems was answered by the "Thousand Plan" operation against Cologne at the end of May, 1942. The second problem was partially solved, as a much higher concentration than had been tried before was successfully achieved, although many new crews, operating for the first time, took part in the attack. The third problem proved insoluble until the new radar bombing aids and the marker (target indicator) bomb became available at the beginning of 1943, although valuable experience was gained in marking targets throughout 1942 (*see* Appendix B).

Cologne

36. It became more and more evident that against large and heavily defended targets a force of 250/350 aircraft was simply not large enough to achieve the concentration in time and space necessary to swamp the enemy's radar-controlled guns and fighters, and to produce mass destruction around the aiming point. It was therefore decided to try out the possibility of an attack on a far greater scale than anything previously attempted. The aim was to send 1,000 aircraft in one attack against a single objective, and preparations to achieve this were made during May, 1942. The organisation of such a force – about twice as great as any the Luftwaffe ever sent against this country – was no mean task in 1942. As the number of first line aircraft in squadrons was quite inadequate, the training organisation and conversion units had to make a very substantial contribution. No. 3 Group alone despatched some 250 aircraft – a number usually regarded at that time as a strong bomber force in itself. Operational Training Units put up 302 aircraft in addition to 64 others attached to Nos. 1 and 3 Groups. Apart from 4 aircraft of Flying Training Command, the whole force which attacked

Cologne was provided by Bomber Command. A diversionary attack on enemy fighter airfields was carried out by 34 Blenheims of No. 2 Group in co-operation with 15 light aircraft of Army Co-operation Command. Fighter Command also supplied 39 aircraft to attack airfields on the route to the target. On 30th May full moon, good weather conditions at home bases, and the fact that the necessary forces were standing by, made it important to carry out the operation with the least possible delay, although thundery cloud was known to cover much of Germany. Cologne was selected as the target because the weather there was more promising than at any other suitable objective. Accordingly 1,047 aircraft were despatched to that city and, although very dirty weather was experienced over the North Sea, clear conditions were found over Holland and Western Germany. Nearly 900 aircraft dropped 1,455 tons of bombs (of which incendiaries comprised two-thirds of the weight) within the space of 90 minutes. Photographic reconnaissance later showed a total of 600 acres of damage, half of this total lying in the area of the central city. This was nearly equal to the aggregate of damage in Lübeck, Rostock, and all other German cities attacked up to that time (780 acres), and proved that in a successful operation the damage increased out of proportion to the numbers involved. It also showed that the destruction of German industrial centres by bombing was a realisable aim if sufficient resources were devoted to achieving it. The loss rate for the operation, which was 3·8 per cent. as against an average of 4·6 per cent. for attacks during the previous twelve months on Western Germany under similar conditions of weather and moonlight, also showed a favourable trend. Owing to the fact that the enemy fighter effort was considerably greater than usual, and that optimum conditions prevailed for "cat's-eye" interceptions, it was not surprising that the loss rate of the medium bombers was 4·5 per cent.; but the loss rate for the third wave of the attack, which comprised heavy bombers, and in which the bombing concentration was highest, was only 1·9 per cent. Detailed analysis revealed that the large numbers of aircraft did not prevent the enemy's location devices from selecting and following single targets all through the attack but, owing to the concentration of aircraft, the guns were prevented from engaging more than a very small proportion of the total.

The Ruhr

37. The reasons for the disappointing results obtained from "GEE" as a bombing aid in the Ruhr area have already been referred to (para. 16). Essen, which was repeatedly attacked from 8/9th March culminating in a mass attack on the "Thousand Plan" proved to be virtually unidentifiable at night owing to the persistent haze. The mass operation (1st/2nd June, 1942) would certainly have achieved better results than most of these attacks but for the fact that low stratus cloud covered the area on that occasion. Although considerable industrial and residential damage was inflicted in most of the important Ruhr cities (particularly in and around Duisburg) in the course of the year, it was scattered and not to be compared with what was to follow the introduction of "OBOE."

38. As in the case of the three raids on the "Thousand Plan," Operational Training Units had to be called upon to give weight and numbers to the attack on Düsseldorf on 31st July/1st August, 1942. Nearly 500 crews completed the operation, which like the big Cologne attack, was executed in bright moonlight and good weather. As an indication of the improvement in weight-lift, it may be mentioned that one-hundred-and-seventy 4,000-lb. bombs were dropped. This, and a subsequent attack (10/11th September) led by the newly-formed Pathfinder Force, caused very extensive damage in the centre of the city, and profitable damage was inflicted on a number of industrial plants and railway facilities. In relation to its size, Düsseldorf was more heavily damaged than Cologne.

Other Targets in Germany

39. The foregoing were the outstanding incidents in the night operations against Germany prior to the introduction of "OBOE." The ports of Hamburg, Kiel, Bremen, and Emden, were all attacked persistently but (apart from Emden) suffered no really significant damage. Among other inland objectives attacked, Saarbrücken, Mainz and Karlsruhe received quite appreciable damage. Yet, as a whole, German war production was not seriously affected prior to 1943.

40. It could hardly have been otherwise since, in the absence of a blind bombing aid, Ruhr targets could not be hit effectively at night; and, owing to the continuously increasing strength of the German defences, previous ideas of what constituted a strong bomber force were rendered obsolete. The employment of training units on operations to augment the scale of attack was justifiable only on the grounds that it proved what might be done with adequate means. It interfered seriously with the training programme, and O.T.U.s were not employed after September, 1942.

41. Berlin remained on the list of priority targets throughout 1942, but I was unwilling to attack it until the strength of the Command had sufficiently increased. Therefore it was left alone for a period of 13 months following the operation of 17th December, 1941, when 10 per cent. losses had been incurred. The termination of the long immunity from air raids which the Reich capital had enjoyed was marked by two attacks on successive nights in January, 1943, when a total of 388 heavies (nearly all Lancasters) were despatched against this target for the loss of 5·9 per cent. These attacks are referred to in the discussion of subsequent operations against Berlin (page 20).

Daylight Operations

42. The carefully-planned attack on the M.A.N. works at Augsburg (17th April, 1942), in which seven out of 12 Lancasters were lost, showed the impracticability of daylight operations against Germany in anything but small numbers and on rare occasions,

without long-range fighter cover. The U-Boat building yards at Flensburg, Lübeck and Danzig, were also attacked at dusk by relatively small forces of heavies making use of thick cloud cover on the outward journey, but only at Flensburg did they succeed in hitting their target.

Factories in German-occupied Europe

43. When the Command was required to attack such targets as the Renault works (Billancourt), Gnome & Rhone works (Gennevilliers), Ford works (Poissy), Schneider works (Le Creusot), and Philips works (Eindhoven) excellent results were obtained whether by night or day. The comparative weakness of the opposition enabled crews to come in low in bright moonlight, or even by day, and positively identify their objective. Apart from serious material damage, there is no doubt that the results did much to discourage the workers in occupied countries from helping the enemy war effort.

Operations against Italy

44. In conjunction with the land offensive in the Mediterranean theatre in the late autumn of 1942 the Command was required to bomb the industrial cities of Northern Italy. Six night attacks were delivered against Genoa between 22nd/23rd October and the end of the year, seven against Turin, and one daylight attack on Milan. Except for the great distance of the targets, conditions more resembled attacks on French objectives than on those in Germany. The ineffectual opposition from Italian guns and fighters made it possible to operate in bright moonlight, and even by day, and many of these attacks were extremely well concentrated.

U-Boat Bases in Western France

45. By the beginning of 1943 the Command was ready to employ "OBOE" and "H.2.S." against German industrial centres. For the first two months it was only possible, however, to devote a relatively small part of our total effort to the main task, as the Command was required[9] to devastate the French cities of Lorient and St. Nazaire. Between mid-January and mid-February, 1943, about 2,000 sorties were despatched against Lorient in the course of nine night attacks. St. Nazaire was bombed by over 400 aircraft on the last night of February, and suffered two further attacks during the following month. These attacks were generally very well concentrated, and left little undestroyed in either town except for the U-Boat bases, which were protected by the heaviest concrete shelters. At the beginning of these operations I protested against the misemployment of my force on a type of operation which could not achieve the intended object.

46. During 1942 the sea-mining campaign began in earnest. Hitherto minelaying operations by Bomber Command had been carried out exclusively by No. 5 Group. The value of these operations had become apparent to me during my period in command of that Group and, as Bomber Command was now responsible for all aerial minelaying in enemy waters in northern and western Europe, I realised the importance of extending the effort to all groups. My proposal that the Command should lay an average of 1,000 mines per month was welcomed by the Admiralty and agreed by the Air Ministry (25th March, 1942) on the understanding that this would not entail reduction of the main bombing offensive. How this was done, with very successful results, is described in Appendix H.

Whereas only 1,055 mines were laid during 1941, the total for 1942 rose to 9,574, the effort representing 14.7 per cent. of the total sorties.

Operations against Ships and U-Boats

47. While attacks on enemy shipping increased in respect of the sea-mining effort, the bombing effort against ships in daylight (by No. 2 Group) was curtailed. Limited mainly to operations against valuable merchant vessels docked in one or other of the Channel ports, a small number of useful attacks were made. An appreciable part, however, of the Command's effort was directed to assist Coastal Command's anti-submarine patrols. From May, 1942, to the end of February, 1943, nearly 1,600 sorties were made by Whitley, Wellington, Halifax and Lancaster squadrons loaned to Coastal Command for this task. Fuller details will be found in Appendix H.

THE MAIN OFFENSIVE OPENS, MARCH, 1943-MARCH, 1944

48. On the night of 5/6th March, 1943, "OBOE" was first used in a main operation against Germany. From this time onwards there was a very marked improvement in bombing concentration on all targets within "OBOE" range, about 300 miles from the ground stations. It now became possible to carry out the task assigned to the Command a year earlier.[10] (This task had been expanded by the directif issued by the Combined Chiefs of Staff on 21st January, 1943, to include the general disorganisation of German industry, giving priority to U-Boat building yards, aircraft industry, transportation, oil, etc.). Whereas only isolated successes had been achieved before the use of "OBOE," a continuous series of significant blows against the West German industrial centres followed the introduction of this device.

49. The range limitation of "OBOE," and the possibility that enemy jamming would restrict its use as in the case of "GEE," had made it necessary to speed up the development of "H.2.S.", which was not subject to these limitations. But in the

meanwhile "OBOE" was exploited to the full in the "Battle of the Ruhr" during the spring and summer of 1943.

50. The chances of making a successful attack in moderate or even in poor weather conditions were much improved by the use of "OBOE." This relative freedom from meteorological limitations in turn made possible a considerable increase in the number of night bombing sorties carried out and this, combined with an expansion of first line strength and the greater proportion of heavies in the force, enormously raised the tonnage of bombs dropped on Germany.

51. Towards the close of the "Battle of the Ruhr," on 10th June, 1943, an Air Ministry directif re-allocated the tasks to be shared between Bomber Command and the recently-expanded U.S. Eighth Army Air Force. This took note of the fact that "the increasing scale of destruction (which was) being inflicted by our night bomber forces and the development of the day bomber offensive (had) forced the enemy to deploy day and night fighters in increasing numbers on the Western Front. Unless this increase in fighter strength (was) checked we (might) find our bomber forces unable to fulfil the tasks allotted to them ... To this end the Combined Chiefs of Staff ... decided that first priority in the operation of British and American bombers based in the United Kingdom shall be accorded to the attack of German fighter forces and the industry upon which they depend."

52. The primary object was defined as before: "the progressive destruction and dislocation of the German military, industrial and economic system, and the undermining of the morale of the German people to a point where their capacity for armed resistance is fatally weakened."

53. Priorities were re-allocated, giving preference to the sources of the enemy fighter strength, and it was laid down that: "while the forces of the British Bomber Command will be employed in accordance with their main aim in the general disorganisation of German industry their action will be designed as far as practicable to be complementary to the operations of the Eighth Air Force." During the remainder of the period under review, therefore, the Command paid particular attention to the main industrial centres associated with aircraft production. This successful phase of the campaign, during which bombing efficiency and strength steadily improved, ended with the decision to divert the Command from its main task of smashing the industrial cities of Germany to a bombing plan designed to create the requisite conditions for a successful military invasion of the continent of Europe.

THE COMPOSITION OF THE FORCE

54. During the first four months of 1943, a moderate expansion of front line strength was achieved. At the close of 1942 there were 29 operational and seven non-operational heavy squadrons and 16 medium squadrons in service. By the end of April, 1943, there were 36 operational and two non-operational heavy squadrons and 14 medium squadrons. The average strength of squadrons also increased during the period, from 17 to 21 aircraft and this, together with the reduction in the number of

non-operational squadrons, contributed to the continued increase in the striking power of the Command. The R.C.A.F. contribution to the size of the Command was very considerable, nor was it limited to their own No. 6 Group, formed 1st January, 1943.[11]

55. Whereas the average effort of Lancaster squadrons had been 78 sorties per month during 1942, they were able to make an average of 112 sorties in April, 1943. As the year progressed the Lancaster became the mainstay of all operations against Germany, and particularly Berlin. The Halifax, Marks II and IV, on the other hand, continued to be unsatisfactory, and it was not until the Mark III version became available in considerable numbers, about February, 1944, that this aircraft could begin to hold its own against the formidable fighter defences of the Reich. The Stirlings and Wellingtons were obsolescent, being unable to achieve the ceiling necessary to avoid accurate heavy flak. After October/November, 1943, they were not employed on German targets.

56. The small light bomber force of No. 2 Group, which had made some spectacular daylight attacks on small targets in Occupied Territory since re-arming with Mosquitos, was transferred to Air Defence of Great Britain at the end of May, 1943. On the other hand, No. 617 Squadron (5 Group) equipped with Lancasters, specially trained to bomb precise targets at night, operated, for the first time during the same month, against the Ruhr dams.

DEFENSIVE TACTICS

57. The gradual expansion of the bomber force from small beginnings was more than matched by the massing of guns and, above all, radar-assisted fighters on the part of the enemy. The Germans fully realised the implications of the bomber offensive even before the spring of 1943, which was by then creating havoc in the Ruhr industries. They knew that they must, if in any way possible and at all costs, make bombing too expensive for us. To do this they were prepared ruthlessly to rob their battle-fronts of guns and fighters. Up to a point they succeeded, and our losses were almost 5 per cent. of total sorties during the spring and summer of 1943, in spite of the introduction of various radar countermeasures. Although concentration in time and space had undoubtedly prevented very serious losses in 1942 and the first half of 1943, our casualties stood higher than ever before. For some time I had pressed for the release of a countermeasure called WINDOW which was known to be effective against the enemy's defence organisation. Permission to employ it was withheld on the grounds that the enemy might retaliate and that our own defensive system was particularly vulnerable to such a countermeasure. At last, at the end of July, WINDOW was released and was first used during the highly successful series of attacks on Hamburg. It immediately put an end to the enemy's accustomed system of defence and caused the bomber loss-rate to swing back to something very near the 1941 level. This remarkable improvement took place at a time of the year when past experience showed that we might expect, not a fall, but a further increase in the loss rate. Coupled with appropriate tactics, the introduction of WINDOW probably saved something

like 200 bombers and their crews within a period of just over two months (during which, incidentally, 1,600 sorties were made against Berlin). A valuable effect of WINDOW on the enemy ground-location devices was a phenomenal decline in the rate of flak damage, which helped squadrons to maintain a high standard of serviceability.

58. The enemy's freelance fighters, aided by flares and searchlights, saved the situation from developing into a debacle, and he gradually improved a system of directing the fighter "pack" towards the bomber stream. But this method of defence was open to serious error, and in planning our operations we exploited this weakness to good effect in our routeing, and by the use of "feint" attacks (for further details of these developments, *see* Appendix D).

BOMBING TECHNIQUE

59. The lessons learned during the "preliminary phase" of the campaign stood us in good stead when we were at last able to use "OBOE" against the Ruhr. Technical refinements in bombing methods developed during 1943 were really elaborations of methods used in conjunction with "GEE" the year before and, important though they were, there is no need to describe them here. The subject is discussed in detail in Appendix B.

60. Beyond "OBOE" range, which was practically limited to the Ruhr area until ground stations were established on the Continent late in 1944, navigational and blind bombing difficulties were still very troublesome. While "H.2.S." proved of considerable value as a navigational aid beyond the now restricted "GEE" limit, and thus assisted the routeing and timing of longer range operations, it could not be compared with "OBOE" as a blind bombing instrument. As I pointed out in a letter[12] to Air Ministry five months before it was first used operationally, the reliable interpretation of "H.2.S." calls for considerably more skill and practice on the part of aircrews than is required for "OBOE." Operational use not only proved the correctness of this forecast, but also showed that many inland targets gave so poor an "H.2.S." response that even the most experienced operators could fail to recognise them. This was a serious disappointment, as all heavies were being fitted with "H.2.S." and no alternative was available, but experience and gradual improvement of P.F.F. technique enabled some very useful attacks to be delivered against inland targets which we had never before been able to locate.

61. As mentioned already (para. 56 above) this period was notable also for the exploits of No. 617 Squadron, specially trained and equipped for bombing precise targets at night. The technique evolved produced outstanding results in relation to the scale of effort, but could rarely be applied to vital targets in Germany.

OPERATIONAL FACTORS

62. The period March, 1943-March, 1944, was one of outstanding achievement, particularly when compared with previous results. For the first time the Command found itself in a position, under suitable conditions, to inflict severe material damage on almost any industrial centre in Germany.

63. In practice, there were, of course, many limitations on target selection, some of which had been in existence since the early days of the war. Apart from the geographical distribution of concentrated flak zones and of the night fighter system, the short nights of the summer months imposed a limiting radius beyond which operations could only be carried out at the risk of heavy losses from enemy fighters. In June, for instance, the only useful German targets left exposed to attack within the arc were Emden, the Ruhr as far as Dortmund, and the Rhine as far as Bonn. Moreover, coastal targets were liable to prove costly even within the "operational arc" because the northern sky was sufficiently light to silhouette aircraft even on a dark night. But Lancasters could go, on occasions, some 50 miles beyond the arc, owing to their speed and because a small force would require less time over the target.

64. Within this arc, the selection of targets was normally governed by a combination of weather factors and the performance of radar aids available for bombing and navigation. On a cloudy night, when "sky marking" technique would have to be employed, either a large town or a scattered area target (such as Duisburg or Gelsenkirchen) would be preferred since a good concentration of bombing could not be hoped for, particularly if the wind was strong.

65. While "OBOE" proved to be relative precise when employed with ground marking, "H.2.S." was incapable of really precise marking under any conditions. Only against a compact and isolated target such as Münster was the response clearly recognisable. (The whole Ruhr area from Duisburg to Dortmund produced a confusing blaze of reactions.) Against the largest cities, such as Berlin and Hamburg, "H.2.S." could not be used to ensure hitting either the centre or a particular part of the town but, generally speaking, it made it possible to put a considerable proportion of the bomb load into the town somewhere. Over Berlin the "H.2.S." responses seemed to be more apparent in the suburbs than in the centre – possibly due to the prevalence of steel-frame structures in the outlying areas.

66. The characteristics of the radar aids also affected the choice of target in other ways, but one of the most important considerations in regard to target marking was the low ceiling of the Stirling, Wellington and Halifax, in that order, as compared with the Lancaster. For while the "OBOE" Mosquitos could operate at great heights above the clouds, the number of main force aircraft able to bomb on the sky-markers was progressively reduced as the height of the cloud tops increased. The whole force could be employed provided the clouds were below 12,000 ft., but only Lancasters if cloud tops were at 17,000 ft. Thus to maintain the offensive in periods of cloudy weather I had sometimes to employ a smaller force than I would have liked.

67. Finally, it was obviously undesirable to continue to attack the same region over a long period, as the enemy would concentrate his defences there. Mosquitos, and

sometimes a small Lancaster force, would therefore be despatched to more distant targets as often as possible, to compel the enemy to spread his defences. One advantage of an operation like the "shuttle" attack on Friedrichshafen and Spezia during June, 1943, was that it caused the inhabitants of places outside normal short-night operational range to protest vigorously if they were denuded of their anti-aircraft defences to benefit other places. In the same way, attacking a second-class target like Wuppertal, which had practically no defences, would no doubt make Solingen, Remscheid, Hagen, etc., clamour for protection.

SUMMARY OF OPERATIONS

The Battle of the Ruhr

68. Although 10 per cent. of our whole bombing effort in 1942, namely 3,724 sorties, had been directed against Essen, no important damage had been inflicted on the Krupp works and little on the town. In the course of 1943, however, this huge and most important target was virtually ruined by a smaller number of attacks, all of them successful, representing only 5·6 per cent. of the total effort (*i.e.,* 3,261 sorties and, in spite of the greater intensity of the opposition, for a loss of fewer aircraft (138 missing, as against 201 missing on Essen in 1942. In fact, the captured municipal records now reveal that a high proportion of the bombs dropped in all big raids from March, 1943, onwards fell in the target area. (O.R.S. (B.C.) Report No. 233, "The Effect of Air Attack on Essen and District," para. 19.)

69. On 5/6th March, 1943, a force of 442 aircraft was despatched against Essen and found good weather over the Ruhr area apart from the usual industrial haze. The "OBOE" ground-marking technique was unanimously reported to have been very well executed by the Pathfinders.

"Red target indicators were well positioned and the backers up, with green target indicators, bombed with great accuracy, focussing the attack on the centre of the target. Innumerable fires were seen well concentrated around the markers, there being an almost solid circle of fires two miles in diameter."

Nothing like this had ever happened to Essen in any previous attack and, as a result of the bombing concentration achieved, only 14 aircraft were missing from this operation. Years of endeavour, of experiment, and of training in new methods had at last provided the weapon and the force capable of destroying the heart of the enemy's armament industry. It was an achievement comparable only with the "Thousand Raid" on Cologne, and marked an important turning point in the Bomber campaign.

70. As a result of this attack, and two others which followed within a month of it, about 600 acres of the built-up area of Essen were damaged or destroyed. In the course of these three attacks about half of the 300 separate buildings in the Krupp works were damaged. By the end of July, 1943, three more attacks had reduced this great industrial complex to a veritable shadow of its former self – the best of these

attacks (25/26th July) executed by about 700 aircraft, inflicted as much damage on the Krupp works as in all previous attacks put together. Essen was then left alone for a period of nine months and, although repairs were pushed forward on first priority during the winter of 1943/44, many buildings were never rebuilt. Among these was the largest single unit in the whole works, the huge "Hindenburg Hall," where locomotive construction ceased after the second "OBOE" attack in March, 1943, and never restarted – in spite of the fact that locomotive construction then had equal priority with aircraft, tanks and submarines. (Apart from Kassel, the Essen plant had the largest locomotive output of any works in Axis Europe). Other major war requirements, the production of which ceased as a result of these attacks from March-July, 1943, included large shells (previous output 400 per month) and fuses (200,000 per month); while output of guns, gun tubes and liners dropped to half the previous level, and aero-engine crankshafts – an especially important item at this period of the War – previously produced at the rate of 1,000 per month, followed the general downward trend.

Other Ruhr Targets

71. During these five months, while Essen was receiving this tremendous punishment, all the chief industrial cities of the Ruhr were attacked in turn. Dortmund, one of the chief centres of German heavy industry; Duisburg, the great inland port with its complex of industrial satellite towns, rolling mills, etc.; Bochum and Gelsenkirchen; Oberhausen and Mulheim; as well as subsidiary outlying towns such as Wuppertal (Barmen-Elberfeld), Krefeld and Munster; Aachen; Remscheid and München-Gladbach; were all damaged – most of them very heavily – within this period. In all, some 14,000 sorties were despatched in the course of the "Battle of the Ruhr," if we include attacks on Düsseldorf and Cologne.

72. Düsseldorf was the leading commercial city of Western Germany and was the seat of the general administrative departments of practically all the important iron and steel, heavy engineering and armaments concerns of the Ruhr and Rhineland, as well as a very important engineering and armaments centre in itself. It received two attacks, each by about 700 aircraft, in the course of the "Battle of the Ruhr." The first (25/26th May) was marred by the presence of cloud up to 20,000 ft., which obscured the markers. The second attack (11/12th June), in good weather, achieved a very heavy concentration round the aiming point. The A.R.P. services were completely overwhelmed, and an immense conflagration raged unchecked over the main part of the city. Some buildings were still smouldering a week after the attack. Many engineering, armaments and rail transportation targets were included in the indescribable devastation revealed by photographic reconnaissance.

73. Since the "Thousand Plan" operation in May, 1942, strenuous efforts had been made to re-habilitate Cologne, both as an administrative and production centre. An outstandingly successful "blind" attack by some 600 aircraft, employing "OBOE" "sky-marking" technique, caused considerably more damage than the well-known

attack of the previous year, and within the next ten days further attacks smashed, first, the very important industrial district on the east bank of the Rhine and then the northern area, including the extensive railway facilities there. Indeed, in its subsequent laments for Cologne Cathedral, German propaganda drew attention to one of the few buildings of importance which had received only minor damage.

74. The successful breaching, on the night of 16/17th May, 1943, of the famous Möhne Dam[13] by Lancasters of No. 617 Squadron, which released a flood of 130 million gallons of the upper waters of the river Ruhr, was merely one outstanding incident in what must have been a period of indescribable strain for the three million inhabitants of the great industrial region of the Ruhr. On the same night, the Eder Dam was also destroyed, and Kassel partially flooded.

75. By the middle of July, 1943, conditions in the Rhineland and the Ruhr had reached a state of chaos to which it was only necessary to contribute occasional "topping-up" attacks, to dissuade the authorities from parting with their defences in response to clamour from other regions.

The Destruction of Hamburg

76. If the five months of the "Battle of the Ruhr" were months of severe trial for the enemy, the virtual annihilation of the second city of the Reich within six days at the end of July, 1943, was incomparably more terrible. This was accomplished by 2,355 Bomber Command sorties (on the nights of 24/25th, 27/28th, 29/30th July) and two small-scale daylight attacks, totalling 235 sorties, by the U.S. Eighth Air Force (25th and 26th July). Excluding a further attack on 2nd/3rd August, which went astray owing to extremely bad weather, Bomber Command aircraft dropped over 7,196 tons of H.E. and incendiaries on the city, while the U.S. aircraft contributed 254 tons, mainly H.E.

77. Official German reports make plain the magnitude of the "catastrophe" which these attacks wrought upon Germany's greatest maritime centre which, up to this time, had a population of nearly two millions. The extracts[14] which follow are translated from a publication intended for German official use only:

Effect of Attack

(24/25th July) "The first attack caused gigantic fires which could not be put out even after 24 hours had elapsed. Coal and coke supplies stored for the winter in many houses caught fire and could only be extinguished weeks later. Essential services were severely damaged and telephone communications were cut early in the attack. Dockyards and industrial installations were severely hit. At mid-day next day there was still a gigantic dense cloud of smoke and dust hovering over the city which, despite the clear sky, prevented the sun from penetrating through. The Police

Presidium burned down . . . The Central Control Room was completely engulfed by fires and had to be evacuated in the early morning under great difficulties.

"An auxiliary control post formed at the Bd0 control never failed. Numerous other control rooms and police service stations as well as RLB offices were destroyed or put out of action. Communications were maintained by motor-cyclists. Every minute Control Centre was flooded by reports of large-scale fires, of the fall of dropped blockbusters and H.E.s. Officers on damage recce, could not on account of long detours get back with their observations and reports for hours. Despite employment of all available forces, big fires could not be prevented from flaring up again and again . . .

(27/28th July) "The continuation of the first attack by daily and nightly nuisance raids made the enemy's intention to destroy Hamburg systematically quite plain. Therefore the fact of a fifth raid in the night from July 27th to the 28th was not surprising. Its magnitude and consequences, however, were far beyond all expectations. At least 800 planes attacked the city in several waves from all sides. The main weight of the attack was this time at the left shore of the Alster. Within half an hour the whole left side was in a terrible situation by a bombardment of unimaginable density and almost complete annihilation of those town districts was achieved by the enemy in a very short time. Extensive parts of that area were enveloped in a sea of fire within half an hour. Tens of thousands of small fires united within a short period of time to conflagrations which developed to firestorms of typhoon-like intensity, in the course of which trees of 3 ft. in diameter were pulled out of the ground. As a consequence the War Minister asked women and children for a voluntary evacuation of the town. Hundreds of thousands left, so that in the next attack the enemy found only LS forces present in the town . . .

(29/30th July) "Compared with the number of planes and bombs dropped this was the heaviest attack, and it was chiefly on those parts of the town which had not been affected up till now. The port was severely hit and the remaining part of the thickly populated district of Barmbeck was completely destroyed by fire. Damage was gigantic.

"The failing of the water system, and the fighting of fires which still remained from earlier attacks, hampered all work severely. The whole of Hamburg was on fire. Rescue, evacuation, clearing of vital roads, fire fighting, etc. asked the impossible from all available LS forces. Economically, Hamburg was knocked out, as even the undamaged parts had to stop work on account of the destruction of water, gas and electricity supplies."

78. A secret document entitled *"Fire Typhoon – Hamburg, Night 27/29th July, 1943,"* begins thus:—

"The cause of the terrific damage lies in the fire-storms. The alternative dropping of blockbusters, H.E.s and incendiaries made fire-fighting impossible, small fires united into conflagrations in the shortest time and these in their turn led to the fire-storms. To comprehend these firestorms, which go beyond all human imagination, one can only analyse them from a physical meteorological angle. Through the unison of a number of fires, the air gets so hot, so on account of its decreasing specific weight, receives a terrific momentum, which in its turn causes other surrounding air to be sucked towards the centre. By that suction combined with the enormous difference in temperature (600-1,000 degrees centigrade) tempests are caused which go beyond their meteorological counterparts (20-30 degrees centigrade). In a built-up area the suction could not follow its shortest course, but the overheated air stormed through the streets with immense force, taking along not only sparks but burning timber and roof beams, so spreading the fire further and further, developing in a short time into a fire typhoon such as was never before witnessed, against which every human resistance was quite useless."

79. Further indications of the industrial effect of this series of attacks are given in Part III, paras. 175-187. When the smoke had cleared sufficiently to permit photographic reconnaissance, on 1st August, it was seen that the heavily damaged areas covered no less than 6,200 out of the 8,380 acres which comprised Hamburg's closely built-up residential districts – *i.e.,* 74 per cent. Practically all parts of the city and docks were shattered, all the four main ship-building yards (including the U-Boat yards) were directly damaged, and every type of power and transportation service brought to a standstill.

80. The loss of 57 aircraft (2·4 per cent.) on the three night attacks in July, which achieved the bulk of these annihilating results, can only be regarded as minute. Previous attacks on Hamburg had entailed far heavier casualties (about 6 per cent. of sorties despatched) and the low casualties incurred in the July operations were due to the disorganisation of the German defences by "WINDOW" employed from this time onwards with outstanding success. It is true that the last of the series of attacks, which took place in very bad weather on 2nd/3rd August, achieved no worthwhile concentration over the target, and as a result of this and severe icing conditions, casualties (4·1 per cent.) were rather heavier. Even including this last attack, losses on these four Hamburg operations were less than half the previously expected rate for this heavily-defended target.

81. Incidentally, on the night after the first Hamburg attack when we returned to Essen with highly effective results, a German ground controller was overheard to inform the fighter pilot he was supposedly controlling: "I cannot follow any of the hostiles, for they are very cunning." Such testimonials to "WINDOW" were frequently intercepted about this time, and the disorganisation of the Hamburg defences showed that they were by no means undeserved.

Operations against Berlin, 1943/1944

82. Like Essen and Hamburg, the German capital had suffered little before 1943. Indeed, I had refused to attack Berlin in 1942 because I considered that I had not enough heavy bombers to achieve the concentration necessary to saturate its defences. In practice, even in 1943, the strength of the force was insufficient. By the summer of 1944, when the force had increased to a size which would have enabled me to

tackle Berlin under reasonable conditions, the Command had been diverted to the support of the invasion of France.

83. Berlin was, of course, a very different proposition from the Ruhr or coastal targets. It entailed many more hours flying over heavily-defended regions, whatever the direction of approach – four flying hours at the very minimum. It was the target which above all the Luftwaffe was bound to defend, and no chances would be taken with it even if that involved leaving lesser places like Stettin and Hanover to look after themselves. The flak defences were proportionately powerful. Finally, the mere size of this sprawling city of four million inhabitants – the closely built-up zones alone contained 18,000 acres, as compared with 8,380 at Hamburg – meant that no noticeable impression could be made on it except by a strong force of heavy bombers.

84. When, in the autumn of 1942, I was urged to attack Berlin in strength, I had about 70 to 80 Lancasters available. This force was obviously quite insufficient for the purpose. Moreover, the Lancasters then suffered from fuel installation troubles, which made them unable to exploit their full altitude. By New Year 1943, those troubles had been overcome, and between 150 and 200 Lancasters were available. Such a force would be able to drop some 400 or 500 tons of bombs on Berlin, and I judged that little would be gained by adding the 100 odd Halifaxes and the 50 odd Stirlings then available since they would be forced to operate between 14,000 and 18,000 ft. At that height they would attract the whole weight of the flak defences, and could in any case only contribute a little over half of the load carried by a Lancaster at that range. In order to secure adequate concentration over the defences, either the Lancasters would have to be pulled down from the comparative immunity of high altitudes to the average altitude of the Halifax and Stirling attack, thereby exposing the Lancasters also to a vastly increased risk, or, alternatively, the Halifaxes and Stirlings would have to bear the brunt far below the Lancasters, with consequent risk of very serious casualties.

85. I therefore resolved at the outset to employ the whole force of approximately 400 aircraft, but only half of it on the main objective. It so happened, however, that the diversionary forces could not be employed during the first two attacks on Berlin, which were therefore executed, by the Lancasters only, on consecutive nights in mid-January 1943. Haze and snowcover prevented the Pathfinders from identifying the target (no radar aids were employed) and although some important factories were hit no great damage was done. Only one aircraft was lost on the first operation, although the flak was heavy; but many German fighters were able to operate in moonlight on the next night and 22 bombers were lost. In the absence of any increase in the proportion of Lancasters, whose numbers were still insufficient either to saturate the defences or to inflict adequate damage on so large a target, I was obliged to include Halifaxes and Stirlings in subsequent operations.

86. The most successful of these early 1943 attacks was that of 1st/2nd March, when "H.2.S." was employed against Berlin for the first time. "H.2.S." operators reported that the responses from the built-up areas entirely filled the screen, making it impossible to recognise the aiming point. Most of the bombing was centred on the

south-western outskirts of Berlin, where heavy damage to industrial plants and business and residential property was revealed by photographic reconnaissance.

87. Two further attempts at the end of March were unfortunately ineffective because, on the first occasion the markers were wrongly placed, while on the second (29/30th March) the "H.2.S." aircraft of the P.F.F. achieved a remarkably good grouping of markers around the aiming point but the main force arrived too late to use them.[15] The overall loss rate on these five preliminary attacks on Berlin in January and March, 1943, was 4·6 per cent., which was light considering the target.

88. After March, no attacks could be carried out so far east as Berlin until the end of August, when the German capital again came within the operational radius. Then, following the destruction of the second city of Germany (Hamburg) a month earlier, 1,647 sorties were despatched against the capital in three attacks within 10 days. The annihilation of Hamburg had inspired such respect for the R.A.F. that, although none of these attacks was well centred on the aiming point, the panic evacuation which followed was compared by some observers to that experienced in Hamburg. Heavy industrial damage was inflicted on the Siemensstadt and Mariendorf districts, and the total built-up area destroyed or severely damaged up to the end of this period approached 500 acres.

89. The "Battle of Berlin" started in earnest in mid-November, 1943, and continued unabated throughout the winter until the second half of March, 1945. In view of the importance of the target, its distance, and the greatly strengthened German defences, it was to be expected that losses would be higher than for other targets at shorter range. In fact, 500 aircraft were missing on 16 major raids on Berlin during this period, the loss measured in terms of aircraft despatched was 6·2 per cent. As this was approximately equal to the pre-"WINDOW" loss-rate on Hamburg it could not be regarded as excessive in relation to the magnitude of the task.

90. Meteorological conditions were, however, invariably poor on all 16 occasions, necessitating "sky-marking" above cloud by P.F.F. aircraft using, on 18/19th November, 1943, "H.2.S." Mark III.[16] Some of these attacks evidently went astray, but from the extent of the damage revealed by reconnaissance it is equally evident that several of them achieved a large measure of success. To the 480 gross acres of devastation in Berlin before, these operations added a further 2,180 gross acres of devastation – an aggregate of rather more than four square miles – excluding considerable additional damage in the outlying suburbs. The greater part of the damage lay in the western half of the city and was particularly heavy in the districts bordering the Tiergarten. In the eastern half of Berlin the damage was more scattered. A large number of important war industries were affected by direct damage to factories, including (for example) Daimler-Benz A.G., producers of tanks, tractors and aero-engines, the B.M.W. aero-engine works, and many others. Damage to the complex of Siemens factories was particularly extensive. State, Ministerial and public buildings suffered much damage, and some State departments were evacuated to provincial towns.

Other Industrial Centres in Germany

91. By August, 1943, the short-range targets in the Ruhr and Rhineland had been very severely dealt with. It then became practicable to concentrate on important industrial cities beyond "OBOE" range, for which "H.2.S." was available as an aid to navigation and marking. Operations against Hamburg and Berlin have been described above, but there remained many other industrial centres, among them some considered to be of special importance as centres of German aircraft production. The directif of 10th June, 1943, having assigned first priority to the joint attack of such targets by the R.A.F. and U.S. Eighth Air Force, Bomber Command sent strong forces against Stuttgart, Kassel, Augsburg, Schweinfurt, Leipzig, Frankfurt, Magdeburg, and other centres upon which the aircraft industry depended. "H.2.S." had by no means solved navigational and blind-bombing problems of long-range operations to the extent that "OBOE" had done for short-range targets in Western Germany. It had, however, much improved the chances of success against those objectives which were previously unassailable. While full success was not achieved by the majority of attacks dependent on "H.2.S." marking, when the marking was well executed tremendous punishment was inflicted which surpassed all previous efforts against those targets.

92. Outstanding attacks were delivered against Kassel (22nd/23rd October), when over 90 per cent. of the bombs dropped fell on the built-up area, Leipzig (3rd/4th December) when heavy damage was inflicted through cloud-cover, Augsburg (25/26th February), Frankfurt (18/19th and 22nd/23rd March), Hanover (8/9th October), Mannheim (5/6th September). Extremely heavy direct damage was caused to a number of aircraft assembly and component factories in these night raids, one most impressive example being the wrecking of 26 engineering workshops of the Junkers Company on the World's Fair site at Leipzig. Several buildings here were completely razed to the ground, while in others the contents were gutted, leaving only the roofless walls standing. Of the 17 large buildings on the site, not one escaped damage, and the largest hall, which boasted an unsupported roof-span of 320 ft., was completely shattered. At Stuttgart the heaviest industrial damage occurred in the Robert Bosch sparking-plug factory and main foundries, the large ball-bearing plant of V.K.F., and the Daimler-Benz aero-engine and armaments plant also suffered severely. At Kassel (the attack on 3rd/4th October) the F.W.190 aircraft factory (Bettenhausen plant) was heavily damaged. But it would be impracticable to give here a full list of the important industrial concerns involved in the ruin of these great centres of German war production.

93. Two attempts were made, in April and May, 1943, to eliminate the Skoda Works at Pilsen, the importance of which had become enhanced by our success against Krupp at Essen. Especially on the second attack the bombing concentration was outstandingly good, but unfortunately on both occasions the marking was displaced a little distance from the aiming point.

94. Two other notable operations against specific German factories at long range must be mentioned. The former Zeppelin Works at Friedrichshafen on Lake Constance, was attacked by No. 5 Group Lancasters in the first "shuttle raid" on

20th/21st June, 1943. The plant, which was producing radar apparatus, received heavy damage and about half of the equipment of the factory is said to have been destroyed. The neighbouring Maybach tank-engine factory was also much damaged, but not so severely as it was in the very successful Bomber Command attack 11 months later.

95. The experimental "V Weapon" establishment at Peenemünde on the Baltic coast was attacked by a force of nearly 600 heavies on 17/18th August, 1943. To ensure the bombing pattern needed to knock out the many small buildings dispersed over a large area, the attack was delivered in full moonlight, although this gave maximum opportunity to enemy night fighters. As the route to the target was largely identical with that used in previous attacks on Berlin, a harassing raid on the capital by Mosquitos was arranged to deceive the defence, at least for a time, as to the real objective. This ruse was initially successful, but as soon as the enemy realised the real target, night fighters were brought up from covering Berlin and as far as the Ruhr to intercept the bombers on their return route. The last of the three waves of bombers suffered rather heavy losses. In all, 40 aircraft were missing on the Peenemünde operation, but the bombing achieved outstanding results. In the living and sleeping quarters of the establishment 90 detached huts and three large barracks were destroyed or severely damaged, while in the northern section the senior officers' mess and 35 other buildings were shattered. Units of the factory workshops were also hit, and it is known that casualties were very heavy and included some important scientists and leading members of the staff of the experimental establishment. German threats of attack against this country by "secret weapons" thereafter became noticeably less specific as regards dates.

Attacks on Factories in Occupied France

96. The requirement to destroy French factories associated with G.A.F. production was met by a special low-level marking and bombing technique evolved by No. 5 Group (*see* Appendix B). The first of these attacks was carried out in clear weather on the Gnome and Rhone aero-engine factory at Limoges on 8/9th February, 1944, when 12,000-lb. bombs were dropped with highly satisfactory results.

97. In the space of seven weeks, up to the end of March, 12 small but important French targets were bombed and only one of these – in this case a viaduct – escaped damage. Four of the factories were so thoroughly wrecked that no attempt was made to rebuild them. All the others suffered extensive damage. These remarkable results were obtained for a total effort of less than 350 sorties, and a single missing aircraft.

98. Perhaps the most impressive testimony to the bombing technique employed was the execution of the attack on the needle-bearing works at St. Etienne/La Ricamerie. This time weather was described as "greatly hampering the attack" so that the planned procedure had to be modified. The leader reported that "cloud made it impossible to see the target except from directly overhead. Flares could not be used since their setting would have caused them to burn above the clouds" – which were at 6,000-8,000 ft. He therefore marked with 30 lb. incendiaries the west and eastern

edges of the target and ordered the other 15 Lancasters to bomb the incendiaries through cloud. In the circumstances it would not have surprised anyone acquainted with the difficulties of night bombing if a factory which only covered an area of about 170 yards by 90 yards had escaped serious injury. However, reconnaissance showed it almost entirely destroyed, and the ruins formed the centre of a compact group of bomb-craters.

Last Attacks on Italy

99. The last stages in the bombing of the industrial cities of Italy were extremely successful, both in causing material damage and in finally destroying what little inclination remained in that country to continue a disastrous war.

100. The chief naval base, at Spezia, was heavily damaged by two attacks in April, 1943, and the "shuttle raiders" visited this target on their return from North Africa.

101. During the last month immediately preceding the Italian capitulation Bomber Command despatched 1,708 sorties against Milan, Turin, Genoa, Leghorn, and switching and transformer stations in Northern Italy. Milan fared worst in these attacks. All forms of transport broke down and mass evacuation was carried out largely on foot. The bombing produced quite hysterical accounts of woe in the press and radio, and there is little doubt that it was the principal factor contributing to the downfall of Mussolini's regime.

Sea Mining

102. During the year 1943 no less than 13,835 sea mines were laid by Bomber Command. A further 4,234 were laid in the first quarter of 1944, for a loss of only 0·8 per cent. of sorties, an improvement largely due to the development of the high-altitude dropping technique. The results of these very successful operations are summarised in Appendix H.

THE FINAL YEAR
APRIL, 1944, TO THE END

103. The heavy and sustained bombing of Germany had begun in earnest in March, 1943. This bombing campaign, designed to weaken the enemy's will to resist and to deprive him of the weapons necessary to wage a successful war, was at its height a year later when the invasion plan began to make its influence felt on bombing operations. The plan ("Overlord") required the employment of a large part of all available bomber forces, on tasks directly related to the invasion, for a period of three months preceding D-Day. During the period 14th April-25th September, 1944, all strategical bomber forces of the R.A.F. and U.S.A.A.F. engaged on operations related

to the invasion and the reduction of the G.A.F. were placed under the direction of the Supreme Allied Commander. (Directif letter C.M.S. 342/D.C.A.S., dated 13th April, 1944.)

104. The invasion of the Continent involved the solution of three great military problems. The three problems may be shortly summarised as follows:—

(*a*) The coastal fortifications had to be breached and one or more beachhead positions secured.

(*b*) The build-up of our forces in the beachheads had to be more rapid than the concentration of the enemy's reserve force at the threatened place.

(*c*) When the build-up of our forces was sufficient for the purpose, the armies had to break out of the beachheads and gain room for manoeuvre.

In the solution of each of these three problems Bomber Command was able to make a vital contribution.

105. The first of the preparatory operations, the bombing of the railway centre at Trappes, took place on 6/7th March, 1944, and by the beginning of April "Invasion" targets became the primary objective of the Command. As the date of the invasion approached, the demands for attacks on tactical targets increased to such an extent that, whereas in April it was still possible to direct about 40 per cent. of the total weight of attack against Germany, during June only 8 per cent. was available for the purpose. Indeed, during the five months, May to September 1944, the tottering German home front experienced a virtual respite from bombing since many new commitments absorbed over 85 per cent. of Bomber Command's effort during that period.

THE STRIKING POWER OF THE COMMAND

106. The following table gives an indication of the increased striking power of the Command during 1944 as compared with the previous year. In making the comparison it should be remembered that the year 1943 was itself a year of high achievement, since the tonnage dropped was 72 per cent. greater than for the whole of the 3¼ years September 1939 to December 1942.

Average number of aircraft with crews available.	1943.	1944.
Heavy bombers	590	1,119
Medium bombers	106	nil
Light bombers	41	97
TOTAL	737	1,216 (excluding Bomber Support A/C).
Total sorties	65,068	166,844
Sorties on bomb raids	57,880	126,347
Total tons dropped	157,434	525,518

With a 65 per cent. increase in aircraft with crews, the effort in terms of bombing sorties despatched was 118 per cent. greater, and the tonnage dropped increased by 234 per cent., and passed the half-million mark.

The rate of effort works out at 137 sorties per aircraft available with crew, compared with 89 for the previous year. Despite the great increase in the rate of effort, serviceability of aircraft was maintained at an average throughout 1944 of 82 per cent. of strength.

PREPARATION FOR INVASION

107. Apart from the destruction of coast defences, dealt with later, the Allied military leaders considered that the success of the invasion of Northern France would be jeopardised unless the possibility of major reinforcement by rail was denied to the enemy. As an essential preliminary, therefore, the bomber forces were required to paralyse the whole railway system from the Rhine westwards to the assault area. Unless this was done, the rate of the enemy's build-up in Normandy could easily exceed our own. Seventy-nine railway centres mainly in Northern France, but also in Belgium and Western Germany, were scheduled for attack by Bomber Command, the U.S. Eighth Air Force, and the A.E.A.F. Of the three forces, Bomber Command was assigned the largest share, *i.e.,* about half of the total number of targets. (In addition, the Mediterranean-based 15th Air Force was allotted a number of targets in Southern France and Germany, but was able to operate for three days only at the end of May.)

108. The primary object of the pre-invasion plan was the destruction of rail depots together with the associated repair and maintenance facilities. Any damage to marshalling yards, rolling stock, or through main lines was to be regarded as a

welcome but incidental bonus. Targets and the aiming points within these were selected to fulfil the primary objective.

109. As Bomber Command had little experience of attacking railway centres or other similar targets many new problems had to be investigated before this series of night operations could be economically and successfully undertaken. Transportation experts advised that the aim should be to put down a concentration of 500-lb. bombs, around a chosen aiming point, sufficient to achieve a stated overall density of bomb-strikes. The estimated density of strikes, they believed, would cause damage to the priority buildings and to most of the essential repair and operating facilities throughout the area.

110. There were a number of difficulties from the operational angle. The most serious problem, was to know beforehand the weight of attack necessary to achieve the required density of hits. To answer this an estimate of the overall accuracy to be expected was needed and the number of bombs required to be dropped in each case. This was obtained by theoretical assessment based upon scientific analysis of crater distribution resulting from night attacks on a number of small objectives such as flying bomb sites, and factories at Friedrichshafen, Le Creusot, etc. A detailed explanation of the method used is given in Appendix B. The number of bombs required to be aimed at each target was calculated.

111. In view of the possible vagaries of weather and of marking aids, and the small size of the sub-targets (which were the real objectives), it was obvious that the estimated tonnage of bombs could not produce the required result every time. The proportion of successful attacks could, of course, be increased by despatching more than the required number of bombs. Moreover the time factor had always to be borne in mind and, to take full advantage of a short spell of favourable weather, one heavy attack was sometimes preferable to a number of smaller ones.

112. By D-Day all 37 of the railway centres assigned to Bomber Command had been damaged to such an extent that no further attention from heavy bombers was deemed necessary. The "long-term" requirement having been fully completed other rail facilities were then included in the plan, with particular emphasis on smashing rail junctions and cross-overs, and the cutting of tracks. In all, from the first attack on Trappes on the night of 6/7th March, to the end of June, Bomber Command carried out 81 attacks on rail centres. Twenty-one further attacks were directed against the "short-term" objectives (junctions, tunnels, etc.) from the end of May to the end of June. All groups in the Command were absorbed in the campaign, but Halifaxes of No. 4 and No. 5 Groups provided the major part of the effort.

113. In every instance success in these operations depended on accurate placing of target markers. The markers were generally laid from a high altitude by Pathfinder Mosquitos, using "OBOE." Main force crews were invariably instructed not to bomb if markers were not seen, and on many occasions they were forbidden to bomb until the position of the markers had been assessed by a "master bomber." Marking by visual means and from a lower level was also carried out on 28 occasions, sometimes by aircraft of the Pathfinder Group or of No. 1 Group but mainly by crews of No. 5 Group using the methods successfully developed by that group for attacking factories

as described above. A total of 13,349 sorties, dropping 52,547 tons of bombs, were made up to the end of June, for a loss of about 2·6 per cent. of the aircraft despatched.

114. In most of the attacks the bombing accuracy was of a high, and in many, of an outstandingly high, order. For instance, at two important centres near Paris – Juvisy and La Chapelle – the whole railway complex was almost annihilated as the result of single attacks, engine round-houses and depots, marshalling yards, rolling stock, and nearly all the other facilities had almost entirely disappeared. Reconnaissance showed complete wildernesses resembling nothing so much as a telescopic view of the extinct craters of the moon.

115. By D-Day, as a result of the combined efforts of Bomber Command, U.S. Eighth Air Force and the Allied Expeditionary Air Force, 51 of the 80 targets on the list were assessed as "damaged to such an extent that no further attacks were necessary until vital repairs have been effected," while all but four of the remainder were "very severely damaged, but with some of the locomotive facilities still serviceable." All the targets attacked by Bomber Command fell within one or other of these categories.

116. The best indication of the success of the three months' offensive against the railways is the fact that the enemy's major reinforcements reached the battlefront too late to prevent the firm establishment of the invading armies in Normandy. When they did percolate through to the front they found themselves operating in conditions of extreme disadvantage. Not only were they fighting under the shadow of overwhelming Allied air supremacy against which their own fighters hardly dared to put in a fleeting appearance, but they were attempting to hold a front behind which, for three or four hundred miles, the vital rail system was in a state of wreckage and complete confusion. Many instances could be quoted to show the chaotic conditions under which the enemy had to try to move his divisions, their equipment and supplies. The chaos was tremendously increased by a succession of attacks on rail junctions, crossings and bridges during the week before D-Day, and maintained after the battle had been joined in Normandy.

117. Although many other tasks were allotted to the Command after D-Day, the attacks on the rail transportation system were still sustained, in co-operation with the Eighth U.S.A.A.F. The principal object of these attacks was to isolate the battle zones from outside supply and reinforcement, and the targets attacked were the main junctions in the following areas:—

(*a*) Nantes-Angers-Saumur-Tours-Orleans area, to cut rail traffic from southern France.

(*b*) Orleans-Chateaudun-Chartres-Etampes-Dreux area, to cut rail traffic from south-eastern and eastern France.

(*c*) Paris junctions, to cut rail traffic from north-eastern and eastern France.

(*d*) Rennes-Pontaubault area, to cut rail traffic from Brest and the Brest Peninsula.

In addition, a large number of fighter-bomber and armed reconnaissance sorties were flown by A.E.A.F. against smaller junctions, bridges, rail traffic, etc., within the same area.

118. One of the most spectacular of this series of attacks was accomplished on the night of 8/9th June by 16 Lancasters, each carrying a 12,000 lb. bomb. The aim was to block the main line from the south-west at Saumur tunnel. The entrance to the tunnel was effectively blocked and remained so until it fell into our hands. To sum up, it may be said with justification that these attacks on rail centres by Bomber Command played a major part in creating the local conditions which made the invasion of France possible, and thus prepared the way for the rapid advance of the Allied armies.

Attack on Coastal Fortifications

119. For many weeks before the actual date of the invasion, the coastal defences from the Brest peninsula to the mouth of the Scheldt were unceasingly hammered. A total of 14,000 tons of bombs was dropped on these targets. It was not possible to concentrate on the place where the invasion was planned owing to the need for keeping the enemy guessing, and it was therefore made a rule that for every coastal battery or defence work bombed in the actual invasion area at least two had to be bombed in other districts. This trebled the magnitude of the task. Nevertheless, before the invasion, the great bulk of the coastal defences had been very heavily damaged, and the final attack, in which more than 5,000 tons of H.E. bombs were dropped on the coastal batteries covering the beaches where our troops landed, effectively silenced all opposition.

G.A.F. Targets

120. In continuation of the operations against factories associated with aircraft production and repair, the Command attacked a further number of such factories in occupied countries during April and May. In all, from the beginning of these attacks in February, very severe damage – in 11 cases virtual destruction – was inflicted on 23 out of 24 factories attacked. These included the major aircraft repair centres in France, Belgium and Norway. The loss of his most conveniently situated aircraft factories in occupied territory forced the enemy to go further afield to find undamaged repair facilities but, even when found, their value was diminished as a result of the attacks on rail communications.

121. But this represented only a small part in Bomber Command's contribution to the joint offensive to reduce the strength of the Luftwaffe below the planned scale. From the opening of the main Bomber Command offensive in March, 1943, to the end of May, 1944, no fewer than 70 factories in Germany known to be producing aircraft or aircraft components were shown by reconnaissance to have been destroyed or seriously damaged. This was achieved in the course of the Command's effort

against German industrial centres, especially those associated with the aircraft industry. In Berlin alone 27 factories identified as directly connected with aircraft production were for the most part severely damaged; while in Stuttgart 11, Leipzig 9, Frankfurt 7, and Friedrichshafen 6, works were similarly dealt with.

Other Military Targets

122. While Bomber Command continued its attacks on rail transportation, coastal defences and G.A.F. targets in occupied countries during the two months preceding the landing in Normandy, from the end of April demands were made for attacks on purely military objectives. The military depôts at Bourg Leopold and Mailly Le Camp were wrecked by heavy attacks during May. The destruction of Mailly was regarded as of particular importance, and this large depôt and tank park (it was one of the chief tank training centres in France, and the depôt of 21 Panzer Division) received 1,776 tons of bombs on 3/4th May. To ensure accuracy, the operation was carried out in brilliant moonlight, and enemy fighters were able to inflict considerable losses on our aircraft while they awaited the master bomber's instructions to bomb. Forty-two of our aircraft were missing out of 338 despatched, but the job was done. In the words of the Officer Commanding the Division, "the main concentration was accurately aimed at the most important permanent buildings, the ammunition stores and an A.A. battery ... In that part of the camp which was destroyed, the concentration of bombs was so great that not only did the splinterproof trenches receive direct hits, but even the bombs which missed choked them up and caused the side to cave in." German losses in personnel and equipment were severe. Five of the most important ammunition and ordnance depots used by the Wehrmacht and Luftwaffe in France were wrecked by Bomber Command during May, and the State Explosive Works at St. Medard en Jalles was successfully attacked at the end of April.

The Final Preparation

123. As D-Day approached attacks were made on targets directly associated with the landing operations, namely W/T and radar stations. The three W/T stations and the radar installation assigned to the Command for attack were put out of action. These operations culminated on the eve of D-Day with large-scale attacks on 10 batteries in the assault area: 1,136 aircraft took part and dropped a total of 5,315 tons of H.E. bombs. With a single exception, the batteries offered no serious resistance to the warships approaching the coast or to the invading forces. Most of them were completely silenced by the air bombardment.

124. Some 110 aircraft of the Command took part in a diversion aimed at deluding the enemy into believing that landings were to be attempted on the beaches near Cap d'Antifer and Boulogne. By means of a special type of "WINDOW" the approach of a large convoy was simulated in these areas, while dummy parachutists and special

apparatus were dropped at Yvetot, Maltot and Marigny. This operation was completely successful.

125. The approach of airborne forces of No. 38 Group and IX Troop Carrier Command was masked by a Bomber Command "MANDREL" force affecting the whole of the enemy's coastal radar system. The enemy's V.H.F. night fighter control system was also effectively jammed by "A.B.C." aircraft during the period when airborne forces were operating.

SUPPORTING THE ARMIES
(a) The Summer Battle

126. After the landings on 6th June, operations in direct support of the Armies remained the prime commitment of the Command. During the next fortnight weather conditions were particularly unfavourable, generally 6/10ths to 10/10ths low cloud, which made bombing difficult both by day and night. In consequence the U.S. heavy bombers were severely handicapped – cancellations were frequent and many of their sorties were abortive. It was all the more important, therefore, that at this critical stage Bomber Command was able to operate on every one of the seven nights following D-Day. No operation was cancelled owing to weather conditions, and all targets were bombed. These were mainly rail and road targets selected in accordance with the military situation. On most occasions it was necessary to bomb from below the clouds at altitudes of from 2,000 to 6,000 ft. Although marking was difficult and not always accurate at the first attempt, correction by the master bombers prevented stray bombing and ensured success in nearly all the attacks.

127. No sooner were the Armies established in Normandy than Bomber Command was called upon for attacks on an increasing variety of targets, first on synthetic oil plants in Germany and then, on 29th June, the A.E.A.F. "Crossbow" directif was received. From that date until mid-August flying-bomb launching sites and depôts became a high priority commitment, though the requirements of the Armies still had prior claim.

128. As a result of my decision in June 1944 to operate by daylight with fighter cover, as well as at night, the Command was able to undertake a very large part of the heavy demands made upon it. (For further details of these attacks, *see* Appendix D.) The first large-scale daylight operations were carried out against the dock areas of Le Havre (14th June) and Boulogne (15th June). Great importance was attached to the execution of these attacks, which were directed against the enemy surface vessels based on the two ports, at a time when it was essential that supplies should reach the Normandy beachhead in an uninterrupted flow. By attacking in daylight, just before sunset, the accuracy of the attack was increased and, in addition, it ensured maximum effect as the enemy vessels would be present and preparing to operate at sea during the hours of darkness.

129. The results achieved were a most valuable contribution to the success of our naval and military operations. At Le Havre the whole area of the docks was plastered

and practically all the naval vessels in the docks, totalling about 60 ships, were either sunk or damaged. At Boulogne results were similar, 28 vessels being reported sunk and several others damaged. The E-Boat pens at Le Havre were also attacked and seriously damaged by a small force using 12,000-lb. bombs. With the bulk of his light naval forces out of action, as a result of these attacks, the enemy was unable to interfere effectively against our sea communications across the Channel.

Attacks on Troop and Armour Concentrations in the Battle Area

130. It was at this stage, also, that for the first time my heavy bombers were called upon to give direct support to the army by striking at enemy troop concentrations in the battle area. On the night of 14/15th June, 1,168 tons of bombs were dropped on the road junction of Aunay-sur-Odon, 18 miles south of Bayeux, where Army Intelligence reported a concentration of enemy motor transport and troops. The road junction, the village, and anything of military importance which it may have contained, were entirely obliterated. Equal success was achieved at Evrecy on the same night.

131. Further operations of this type were called for at critical periods throughout the battle in Normandy. On 30th June, for instance, it was reported that 2nd and 9th S.S. Panzer Divisions were moving up to the fighting zone through Villers Bocage. This locality was the enemy's general supply point for the area and a road centre very difficult to by-pass. More than 1,100 tons of bombs dropped with great accuracy in a daylight attack by this Command blocked all roads and cratered the whole target area, preventing the attack by the S.S. Divisions which had been planned for that night.

132. A week later, in spite of pressure from the 1st Canadian and 2nd British Armies, the enemy still maintained his "hinge" position at Caen. A further Bomber Command attack was therefore called for against troop positions and strongpoints in the Caen area on 7th July. Four hundred and fifty-seven heavy bombers dropped in daylight 2,350 tons of H.E. in the space of 38 minutes.

133. The number of enemy troops killed in this attack was apparently not great, but all reports from prisoners showed that the morale effect was shattering. There was great confusion in the enemy lines and complete loss of offensive power. (After one such bombing attack it was said that a division was without food or supplies for a whole day.) It cannot be doubted that if the army had been able to follow up immediately this air bombardment in the Caen area the enemy would have been found in a state of chaos. As it was, even though our armour did not begin their limited advance until the following morning, the opposition was still so broken and confused that the first objectives were taken with the minimum loss of life to the attackers.

134. It was soon after this attack that the Chief of Ops. and Plans, A.E.A.F., expressed the view (13th July, 1944) that the Army had in the past rarely taken advantage on the immediate front of heavy bombing assistance, and that it also appeared, from enemy reports, that they were failing to exploit our continuing air

attacks on enemy rail communications. The latter were depriving the enemy's fighting troops of fuel and motor transport, seriously delaying his reinforcements, and causing a serious wastage of his armour by compelling it to make long road journeys. The Chief of Ops. and Plans considered that, unless the Army took advantage of these attacks, the air effort expended might be better employed on a return to attacks on German industries and the main bottle-necks of his flying-bomb organisation. (A.E.A.F. Operations Record Book.) Nevertheless Bomber Command was required to continue attacks on French rail communications until mid-August, and to be ready to blast a way for the Army through the enemy's lines practically whenever serious resistance was offered to our advance.

135. On 18th July a combined effort, including U.S. Eighth Air Force and A.E.A.F. was called for against three groups of enemy forces and installations to assist the 2nd Army advance south of Caen. Bomber Command despatched more than 1,000 sorties, contributing 5,000 out of the total of 6,800 tons of bombs dropped in this operation. As an indication of the effect of these attacks, the Bombing Analysis Unit found that a concentration of German tanks consisting of a Panzer Company with some Battalion H.Q. vehicles dispersed in an orchard was completely knocked out and ceased to exist as a fighting unit.[17] At the most only two tanks escaped serious bomb damage, and even if these had in fact been able to move under their own power (which is doubtful) they would have been unable to leave the area owing to the density of the craters. It was considered that a high proportion of the German personnel present during the attack became casualties. Large numbers of Germans suffering from shock and wandering about helplessly, were picked up by our troops in the other areas attacked on the same occasion.

136. In all there were eight occasions during the three months' battle in Northern France when this type of attack was called for, and some 17,560 tons were dropped on concentrations of German troops in the battle-field between D-Day and the middle of August.

137. But this was not by any means the limit of Bomber Command's assistance to the land forces. The by-passed coastal strongholds of Havre, Brest, Ile de Cezembre (part of the defences of St. Malo), Boulogne, Calais, and Cap Gris Nez, were all occupied with the help of the heavy bombers of my Command. The importance to the enemy of denying our armies the use of these places was so great that he was prepared to sacrifice their garrisons to the last man. Le Havre was bombed seven times a week, and altogether 9,750 tons of bombs were dropped on the defended areas of the port. This resulted in the capture by the Army of its garrison of 11,000 men for a loss of 50 soldiers. One attack – by 762 bombers, which dropped 3,347 tons of H.E. – was sufficient at Boulogne, which surrendered with 8,000 prisoners within a week. Calais was bombed six times, receiving a total of some 8,000 tons of H.E., with a similar result. Brest was bombed by U.S. heavies as well as our own, and action was co-ordinated with the naval plan of the period, principally concerned with preventing the escape of enemy surface and underwater vessels, and the sinking of any vessels which might be used as blockships.

138. At the end of September two attacks were made on the defended area and

gun positions at Cap Gris Nez. After some 3,700 tons of bombs were dropped, the Army was able to mop up the positions and the Straits of Dover were opened. Dover and other south coast towns were thus relieved of the sporadic shell-fire they had endured for years.

139. The coming of autumn found these operations nearing completion and the Germans on the run everywhere, except at the mouth of the Scheldt, from which position they controlled the entrance to the port of Antwerp. Bomber Command was again called in to bomb them out of the island fortress of Walcheren.

The Reduction of Walcheren Fortress

140. The capture of this island fortress, whose gun batteries commanded the sea approaches to the great port of Antwerp (occupied by the 2nd Army without a struggle on 4th September), was judged to be impracticable unless the guns had first been silenced. Bomber Command was required to attack not only the gun emplacements themselves, but the sea-wall of the island, most of which lies below sea-level.

141. Weather conditions were often difficult, the targets were small, but when suitable opportunities presented themselves the gun batteries were attacked with success. There were eleven opportunities in the latter half of September and during the following month, and a total of 6,000 tons of H.E. was dropped on the batteries.

142. The formidable task of progressively breaching the huge sea-wall at four selected points was assigned also to Bomber Command. On 3rd October the first attack was made, at the south-west corner of the island. Although the wall was 204 ft. thick at its base, sloping upwards to a thickness of 60 ft. at the top, 243 Lancasters attacking in successive waves effected a breach within an hour. Lancasters which followed up with 12,000 lb. bombs returned to base, as by then the object of the attack had been achieved.

143. The inrush of the sea drowned four gun emplacements, and by 7th October, when new breaches were on either side of Flushing, seven other batteries were seriously imperilled. The further successful breaching of the wall on the north-east coast on 11th October virtually completed the flooding of the low-lying parts of the island. In preparation for the final assault on the island, which began on 1st November, enemy positions still remaining above water received further attention from Bomber Command. By 6th November the approaches to Antwerp were virtually clear of the enemy, and the way was open for the supplies urgently needed by the Allied armies.

144. With France, Belgium and Southern Holland in Allied hands, the final phase of military operations appeared to be in sight. After the failure of the attempt to cross the Lower Rhine at Arnhem, in September, the American armies prepared to drive to the Cologne Plain. In conjunction with the U.S. Eight Air Force, Bomber Command renewed its attacks on enemy rail communications behind the front line – this time on German soil – and dropped more than 20,000 tons on German rail centres during November and December alone.

145. As the enemy had established strong positions on the line of the river Roer, covering the approaches to the Cologne plain, three fortified towns on the Roer (Düren, Jülich and Heinsburg) were allocated to Bomber Command for attack. The weather was clear on 16th November and the three towns received a total of 5,689 tons between them. It had been intended to make repeat attacks at Düren and Jülich, but the destruction was on such a scale that the Army stated that no further attacks were required.

The same type of attack had previously been delivered on the towns of Kleve and Emmerich, which were important points on the flank of the British 2nd Army. Three hundred and fifty aircraft were despatched to both targets in clear weather. Both targets were obliterated.

On five occasions between 3rd and 11th December, 1944, the Roer dams at Urft and Schwam-menauel were attacked, as the U.S. armies on the central sector of the front found their advance exposed to a potential threat of flooding. As in the case of the Sorpe dam (which was also bombed accurately but without conclusive results), the structure of the Roer dams was such that it was known to be impossible to cause immediate breaches with the heaviest bomb then available. It was hoped that sufficient damage might be done to cause seepage and consequent disintegration. Many direct hits were in fact scored. This was not sufficient, although photographs showed that the top of the Urft dam was deeply chipped at three points. In one case the chip extended almost down to the water-level, which at the time of reconnaissance was 13 ft. from the top. The enemy evidently manipulated the water-level so as to avoid erosion of the dam and spillway.

Rundstedt's Counter-offensive

146. Rundstedt's powerful counter-thrust, which opened on 16th December, coincided with a period of continuous and widespread fog and low cloud. Only in such conditions could the Germans hope to achieve success, for they had by then much practical experience of the truth of Field-Marshal Keitel's analysis, made 12 months earlier, that the strength of "the enemy lies firstly in his Air Force." Although weather seriously hampered air operations, during the first week of the offensive Bomber Command operated in strength on four nights and twice by day, attacking enemy rail communications in the general area for the concentration of troops and supplies. These attacks, and others by the U.S.A.A.F., continued at maximum intensity until the German withdrawal was in full swing. Some of the attacks on the railway centres were highly effective; for instance the night attack on 24/25th December on the Nippes yard at Cologne. There nearly all rail tracks were hit, much rolling stock destroyed and the yard itself was 100 per cent. unserviceable next day. Owing to poor weather some of the other railway centres were less seriously damaged, but all lines running westwards from Cologne, Bonn, Koblenz and Bingen were affected in varying degrees. In considering the effects of this type of operation, it may be noted that attacks on German road and rail communications up to the beginning of

November, 1944, are reported to have inflicted casualties to troops amounting to the equivalent of two divisions. This was before attacks on transportation were stepped up in response to Rundstedt's counter-offensive.

147. A particularly successful attack was made on the vital centre of the enemy's road communications at St. Vith on 26th December. This was the hub of the road network in the eastern Ardennes, and was attacked as soon as weather conditions were suitable. Prisoners of war subsequently reported that every single road was completely blocked and that the cratered area was so extensive that it was not even possible to clear detours through side streets around the great piles of rubble in the centre of the town. After the attack, a German engineer battalion was employed for a week on the task of restoring the roads. During this period two divisions, one *en route* to buttress the attack on Bastogne and the other rushing to the defence of Vielsale, were forced to by-pass the town. The delay caused by the detour resulted in many units arriving too late to dig in before the Allied counterattack. The roads were only partly usable 16 days after the attack, and the main roads were not in fact cleared until 3rd February, more than a week after the Allied occupation. There is much evidence that Rundstedt's offensive was crippled by shortages of supplies of all kinds.

148. Troop concentrations at the road junction of Houffalize were also bombed on the night of 30/31st December and again on 5/6th January. The town was virtually destroyed and a wide area heavily cratered.

149. In conjunction with his thrust on the ground the enemy used his air force in greater strength than at any time since D-Day. As part of a plan principally carried out by the U.S. Eighth Air Force, to immobilise the enemy's fighters, Bomber Command attacked airfields near Essen, Dusseldorf and Bonn on 24th and night of 24/25th December. All these airfields were heavily crated and rendered unserviceable, and a number of aircraft were destroyed on the ground.

150. In considering the part played by Bomber Command in the failure of the Ardennes counter-offensive, the story would not be complete without some reference to the effect on the offensive of the strategic bombing of Germany.

For this last all-out effort of the Germans to defeat the Allied armies, Rundstedt's divisions were equipped with tanks which, from the point of view of performance, were among the best produced by either side in this war. The blow was skilfully planned and might have achieved very considerable success, but for serious inadequacies of tank production. This situation first became apparent after the heavy damage inflicted on the main tank-transmission producer (Zahnradfabrik) and one of the two main tank-engine producers (Maybach) in the very effective Bomber Command attack on Friedrichshafen, in April, 1944. Soon after this, Reichsminister Speer assigned to the manufacture of tank engines, tank transmissions and assault guns equal priority with fighter aircraft production; and about a month later the Hauptausschuss Panzerwagen was informed that higher priority for production of Panther and Tiger tanks could not be applied for and that every effort must be made to get along without it.

151. Prisoners taken in the Ardennes battle reported that tank crews were sent to Panzer bases and depots inside Germany as long as seven weeks before the offensive,

but received their tanks only a day or two before they were due to take part in the operation. We know also that many tanks failed to reach the battle area owing to lack of fuel, and for the same reason sustained operation was impossible for those that got there. Innumerable cases of engine trouble and other mechanical defects were experienced during battle owing to inadequate running-in; and the enemy clearly had great difficulty in fitting out and maintaining armoured divisions at a strength which was sometimes below 60 and never much higher than 80 tanks. Such low tank holdings were by no means the result of any military tactical doctrine, but were merely the highest average that enemy production could maintain.

152. "Transport difficulties were decisive," said Speer, Hitler's War Production Minister, "in causing the swift breakdown of the Ardennes offensive . . . the most advanced railheads of the Reichsbahn were withdrawn further and further back during the offensive owing to the continuous air attacks."

Von Rundstedt himself (and Kesselring, too, for that matter) was equally aware that it was the Allied bombers which had encompassed his downfall and that of the Reich: "Air power was the first decisive factor in Germany's defeat. Lack of petrol and oil was the second, and the destruction of railways the third. The principal other factor was the smashing of the home industrial areas by bombing."

(c) The Crossing of the Rhine – The Last Phase

153. When at last the Allied armies closed up to the Rhine in February and March, 1945, heavy bombers were called in once more. The shattered industrial cities of Cologne, Duisburg, Dortmund and Essen were again very heavily and successfully attacked by Bomber Command, in daylight, to create chaos in the rear of the German armies on the east bank of the Rhine.

154. Wesel, on the same side of the Rhine below its junction with the Ruhr, was pulverised in a series of attacks during the second half of February. It was again attacked on 6th and 6/7th March, since it was packed with troops and equipment which had succeeded in getting away across the Rhine. (At least 3,000 vehicles were said to be parked in the town.) Owing to the extent to which Wesel had been wrecked by previous raids it was difficult to assess new damage from reconnaissance photographs. All roads were blocked.

155. During the one week ending 25th March, seventeen further attacks were made by Bomber Command in preparation for and support of the 21st Army Group crossing of the Rhine north and south of Wesel. They comprised five attacks on railway centres, five attacks on bridges and seven attacks on enemy troop concentrations and strongholds. These operations were outstandingly successful and the following extract from a message received from Field Marshal Montgomery pays tribute to their accuracy and effectiveness:—

"My grateful appreciation for the quite magnificent co-operation you have given us in the Battle of the Rhine. The bombing of Wesel last night (23/24th

March) was a masterpiece and was a decisive factor in making possible our entry into that town before midnight."

Another message from the Commando Force which occupied the town, refers to the operation as "a very fine attack. Only, one stick of bombs fell away from the aiming point and did no damage. Wesel was taken with only 36 casualties."

Having crossed the last German defence line in strength the Allied armies proceeded to occupy the devastated industrial areas while the last remnants of organized resistance lying in their path, between them and the Russians, were quickly reduced to impotence by heavy Bomber attacks by night and day on centres of administration and of rail and road communications.

THE OFFENSIVE AGAINST AXIS OIL

156. Throughout the whole period of the land battles from the week following D-Day, Bomber Command was committed to the offensive against German supplies of liquid fuel as well as to the destruction of enemy communications and to the direct support of our armies in the field.

The loss, in the latter part of summer 1944, of the Roumanian oil-fields, and the refineries there and in Poland, placed a premium upon the enemy's own refineries and synthetic oil plants, which had then to bear the burden of all demands for fuel for all services.

Thereafter the Ruhr synthetic oil plants were repeatedly attacked on high priority while U.S.A.A.F. continued to attack plants further afield. Up to the end of September the Command had dropped more than 12,600 tons of bombs on these plants, and oil production all over Germany had fallen to a very low level.

157. Repairs were, however, executed with great determination and a long period of bad weather raised the enemy's hopes of staging a big come-back by the oil industry during the winter. Reichsminister Speer circulated a telegram to this effect during September, in which he forecast that during the season of predominating bad weather and fog "the bombing of synthetic oil plants cannot then be carried out with the same precision ... in spite of the really considerable damage done, we can in a period of five to six weeks restore production to about two-thirds of the level. . . prior to the attacks."

On the contrary, Bomber Command, now using "GEE-H" marking, continued its attacks on the Ruhr synthetic oil and benzol plants throughout the winter. One by one these plants (and others attacked by the U.S. Eighth Air Force) were crippled beyond repair and fell out of the battle, destined to remain inactive for the rest of the War. Moreover, we carried out highly successful attacks during January and February, 1945, against the more remote plants at Pölitz, Leuna and Brux.

Speer himself later remarked that these attacks "were more effective in their results than day attacks (*i.e.,* by U.S. bombers) by reason of the fact that the superheavy bombs caused shattering damage to these plants." The same authority admitted that from June, 1944, onwards, aviation spirit was produced in such small quantities that it was not possible to meet the demands of the Luftwaffe. After October even the minimum emergency requirements of the G.A.F. could not be met.

In all, Bomber Command dropped more than 96,000 tons of bombs with decisive effect on Axis oil targets from D-Day to the end of the War.

THE FLYING BOMBS

158. Long before the first flying bomb was launched against this country, on the night of 15/16th June, 1944, my Command had taken effective action against this new weapon, by destroying a large part of the experimental station at Peenemunde in August 1943 (*see* para. 94 above), and by subsequent bombing of supply and launching sites in Northern France. The original system of 56 sites in the Pas de Calais area and eight sites in the Cherbourg area, after bombing attacks by my Command and U.S. Eight Air Force starting in December, 1943, was found by the enemy to be too vulnerable and had to be abandoned. The delay thus caused was of the greatest importance.

159. As soon as flying-bomb attacks began, during the week after the invasion, the attack of the new system of simplified launching sites, and the supply depots, became a high priority commitment for Bomber Command. During the latter half of June alone nearly 16,000 tons of bombs were dropped on these targets, and a further 44,000 tons up to the 3rd September, when the last flying-bomb was launched from a ground site.

160. The launching sites were very small and well concealed. For more than half the period of these operations there was cloud over the target area below 5,000 ft. Nevertheless, the majority of the sites were made inoperative. When the launching sites were reconstructed or removed elsewhere I was directed to destroy the dumps and depots in which the missiles were stored. The limestone coves and reinforced concrete structures which served as storage depots were heavily bombed with 1,000 lb. and 12,000 lb. H.E. bombs. Very severe damage was inflicted on the depots, repair work was wrecked or hindered and road and rail communications completely disrupted. As a result of all these attacks – and those against German industrial centres – the enemy's flying-bomb programme was so much delayed and reduced in scope that, although a serious trial to the people of London, it never had a chance of influencing decisively the course of the war.

THE BOMBING OF THE INDUSTRIAL CENTRES RESUMED

161. From April, 1944, for nearly half a year, the German home industrial centres experienced a virtual respite from bombing. In the few intervals between demands for assistance to the armies, or for the attack of flying-bomb targets, rail centres, oil plants, French aircraft factories, U-boat bases, etc., or when weather prevented operations over Western Europe, I carried out attacks on targets in Germany in

accordance with the current directif. During the period May-September, 1944, however, other commitments absorbed over 85 per cent. of Bomber Command's effort. Indeed, for a period of two months, which included D-Day, it proved impossible to attack any German city in strength.

162. As a result, determined efforts by the Nazi leaders to revive vital war production by patching up bombed factories and providing emergency living conditions for thousands of homeless workers made much headway during the spring and summer. Whilst the German armies were reeling back across France and Belgium, their heavy losses of war material were partly offset by a relative increase in the supply of new equipment coming from reorganized industry at home. This period was one of critical importance as new types of weapons were coming into production.

163. By the latter half of September military demands on my effort, though still considerable, were less than they had been; and the flying-bomb sites had been occupied. It became possible therefore, for me to resume the campaign against German industrial cities. On 25th September, 1944, the return of Bomber Command to its proper strategic role was accompanied by the re-transfer of operational control from the Supreme Allied Commander to the Chief of the Air Staff.

164. During the next seven months a tremendous effort, amounting to 153,000 tons of H.E. and incendiary bombs, was directed against the enemy's industrial cities. October was a month of record achievement in this respect as the bomb load dropped on industrial cities (42,246 tons) was not only higher than in any other month of the War, but also more than twice the pre-invasion record. The increased effort required against the petroleum industry in November, and against Rundstedt's communications in December and January, followed by bad weather at bases, prevented me from maintaining the campaign on quite the same scale. By the end of 1944, however, 80 per cent. of the 57 German towns with a pre-war population of 100,000 or more had been either virtually destroyed or heavily damaged by Bomber Command's attacks. New targets were attacked and old ones further disintegrated during the last half-year of the War. Of the latter, the Ruhr and Rhineland cities were finally wrecked, and it is now known that production virtually ceased at Krupp's and at the Bochumer Verein steelworks after the attacks in October and early November respectively. (No complete gun of any kind left Krupp's during the last 12 months of the War.)

165. With "GEE-H" and "OBOE" ground stations situated on the borders of Germany, a great number of targets could be attacked with certainty of success even in 10/10ths cloud. Deep penetrations could even be made to remote targets like Dresden and Chemnitz without incurring heavy losses, since the enemy's fighter defence system had lost its sting.

166. The attack on Dresden, the largest city (630,000 population) that had not previously been bombed, may be mentioned as one among many other highly effective operations. Apart from its industrial significance, Dresden had become of great importance as a communications centre and control point in the defence of Germany's eastern front. On the night of 13/14th February, 1945, a double attack was made on the city by a total of 805 aircraft. There was cloud over the area for the first

attack, but it had cleared for a distance of 10 miles from the target before the second attack developed. Next day reconnaissance showed a vast pall of smoke from innumerable fires still burning in the city. As a result of these attacks (and two smaller Eighth U.S.A.A.F. daylight attacks on the two succeeding days) more than 1,600 acres of the closely built-up sections of Dresden were destroyed. The effect, not only on the local population, but on the whole nation is now known to have been very great. Speer mentions this attack as having a moral effect comparable to that produced by the destruction of Hamburg in 1943. Other important industrial centres in Eastern Germany previously beyond effective operational range, such as Dessau, the heart of the Junkers concern, and Chemnitz, "the Manchester of Saxony," were all attacked with outstanding results.

167. Many smaller undamaged towns, like Solingen, were dealt with in accurate attacks. On the night of 23rd/24th February, 1945, it was the turn of Pforzheim, a town of 80,000 inhabitants, in which almost every house was a small workshop engaged in the production of precision parts for instruments, small arms and fuzes. Hardly a building remained intact throughout the whole town and, apart from the tremendous fire damage, many areas of buildings were levelled by 4,000 lb. H.E. bombs. The railway facilities were severely damaged also; two of the bridges over the river collapsed, the road bridge over the marshalling yard was hit, and the goods yard completely burnt out.

168. Of successful attacks on important factories during the final year numerous examples could be mentioned. The Opel works at Russelsheim, the largest pre-war automobile factory in Germany, which had been converted to the manufacture of aircraft components and military M/T vehicles, was one of the chief targets in this category. Following a relatively light attack by the U.S. Eighth Air Force in July, 1944, Bomber Command delivered two heavy attacks in August. While the first did not achieve much success, the second and heavier attack on 25/26th August was outstanding. Half the total plan-area of this large factory was affected, and it is reported that all machine tools were either damaged or made idle as a result of the attack.

169. In one of the most outstanding attacks of the War, all six factories of importance in the small town of Friedrichshafen were almost completely destroyed. This was the second Bomber Command attack on Friedrichshafen, and was carried out shortly before D-Day. The damage included the four high priority factories; Maybach-Werke, through which passed 60 per cent. of all German tank engines; Zahnradfabrik, the chief manufacturing plant of gears, gear boxes and aircraft reduction gears; the Zeppelin works, producing radar equipment, etc.; and the Dornier-Werke factories.

THE DISRUPTION OF COMMUNICATIONS IN GERMANY

170. Linked with the effects of the crescendo of devastation which descended over all but the most remote industrial areas of Germany, was the chaos produced by the

disruption of her communications. The tremendous tonnage of bombs directed against rail facilities had a far-reaching effect on military supplies and distribution of coal, but the cutting of the Dortmund-Ems and Mittelland canals was perhaps the most telling blow. The Dortmund-Ems Canal was breached by Bomber Command on 23rd/24th September, 1944. Thereafter it was maintained by repeat attacks in an unserviceable state, except for a few days, until the end of the War. The severing of the Mittelland Canal began with the highly successful attack from below cloud on 21st/22nd November, and later attacks were equally well executed. The extraordinary energy with which repairs were put in hand after each attack testified to the vital importance of the two canals in German war industry and system of communications. But repair work never succeeded in catching up with destruction.

THE LAST YEAR OF SEA-MINING OPERATIONS

171. Shortage of mines limited the scope of sea-mining operations during the final year, but by laying mines in particularly vulnerable areas Bomber Command reduced German sea communications to an equally chaotic state; Although no less than 40 per cent. of German naval personnel was employed on minesweeping and escort duties during this period, the enemy minesweeping forces were unable to cope expeditiously with the sweeping of the necessary channels. Danzig Bay, for instance, was closed to traffic for one period of 15 days, and the East Prussian ports of Konigsberg and Pillau were closed for 13 days after the brilliant operation of 9/10th April, 1944, when No. 5 Group Lancasters mined the ship canal between the two ports. The mining of the Kiel Canal on 12/13th May by P.F.F. Mosquitos from altitudes ranging between 300 and 400 ft. was executed with equal precision, and again on 5/6th October, when reconnaissance showed concentrations of shipping held up at each end of the canal.

THE END OF THE GERMAN NAVY

172. While the minelaying programme directed against industrial sea traffic was extremely successful, an increasing effort was directed against the U-Boat bases and training areas. From the autumn of 1944 onwards the Command was required to prevent what remained of the German submarine and surface fleet from playing any further part in the War. The departure of U-Boats from their beleaguered bases in Western France was hindered both by mining and by attacks on the concrete shelters with 12,000 lb. bombs. The battleship "Tirpitz" was hit and put out of action as a naval unit in September, and on the third attempt was sunk by direct hits with 12,000 lb. bombs on 12th November, 1944. Further crippling losses were inflicted on the chief remaining naval units during the following months, as described in Appendix H. The U-Boats' last places of retreat in the heavy concrete shelters in Norway and Germany were hit and penetrated by 22,000 lb. bombs in the last months of the War.

Particularly valuable were the attacks from August onwards against the concrete advanced bases of the midget submarines which operated against the left flank of Allied sea communications.

1 A.W.A. Report BRA/3.

2 O.R.S.(B.C.) paper entitled "Note on Attack on Essen, 8/9th March-8/9th June," dated 26.7.42.

3 D.O. letter to C.A.S., 2.3.42.

4 O.R.S. (B.C.) paper entitled "The Success of Night Bombing Operations: an Appreciation," dated 22.12.41.

5 May, 1942.

6 15th July, 1942.

7 "H.2.S." first used 30/31st January, 1943, against Hamburg.

8 First used 16/17th January, 1943, against Berlin.

9 Air Ministry directif letters of 14.1.43 and 23.1.43. See Appendix L, No. 26.

10 Air Ministry directif letter of 14th February, 1942.

11 In January, 1943, 37 per cent. of pilots in Bomber Command Squadrons were provided by the Dominion Air Forces. Canadians formed about 60 per cent. of these, the balance being provided by R.A.A.F. and R.N.Z.A.F. personnel. By January, 1945, 46 per cent. of pilots were Dominion personnel, of which 55 per cent. were Canadian.

No. 6 (R.C.A.F.) Group contributed 14·5 per cent. of the total tonnage of bombs dropped by the Command from the time of the formation of the Group till the end of the War in Europe. The cost of the Group (attached R.A.F. personnel only excepted) was borne by the Canadian Government, and the full upkeep of its operational squadrons, including expenditure for fuel and ammunition, was defrayed from Canadian taxes and domestic loans.

12 10th August, 1942.

13 O.R.S. Night Raid Report No. 330 describes this operation in detail.

14 21st Army Group Report (Appendix G. to 1/G/PAD), dated 18th June, 1945.

15 See Appendix B, para. 47.

16 See Appendix B, paras. 44 and 48, and Appendix A, para. 83.

17 B.A.U. Report No. 22. "Ground Survey of the Results of an Attack by Heavy Bombers on a German Tank Concentrations."

PART III.
SUMMARY OF THE BOMBING EFFORT AND RESULTS

THE BOMBING EFFORT

173. The progress of Bomber Command and the development of striking power is revealed in the following figures, which show the increase of effort in terms of sorties flown and tonnage dropped during the period.

	Sorties.	Monthly Average.	Tons of Bombs, including Sea Mines.	Monthly Average.
September, 1939, to February, 1942, inclusive (30 months)	58,808	31,606	65,068	166,844
1942 (less January and February)	67,483	1,960	3,161	5,422
1943	13,904	16,871	49,534	48,379
1944	166,593	538,688	185,113	1,651
1945 (4 months)	4,838	13,882	44,891	46,278
Whole War (68 months)	**389,809**	**5,732**	**988,307**	**14,534**
February, 1942 to May, 1945 (38 months)	331,001 (85·1 per cent)	8,711	938,773 (94·9 per cent)	24,705

This great increase in striking power was accompanied by a corresponding increase in the accuracy of bomb aiming (*see* Appendix B).

The sorties flown prior to February, 1942, represented 15 per cent. and the tonnage dropped 5 per cent. of the totals for the whole War, although the period was 44 per cent. of the whole. Whereas the average bomb load per attacking aircraft for the year 1941 was 2,889 lbs., by 1944 it had risen to 9,155 lbs. The bomb load was therefore more than three times as great. The figures emphasise the very great increase of effort throughout the period. By 1944 the Command had achieved a really effective striking power, but of the tonnage dropped during the first nine months of 1944 only 34·4 per cent. was despatched against Germany, owing to the demands of land operations. During the last three months of 1944 a greater tonnage of bombs was dropped than in the whole of 1943. Of this load, 53 per cent. was dropped on German industrial cities.

Throughout the War, 45 per cent. of the total tonnage of bombs dropped was despatched against the German industrial cities. The overall weight of attack against German industrial and administrative cities during the period 23rd February, 1942-8th May, 1945, was 417,133 tons of bombs. In all, 70 cities were attacked and many smaller towns.

CASUALTIES

174. These results were not achieved without painful losses. The total of aircraft lost on all operations during the period of my command was 7,122. The personnel casualties, so far as can be estimated, in the absence of final figures which the Air Ministry has not yet supplied, are 43,786 aircrew killed, and some 4,000 injured. In addition, more than 10,000 men were held prisoner by the enemy. (*See* Part V, Table 15.)

The rate of loss was highest in the first year, 1942 (4·1 per cent.), before our tactics and counter-measures were fully developed. The loss rate fell to 3·7 per cent. in 1943, and to 1·7 per cent. in 1944, and in the last months of the War, in 1945, to 0·9 per cent. The rate of loss for the whole period was 2·1 per cent.

THE RESULTS

Devastation of the German Industrial Cities

175. Despite the fact that only 45 per cent. of the Command's total effort was directed against the cities, nearly half the total acreage of the cities attacked was destroyed. The general effect of these devastating attacks on the German industrial cities can fairly be described as causing "the progressive destruction and dislocation of the German military, industrial and economic systems, and the undermining of the morale of the German people to a point where their capacity for armed resistance was fatally weakened."[1] By the widespread creation of bottlenecks, the enemy's industrial planning was severely disorganised, and the execution of any industrial project made unreliable and hazardous. By the creation of weak links in every chain of industry the whole system became critically weakened.

Evidence in support of this is now being produced by ground investigation and by interrogating leading industrialists. With regard to bottlenecks, Reichsminister Albert Speer stated, "For the year 1943-1944 some 1,000,000 to 1,500,000 persons may be reckoned to have been engaged on A.R.P. and in bomb damage repair organisations. Needless to say, this is one reason why industry was unable to make good its shortages of manpower. It is *not*, however, to be assumed that a materially greater supply of armaments would have been attained, even had the necessary manpower been available, since the bottlenecks in material (raw steel, etc.) would still have persisted."

176. The following significant statement was also made during interrogation by Albert Speer:—

"The first heavy attack on Hamburg in August 1943 made an extraordinary impression. We were of the opinion that a rapid repetition of this type of attack upon another six German towns would inevitably cripple the will to sustain armament manufacture and war production. It was I who first verbally reported to the Fuhrer at that time that a continuation of these attacks might bring about a rapid end to the war."

177. In the absence, to date, of complete scientific investigation and assessment of the effect of bomb damage all over Germany, no adequate appreciation of the whole effect of the campaign can be made. Unless and until this is done, while the essential information is still obtainable, we may never know the final answer. The completion of these investigations is therefore a most urgent requirement.

From preliminary investigation, however, it is clear that the effect of bombing on production was very great. The following examples, chosen because it has been possible to obtain some of the facts concerning them (from investigation of documents), are representative of the scale of damage inflicted and its effects on German war economy.

Summary of Effects of Bombing of German Cities (from ground assessment by the Operational Research Section, Bomber Command)

178. *Essen.* – (i) From March 1943 the industries in Essen, which employed about 240,000 workers, had their production reduced by 30 per cent.

(ii) During the last two years of the War, Krupp's works lost at least one year's production. Production of locomotives and of fuses had ceased in March 1943, output of large shells stopped in July 1943. During 1943 and 1944 output of armoured gun-turrets and of aero-engine crankshafts steadily declined until October 1944, when there was virtually a complete stoppage of production throughout the works. No complete gun left Krupp's during the last year of the War. By the end of the War, over half the workshops had been destroyed or very heavily damaged, and all the remaining buildings damaged. Forty per cent. of the machines in the works were destroyed or heavily damaged; and, at the time of the occupation, production could not have been restarted for a very considerable time.

(iii) Ninety per cent. of the houses in Essen were destroyed or seriously damaged.

179. *Bochum.* – (i) From May 1943 to the end of the War, the production of the town amounted to only 55 per cent. of its pre-raid level. During the last five months of the War production was at only 14 per cent. of capacity and it would have taken a long time to recover to any significant extent.

(ii) The great Bochumer Verein steel works, which prior to the bombing produced 100,000 tons of raw steel and 60,000 tons of pig iron per month, lost 50 per cent. of its production during the rest of the War and since November 1944 produced less than 15 per cent. of its normal production. Munitions in the form of guns and shells were reduced to 70 per cent. over the last two years and to 40 per cent. for the last six months.

(iii) Housing damage amounted to 80-90 per cent. destroyed or seriously damaged.

(iv) The coal mining industry which produced 1,350,000 tons per month declined steadily and by the end of 1944 was only at 50 per cent.

180. *Dortmund.* – (i) Since May 1943, to the end of the War, the production of the important steel and engineering centre of Dortmund was reduced by about 30 per cent. Production during the last seven months of the War was at only 40 per cent. and the town was completely knocked out in March 1945.

(ii) The coal mining industry lost 10 per cent. of its production through air attack in 1943 and 50 per cent. during the last seven months of the War.

(iii) Ninety per cent. of buildings in the main town are rendered uninhabitable.

181. *Düsseldorf.* – (i) Since May 1943, production was reduced on the average to 70 per cent. of the pre-raid level.

(ii) 50 per cent. of the houses were destroyed.

182. *Hamburg.* – (i) As a result of the heavy attacks in July 1943, the larger factories lost two months production and the smaller ones six months; 61 per cent. of the total houses were destroyed and 180,000 tons of shipping sunk; 130,000 tons of goods were destroyed in the warehouses.

(ii) The loss in U-Boat production throughout the War is estimated at 25 per cent., or 130 boats[2], including loss consequent upon bombing sub-contractors' factories all over Germany.

(iii) Oil production was reduced to 25 per cent. of normal from mid-1944.[3]

Survey from Air Photographs: Acreage of Devastation

183. Of the 70 cities attacked by Bomber Command, 46 were approximately half destroyed, and of these 23 were more than 60 per cent. destroyed in terms of built-up area. These 23 towns are listed below; where more than 500 acres have been destroyed, the town is underlined.

184. More than 500 acres of the following towns have been destroyed, but the percentage of destruction is less than 60.

The number of industrial and administrative cities of which more than 500 acres of built-up area have been destroyed is 31. This is on the basis of photographic evidence only. We now know that actual damage was greatly in excess of damage revealed by vertical photography.

185. The progress of this devastation is shown by the following figures which show the proportion of the cumulative total of target areas attacked which had been destroyed at the start and mid-period of each year.

	Acreage Destroyed.	Percentage of Built-up Area Destroyed
Wuppertal/Elberfeld	870	94
Würzburg	422	89
Bochum	532	83
Pforzheim	304	83
Remscheid	281	83
Heilbronn	351	82
Bremerhaven	297	79
Hamburg	6,200	75
Hildesheim	263	70
Darmstadt	516	69
Hanau	190	69
Kassel	620	69
Friedrichshafen	99	67
Osnabruck	441	67
Hagen	325	67
Münster	650	65
Düsseldorf	2,003	64
Mannheim/Ludwigshafen	1,213	64
Mülheim	193	64
Witten	129	62
Cologne	1,994	61
Dessau	331	61
Mainz	593	61
Bremen	1,042	60
Hanover	1,517	60

	Acreage Destroyed.	Percentage of Built-up Area Destroyed
Aachen	605	59
Berlin	6,427[3]	33
Brunswick	655	47
Chemnitz	590	41
Dortmund	923	54
Dresden	1,681	59
Duisburg	1,424	48
Essen	1,319	50
Frankfurt-am-Main	1,145	52
Kiel	725	50
Krefeld	714	47
Leipzig	625	20
Magdeburg	774	41
München-Gladbach/Rheydt	633	54
Munich	1,547	42
Nuremberg	1,146	51
Stettin	736	53
Stuttgart	1,152	46
Wuppertal/Barmen	655	58

186. In assessing the conclusions of German generals and industrialists as to the effect of bombing on the collapse of the German war effort, it must be borne in mind that the enemy was not always able to distinguish between targets aimed at and targets hit, and therefore was not in a position to decide whether concentration upon special targets was in fact the best means of hitting them. In the course of attacks on cities, vital factories encompassed in the bomb pattern were destroyed. So far as the Germans were concerned, however, this might well appear to be an attack on a specific target as distinct from an attack on a town. An example of this was the heavy attack (937 tons) of 15/16th March, 1945 on Hagen by Bomber Command, in the course of which the

	Percentage Destroyed of Total Acreage Attacked to Date.	
	January	June
1942	Negligible	2-2
1943	3-1	11-9
1944	28-2	31-4
1945	44-6	48-6

accumulator factory there was destroyed.[4] The importance of this has been emphasised by Albert Speer as follows: "Output at U-Boat shipyards was conditioned by the delivery of electric motors and batteries, so that attacks on the shipyards themselves did nothing (extra) to reduce the output of U-Boats. The electrical industry which was responsible for manufacturing the electric motors, and the factories manufacturing batteries constituted bottlenecks because the new U-Boats required triple the quantity of equipment per boat. The factories at Hagen and Vienna manufacturing accumulator batteries were destroyed and Posen was lost to us, but the largest accumulator factory (Acfa) at Hanover remained intact. If the last-named factory had been destroyed, the construction of U-Boats would have had to be abandoned four weeks later." Incidentally, the remaining factory, on which continuance of U-Boat production is stated to have depended, was not listed as a specific target for attack.

187. It should be borne in mind too that while dispersal of industries gave temporary immunity, the increased dependence upon communication facilities that resulted proved a fatal weakness when the transportation system was heavily attacked. According to General-Engineer Spies "the transport system was slowed down to such an extent that industry had great difficulty in functioning. Ultimately, delay in getting semi-finished products to the assembly factories progressively slowed down production until it came almost to a standstill early this year (1945). The fact that semi-finished products had to be carried over long distances was due, in the first place to the bombing of factories which forced dispersal, and secondly the attacks on transport, which still caused delays in production." It was as a vital part of these attacks on communication that the Command put the Dortmund Ems and Mittelland Canals out of action in September, 1944. In this connection Reichsminister Speer may again be quoted:—

> "After the transport of coal by rail had fallen off owing to traffic difficulties
> its transportation by canal became decisive in the maintenance of industry
> in Central Germany."

Although some vital emergency supplies were on occasions pushed through between our attacks, he stated that "the attacks were of extraordinary importance."

As an added testimonial to the effects on transportation of these attacks, there is the further statement by him that "Despite the greatly reduced raw steel production the stocks actually held by the steel plants increased from month to month from the summer of 1944 onwards. This is the best demonstration of the extent to which deliveries to industrial producers were limited by transport difficulties."

The Results of Attacks on Oil Plants

188. The attacks on specific oil targets began in June 1944, and between that date and the end of the War 95,553 tons of bombs were dropped on these targets. Although in conjunction with the Americans we succeeded in reducing the enemy's supplies

of liquid fuel to a critically low level, there was a danger that under cover of winter fog and bad weather, the output of the plants could be restored. Speer in a telegram circulated on September 12th, 1944, said "we may from experience expect a season of predominating bad weather and fog. The bombing of synthetic plants cannot be carried out with the same precision ... in spite of the really considerable damage done, we can, in a period of five or six weeks, restore production to about two-thirds of the level attained by synthetic plants and refineries before attacks."

In December and January unexpected local improvements in the generally unfavourable weather conditions, however, made it possible to smash some of the most important and most remote synthetic oil plants, at Brux, Leuna and Pölitz. Owing partly to this occasional luck with the weather and partly to the availability of "GEE H" ground stations on the borders of Germany for blind bombing of the nearer plants, results of these attacks exceeded my expectations, and frustrated the German hopes. The successful night attacks on the synthetic oil plants at Leuna and Pölitz (and a U.S.A.A.F. attack on the former) reduced their normal output by 98·8 per cent. And 95·4 per cent. respectively. The synthetic plant at Brux was put right out of action in January 1945 in another night attack. The success of these attacks and the immobilisation of the Silesian synthetic oil plants, four weeks prior to their capture by the Russians, ensured that "the final outcome of the oil offensive was never in doubt." (Review of the Air Offensive against Axis Oil Supplies – Combined Strategic Targets Committee Working Committee (Oil) Bulletin No. 1945-19).

189. The combined offensive against oil targets which was continued during January to April, 1945 resulted in practically the whole industry being immobilised by the beginning of April. The overall result of this successful campaign was to deprive the enemy of effective use of his most powerful means of defence against the advancing Allied Armies, his Air Force and his Panzer Divisions.

190. The decisive part played by Bomber Command in the oil campaign is shown by the tables set out below.

SYNTHETIC OIL PLANTS AND REFINERIES (GERMANY)

Number of plants attacked	42
Number of attacks by Bomber Command	82
Number of attacks by Eighth Air Force	170
Tons of bombs dropped by Bomber Command	63,674
Tons of bombs dropped by Eighth Air Force	45,617

	Attacked by Bomber Command Only.	Attacked by 8th U.S.A.A.F. Only.	Attacked by Both Forces.
Ruhr	3	-	8
Others	-	14	17
Total	3	14	25

Benzol Plants (Germany)

Number of plants attacked	30
Number of attacks by Bomber Command	44
Number of attacks by Eighth Air Force	18
Tons of bombs dropped by Bomber Command	17,086
Tons of bombs dropped by 8th Air Force	3,991

Plants attacked by Bomber Command only.	Plants attacked by 8th Air Force only.	Plants attacked by both Forces.
14	3	13

In all 92·6 per cent. of the full production from 55 oil plants was lost to the enemy in these combined attacks (excluding the loss from plants attacked by the U.S.A.A.F. only).

Bombing Forced the Enemy on to the Defensive

191. In 1942 Germany's armed forces, equipped for the offensive, were stronger than those of any other Power. With practically the whole production capacity of Europe at her disposal and ample quantities of foreign slave labour, her offensive strength appeared certain to develop to a prodigious extent.

192. The growing effectiveness of Bomber Command's operations (later augmented by U.S. operations) against the Reich cities and German-controlled installations and war plants in the West kept alive the spark of hope, and therefore resistance, among the workers of occupied Europe. Gradually enemy production was forced to switch from offensive weapons to fighters and flak, and a great army of at least two million men was employed in a purely defensive role, in the Flakartillerie, night-fighter Gruppe, the Air Raid Precautions organisation, mine-sweeping, and in essential repair work.

193. The fighter force and flak were gradually but steadily withdrawn from the

Fronts, to defend the Reich itself from air attacks, until three quarters of their total strength in these arms was engaged in this task. The fighting fronts were denuded, and the enemy armies robbed of that air support which had contributed so much to their early victories. Finally, when the Allied Armies took the offensive on the Continent, they had overwhelming air superiority, with all that that means in modern land warfare.

Bombing Caused Shortage of War Materials on all Fronts

194.

(i) Tank production seriously declined, especially after bombing of Friedrichshafen, in April, 1944.

(ii) The pre-fabricated U-Boat campaign was wrecked by bombing. While a total of less than 230 U-Boats[5] are claimed to have been sunk, or probably sunk, during the whole War by shore-based aircraft of all Allied air forces engaged on anti-submarine patrols or escort, as a consequence of bombing the fall in U-Boat production at Hamburg alone was equivalent to 130 U-Boats lost.

This was attributable not only to direct attacks on Hamburg by Bomber Command and Eighth U.S.A.A.F., but also indirectly to attacks on other German industrial centres. It is known that the factories of Blohm & Voss' sub-contractors all over Germany suffered bomb damage and that as a direct consequence component U-Boat sections were sent uncompleted to Blohm & Voss, who, through shortage of labour and materials, were unable to complete them for assembly. This estimate of 130 U-Boats lost takes no account of the decline in production at Bremen, Kiel, etc. Moreover, in addition to actual reduction of output there was abortion by air attack of the forecast increase of production, and consequent disorganisation of planning.

(iii) A vital six months delay in production of "V" weapons resulted from the bombing of Peenemünde, August 1943, and of the launching sites during the winter of 1943/44.

A further large contribution was made when the "V" weapons became operational in 1944. Between August 1943, and September 1944 some 64,522 tons of bombs were dropped on targets associated with production, storing and launching of flying bombs. As a result of these attacks, the enemy's programme was so severely interrupted and delayed that he was able to launch only a very small proportion of his planned attack against our cities before the launching area was occupied by the Allied armies.

(iv) Indirect effects of all kinds resulted from wrecking industrial cities. These have been discussed in paras. 187 and 188, and a further point arises in connection with "V" weapon production.

It now appears that, although the U.S.A.A.F. attack on the "V.I" factory at Fallersleben on 20th June, 1944, caused the transference of a large proportion of its activity to other factories, production of flying bombs was hampered far more by bombing of the Ruhr cities and the transportation system. The lack of sheet metal supplied by the Ruhr factories, together with the dislocation of transportation, was responsible for a deficit of between 20 per cent and 30 per cent. as compared with the scheduled programme figures. In the same way, output of "V.2" rockets was reduced by between 10 and 15 per cent. as a result of bomb-damage to the transportation system.

(v) The damage to communications accentuated the shortage of war materials, by making it impossible to send equipment rapidly to the places where it was most urgently needed.

Results of Operations against Italy

195. By comparison with the tremendous weight of attack against Germany, the total effort directed against Italy, namely 9,089 tons of bombs, might at first sight appear relatively insignificant. (All but 259 tons of this effort was contributed during the first eighteen months of my period of Command). In reality, the return for a comparatively modest scale of attack on Italian cities was vastly greater than in the case of Germany for a number of reasons. On the operational side, weather conditions were generally good for visual bombing and this, combined with the negligible opposition from flak and fighters, resulted in the attacks being more concentrated and effective than most attacks up to that time on Germany. Moreover, their effectiveness cannot be measured in terms of factories or town areas damaged, though these were fairly considerable; the psychological reaction of the Italian population was clearly of far greater importance. While the German leaders have now admitted that morale was bad following our attacks on their own towns, they distinguished between "morale" and "conduct" and the latter (they claim) was unimpaired in the case of the German workers. For the Italian leaders, however, no pretence of stoic heroism was possible so hysterical was the behaviour of the populations in the bombed cities. The controlled Italian press made no attempt to conceal the utter disorganisation which followed our attacks, and after repeated operations against Genoa, Turin and Milan in the early winter of 1942, Mussolini publicly declared that it was necessary to organise a semi-permanent or possibly a nightly exodus from all Italian industrial zones, so that only military personnel would remain in the cities at night.

196. Some 300,000 people, or half the total population, had already fled to safe areas from Turin after the second raid on that city in November 1942, and the Lancasters' attack on Milan in daylight the previous month caused equal, if not greater, panic. The attacks on the naval base of Spezia during April and June 1943, added to the prevailing gloom and despondency of the Italian population. The final attacks on the industrial cities in July and August of that year were so successful that they deprived the Italians of what little inclination they retained for continuing a war which they had entered only in expectation of easy victory.

197. The whole series of Bomber Command attacks on the Northern Italian cities, from the very night of their entry into the war, consequently played a large part in bringing about the quick collapse of Mussolini's regime.

Bomber Command's Contribution to the
Land Battles of 1944/45

198. As has already been described in Part II, paras. 30-40, Bomber Command played a decisive role in the rout of the German armies in France and, finally, in Germany

The Results of Sea-Mining and Attacks on Enemy Naval Units,
Shipping and other Naval Targets

199. These very successful operations are dealt with in detail in Appendix H.

1 A.M. Directif dated 4th February, 1943.

2 Includes the effects of the VIII Bomber Command attacks.

3 Berlin: includes approximately 750 acres of American damage.

4 The same factory had been heavily damaged as a result of a previous attack on Hagen in October, 1943.

5 Note. – The figure would be 235½ (227½ + 8 Italian) including Italian submarines. A further 30 (+ 4 Italian) claimed by shore-based aircraft and surface ships.

PART IV. – CONCLUSIONS

200. To sum up, it can be said that Bomber Command successfully achieved the tasks allotted to it, notwithstanding the limitations imposed by inadequacy of means. The progressive solution of the numerous outstanding problems, as related in the attached appendices, eventually brought the force to a state of effectiveness which, had it been available a year or more earlier, would undoubtedly have ended the German war as abruptly as the Japanese war was ended, by concentrated and overwhelming bombing without need of an invasion by land forces.

201. The extent to which the Command was able to contribute to the solution of most of the great problems of the war is indeed remarkable. When still small and ill-equipped it nevertheless smashed the invasion ports on the French coast in 1940; its early expansion provided numerous squadrons for the Middle East and for Coastal Command (where their intervention was decisive); and while struggling to expand and to solve its technical problems, it nevertheless foiled the German attempt to convert most of Europe into a German arsenal. Later, when it began to be able to hit hard, it dealt mighty blows at German war production, devastating the German industrial cities, and by so doing hampered and reduced the production of every war necessity. The production of submarines, tanks, aircraft, flying bombs, guns, motor vehicles, were all alike involved.

202. When called upon to prepare the way for the invasion of the Continent, it succeeded so well that this great undertaking was accomplished with far less difficulty than had been foreseen by even the most optimistic. When the Allied Armies joined battle with the enemy, new means were found to enable the heavy bombers to blast obstructions from the path of the soldiers, and to enable them to overcome the strongest German defences with but little loss. The important task of clearing the Channel ports became for the Army, after bombing, merely a mopping-up operation, and the Island of Walcheren, which has a notorious place in British military history, after due preparation from the air, fell in a few hours to the first assault. The bombing of Wesel, where a costly operation was expected, put our troops across the Rhine for 36 casualties.

203. The sea-mining campaign, carried out as a side-line without diverting bombers from Germany, yielded a harvest of over 900 known ships sunk or damaged, and, besides imposing great delays on enemy sea communications, tied down a great force of mine-sweepers and sperrbrechers. Nor did the big ships of the German Navy escape, although they took great care to offer the minimum chances of attack to my bombers. The list of heavy ships sunk by Bomber Command is approximately equal to that sunk by all other methods employed during the War. (*See* Appendix H.)

204. In the last phase, Bomber Command in conjunction with the U.S.A.A.F., destroyed one by one the German synthetic oil plants until, by the spring of 1945, the enemy had practically no liquid fuel at his disposal.

205. But, in addition to all these direct achievements, Bomber Command made a further very great contribution to the Allied victory. To counter the combined bomber offensive the enemy was obliged to employ a most considerable part of his army, navy and air force, and of his potential man-power for war production, in a purely defensive rôle. Fighter squadrons and flak regiments were retained in large numbers for the defence of the home front, and 40 per cent. of German naval personnel were diverted from profitable employment in an attempt to cope with my sea-mining campaign. A veritable army of at least 2,000,000 men was engaged in A.R.P., railway repair work, repair of factories, repair of power supply and municipal transport services, re-housing, shipping repairs, etc. Not only man-power, but war materials, too, were consumed in the air defence. Flak comprised 30 per cent. of the total 1944 output of guns from German armaments factories. The fighting power of the Wehrmacht was, according to their Armaments Minister, "considerably weakened" by the diversion of these valuable anti-tank weapons (and their ammunition), which, in consequence of the home defence requirement, scarcely played any part in the final battles.

206. Before the War, doubt had been expressed as to the possibility of one Command being able to compete with the strategic bombing of German industry, close support of land forces, the destruction of enemy heavy warships and the carrying out of a vast sea-mining campaign. It was argued that each of these activities required specialised training, and it would therefore be necessary to have one bomber force trained in strategic bombing, another trained for army co-operation, and yet another trained and equipped to undertake tasks in co-operation with sea warfare. The War

has proved this view to be wrong. It has shown that one Command, if trained and equipped on the right lines, can successfully carry out every task allotted to it. Indeed, this very flexibility may be a danger, in that many demands will be made for the bombers to attack targets of secondary importance which are causing annoyance to one or other Government department. The largest force if so dissipated can become ineffective, and one of the problems which persisted throughout the War, and was never satisfactorily solved, was the selection of primary targets. I maintained, and I contend that the experiences of this War have proved, that apart from a very small number of targets of special importance, the enemy's sinews of war were to be found in his industrial cities. German propaganda tried very hard to convince us that German war industry was wholly dispersed, or was underground, or concealed in forests, or indeed was anywhere except where one would expect to find it – in the great industrial cities.

207. The above paragraphs record my conclusions after spending more than three years directing the effort of Bomber Command. While there are many lessons to be learned from a study of these operations, we are ending this War on the threshold of tremendous scientific developments – radar, jet propulsion, rockets, and atomic bombing are all as yet in their infancy. Another war, if it comes, will be vastly different from the one which has just drawn to a close. While, therefore, it is true to say that the heavy bomber did more than any other single weapon to win this War, it will not hold the same place in the next. The principles will, however, hold true; the quickest way of winning the War will still be to devastate the enemy's industry and thus destroy his war potential. But the means by which that end is achieved will certainly be different from those which were used, with such far-reaching effect, to destroy the most powerful enemy we have faced for centuries.

PART V. – STATISTICS AND GRAPHS

The following graphs show the growth of the bomber offensive, the geometrically increasing weight of attack, the progressive improvement of accuracy, the diminution of casualty rate and the bombing results obtained.

Six of the graphs, showing cumulative totals, have been drawn to logarithmic scale. The figure plotted for each month in these cases represents the cumulative total from the start of the war.

2. As the scale is logarithmic, equal vertical distances in every case represent not an equal amount but an equal multiplication. Thus the distance on the scale separating 2,000 and 4,000 is equal to that separating say, 6,000 and 12,000 since the ratio of the numbers is the same in both cases. It follows that:—

(a) The ratio of a higher to a lower figure is given by transferring the vertical distance between them to the left-hand scale and measuring upwards from 1, 10, 100 or 1,000, etc. as convenient, regarding the datum in each case as 1. Thus the number of tons per aircraft despatched and per aircraft missing from the start of the war, on bomb raids at any month, can be read in this manner from Graph No. 4.

(*b*) The percentage increase for a given period is obtained by measuring the vertical distance as above and evaluating ratios of 2/1 as 100 per cent., 1·6/1 as 60 per cent. and 1·5/1 as 50 per cent. increase respectively.

(*c*) The percentage relationship of the lower of two figures to the higher can similarly be read by measuring the distance separating them against the left-hand scale, reading in this case downwards from any convenient 1,000, 100,000 datum, etc., which will then represent 100 per cent., while the lower reading on the scale will give the lower number as a percentage of the higher.

3. It will be seen that as the distance separating two curves shows the percentage relationship of the lower to the higher, and the ratio of the higher to the lower, the changes of these throughout the war are readily determined, but it is necessary to remember that the comparison is based in all cases upon cumulative totals.

4. To assist interpretation, chronological notes are given below. A study of the graphs as a whole, relating one to the other in conjunction with the chronological notes and Parts I-IV, provides a clear picture of the progress and trends of development.

5. Each graph is supplemented by a statistical Table.

Growth of the Command, February, 1942-May, 1945

Graph No. 1.   Cumulative tonnage monthly, shown separately, for all targets, German targets, enemy occupied territory, Italy.

Graph No. 2.   Monthly average number of aircraft available with crews, shown separately, for: total, heavies; medium; light.

Graph No. 13.   Operational status of squadrons.

Graph No. 3.   Monthly average effective bomblift available.

Note. – This has been assessed as the product of (*a*) the number of aircraft available with crews, and (*b*) the average tonnage dropped by each category of aircraft monthly.

Effort and Casualties

Graph No. 4.   Cumulative monthly totals, shown separately, for; tonnage of bombs dropped; sorties despatched; aircraft missing.

Graph No. 5.   Cumulative monthly totals of sorties despatched and aircraft missing, shown separately, for: all operations; bomb raids; sea mining; countermeasures (R.C.M. and bomber support); miscellaneous.

Graph No.5A.   The relationship of R.C.M. measures to the progressive reduction of percentage loss of aircraft in night raids on Germany.

Distribution of Effort

Graph No. 6.   Cumulative monthly totals of tonnage of bombs reported dropped on various targets, shown separately for: all targets; German industrial towns; troops and defences; transportation; naval targets; oil targets; airfields and aircraft factories; specific industries; military installations (V weapons); sea mining; miscellaneous targets.

Graph No. 7.   Cumulative monthly totals showing effort expended on sea mining, in terms of number of mines laid, sorties despatched, aircraft missing.

Accuracy and Results

Graph No. 8.   Cumulative monthly totals of tonnage of bombs reported dropped on German industrial towns; cumulative total of acreage attacked; cumulative total of acreage devastated in strategic bombing of industrial towns only.

Graph No. 9.   The progress, decline and revival of the German armaments industry (index figures from German source; *see* supplement attached to graph).

Graph No. 10.   The percentage of aircraft attacking target area (photographic evidence).

Graph No. 11.   The devastation of German industrial towns. A comparison of towns of which more than 500 acres have been destroyed and/or which are more than 50 per cent. devastated, classified by size of population. (Strategic bombing only.)

Flying Control

Graph No. 12.   Aircraft diversions, showing separately those provided for and those carried out.

Enemy Opposition

Graph No. 14.   The number of guns (heavy and light) and searchlights deployed by the enemy (January, 1940 to March, 1945).

Personnel Casualties

Table 15.   3rd September, 1939, to 8th May, 1945.

CHRONOLOGICAL NOTES
Some dates of particular interest
23rd FEBRUARY, 1942-8th MAY, 1945

1942.

March
3rd/4th	Night attack on Renault factory.
	Lancaster first operated (sea mining).
8th/9th	GEE first employed. Target, Essen.
10th/11th	Lancaster first operated on a bomb raid.
27th/28th	Bombers used in combined operations at Brunewald.

April
10th/11th	First 8,000-lb. bomb dropped. Target, Essen.
17th	Day attack on Augsburg by Lancasters.
29th/30th	Last operation by Whitley (except O.T.U.).

May
30th/31st	First raid of over 1,000 bombers. Target, Cologne.
	O.T.U.s first employed on bomb raid.
31st	Mosquito first operated.

June
1st/2nd	Raid of over 1,000 aircraft. Target, Essen.
25th/26th	Raid of 960 aircraft. Target, Bremen.
	Last operation by Manchester.

August
15th	P.F.F. formed in 3 Group.
17th	VIII Bomber Command first operated. Target, Rouen railway centre.
17th/18th	Last operation by Blenheim.
18th/19th	First P.F.F. attack (Flensburg).
19th	Bombers used in combined operations at Dieppe.

September
10th/11th	First 4,000-lb. incendiary dropped, on Düsseldorf.
14th/15th	Last operation by Hampden.
October 17th	Day raid on Le Creusot.
22nd/23rd	First raid of over 100 aircraft on Italy. Target, Genoa.
24th	Day raid on Milan by 88 Lancasters.

December
20th/21st	OBOE first employed. Target, Lutterade power station.

1943.

January
16th/17th	Target indicator bombs (250 lb.) used for the first time. Target, Berlin.
25th	No. 8 Group reformed to take over P.F.F.
27th	Copenhagen Diesel Engine Works attacked by eight Mosquitos.
30th/31st	H.2.S first used. Target, Hamburg.

March
  3rd   Knaben molybdenum mines attacked by nine Mosquitos.
  5th/6th   Battle of the Ruhr opened with the first attack on Essen with OBOE ground-marking.

May
  16th/17th   Mohne, Eder, Sorpe and Schwelm dams attacked by Lancasters.
  27th   Jena optical factories attacked by six Mosquitos.
  31st   No. 2 Group, last operation under Bomber Command.

July
  24th/25th   WINDOW used for the first time. Target, Hamburg.

July
  24th/25th to }   Hamburg attacked on four nights, 8,623 tons were dropped for the loss of 87 aircraft.

August
  2nd/3rd }
  16th/17th   Last attack on Italy (Turin).
  17th/18th   Peenemunde Research Establishment attacked. 597 heavies despatched, 571 attacked with 1,938 tons.
  31st/1st   Flares used by enemy fighters for first time. Target, Berlin.

September
  15th/16th   12,000-lb. H.C. bombs dropped for first time. Target, Dortmund-Ems Canal.
  22nd/23rd   First feint attack, the target being Oldenburg. Main target, Hanover.

October
  8th/9th   Wellingtons operated on bomb raids for the last time under Bomber Command, having been used continuously since April, 1940.

November
  3rd/4th   First attack with G.H. (on Dusseldorf).
  18th/19th   Battle of Berlin opened. (Two German towns attacked by large forces in one night for the first time. 444 aircraft despatched on Berlin and 395 on Mannheim/Ludwigshaven.)

December
  16th/17th   Mosquitos and Beaufighters operated as intruders for the first time in Bomber Command.

1944.
February
  8th/9th   First 5 Group attack on French factories, 12,000 lb. H.C. bombs dropped on Gnome and Rhone Works, Limoges.
  15th/16th   Heaviest attack on Berlin, 2,643 tons dropped.
  23rd/24th   Mosquitos dropped 4,000-lb. H.E. bombs for the first time (Dusseldorf).

March
6th/7th   Pre-invasion attacks opened, on Trappes M/YD.
24th/25th   Last attack of Battle of Berlin.

April

                 Only 29·2 per cent. of the total effort made against Germany
                 during the month.

May
12th/13th   Mosquitos laid sea mines for the first time, Kiel Canal.
22nd/23rd   Last attack on German industrial city, Brunswick, until 24th/25th

July.

                 Only 18·6 per cent. of total effort made against Germany during
                 month.

June
5th/6th   D-Day. Invasion of Normandy. 1,333 sorties during the night.
8th/9th   First 12,000-lb. D.P. bombs ("Tallboys") dropped, Saumur
                 railway tunnel.
14th   First of a series of heavy bomber raids by day, Le Havre.
                 Only 8·6 per cent. of total effort made against Germany during
                 month.

July
24th/25th   Offensive against German industrial cities resumed (Stuttgart).

August
27th   First major bomb raid by day on Germany, Homberg synthetic
                 oil plant.

September
8th   Last bomb raid by Stirlings.
23rd/24th   Dortmund-Ems Canal breached.

November
12th   "Tirpitz" sunk.
16th   Close support given to the U.S. army for the first time, in
                 daylight attacks on Julich, Duren and Heinsberg.

December
16th   Rundstedt's offensive opened.

1945.
February
20th/21st   First of 36 raids on Berlin on consecutive nights by Mosquitos.

March
14th   First 22,000-lb. D.P. bombs ("Grand Slams") dropped – Bielefeld
                 Viaduct.
May 8th   Last day of war.

Graph No. 1: Notes

The black line represents a geometric progression, and it will be seen that the successive cumulative monthly totals approximate to it closely. The tonnage dropped in each successive nine months' period equals approximately the total tonnage dropped previously since the start of the war.

The reductions of effort in the winter months are clearly shown, as is also the subsequent increased rate that raised the total approximately to the black line again.

The effect of the pre-invasion bombing and diversion of effort to support of the armies is also clearly shown by the rapid increase of tonnage dropped on enemy occupied territory, and by the comparatively slow increase of the tonnage dropped on Germany from D-Day until July, 1944. The intensfication of attacks on Germany from September, 1944, to the end is made instantly apparent by the increased slope of the curve.

The red percentage scale shows a ratio of a higher to a lower figure on the same curve expressed as a percentage.

The tonnage dropped by April, 1945 (657,420), was slightly more than double the total tonnage that had been dropped on Germany from the start of the war until the end of September, 1944; in other words, during the seven months, October, 1944 to April, 1945, the tonnage dropped on Germany was equal to the total tonnage dropped on Germany previously from the start of the war. During the pre-invasion and army-support period, the high rate of increase in the total tonnage on all targets was in some measure attributable to the increased, more economical H.E. loads, as will be seen from a study of Graph No. 4, where these loads are shown separately.

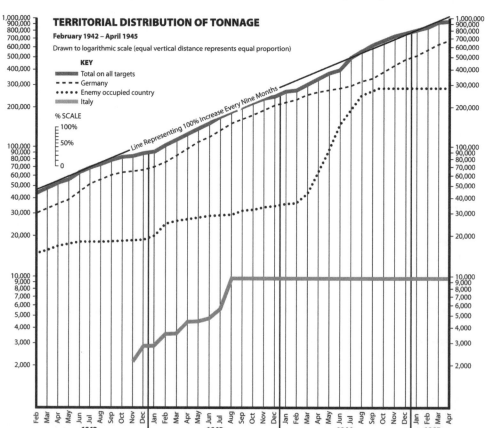

Table 1
TERRITORIAL DISTRIBUTION OF TONNAGE
CUMULATIVE TONNAGE TOTALS MONTH BY MONTH

	Target At Sea's	Germany	Italy.	Enemy Occupied Territory.	Total from Start of War.
1942					
At: February	500	31,714	259	15,598	48,071
March	502	33,611	-	16,374	50,746
April	505	36,708	272	17,694	55,179
May	524	39,446	-	18,171	58,413
June	531	45,920	-	18,535	65,258
July	542	52,128	-	18,684	71,626
August	553	56,078	-	18,885	75,788
September	562	61,564	-	18,985	81,383
October	567	64,556	846	19,223	85,192
November	579	65,386	2,358	19,292	87,615
December	580	67,221	3,098	19,430	90,329
1943					
January	582	70,189	-	20,805	94,674
February	584	75,927	3,734	25,388	105,633
March	594	84,663	-	27,233	116,224
April	597	94,575	4,683	27,836	127,691
May	610	107,170	-	28,148	140,611
June	614	121,394	4,803	29,071	155,882
July	620	136,752	5,804	29,536	172,712
August	-	153,420	9,086	29,735	192,861
September	-	165,690	-	32,320	207,716
October	-	179,370	-	32,413	221,489
November	-	192,296	-	33,982	235,984
December	-	203,654	-	34,426	247,786
1944					
January	622	220,495	-	36,011	266,214
February	626	232,286	-	36,270	278,268
March	-	251,996	-	44,258	305,966
April	627	266,011	9,089	63,735	339,462
May	628	274,558	-	92,439	376,714
June	-	279,460	-	144,804	433,981
July	628	292,682	-	189,197	491,596
August	633	307,121	-	240,608	557,451
September	-	328,167	-	272,149	610,038
October	-	379,700	-	281,820	671,242
November	-	432,561	-	281,981	724,264
December	-	479,213	-	284,369	773,304
1945					
January	-	509,933	-	286,572	806,227
February	-	555,333	-	287,061	852,116
March	634	622,960	-	287,070	919,753
April	-	657,420	-	287,564	954,707
May	634	657,674	9,089	287,647	955,044
% Distribution	0·07%	68·8%	0·94%	30·19%	

Graph No. 2

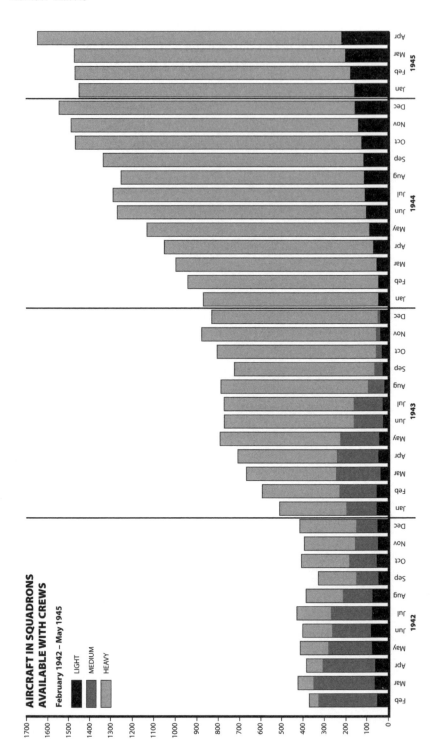

AIRCRAFT IN SQUADRONS AVAILABLE WITH CREWS

February 1942 – May 1945

LIGHT
MEDIUM
HEAVY

Table 2
AIRCRAFT IN SQUADRONS, AVAILABLE
WITH CREWS, DAILY
Monthly Average, February, 1942-April, 1945

	Light	Medium	Heavy	All Types.
1942				
February	55	275	44	374
March	52	301	68	421
April	56	247	86	389
May	70	210	136	416
June	80	181	141	402
July	76	198	153	427
August	62	152	174	388
September	44	109	178	331
October	47	136	225	408
November	45	118	234	397
December	46	111	262	419
1943				
January	53	148	313	514
February	57	173	363	593
March	37	213	413	663
April	44	199	466	709
May	48	182	560	790
June	24	117	632	773
July	26	88	662	776
August	35	67	685	787
September	35	37	654	726
October	41	24	742	807
November	47	16	816	879
December	46	11	776	833
1944				
January	44	7	818	869
February	43	6	897	946
March	58	-	942	1,000
April	72	-	980	1,052
May	84	-	1,048	1,132
June	102	-	1,162	1,264
July	107	-	1,178	1,283
August	110	-	1,135	1,245
September	113	-	1,210	1,323
October	119	-	1,336	1,455
November	137	-	1,339	1,476
December	148	-	1,381	1,529
1945				
January	147	-	1,287	1,434
February	166	-	1,283	1,449
March	192	-	1,262	1,434
April	201	-	1,424	1,625

Graph No. 3: Notes

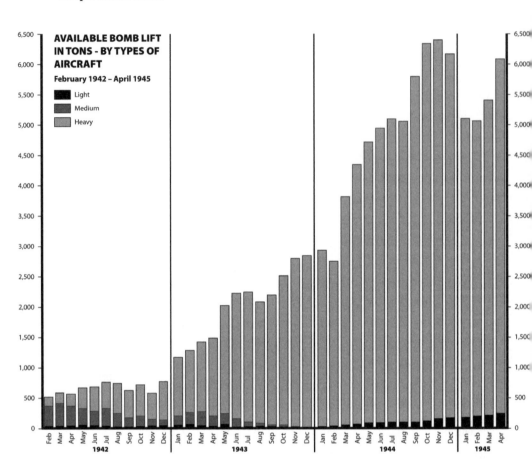

The effective lift shows the maximum striking power available. What is represented is the total effective bomb load of all available crewed aircraft. The bomb load is the average dropped in the month by attacking aircraft of each type. In consequence, where an incendiary load instead of an H.E. was carried, or distant targets were attacked, there is a fall in the bomb load, which shows as a reduction of the available striking power. This largely accounts for the marked drop of striking power shown early in 1945, although the reduced availability (*see* Graph No. 2) was an important factor.

Table 3

AVAILABLE BOMBLIFT IN TONS – BY TYPE OF AIRCRAFT

February, 1942-April, 1945

	Light	Medium	Heavy	All Types.
1942				
February	33	340	137	510
March	39	391	199	629
April	43	311	229	583
May	51	273	381	705
June	58	241	424	723
July	51	287	471	809
August	44	215	538	797
September	39	152	486	677
October	42	187	552	781
November	52	118	469	639
December	63	94	667	824
1943				
January	72	159	915	1,146
February	91	203	1,074	1,368
March	66	254	1,180	1,500
April	61	182	1,325	1,568
May	77	201	1,864	2,142
June	14	153	2,179	2,346
July	17	113	2,225	2,355
August	24	88	2,082	2,194
September	24	59	2,229	2,312
October	28	36	2,542	2,606
November	42	-	2,864	2,906
December	36	-	2,930	2,966
1944				
January	34	-	3,013	3,047
February	37	-	2,682	2,719
March	60	-	3,837	3,897
April	78	-	4,393	4,471
May	92	-	4,768	4,860
June	95	-	4,986	5,081
July	108	-	5,116	5,224
August	101	-	5,086	5,187
September	107	-	5,832	5,939
October	139	-	6,315	6,454
November	167	-	6,354	6,521
December	169	-	6,132	6,301
1945				
January	167	-	5,097	5,264
February	185	-	5,031	5,216
March	198	-	5,356	5,554
April	232	-	6,004	6,236

Note. – *The available bomblift given above is the product of the average number of aircraft available each month and the average tonnage dropped by aircraft reported to have attacked their targets. It is therefore a conservative estimate of striking power.*

Graph No. 4: Notes

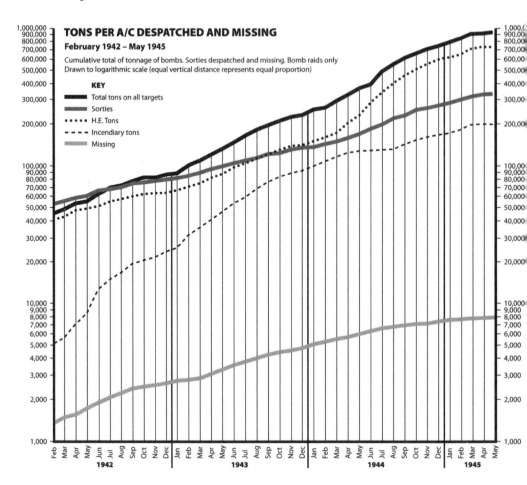

Points to note are the progressively increased load per aircraft and the rapid increase in the proportion of incendiaries carried until the pre-invasion period March, 1944. By that month the cumulative incendiary tonnage dropped had amounted to 40 per cent. of the combined tonnage. When the war ended, the percentage of incendiaries to total tonnage was 20·5 per cent.

The sorties despatched and aircraft missing are for bomb raids only, so that the vertical distance between the curves of aircraft despatched and missing are a measure of the percentage of despatched aircraft lost. The vertical distances separating the curve showing tonnage of bombs dropped from that showing aircraft missing are proportionate to the tonnage of bombs dropped per aircraft missing from the start of the war at any particular month end. The distances in this case should be read upwards from any power of ten on the scale, conveniently regarded as unity.

Table 4

CUMULATIVE MONTHLY TOTALS OF TONNAGE OF BOMBS, SORTIES DESPATCHED, AND AIRCRAFT MISSING
February, 1942-May, 1945

| | Bombing Raids. | | | Bombs(Tons) | |
	Tonnage	Sorties	Missing.	H.E.	Incend.
1942					
February	48,071	53,872	1,439	42,885	5,089
March	50,746	55,921	1,512	44,993	5,624
April	55,179	59,509	1,649	47,997	7,051
May	58,413	61,806	1,750	49,630	8,634
June	65,258	66,230	1,946	52,174	12,928
July	71,626	69,993	2,129	56,357	15,109
August	75,788	72,225	2,271	58,755	16,864
September	81,383	75,387	2,431	61,698	19,511
October	85,192	77,540	2,525	63,450	21,564
November	87,615	79,133	2,577	64,737	22,694
December	90,329	80,619	2,662	65,967	24,177
1943					
January	94,674	82,930	2,746	68,066	26,423
February	105,633	87,869	2,845	73,204	32,242
March	116,224	92,739	2,995	78,647	37,385
April	127,691	97,860	3,234	85,187	42,310
May	140,611	102,904	3,482	92,392	48,103
June	155,882	108,155	3,750	100,651	55,021
July	172,712	113,869	3,940	109,590	62,912
August	192,861	121,044	4,229	120,496	72,155
September	207,716	126,057	4,420	128,507	78,999
October	221,489	130,177	4,578	135,556	85,724
November	235,984	134,830	4,734	143,489	92,286
December	247,786	138,499	4,902	149,718	97,859
1944					
January	266,214	144,148	5,219	160,391	105,614
February	278,268	148,277	5,406	166,774	111,286
March	305,966	156,474	5,686	183,348	122,410
April	339,462	165,034	5,876	209,860	129,304
May	376,714	174,940	6,131	244,197	132,210
June	443,981	190,926	6,459	301,096	132,581
July	491,596	206,549	6,759	357,081	134,211
August	557,451	224,342	6,972	416,290	140,856
September	610,038	238,885	7,089	461,898	147,835
October	671,242	254,314	7,205	512,572	158,364
November	724,264	267,569	7,337	560,628	163,330
December	773,304	281,153	7,449	604,504	168,494
1945					
January	806,227	290,782	7,568	632,736	173,185
February	852,116	305,847	7,721	666,555	185,255
March	919,753	324,699	7,923	723,866	195,581
April	954,707	335,895	7,985	758,218	196,173
May	955,044	336,037	7,985	758,408	196,256

Table 5

DISTRIBUTION OF EFFORT AND CASUALTIES – CUMULATIVE TOTALS

(a) Sorties Despatched and (b) Aircraft Missing on Various Types of Operations

	(a) Sorties.					(b) Aircraft Missing.		
	Bomb Raids.	Sea Mining.	Counter Measures.	Miscle-laneous.	Total.	Bomb Raids.	Sea Mining.	Total.
1942								
Up to-								
February	53,872	2,761		2,173	58,808	1,439	57	1,533
March	55,921	3,027		2,254	61,202	1,512	68	1,617
April	59,509	3,371		2,338	65,218	1,649	78	1,768
May	61,806	3,821		2,399	68,026	1,750	94	1,885
June	66,230	4,337		2,455	73,043	1,946	103	2,090
July	69,993	4,771		2,493	77,256	2,129	114	2,284
August	72,225	5,153		2,530	79,905	2,271	130	2,442
September	75,387	5,621		2,540	83,544	2,431	147	2,621
October	77,540	6,082		2,566	86,198	2,525	161	2,726
November	79,133	6,664		2,657	88,455	2,577	176	2,795
December	80,619	7,085		2,710	90,414	2,662	183	2,886
1943								
January	82,930	7,681		2,765	93,377	2,746	199	2,988
February	87,869	8,221		2,842	98,932	2,845	208	3,097
March	92,739	8,732		2,921	104,392	2,995	226	3,267
April	97,860	9,423		3,027	110,310	3,234	259	3,540
May	102,904	9,791		3,190	115,885	3,482	267	3,798
June	108,155	10,217		3,255	121,727	3,750	274	4,078
July	113,869	10,530		3,555	127,954	3,940	280	4,276
August	121,044	11,032		3,743	135,819	4,229	290	4,578
September	126,057	11,429		3,896	141,382	4,420	293	4,774

	(a) Sorties.					(b) Aircraft Missing.		
	Bomb Raids.	Sea Mining.	Counter Measures.	Miscle-laneous.	Total.	Bomb Raids.	Sea Mining.	Total.
October	130,177	11,796		4,089	146,062	4,578	298	4,937
November	134,830	12,148		4,340	151,327	4,734	306	5,103
December	138,499	12,404	11	4,569	155,482	4,902	311	5,277
1944								
January	144,148	12,777	51	4,817	161,792	5,219	314	5,599
February	148,277	13,547	140	5,295	167,258	5,406	323	5,804
March	156,474	14,065	423	6,175	177,136	5,686	326	6,102
April	165,034	14,919	827	6,907	187,686	5,876	345	6,326
May	174,940	15,745	1,175	7,700	199,559	6,131	354	6,615
June	190,926	16,205	2,194	8,088	217,412	6,459	355	6,959
July	206,549	16,389	4,707	8,748	236,392	6,759	357	7,272
August	224,342	16,803	6,728	9,179	257,051	6,972	369	7,512
September	238,885	16,988	8,503	10,048	274,423	7,089	373	7,652
October	254,314	17,245	10,030	10,397	291,985	7,205	381	7,784
November	267,569	17,415	11,414	10,596	306,993	7,337	382	7,927
December	281,153	17,675	12,754	10,745	322,326	7,449	385	8,047
1945								
January	290,782	17,834	13,873	10,808	333,296	7,568	391	8,179
February	305,847	18,126	15,910	11,023	350,905	7,721	400	8,357
March	324,699	18,402	17,968	11,178	372,246	7,923	405	8,580
April	335,895	18,682	19,525	12,248	386,349	7,985	408	8,652
May	336,037	18,725	19,686	15,362	389,809	7,985	408	8,655

Note. – Total aircraft missing { Counter-measures   116
{ Miscellaneous Sorties   146

Graph No. 5: Notes

The cumulative totals of aircraft despatched on all operations, and shown separately, of aircraft despatched on bomb raids and sea mining operations, are shown in black; aircraft missing in these operations are shown in red. The green curves show cumulative totals of aircraft despatched on counter-measures, including fighter support, intruders, decoy sweeps or mandrel screen; such operations as met. flights, special operations, reconnaissance are shown as miscellaneous. The aircraft lost in these two categories are too few to be recorded on the scale as drawn.

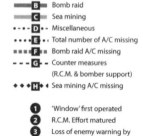

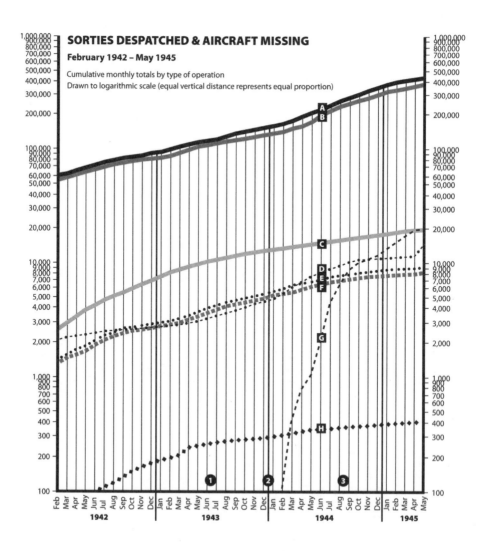

Graph No. 5A: Notes

This diagram represents graphically the percentage loss rate per each 3,000 bomber sorties by night on German targets only. This method of representation gives a clear picture of the effect of R.C.M., how long the effect lasted, and the time taken by the enemy to recover. In order to attempt an accurate survey of the value of R.C.M., it has been considered necessary to disregard all French and Italian targets by night and by day, sea mining, Mosquito attacks, and in fact all aircraft not actually engaged in bombing a German target by night. The overall Command percentage loss rate is, of course, more favourable than that shown by the curve since the general effect of bringing in non-German targets, sea mining and the considerable Mosquito effort – as well as the later highly successful day raids on Germany – is to lower the percentage loss rate. This is, of course, due to the fact that the targets which have been excluded were very lightly defended. Even this requires qualification, for the period immediately before and after D-Day, when the Command was engaged on French targets by day and by night. Until the German retreat through France got under way, these targets were quite strongly defended.

2. Nevertheless, since the main effort of the Command has been by night against Germany and because R.C.M. has always been kept in step with this primary task, all but German targets attacked by night have been excluded.

DIAGRAM SHOWING BOMBER COMMAND LOSS RATE ON GERMAN TARGETS

January 1942 - April 1945

Percentage losses on German targets by night are calculated for each 3,000 sorties. Introduction of each R.C.M. device and other important factors affecting the loss rate are shown at the appropriate dates.

Graph No. 6: Note

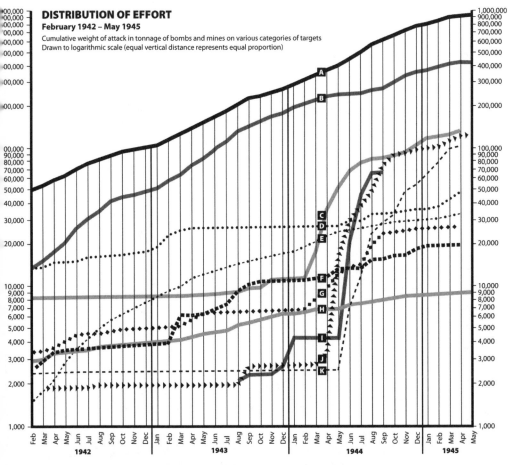

DISTRIBUTION OF EFFORT
February 1942 – May 1945
Cumulative weight of attack in tonnage of bombs and mines on various categories of targets
Drawn to logarithmic scale (equal vertical distance represents equal proportion)

KEY

A	Total
B	Industrial Towns
C	Transportation
D	Naval Targets
E	Mines / Tons
F	Specific Industries
G	Airfields & Ground G.A.F.
H	Miscellaneous
I	Military Installations V. Weapons
J	Troops & Defences
K	Oil

The diversion of effort from Germany in March, 1944 and the distribution of it amongst pre-invasion and invasion support targets is clearly shown. The percentage of the cumulative tonnage dropped on German industrial towns at that date was 68 per cent. By September the percentage had fallen to 44 per cent. and this was also the percentage at the end of the war. (Total tonnage includes tonnage of sea mines). Nevertheless the cumulative total tonnage dropped on German industrial towns at February/March, 1944, was doubled by the end of the war.

The tonnage of bombs dropped on military installations (V-weapon sites and dumps) from August, 1943, to the end of the war was approximately equal to the cumulative total tonnage dropped on the German industrial towns from the start of the war to March, 1943.

DISTRIBUTION OF EFFORT

Cumulative Weight of Attack on Various Categories of Target, Tonnage of Bombs and Mines.

	Industrial towns	Troops & Defence	Trans-portaion	Naval Targets	Oil Targets	Airfieds & Aircraft Industires	Specific Industries	Military Installations	Miscella-neous	Sea Mining	Totals
1942											
February	13,614	-	8,317	13,365	2,295	3,315	2,418	-	2,881	1,464	49,535
March	15,325	1,866	8,387	13,663	-	3,347	2,928	-	3,005	1,702	52,448
April	17,992	-	8,398	14,510	-	3,590	3,325	-	3,214	2,083	57,262
May	20,375	-	-	14,741	-	3,894	3,536	-	3,308	2,767	61,180
June	26,462	-	8,409	14,964	2,306	4,284	3,572	-	3,406	3,549	68,807
July	31,708	-	-	15,860	-	4,383	3,594	-	3,500	4,150	75,776
August	35,536	1,927	-	15,970	-	4,417	3,609	-	3,614	4,798	80,586
September	40,792	-	-	16,073	-	4,542	3,625	-	3,709	5,535	86,918
October	43,916	-	-	16,467	2,307	4,725	3,662	-	3,779	6,176	91,368
November	45,616	-	8,418	17,129	-	4,733	3,671	-	3,814	6,936	94,551
December	48,113	-	8,452	17,153	-	4,740	3,759	-	3,878	7,584	97,913
1943											
January	51,038	-	8,482	18,367	-	4,806	3,808	-	3,941	8,445	103,119
February	57,367	-	8,488	22,768	-	4,822	3,935	-	4,019	9,193	114,826
March	63,973	-	8,561	24,436	2,331	4,837	6,007	-	4,152	9,964	126,188
April	73,070	-	8,669	25,771	-	5,587	6,048	-	4,288	11,180	138,871
May	84,974	-	8,782	25,803	2,352	6,187	6,127	-	4,459	11,931	152,542
June	98,922	-	8,838	25,927	-	6,376	6,878	-	4,612	12,708	168,590
July	115,021	-	9,094	25,933	2,355	6,380	7,269	-	4,733	13,322	186,034
August	130,695	-	9,099	-	-	6,382	9,099	2,072	5,299	14,058	206,919
September	142,761	2,597	9,874	-	-	6,400	10,125	2,225	5,446	14,843	222,559
October	155,862	-	-	25,938	2,361	6,417	10,462	-	5,753	15,563	236,952
November	168,399	-	11,330	25,940	-	6,424	10,681	-	6,027	16,213	252,197
December	179,577	-	-	-	-	6,431	10,778	2,571	6,201	16,720	264,506

	Industrial towns	Troops & Defence	Transportaion	Naval Targets	Oil Targets	Aircraft & Airfields	Sspecific Industries	Military Installations	Miscellaneous	Sea Mining	Totals
1944											
January	196,143	-	11,337	26,018	-	6,451	10,841	4,053	6,413	17,603	283,817
February	207,735	-	11,482	26,030	-	6,590	10,887	4,062	6,524	18,939	297,207
March	227,191	-	17,725	-	-	7,970	11,226	4,076	6,790	20,115	326,081
April	239,188	3,230	36,955	26,036	-	9,145	11,606	4,083	6,858	22,178	361,640
May	244,584	15,864	51,968	26,051	-	11,793	13,094	4,088	6,911	24,204	400,918
June	245,294	29,593	69,401	29,184	6,857	13,139	13,144	19,995	7,374	25,465	459,446
July	254,888	38,440	78,876	29,482	11,264	13,653	13,163	44,287	7,543	25,979	517,575
August	265,069	48,355	83,176	32,470	22,393	18,969	15,706	63,663	7,650	27,103	584,554
September	277,596	74,719	85,309	32,928	27,228	23,416	15,709	64,522	8,111	27,655	637,693
October	319,842	87,085	86,345	33,900	30,910	23,463	16,791	-	8,384	28,478	699,720
November	347,538	92,774	91,237	34,059	45,295	23,482	16,854	-	8,503	29,048	753,312
December	364,265	96,451	109,691	35,588	50,404	25,340	18,458	-	8,585	29,903	803,207
1945											
January	376,196	98,523	118,150	35,717	59,432	-	19,679	-	8,668	30,290	836,617
February	398,084	102,279	123,655	36,278	73,541	-	-	-	8,738	31,366	883,482
March	428,362	110,321	129,884	40,202	92,477	25,345	19,690	-	8,950	32,235	951,988
April	430,684	122,377	137,793	46,728	97,914	25,941	19,694	-	9,054	33,237	987,944
May	430,747	122,532	137,793	46,728	97,914	25,977	19,694	64,522	9,137	33,237	988,281
Percentage of Effort.											
Bombing only	45·1	12·8	14·4	4·9	10·2	2·7	2·1	6·8	1·0	—	
Including Sea-Mining	43·6	12·4	14·0	4·7	9·9	2·6	2·0	6·5	0·9	3·4	

Graph No. 7: Notes

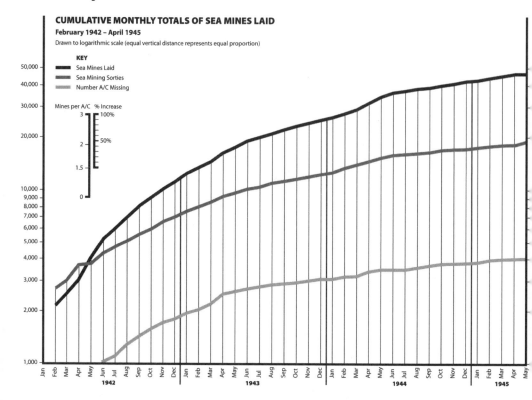

A feature worthy of note is the increase in mines laid per aircraft sortie throughout the period.

The inclusion of all groups in minelaying operations after April, 1942 caused a sharp rise in load carried, as the proportion of 5 Group Hampden (load 1 mine) became smaller.

Stirlings and Lancasters were at that time carrying an average load of four mines each, while Halifaxes and Wellingtons were only carrying two mines.

The upturn in April, 1944 can be accounted for by:—

(i) Cessation of minelaying operations by Wellington aircraft and later Stirlings.

(ii) Increased loads carried by Lancasters (average 5½ mines) and Halifaxes with special carriers (4 mines).

The curve showing aircraft missing shows the steady increase in casualties sustained by aircraft operating within the height range of 600 to 1,000 ft. which was the maximum permissible for height of drop until April, 1943. The improvement of mine and parachute for higher dropping is seen to result in an immediate smoothing of the curve.

Table 7
SEA MINING STATISTICS
Number of sea mines laid, sorties despatched, and aircraft missing.
Cumulative totals, 23rd February, 1942-8th May, 1945

	Aircraft Despatched.	Aircraft Missing.	Number of Mines Laid.*
1942			
February	2,761	57	2,185
March	3,027	68	2,541
April	3,771	78	3,110
May	3,821	94	4,133
June	4,337	103	5,300
July	4,771	114	6,197
August	5,153	130	7,165
September	5,621	147	8,266
October	6,082	161	9,248
November	6,664	176	10,404
December	7,085	183	11,391
1943			
January	7,681	199	12,676
February	8,221	208	13,805
March	8,732	226	14,964
April	9,423	259	16,833
May	9,791	267	17,981
June	10,217	274	19,155
July	10,530	280	20,082
August	11,032	290	21,185
September	11,429	293	22,373
October	11,796	298	23,449
November	12,148	306	24,425
December	12,404	311	25,225
1944			
January	12,777	314	26,326
February	13,547	323	27,987
March	14,065	326	29,459
April	14,919	345	32,102
May	15,745	354	34,862
June	16,205	355	36,640
July	16,389	357	37,348
August	16,803	369	38,934
September	16,988	373	39,682
October	17,245	381	40,815
November	17,415	382	41,565
December	17,675	385	42,725
1945			
January	17,834	391	43,393
February	18,126	400	44,747
March	18,402	405	45,945
April	18,682	408	47,307
May	19,025	408	47,307

* *For cumulative tonnage of Sea Mines see Table 6.*

Graph No. 8

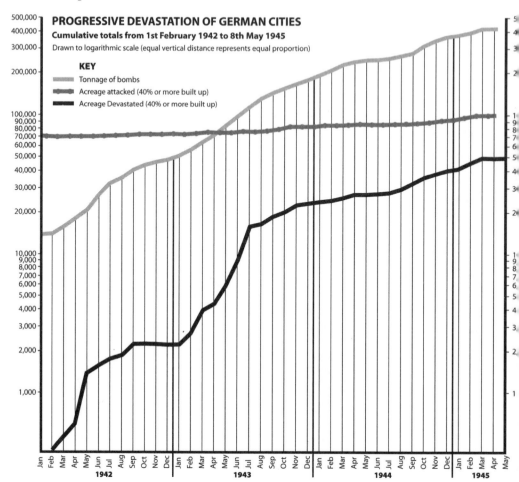

PROGRESS OF THE BOMBER OFFENSIVE AGAINST
GERMAN INDUSTRIAL TOWNS ASSESSED IN TERMS OF
ACREAGE DESTROYED
Explanatory Notes and Definitions

1. Basis of Calculations

Monthly figures for weight of bombs claimed dropped on towns attacked are as given
by Air Ministry War Room.

Figures for acreage 40 per cent. or more built up (Target) area of towns attacked
are those calculated, in accordance with the definitions given below, by Headquarters,
Bomber Command, and agreed with A.C.I.U., Medmenham.

Figures for acreage destroyed are those calculated by A.C.I.U., Medmenham, in the manner described below.

2. Definitions

(i) *Towns attacked.* – These include all German towns on which *strategic* attacks were made by Bomber Command. The list does *not* include a number of small towns on which, at one time or another, tactical attacks were made, and which, in the course of these attacks, were almost entirely destroyed.

(ii) *Cumulative total tons of bombs claimed dropped on towns attacked.* – The tonnage included under this heading is *only* that claimed dropped in attacks where the objective was specified as the town area. It does *not* include the tonnage claimed dropped on individual targets in or near the town area, but it must be pointed out that these latter attacks may have contributed some small part of the destruction in the town.

(iii) *Cumulative total acreage* (40 *per cent. or more built up) of towns attacked.* – Under this heading the built-up (Target) area of a town is added when the town is *first* attacked. The cumulative total thus represents the combined acreage of all towns attacked up to any date, regardless of how many attacks have been made upon any town.

(iv) *Cumulative total acreage of devastation in built-up target area.* – This means the total area of devastation within the target area as defined in 2 (iii) above. It excludes damage to factory buildings, marshalling yards and docks (the significance of which cannot be measured in terms of area alone) and also damage to non-industrial areas less than 40 per cent. built up.

In some cases daylight photographic cover of a town (upon which all calculations of results are exclusively based) has not been obtained until the end of a series of raids which extend over a period of more than one month. Where possible adjustments have been made *pro rata* with the probable success of the intermediate attacks. Where such adjustment has not been possible the results of the whole series of raids have been included in one month, generally that in which the last raid of the series took place, but occasionally that in which the majority of the raids took place.

It should be noted that the results figures include in some cases (where it is impossible to separate it out) damage inflicted upon non-industrial areas during the course of U.S.A. attacks on specific objectives. Since, however, in cases where this was large, it was nearly always possible to make a separation, the error introduced will only have a negligible effect on the results and can be ignored.

3. Notes

It will be seen that whereas in 1942 more than 20 tons of bombs were required to devastate an acre, this figure fell to less than eight tons per acre at the end of 1943 following the heavy and successful Battle of Hamburg.

The vertical distances separating the red and black lines are proportionate to the cumulative tonnage dropped per cumulative acreage destroyed at any month end.

The rapid increase of devastation with the opening of the main offensive in 1943 is well emphasized. Between January and August of that year the devastation was increased eightfold, while the tonnage was only two-and-a-half times greater. To measure the increased accuracy and effectiveness, account must be taken of diminishing returns, i.e., the percentage of attack that fell in target areas already devastated.

The percentage of total attacked area devastated at any period is given by the vertical distances separating the green and black lines.

Table 8
PROGRESS OF STRATEGIC BOMBER OFFENSIVE AGAINST GERMAN INDUSTRIAL TOWNS
(See also Table 11)
CUMULATIVE TOTALS FROM FEBRUARY, 1942 TO MAY, 1945

	Tonnage of Bombs. Cumulative Total of bombs claimed dropped on towns attacked.	**Acreage Attack** Cumulative Total acreage (40 per cent or more built-up) of towns attacked	**Acreage Devasted.** Cumulative total acreage destroyed in built-up (Target) area	Cumulative per cent of built-up (Target) area destroyed
1942				
Up to the end of-				
February	13,614	70,112	Negligible	-
March	15,325	70,745	190	0·27
April	17,992	70,745	390	0·55
May	20,375	70,745	1,380	1·95
June	26,462	70,745	1,574	2·23
July	31,708	71,611	1,747	2·44
August	35,536	72,582	1,911	2·64
September	40,792	72,582	2,276	3·14
October	43,916	74,111	2,276	3·07
November	45,616	74,111	2,276	3·07
December	48,113	74,111	2,276	3·07
1943				
January	51,038	74,111	2,276	3·07
February	57,367	74,111	2,730	3·68
March	63,973	74,751	4,066	5·44
April	73,070	74,751	4,490	6·02
May	84,974	75,890	6,062	7·99
June	98,922	77,624	9,266	11·92
July	115,021	77,963	16,352	20·9
August	130,695	79,139	17,118	21·6
September	142,761	79,884	19,274	24·1
October	155,862	83,553	20,741	24·8

November	168,399	83,553	22,961	27·5
December	179,577	83,553	23,596	28·2
1944				
January	196,143	85,437	24,111	28·2
February	207,735	87,265	24,581	28·2
March	227,191	87,265	25,768	29·5
April	239,188	87,413	27,102	31·1
May	244,584	87,413	27,414	31·4
June	245,294	87,413	27,414	31·4
July	254,888	87,413	27,979	32·0
August	265,069	88,237	29,979	33·8
September	277,586	88,981	33,081	37·2
October	319,842	89,914	36,609	40·7
November	347,538	91,760	38,529	42·0
December	364,265	94,204	40,144	42·6
1945				
January	376,196	94,479	42,104	44·6
February	398,084	100,077	46,460	46·4
March	428,362	101,474	49,286	48·6
April	430,684	101,474	49,326	48·6
May	430,747	101,474	49,326	48·6

Graph No. 9

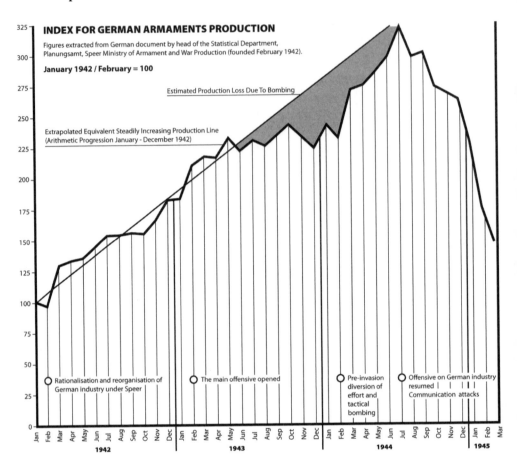

The effect on the German armaments production of the combined bomber offensive is estimated by an extrapolated line. This does not pretend to give more than an indication of the rate of progress which the Germans were able to maintain in 1942 after Speer's reorganisation. It represents an arithmetical progression, the total of which equals the total for that year. Attention is drawn by the shaded area to the coincidence of the July, 1944, intersection of this line with the production figure. The steep rise to this figure took place during the diversion from strategic to tactical bombing.

Table 9
INDEX FOR GERMAN ARMAMENTS PRODUCTION
January-February, 1942 = 100

These figures have been extracted from a manuscript prepared by Dr. Wagenfueher, who during the War was head of the statistical department of the Planungsamt of the Speer Ministry of Armament and War Production.

	1942	1943	1944	1945
January	103	182	241	277
February	97	209	231	175
March	129	216	270	145
April	133	215	274	
May	135	232	285	
June	144	220	297	
July	153	229	322	
August	153	224	297	
September	155	234	301	
October	154	242	273	
November	165	231	268	
December	181	222	263	
Average	142	222	277	182

Graph No. 10

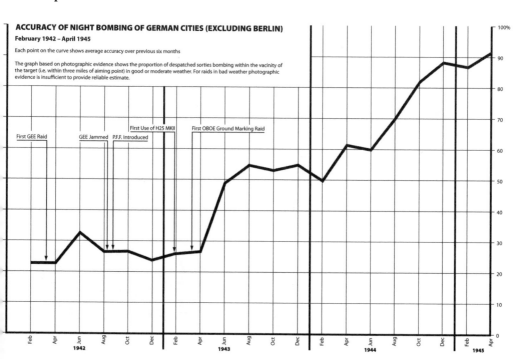

Table 10
ACCURACY OF BOMBER COMMAND NIGHT ATTACKS ON GERMAN CITIES
(EXCLUDING BERLIN)

Period	Total Number of Photos Plotted			Photos Plotted within 3 miles of A.P.			Percentage Plotted within 3 miles of A.P.		
	Weather		Total	Weather		Total	Weather		Total
	Good	Mod		Good	Mod		Good	Mod	
1941									
August-September	121	90	211	47	20	67	39	22	32
October-November	61	31	92	13	2	15	21	6	16
December-January	52	74	126	39	17	56	75	23	44
1942									
February-March	69	185	254	54	24	78	78	13	31
April-May	370	152	522	247	16	263	67	11	50
June-July	475	487	962	175	97	272	37	20	28
August-September	386	902	1,288	152	295	447	39	33	35
October-November	88	192	280	22	48	70	25	25	25
December-January	18	88	106	11	20	31	61	23	29
1943									
February-March	581	416	997	148	208	356	25	50	36
April-May	2,070	403	2,473	1,475	147	1,622	71	36	66

June-July	3,399	33	3,432	2,277	17	2,294	67	52	67
August-September	2,027	534	2,561	829	260	1,089	41	49	43
October-November	1,290	674	1,964	1,106	397	1,503	86	59	77
December-January	261	496	757	180	108	288	69	22	38
1944									
February-March	973	624	1,597	667	466	1,133	68	75	71
April-May	607	477	1,084	562	261	823	93	55	76
June-July	-	287	287	-	271	271	-	94	94
August-September	1,625	675	2,300	1,547	502	2,049	95	74	89
October-November	1,715	684	2,399	1,624	671	2,295	95	98	96
December-January	1,381	354	1,735	1,258	344	1,602	91	97	92
1945									
February-March	1,633	269	1,902	1,613	252	1,865	99	94	98

N.B. – (i) Raids on Berlin are excluded from the above table as, owing to the very large size of this target, the percentage within 3 miles does not provide a satisfactory measure of success.

(ii) There is insufficient photographic evidence for the success of raids in poor weather to warrant their inclusion.

(iii) The results for 1941 and the early part of 1942 are likely to be favourably biased as the few cameras available were usually carried by the best crews.

Graph No. 11

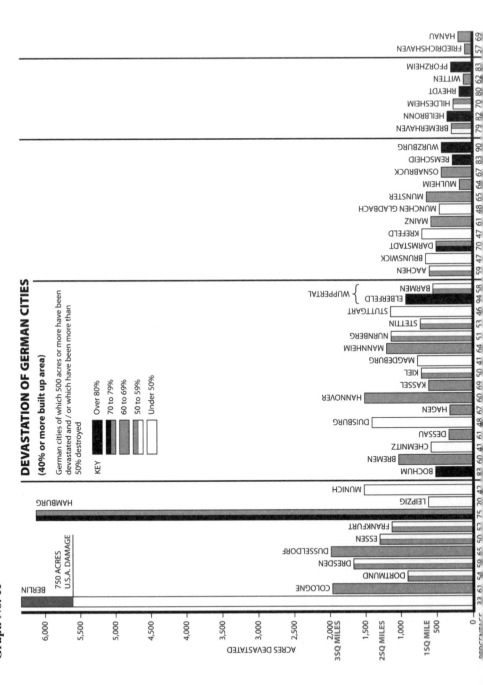

DEVASTATION OF GERMAN CITIES
(40% or more built up area)

German cities of which 500 acres or more have been devastated and / or which have been more than 50% destroyed

KEY

Over 80%
70 to 79%
60 to 69%
50 to 59%
Under 50%

Table 11

PROGRESS OF THE BOMBER OFFENSIVE AGAINST GERMAN INDUSTRIAL TOWNS SCHEDULE, BY TOWNS, OF ATTACKS AND DEVASTATION RESULTING

Town	Date of First Main Force Attack	Date of Last Main Force Attack	Total Number of Main Force Attacks	Acreage 40 percent or more Built-up (Target) Area.	Acreage Destroyed In Built-up (Target) Area.	Destroyed Percentage Of Built-up (Target) Area.
Aachen	5/6.10.42	13/14. 7.43	2	1,030	605	59
Augsburg	25/26. 2.44	-	1	1,535	445	29
Berlin	16/17. 1.43	24/25. 3.44	24	19,423	6,427*	33
Bochum	29/30. 3.43	4/5.11.44	6	640	532	83
Bonn	18.10.44	4/5. 2.45	5	708	240	34
Bremen	3/4. 6.42	22. 4.45	12	1,744	1,042	60
Bremerhaven	18/19. 9.44	-	1	375	297	79
Brunswick	14/15. 1.44	-14/15.10.44	5	1,400	655	47
Chemnitz	14/15. 2.45	5/6. 3.45	2	1,452	590	41
Coblenz	6/7.11.44	-	1	523	303	58
Cologne	13/14. 3.42	2.3.45	22	3,250	1,994	61
Darmstadt	25/26. 8.44	11/12. 9.44	2	745	516	69
Dessau	7/8. 3.45	8/9. 4.45	2	542	331	61
Dortmund	14/15. 4.42	12. 3.45	9	1,720	923	54
Dresden	13/14. 2.45	-	1	2,844	1,681	59

Town	Date of First Main Force Attack	Date of Last Main Force Attack	Total Number of Main Force Attacks	Acreage 40 percent or more Built-up (Target Area.)	Acreage Destroyed In Built-up (Target) Area.	Destroyed Percentage Of Built-up (Target) Area.
Duisburg	13/14. 7.42	21/22. 2.45	18	2,955	1,424	48
Dusseldorf	31/1. 8.42	2/3.11.44	10	3,115	2,003	64
Emden	6/7. 6.42	6. 9.44	5	485	270	56
Essen	8/9. 3.42	11. 3.45	28	2,630	1,319	50
Frankfurt a/Main	24/25. 8.42	28/29.12.44	11	2,200	1,145	52
Freiburg	27/28.11.44	-	1	694	257	37
Friedrichshafen	27/28. 4.44	-	1	148	99	67
Gelsenkirchen	25/26. 6.43	22/23. 1.45	4	757	360	48
Giessen	2/3. 12.44	6/7.12.44	2	398	130	33
Hagen	1/2. 10.43	15/16. 3.45	4	486	325	67
Hamburg	15/16. 1.42	13/14. 4.45	17	8,315	6,200	75
Hamm	5.12.44	-	1	355	140	39
Hanau	6/7. 1.45	18/19. 3.45	2	275	190	69
Hannover	22/23. 9.43	25. 3.45	16	2,519	1,517	60
Harburg	11/12.11.44	-	1	286	153	53
Heilbronn	4/5.12.44	-	1	430	351	82
Hildesheim	22. 3.45	-	1	378	263	70
Kaiserslautern	27/28. 9.44	-	1	369	134	36

					Acreage	
Karlsruhe	2/3. 9.42	2/3. 2.45	6	1,237	398	32
Kassel	27/28. 8.42	8/9. 3.45	6	905	620	69
Kiel	27/28. 2.42	23/24. 4.45	10	1,466	725	50
Konigsberg	26/27. 8.44	29/30. 8.44	2	824	435	53
Krefeld	2/3. 10.42	21/22. 6.43	2	1,529	714	47
Leipzig	20/21.10.43	19/20. 2.44	3	3,183	625	20
Lubeck	28/29. 3.42	-	1	633	190	30
Magdeburg	21/22.1.44	13/14. 2.45	4	1,884	774	44
Mainz	11/12.8.42	27. 2.45		971	593	61
Mannheim-Ludwigshaven	14.15 2.42	1. 3.45	13	1,911	1,213	64
Mulheim	22/23.6.43	-	1	303	193	64
Munchen-Gladbach and						
Rheydt	30/31. 8.43	1. 2.45	4	1,176	633	54
Munich	19/20. 9.42	7/8. 1.45	9	3,634	1,547	42
Munster	28/29. 1.42	25. 3.45	6	997	650	65
Neuss	23/24. 9.44	28/29.11.44	4	225	17	8
Nuremburg	28/29. 8.42	16/17. 3.45	11	2,255	1,146	51
Oberhausen	14/15. 6.43	4.12.45	3	502	100	20
Osnabruck	9/10. 8.42	25. 3.45	5	658	441	67
Pforzheim	23/24.2.45	-	1	369	304	83
Plauen	10/11. 4.45	-	1	712	365	51
Potsdam	14/15. 4.45	-	1	559	75	13
Remscheid	30/31. 7.43	-	1	339	281	83

Town	Date of First Main Force Attack	Date of Last Main Force Attack	Total Number of Main Force Attacks	40 percent or more Built-up (Target) Area.	Acreage Destroyed In Built-up (Target) Area.	Destroyed Percentage Of Built-up (Target) Area.
Rostock	23/24.4.42	26/27. 4.42	4	634	200	32
Saarbrucken	29/30. 7.42	5/6.10.44	4	866	418	48
Schweinfurt	24/25. 2.44	26/27. 4.44	2	293	126	43
Solingen	4.11.44	5.11.44	2	343	169	49
Stettin	20/21. 4.43	29/30. 8.44	4	1,386	736	53
Stuttgart	4/5. 5.42	12/13. 2.45	18	2,514	1,152	46
Trier	21.12.44	23.12.44	2	492	48	10
Ulm	17/18.12.44	-	1	562	155	28
Wiesbaden	2/3. 2.45	-	1	605	90	15
Witten	18/19. 3.45	-	1	207	129	62
Wilhelmshaven	10/11. 1.42	15/16.10.44	9	972	130	13
Worms	21/22. 2.45	-	1	328	127	39
Wuppertal-Barmen	29/30. 5.43	13. 3.45	2	1,139	655	58
Wuppertal/Elberfeld	24/25. 6.43	-	1	929	870	94
Wurzburg	16/17. 3.45	-	1	477	422	89

* Includes approximately 750 acres of American damage.

Graph No. 12

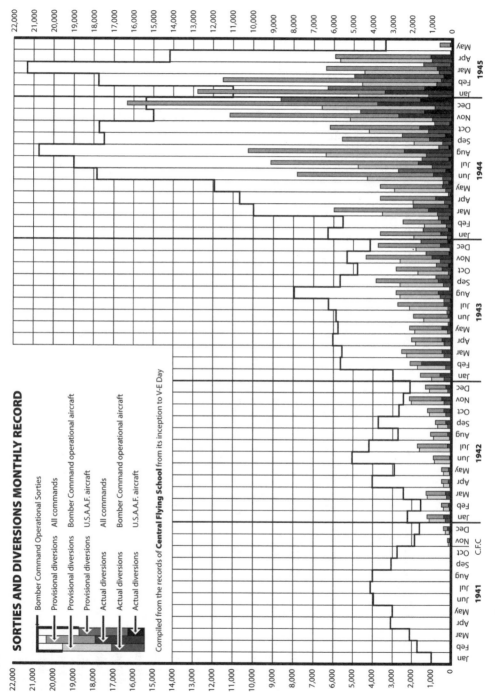

SORTIES AND DIVERSIONS MONTHLY RECORD

Bomber Command Operational Sorties

Provisional diversions   All commands

Provisional diversions   Bomber Command operational aircraft

Provisional diversions   U.S.A.A.F. aircraft

Actual diversions   All commands

Actual diversions   Bomber Command operational aircraft

Actual diversions   U.S.A.A.F. aircraft

Compiled from the records of **Central Flying School** from its inception to V-E Day

Table 12

(See Appendix "K")

SORTIES AND DIVERSIONS, MONTHLY RECORD – FEBRUARY, 1942, to MAY, 8th, 1945

Bomber Command Operational Aircraft

	Sorties				Provisional Diversions				Acctual Diversions			
	1942	1943	1944	1945	1942	1943	1944	1945	1942	1943	1943	1945
January	*2,226	2,963	6,310	10,970	*1,044	1,012	1,812	4,205	*304	426	281	1,218
February	*1,506	5,555	5,466	17,609	*373	1,612	1,414	4,374	*65	295	364	861
March	2,394	5,460	9,878	21,341	1,182	2,225	3,411	4,329	257	345	781	750
April	4,016	5,918	10,550	14,103	425	1,817	2,087	5,440	45	444	2,403	1,004
May	2,808	5,575	11,873	3,460	454	1,693	2,908	20	107	273	399	-
June	4,997	5,842	17,853	-	843	1,405	4,090	-	10	97	496	-
July	4,233	6,227	18,980	-	1,581	1,926	4,619	-	90	216	1,019	-
August	2,649	7,865	20,659	-	945	2,474	6,072	-	128	555	1,351	-
September	3,639	5,563	17,372	-	695	2,553	1,907	-	205	532	539	-
October	2,644	4,680	17,562	-	1,068	1,631	4,071	-	344	260	1,464	-
November	2,267	5,265	15,008	-	1,828	2,510	4,990	-	420	624	1,038	-
December	1,959	4,155	15,333	-	1,023	1,793	6,306	-	206	164	1,721	-
Actual Total	31,606	65,068	166,844	67,483	10,044	22,681	43,687	18,368	1,812	4,231	9,856	3,833
Grand Total 1942-1945	331,001				94,780				19,732			

* *Note. – January and February, 1942, not included in totals.*

Graph No. 13.

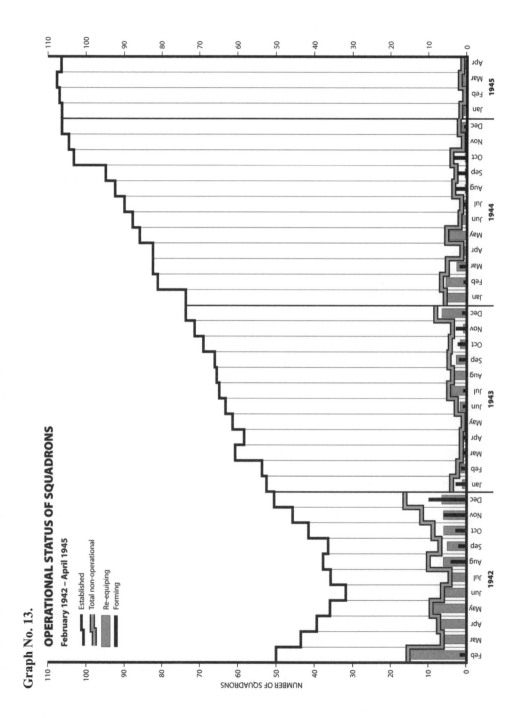

OPERATIONAL STATUS OF SQUADRONS

February 1942 – April 1945

Established
Total non-operational
Re-equiping
Forming

NUMBER OF SQUADRONS

Table 13
PERCENTAGE STRENGTH OF COMMAND NON-OPERATIONAL OWING TO FORMATION OR RE-EQUIPMENT OF SQUADRONS, MONTHLY

	No. Of Sqdns Estab.	Sqdns. Non-Op. for Re-equipping	Est. Sqdns. Non-Op. for Re-equipping	Squadrons Forming	Est. Sqdns. Non-Ops. Forming
1942					
February	51	14	27·4	1	2.0
March	44½	6	13·4	-	-
April	40½	7	17·3	-	-
May	37	9	24·3	-	-
June	33	6	18·5	-	-
July	37	4	10·8	1	2·7
August	39	6	16·0	4	10·2
September	38	5	13·1	2	5·2
October	43	6	14·0	3	7·0
November	47	6	12·7	6	12·7
December	52	6½	12·5	10	20·0
1943					
January	54	1	2·0	3	5·4
February	55	1½	2·8	1	1·9
March	62	½	0·8	1	1·6
April	59½	½	0·9	1	1·8
May	62½	-	-	1	1·6
June	64½	2	3·1	1	1·5
July	66	4	6·0	1	1·5
August	66½	4	6·0	-	-
September	67	3	4·4	2	3·0
October	70	2	2·8	2½	3·5
November	72½	1	1·4	3	4·1
December	74½	7	9·4	1½	2·0
1944					
January	74½	6	8·0	-	-
February	82	6	7·3	1	1·2
March	83	3	3·7	2½	3·0
April	83	1	1·2	½	0·6
May	86½	5	5·8	½	0·5
June	88½	2	2·2	-	-
July	90½	½	0·5	1	1·1
August	93	½	0·5	3	3·2
September	95½	½	0·5	2½	2·6
October	103½	½	0·48	3½	3·4
November	105	-	-	1	0·9
December	107	1½	1·4	½	0·5
1945					
January	107	1	0·9	½	0·45
February	107½	-	-	½	0·45
March	108	1	0·9	½	0·45
April	107	1	0·9	-	-

Note. – *Numbers of squadrons are expressed in terms of standard 2-flight squadrons of 16 + 2, 16 + 4 and later 20 U.E. aircraft.*

Graph No. 14.

ENEMY GROUND DEFENCES AGAINST STRATEGIC AIR ATTACK

January 1941 - March 1945

The development of G.A.F. flak defence as indicated by the deployment of guns and searchlights (Naval flak defence in Germany and the west increase these figures by 15% heavy & 10% light guns)

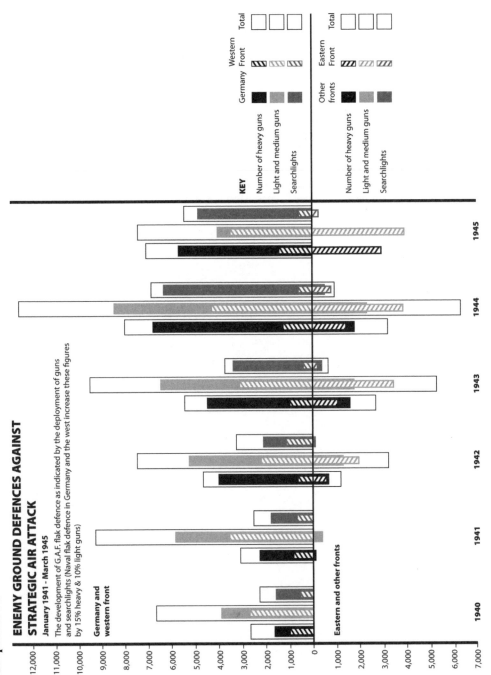

Table 14.
ESTIMATE OF G.A.F. FLAK GUNS, SEARCHLIGHTS AND BALLOONS DEPLOYED IN GERMANY AND IN OCCUPIED TERRITORIES, 1940-1945.

Notes: 1. This information is based on known numbers of *units* deployed and in view of variations in establishments, the resultant *equipment* figures can only be considered as informed estimates.

2. It will be observed that the figures relate to G.A.F. Flak only, no detailed information on Army and Naval Flak being yet available. From the point of view of opposition to strategic air attack the only appreciable factor in Army and Naval Flak is that represented by Naval Flak defences in Germany and the West, for which, as a rough approximation, 15 per cent. should be added to the G.A.F. Flak figures in respect of heavy and light guns, and 10 per cent. in respect of searchlights.

3. Western Front includes France, Holland and Belgium.

	Heavy Guns.	Light and Medium Guns.	Searchlights.	Barrage Balloons.
July, 1940				
Germany	1,692	3,996	1,716	Figures not available
Western Front	936	2,724	540	
Total	2,628	6,720	2,256	
January, 1941				
Germany	2,300	5,832	1,824	Figures not available
Western Front	804	3,540	696	
Total	3,104	9,372	2,520	
Other Fronts	156	468	36	
Grand Total	3,260	9,840	2,556	
January, 1942				
Germany	3,999	5,256	2,088	
Western Front	617	2,196	1,188	
Total	4,616	7,452	3,276	
Other Fronts	670	1,308	108	
Eastern Front	604	1,944	-	
Grand Total	5,890	10,704	3,384	
January, 1943				
Germany	4,491	6,456	3,330	1,680
Western Front	930	3,072	396	96
Total	5,421	9,528	3,726	1,776
Eastern Front	1,075	3,456	204	-
Other Fronts	1,645	1,854	456	72
Grand Total	8,141	14,838	4,386	1,848
January, 1944				
Germany	6,716	8,484	6,320	1,968
Western Front	1,225	4,200	560	288
Total	7,941	12,684	6,880	2,256
Eastern Front	1,430	3,912	576	96
Other Fronts	1,815	2,412	384	24
Grand Total	11,186	19,008	7,840	2,376
March, 1945				
Germany	5,614	3,984	4,880	1,464
Western Front	1,384	3,398	544	12
Total	6,998	7,382	5,424	1,476
Eastern Front	2,952	3,942	256	48
Grand Total	9,950	11,324	5,680	1,524

PERSONNEL CASUALTIES
Table 15
Figures promulgated, up to and including Air Ministry Casualty Circulation List No. 1798, dated 30th June, 1945, for casualties to Bomber Command personnel, 3rd September, 1939, to 8th May, 1945.
(Figures for 23rd February, 1942, to 8th May, 1945, not available.)
SUMMARY. (Net Figures.)

	Killed.	*Missing.*	*P.O.W*	*Total.*	*Wounded.*
1. *Flying Battle.*					
(All operational sorties)					
Aircrew	39,248	8,595	1,742	49,585	4,144
Groundstaff	43	43	5	91	23
	39,291	8,638	1,747	49,676	4,167
2. *Flying Accident.*					
(Non-operational Sorties)					
Aircrew	7,862	244	11	8,117	3,985
Groundstaff	226	6	-	232	110
	8,088	250	11	8,349	4,095
3. *Ground Battle.*					
(Including Enemy Action)					
Aircrew	40	3	3	46	37
Groundstaff	205	27	1	233	163
	245	30	4	279	200
4. *Ground Accident.*					
(Non Enemy Action)					
Aircrew	136	-	-	136	141
Groundstaff	560	-	-	560	478
	696	-	-	696	619
5. *Total.*					
Aircrew	47,286	8,842	1,756	57,884	8,307
Groundstaff	1,034	76	6	1,116	774
	48,320	8,918	1,762	59,000	9,081

Notes:—

(i) The figures for Missing refer to those still unaccounted for and not yet reclassified as Presumed Dead, Died of Wounds or Injuries, or as P.O.W.

(ii) The figures for P.O.W. include those recorded as P.O.W. at 30th June, 1945, and are subject to reclassification.

(iii) The figures for wounded are for casualty incidents not for number of individuals wounded, e.g., a man wounded on three separate occasions is recorded as 3.

(iv) The Total of all these figures, including wounded (see (iii) above)	*68,081*
Add: *Died of natural causes*	*525*
Add: *Returned prisoners of war*	*10,541*
Gross Total	*79,147*

APPENDICES
APPENDIX A

RADIO AIDS TO NAVIGATION AND BOMBING

The account which follows deals with the operational development and practical use of the various Signals devices and equipments in the radar and non-radar fields during the period February, 1942, to May, 1945. Though an integral part of the Bomber Command Signals organisation, the subject of Radio Countermeasures has been dealt with separately in Appendix E.

2. The early part of the year 1942 found Bomber Command still entirely dependent upon non-radar aids to safety and air navigation. The planned radar equipments – Gee and H.2.S. – had not yet made their appearance.

3. Within their known limitations, the service given by these non-radar aids – H.F. D/F, M.F. D/F, Darky (R/T Guard), M.F. Beacons and Jay Beams – met requirements fairly well under good weather conditions. Comparatively few bomber aircraft were operated on any single occasion; in February, 1942, the number exceeded 100 aircraft on five nights only, out of the 18 nights upon which operations took place. Although the number of aircraft which could use M.F. Beacons and Jay Beams simultaneously was unlimited, the accuracy of the British Beacons was poor at extreme range, and the system as a whole suffered from enemy interference. Jay Beams gave good range and high accuracy, but their application was restricted due to geographical limitations.

THE NON-RADAR AIDS

The M.F. D/F Organisation

4. The network of M.F. D/F stations provided fixing service for operational aircraft for distances up to about 350 miles east and south of the British coastline. However, due to geographical considerations, it was not possible to arrange each set of stations on a base-line which would ensure reasonable accuracy at the limits of range, and as range increased, so accuracy fell off, particularly over Germany.

5. Nevertheless, as the only fixing service available, the M.F. D/F system was widely used until the advent of the radar aids. During the early part of 1942, it was

not unusual for that part of the organisation which dealt with only operational aircraft to give as many as four fixes per aircraft operating. With 100 aircraft airborne, this would involve up to 400 fixes over a period of perhaps five hours, or 80 fixes an hour. Due to the exchange of signalling which was necessarily involved in getting a fix, any one set of stations, or section, of the organisation could not be expected to give more than 20 fixes per hour, and then only if the requests for service were spread over the hour. As, due to the base-line factor already mentioned – together with the shortage of ground equipment and personnel – not more than five sections could be made available to cover one operation, it is clear that the M.F. D/F organisation was reaching its peak load capacity when, in the absence of other aid, more than 100 bomber aircraft were likely to require assistance. When an emergency arose due to weather or other causes, the rate of requests for fixes would rise even higher over a short period, resulting in serious congestion and delay.

6. The service given by the M.F. D/F organisation was of a very high standard, but its very popularity was an important factor in limiting its usefulness if more than 100 aircraft were operating. Indeed, it was a long time before the older generation of navigators could be persuaded to give up M.F. D/F as the basic navigational aid.

7. Even after the introduction of GEE, which was in general use in the Command by the middle of 1942, the M.F. D/F organisation had an essential part to play in connection with Air/Sea Rescue and the giving of assistance to aircraft which were in difficulties over the North Sea. The "silent" aids were of little use to an aircraft about to ditch, when the important thing was to be able to get in touch with the ground in order that the rescue organisation could be set in motion. The M.F. D/F Service was continued in full measure until the end of the War, and apart from the safety aspect – which eventually became its real function – M.F. D/F was always available as a navigational aid if all else failed.

The H.F. D/F System

8. At one time H.F. D/F stations were provided at every airfield in the Command; this was the policy in February, 1942. Though an H.F. D/F station could not be relied upon to give reliable bearings at ranges much over 100 miles, it could in fact home an aircraft from much greater distances, the accuracy improving as the range shortened, until the final bearings would bring the aircraft right over the airfield. The sequence of using the ground-air aids on the return flight was therefore to obtain two or three fixes on M.F. while over the North Sea and then to change to the home station H.F. D/F for the final homing.

9. Clearly, since ground-air communication was again involved, there was a practical limit in the physical sense to the number of aircraft which any one H.F. D/F station could handle. While, due to the shorter procedure, the number of bearings which could be given by an H.F. D/F station was greater than the 20-fixes-per-hour standard of the M.F. D/F organisation, in general aircraft required more H.F. homing bearings than they did M.F. fixes, so that ultimately the homing capacity of an H.F.

D/F station was about 20 aircraft. Since at that time there was one such station on each airfield, which would normally operate considerably fewer than 20 aircraft on any one night, the H.F. D/F service was, in general, extremely good, difficulties only arising if a number of aircraft required service simultaneously.

10. With the introduction of GEE, which not only gave a very high degree of accuracy for fixing over this country but was also an extremely accurate and easily operated homing aid, the need for H.F. D/F almost ceased. The station was, however, always useful as the channel of wireless communication with base. The service, in an attenuated form, was maintained till the end of the War and was available both as a safety aid and a communication channel.

Darky

11. The two systems already discussed – M.F. and H.F. D/F – relied for their work upon the serviceability of the aircraft W/T equipment and the presence of the W/T operator. It frequently happened that as a result of battle damage and for other reasons, either or both were non-effective. In such circumstances the aircraft would have had no communication with the ground unless some other aid had been provided.

12. This aid was "Darky" – an R/T channel under the control of the pilot, who could speak direct to the ground on pre-set equipment which required no attention from the wireless operator. Stations to provide the ground side of this R/T service were established not only at every airfield in the Command, but also at all other suitable locations throughout the country; the object was to provide a network of such stations, so placed that aircraft flying over this country would always be within range of a ground station capable of answering a "Darky" call.

13. In order to make every such station available to all bomber aircraft, the service had necessarily to be operated upon one common frequency – 6,440 kc/s, which in effect became the Bomber Command R/T Guard – and since in these circumstances there was the serious problem of mutual interference with which to contend, the equipment used both in aircraft and on the ground was the low-power TR9 (later the TR. 1196).

14. A simple uncoded operating procedure was devised and since a returning bomber aircraft came within range of "Darky" after crossing the English coast at almost any point, the pilot could be given either a rough position, or courses to steer and distances from ground station to ground station, until eventually he found his own airfield.

15. The "Darky" service was intended for aircraft lost or otherwise in distress over this country, and until GEE became a universal fit in the bomber force, there is not the least doubt that a great many aircraft were saved from destruction by "Darky." Many more not in actual distress were helped home to base, and before the reliability and accuracy of GEE were developed to the point of providing a certain homing service to all aircraft, "Darky" had become established as the main safety service available to aircraft after crossing the coast inwards, despite the admitted

shortcomings of the equipment which was in use, and the problem of mutual interference, which was never satisfactorily overcome.

16. The "Darky" scheme gave birth to all later developments in the local control and landing organisation; for it was the fundamental conception of a common control frequency for a given number of aircraft that inspired the ideas upon which the procedure of Regional Control – (later to become Flying Control) – were based in Bomber Command.

M.F. Beacons

17. Yet another non-radar aid to navigation was the M.F. Beacon system, which early in the War became an established aid to both sides.

18. The British system, as developed by February, 1942, was designed to give any aircraft equipped with an M.F. receiver a method of obtaining bearings or running fixes. Again, as in the case of M.F. D/F, the fixing accuracy fell off rapidly with range due to geographical considerations. Though good bearings could often be obtained up to 400 or 500 miles, nevertheless, at that distance the base-line for any pair of beacons receivable over the interior of Germany gave a very poor cut.

19. In an attempt to prevent the enemy making use of the British beacons, an elaborate coding system was used, which involved changes of callsign and frequency with mast-sites.

20. The Germans also operated a very similar system, in the same frequency band, and were also well aware that their system could be used by bomber aircraft. Since far greater accuracy over Germany could be obtained by the use of the enemy's own beacons, a reporting procedure was developed to keep crews informed as to which of the enemy's beacons could safely be used for navigation at any given time. This involved a constant ground watch in this country for the purpose of breaking the current German beacon code; a later development involved this decode being signalled to bomber aircraft on operations.

21. The whole procedure was necessarily fraught with a certain degree of complication, with the result that crews would never entirely trust the German system, although in fact, this was capable of giving very useful results.

22. The enemy was fully aware of Bomber Command's methods for the use of his beacons and as a result rather over-estimated the actual value which was placed by the Command on the radio beacon method of navigation. In an attempt to "spoil" the British system for returning bombers, he started a systematic interference campaign, very skilfully conducted, the object of which was to make any bearings taken on British beacons, even at quite short ranges, ambiguous and unreliable. Since this constituted a serious danger to our aircraft, a warning procedure was developed, based upon continuous ground monitoring of the British system, by means of which they were informed while in flight as to which of the British beacons were clear of interference at any particular period.

23. The final development was the mustering by both sides of all their available

M.F. transmitters. Our task became then to operate a greater number of transmitters than the enemy had available for his jamming operations. By this time, the M.F. band was crowded from end to end with beacon signals, jammed and unjammed. Such serious interference was caused to the M.F. D/F service and home broadcasting, that M.F. beacons as an aid to navigation became virtually unusable by either side.

24. Bomber Command finally withdrew from the conflict when the widespread fitting of GEE eliminated the need for the beacon system. It was reduced to a few transmitters used for training purposes but continued to serve as an aid to non-operational aircraft not fitted with GEE.

Jay Beams

25. In connection with the introduction of GEE, it was thought that for a time, the enemy might be prevented from discovering our use of this system if he were convinced that for navigational aid Bomber Command was using radio beams. Apart from this purely deceptive employment of radio beams, there was the fact that if "tramlines" of beams could be laid down across the North Sea, they would undoubtedly be a great help to returning aircraft, which could run in on them without having to call for assistance from the ground.

26. Consequently, high-power S.B.A. transmitters, with a sharpened-up aerial system to give a beam as narrow as possible, were set up at various points down the east coast from as far north as Lossiemouth to Manston on the coast of Kent with an additional installation near Lyme Regis to cover the southern approaches. The aerial arrays for these transmitters were mounted on turntables, rotating in azimuth so that within certain limits the radio beam could be aligned on any required bearing. The bearings that were chosen for any particular occasion depended upon the ordered route for the night. In order not to disclose the intended route to the enemy the beams were not switched on until the return flight began.

27. In the aircraft, reception of the beam signal was on the S.B.A. receiver with which all bomber aircraft were fitted. Since several beams were on the air simultaneously, they had to be separated in frequency to prevent mutual interference, and each was identified by a characteristic letter, sounded in morse. The alignment of the beams and the periods of working were given to navigators at the briefing for an operation. On occasion, beams were aligned to cut over the North Sea so as to give a fix; normally, however, the alignments chosen were those which would give the best lead-in to the various Group areas.

28. The Jay beams gave good range – at least 350 miles to an aircraft at 10,000 ft. – and became quite popular as an easy method of homing. All that was required was to select the required frequency on the S.B.A. receiver control box and then keep the aircraft on the starboard edge of the narrow "solid" which was produced by the dots and dashes of the side-lobes. The definition of the edge of the beam was very sharp even at extreme range, and its actual alignment was represented by the bearing of the starboard edge of the beam when heading towards the transmitter.

29. The disadvantage of a long homing on a Jay beam was the fatigue factor – listening continuously to the whine of the beam, which was only varied when the aircraft wandered into the dot or dash sector. Nevertheless, many pilots habitually used the Jay beams for such homings, and navigators could always obtain a position line which, combined with a D/F loop bearing, would give a reasonably accurate fix.

30. Like all the other non-radar aids discussed in the foregoing paragraphs, Jay were no longer of any great practical value once GEE was established, and though two were kept in use until late in 1944 the others were closed down towards the end of 1943.

31. While the advent of the radar aids sounded the death knell of the purely non-radar devices and systems already described so far as their application to operations was concerned, the fact remains that in their time they gave good service and, when later relegated to a stand-by role, they were always available for those who cared to use them.

THE RADAR AIDS

Introduction of GEE

32. The decision to fit GEE to all aircraft of Bomber Command was taken at a conference held by the C.A.S. on 18th August, 1941. Although the matters of policy leading to this decision do not properly come within the scope of this Appendix they will be briefly recapitulated in order to clarify the story.

33. Prior to this decision it had become evident that target location at night by visual means was always extremely difficult and generally impossible. Moreover, navigation by night was uncertain and inaccurate. The proposed expansion of the bomber force to a size which could mount continuous damaging attacks on the enemy was therefore dependent for success upon the development of means to overcome these handicaps.

The Problem

34. The main problem, therefore, was of devising a means of navigation which would enable an aircraft to find its way accurately, deep into enemy territory, despite the enemy defences which were steadily growing in density and improving in execution, and despite the loss of navigational aids on the continent and the presence of decoys and dummies erected for our confusion. The great difficulty of navigating under these conditions was that the navigator was able to fix his correct position only very rarely, thus being deprived of the essential information about wind changes on which accurate track-keeping depended. The normal practice was to compare the plotted position of the bomber with the actual position either by means of observations of

pin-points on the ground, radio fixes or by astro-navigation. Conditions frequently prevented this being done satisfactorily and the necessity to fly at great heights to avoid the enemy defences further hindered any attempts to identify landmarks on the ground.

Operation of GEE

35. A new scientific aid to navigation was urgently required and was provided by GEE, a system which had been devised before the War. The system on which GEE worked was simple. A master station transmitted a pulse signal and simultaneously a synchronised signal was emitted from a "slave" station. The GEE apparatus was able to measure the time difference in the reception of these two signals, and thus determine the difference in its distance from the two stations. This enabled the navigator to place the aircraft somewhere along a line of constant difference in distance between the stations. This line was the hyperbola springing from the two stations, and was shown as a "lattice line" on a specially prepared chart that the navigator carried. Another set of transmissions from the same "master" and a second "slave" station gave a position along one of a second series of hyperbolae, sprung from the master and second slave station. The actual position of the aircraft was the point at which the two curves intersected.

Application of GEE

36. This new aid to navigation could be used in two ways. The navigator could either take a periodical fix to enable him to check and correct his D.R. navigation or, if the course and target suited, it was possible to fly a course along a "lattice line," checking the position at any time from the other lattices as they were crossed.

37. The great advantage of GEE over all previous navigational systems was that a position could be fixed at any time without ground-air communication and irrespective of whether the weather was suitable for the identification of landmarks. A further advantage was that the apparatus itself did not radiate and so could not be plotted or homed upon.

38. The chief disadvantage of GEE which was the cause of the initial reluctance to adopt the system, was its limited range. Accurate fixes could be obtained only within a range of some 350 miles from the home stations. Nevertheless the ability to fix positions with certainty within that range enabled navigators to fly with considerably greater accuracy to targets beyond it.

Progress with GEE

39. At the beginning of 1942 the development trials of GEE were well advanced and by the end of February, the beginning of the period covered by this appendix, the

first ten squadrons to be equipped were standing by for operations. Small scale experimental sorties over enemy territory using GEE had been made in June 1941 but it was subsequently decreed by the C.A.S. that, in order to obtain the best value from GEE before its secrets should be discovered by the enemy, no further operational use should be made of it until it was possible to employ it in some strength.

40. GEE was first used operationally on the night 8/9th March 1942, when Essen was the target. This involved operating at the extreme limit of the GEE range by crews with no previous experience of its operational use at such range and for reasons related in Part II, paras. 16, 17 and 18, the results fell short of expectations. Nevertheless, it became apparent that a new standard in navigation had been set.

41. Another very important benefit obtained from the use of GEE was that it made the theoretically desirable policy of concentration of aircraft in time and space practicable.[1] Concentration of the bomber stream was adopted along routes as a tactical countermeasure to the Radar aids to enemy defences, and over the target to saturate both the defences and the A.R.P. services, thus reducing casualties and increasing the effective damage caused by raids. This policy called for very accurate track and time-keeping and presented the further problem of landing large numbers of bombers in a comparatively short time. Without GEE this could not have been attempted with any hope of success.

42. The value of GEE in assisting the return was immediately noticeable. The accuracy of GEE fixes increased as the aircraft approached nearer home and many of the hazards that had hitherto faced bombers returning to their bases, after long journeys and with tired crews, disappeared. Through this, the development of improved landing procedure, and training (*see* Appendices K. and G.) the losses from crashes, which had previously made up a formidable part of the total wastage, became progressively reduced.

Enemy Interference with GEE

43. It was not expected that GEE would operate for long without interference by the enemy. Early estimates were that the first sets might have a useful operational life of up to five months from the date on which they were introduced. This was one reason why the introduction of GEE was delayed until it could be used in effective numbers.

44. In August, 1942, jamming of GEE began. The effect of the jamming was not to destroy the accuracy of working but to limit the range at which fixes could be obtained. Still, as the range limitation was one of the most important disadvantages under which GEE suffered, this further reduction was a serious matter. Measures to overcome the jamming therefore were quickly initiated, and a modification was made available to Bomber Command by 19th August; by 21st August, 520 sets had been modified with the anti-jamming feature.

45. It was fully realised that further steps would have to be taken to ensure the uninterrupted use of GEE in the future. These were taken along lines which were later followed closely by the Germans in attempting to avoid our own R.C.M.

jamming, namely by increasing and varying the frequency ranges over which GEE operated. Additional stations were erected, in this country, and the frequency bands were widened. For instance, a new frequency was introduced for the first attacks in the Battle of Hamburg, on 24/25th July, 1943, the night when WINDOW was also used for the first time.

46. By June, 1944, there were five GEE "chains" – or sets of master and slave stations – operating in this country, three of which were used constantly by Bomber Command. As advances were made into liberated Europe, so fresh chains were set up on the continent until, at the end of the War, there were a further six giving coverage over nearly the whole of unconquered Germany.

Results with GEE

47. The value of GEE to Bomber Command can be summarised briefly as follows: (*See also* Appendix B, paragraphs 7-19.)

(*a*) In target location. At the time of its introduction GEE was the most effective navigational aid that Bomber Command possessed, but it was subject to limitations of range and an increase in possible errors with the range. It was used first to aid the flare-dropping force of the early Pathfinders, who could illuminate a strip round the target to enable later bombers to identify their aiming point visually. For blind bombing, GEE was not sufficiently accurate. In regard to its value for minelaying, much depended on the nature of the area to be marked; whether or not it was a restricted area in a channel; and, also on the angle of cut of the lattice lines in the target area, and their relation to the margin of error permissible in laying the mines.

(*b*) As a navigational aid. GEE was invaluable in aiding concentration, assisting in wind determination and to ensure accurate tracking for the avoidance of defended areas.

(*c*) In homing and landing bombers. The problem of landing large numbers of bombers in a short time in indifferent weather conditions was greatly reduced by the aid of GEE. It helped to bring about a very considerable reduction in crashes.

48. The intricate navigational problem which was submitted to the Command in connection with the convoy simulation part of the D-Day R.C.M. operations was solved by No. 617 Squadron with the aid of GEE.

OBOE

49. Although the merits of GEE as a navigational aid were well appreciated, so also

were its shortcomings as an aid to blind bombing; and the need for a device to increase the accuracy of bomb-aiming or target marking under all weather conditions remained paramount. During the early part of 1942 development work was proceeding on three such devices – OBOE, H2S. and G.H. The first of these to be used operationally was OBOE.

Development of OBOE

50. OBOE had been developed as a result of the experiences of No. 109 Squadron earlier in the War in their campaign against German navigational beams used for the guidance of enemy night bombers. Briefly, it had been discovered that it was a practical possibility for an aircraft to fly along a certain beam and for its position on that beam to be calculated by measuring its distance from a second point. This principle had been elaborated into the "Trinity" operation which had been employed in an attempt to hit the battleships "Scharnhorst" and "Gneisenau" in their refuge in Brest in late 1941.

51. There were certain disadvantages in this early method; the necessity for the bomber to fly a steady course along the beam, rendered it more vulnerable to ground defences; the susceptibility of the beams to jamming; and the poor serviceability of the aircraft equipment. In short, the system was not sufficiently reliable.

OBOE, Mark I

52. OBOE, Mark I, which operated on a wavelength of 1½ metres, relied on the measurement of the distance of the aircraft from two ground stations by means of re-radiation of radar signals, thus producing a fix – or, in this case, continuous tracking. As it is possible to measure distance much more accurately than bearing, this was a considerable improvement over older systems, all of which depended to some extent on fixes obtained from bearings. Further, the calculations of distances were made at the ground stations and not in the aircraft. The system can be briefly described as follows: one ground station controls the aircraft at a fixed distance equal to the distance from the ground station to the target. Thus, the aircraft is made to approach the target along an arc of the circle which passes through the target, the centre of which is the ground station. Any deviation from this course is signalled to the aircraft by a system of dots or dashes to indicate errors to port or starboard of its course. Meanwhile, the second station makes periodical measurements of the distance of the aircraft, and from these is able to calculate the position and speed of the aircraft and thus determine the precise moment at which the bombs should be released. This in turn is signalled to the aircraft. The possible errors are thus limited to those arising from minor deviations from course, which are liable to be serious only if the aircraft is forced, either by inaccurate track-keeping or by the enemy defences, to weave, and is thus on an incorrect heading when the time comes to release the bombs.

Disadvantages of OBOE

53. The main disadvantages of the system were the need to follow what was for all practical purposes a straight course for some distance in to the target, and the fact that the aircraft itself had to re-radiate a signal and was thus liable to be plotted or homed on. Moreover, the range of the system was governed by the operational height attainable by the aircraft. For this reason alone its high ceiling made the Mosquito the most suitable aircraft to operate OBOE; but its speed was also a determinant, since the combination of height and speed, by rendering it largely immune from both night fighters and ground defences, overcame the disadvantage of increased vulnerability of the operating aircraft. The limitation of function to one aircraft at a time was overcome by employing the OBOE aircraft as a target marker and not, save only in very small scale raids, as a bomber.

54. No. 109 Squadron, which had been concerned throughout with the development of OBOE, was incorporated in the P.F.F. and the first OBOE raid was delivered in December, 1942.[2]

Application of OBOE

55. Although, by reason of being a ground-controlled system, OBOE suffered from a limitation in range, targets in the Ruhr were within the coverage. In that area, a theoretical margin of error of the order of 300 yards was attainable. This enabled the "Battle of the Ruhr" to be successfully fought in March and April, 1943, when, for the first time in the War, the Krupps works at Essen, which had hitherto safely escaped all attempts at visual identification, were hit and severely damaged.

56. It was fully expected that the 1½-metre OBOE would be found to be susceptible to jamming, and consequently development of a 9-cm. OBOE (Mark II) was pressed forward. This was introduced in October, 1943, and although there was a slight loss of range in comparison with Mark I, this was offset by the freedom from interference.

57. Until the end of the war, OBOE-assisted marking for large-scale raids was used wherever possible on German targets within its range. It was especially valuable in early 1944 when more and more targets in France and Belgium came to be attacked in preparation for the forthcoming invasion, and on D-Day itself OBOE marking in aid of attacks on coastal batteries in Normandy resulted in nine of the ten batteries being unable to offer serious resistance to the invading forces.

58. Continental OBOE stations were set up in liberated areas, making deeper penetrations by OBOE raids possible. Ultimately, targets to a depth of 250 miles within Germany itself were brought within range and development of the OBOE technique using repeater aircraft – in effect airborne re-control stations – was in hand, which was expected to bring all German targets within range.

PRECISION BOMBING WITH G.H.

Development of G.H.

59. At the time of the resumed development of GEE, another navigational system known as "H" was devised and in the autumn of 1940 consideration was given to both these methods, to determine which would be the more suitable. It was appreciated that "H" had, theoretically, far greater accuracy than GEE, but on the other hand the system could only be used by a limited number of aircraft simultaneously, approximately 100. Whilst such limitation was not serious at this time, because of the small operating strength of the bomber force, it was foreseen that when Bomber Command expanded, with improved timing and concentration, the "H" system by reason of its limitations, might be unsuitable for the size of the forces that could be operated. It was decided, therefore, to continue with the development and introduction of GEE as the first standard radar navigational aid in bomber aircraft rather than "H."

60. Although the introduction of GEE, early in 1942, immediately produced an increase in the accuracy of navigation throughout the Command, with a consequent improvement in bombing results, it was still apparent that the ability to bomb with a high degree of accuracy in blind conditions remained an unsatisfied requirement. Therefore, development of blind marking devices to supplement GEE was instituted with high priority. In the first instance, this work was directed towards producing equipments capable of meeting the precision-marking requirements of the Pathfinder Force. These were divided into two categories applicable to (*a*) targets within the range of radar systems dependent upon ground control; and (*b*) targets which were at such ranges that the airborne devices would have to be entirely independent of any ground control. These requirements were met by OBOE and H.2S. respectively.

The Problem

61. In the meantime, however, it became clear that a requirement might soon exist for a highly accurate device which could by direct bombing, ensure the effective destruction of small targets unsuitable for H.2S. It had been appreciated that sky-marking (*see* Appendix B, paragraph 21) was not entirely satisfactory for very small targets and, further, it was realised that attacks on such targets might at a later date be required by day or by night when 10/10ths cloud conditions prevailed in the target area. In short, a device with an accuracy closely approaching that of the Pathfinder Force's short range marking equipment (OBOE) but capable of handling a large number of aircraft simultaneously, was becoming a probable need of the future.

62. G.H. has been described as "OBOE in reverse." The initial transmissions are made by the aircraft and are re-radiated by two ground beacons. These beacons are mobile and are capable of being set up in new positions very rapidly. The advantages

over OBOE are that the aircraft itself can determine its own position at any time and not only can the system thus be used for continuous navigation, but also a number of aircraft can use it simultaneously. The principal disadvantage, in comparison with OBOE, is that the accuracy depends much more on the technical efficiency of the aircrew which generally is not as great as that of the ground station. This is offset, however, by the fact that each aircraft can bomb on its own G.H. fixes, whereas OBOE can be used for the control of individual aircraft only; additional errors, particularly where sky-marking has to be used, are inevitable.

Application of G.H.

63. The first introduction of G.H. into four Lancaster Squadrons, fitted with 8,000 lb. bomb doors, was unfortunately later than expected, due to the supply of equipment being behind schedule. It was completed late in October, 1943, which coincided with the start of the long winter nights when Bomber Command's directive called for attacks on targets deep in German territory. The G.H. system being dependent on ground stations, was limited to a range which did not include those targets that were of first importance in the winter of 1943-44. Further, it was this winter that heralded the "Battle of Berlin." Hence, there was no immediate use for this system and to prevent the unnecessary loss to the enemy of equipment, which would give him the chance of preparing appropriate countermeasures before the new technique could be used in force, instructions were issued to the effect that the G.H. sets were not to be carried on operations unless aircraft were detailed specifically for G.H. bombing.

64. On the night of 3/4th November, 1943, however, a portion of this G.H. Lancaster force was detailed to attack a factory near Dusseldorf, during a major attack on the town area. Subsequent photographic reconnaissance revealed that approximately 90 per cent. of the bombs, which were dropped completely blind, had fallen with an accuracy which exceeded expectations. It was this promising start in the operational life of G.H. that led to the later decision to strip the aircraft of all G.H. equipment in order to conserve it until such time as the trend of operations demanded its assistance. Except for the prominent part G.H. played in a small but important mining role, prior to and just after the invasion of Normandy, and also for its major contribution to the success of the feint invasion of the Pas de Calais in connection with D-Day operations, this device did not play its leading role until a later date.

G.H. after D-Day

65. Since G.H. had become a limited requirement for Tactical Air Forces and the 8th United States Air Force, arrangements had been made for the siting of G.H. beacons on the continent. The extreme mobility of these ground stations meant that they could take immediate advantage of every forward move of the Allied Armies, and therefore, the system was likely to be of considerable value to Air Forces engaged in the tactical

support of the Army. In addition to the tactical value of this system, the strategical bombing application was quickly appreciated in relation to the excellent and accurate cover that could probably be provided over Germany and, in particular, over the Ruhr, in the likely event of stations being sited in France, Belgium and Holland at a later date. An urgent requirement was therefore put forward in June, 1944, for greatly extended provisioning of G.H., to allow for its introduction into all aircraft of one Lancaster Group of Bomber Command. No. 3 Group was selected for this re-equipment.

No. 3 Group's G.H. Operations

66. By October, 1944, mobile ground stations were sited and ready for operations on the continent and a fair proportion of the aircraft of No. 3 Group had been equipped with G.H. In order to make full use of the potentialities of the equipment since the percentage of aircraft fitted was still insufficient for direct bombing by each individually equipped aircraft, G.H. crews had been trained to undertake marking duties for night attacks and also to act as formation leaders for daylight attacks.

67. Daylight formation bombing on leaders was initially the chief method of employment of the G.H. force, and between October and November of 1944, this force started its long list of successful attacks against a variety of targets, including Synthetic oil and Benzol Plants, marshalling yards and certain tactical targets. In the first three weeks alone, No. 3 Group undertook nine daylight and two night attacks against targets in the Ruhr and Rhineland, and of the daylight attacks, seven were carried out in conditions of 10/10ths cloud. Amongst these first successes are names which rank high on the list of the outstanding achievements of Bomber Command; Bonn, Leverkusen, Bottrop, Solingen and in particular, Coblenz, where 120 aircraft completely devastated approximately 250 acres of the built-up area attacked, or just over 2 acres per aircraft.

68. In December, 1944, the G.H. force, in one of the worst months of the year, which had hampered other bomber operations, operated on 15 days of the month. Three of these attacks were in support of the Army, during Rundstedt's break through in the Ardennes; the first of these being undertaken in response to an urgent call for tactical support when other air forces in the theatre were unable to operate because of the prevailing weather conditions. On this occasion, an attack was made against Trier, when the target area was entirely fog covered. The success of the attack in the conditions under which it was made earned the personal congratulations and gratitude of the Supreme Commander.

69. From 14th October, 1944, to the last G.H. attack of the War, on 24th April, 1945, No. 3 Group operated on 94 occasions, an average of 15 operations a month, virtually one every other day. In March, 1945, no fewer than 25 attacks were made, of which 18 were in conditions of 10/10ths cloud and only four where the cloud was less than 5/10ths. This scale of effort was not maintained in April only because the rapid advance of the Allied armies necessitated moving the ground stations forward.

70. There can be no doubt that in the closing stages of the war, Bomber Command had, in G.H., an extremely valuable and efficient aid to precision bombing. (*See also* Appendix B, paras. 71-77.)

RADAR BOMBING – H.2.S

71. H.2.S. was in the development stage as a bombing aid in 1942, but the difficulties of design were very great. There were also doubts about the wisdom of using the equipment over enemy territory for fear of jeopardising the security of certain special components necessary for the 9-cm. technique, which was proving to be extremely valuable both in the operation of OBOE and also in the anti-submarine war, then at its height. (*See* Part II, paras. 21 and 22.)

Development of H.2.S.

72. The H.2.S. apparatus was conceived as a result of the discovery that various ground features returned distinctive echoes to a radar transmission from an aircraft. This principle had been successfully exploited in A.S.V., where the problem was to distinguish between a vessel on the sea, which would reflect back radar pulses quite strongly, and the sea itself, which produced only a diffused return due to "scatter" effect. It was subsequently found that towns, or large buildings such as aircraft hangars, gave responses which stood out above the ordinary ground returns and thus enabled an aircraft to reproduce a "picture" of the ground over which it was flying. In this respect, H.2.S. can be stated to be a pure radar device because both the transmission and the reception took place in the same apparatus.

73. The benefits to be obtained from the successful use of such a piece of equipment, provided that it could be developed to the required pitch of efficiency, were obvious. The scepticism in regard to its possibilities and the opposition to its adoption were based on the belief that the apparatus could not be brought to the stage of perfection where it would produce accurate results. However, at that time, early 1942, the need for some technical aid to improve the very unsatisfactory standard of bomb-aiming was so great that almost any expedient was considered worthy of a trial. In July, 1942, the Secretary of State for Air decided to lift the security ban on the use of H.2.S. and proceed with the equipment of two squadrons; but permission to employ them over enemy territory was not given until January, 1943.

74. The later trials had been carried out with the equipment installed in Halifaxes, but the fitting in Bomber Command was made, in the first instance, in Stirlings. By the end of 1942, twelve aircraft in each of No. 7 (Stirling) and No. 35 (Halifax) Squadrons of the P.F.F. had been fitted and the first H.2.S-assisted operation was carried out on 30th January, 1943, when the target was Hamburg. Thirteen H.2.S. aircraft took part in this attack in conditions of 6-8/10ths cloud. A number of technical failures were suffered, but six navigators said they had identified the target by H.2.S.

Its screen appearance was in accordance with expectations, and they claimed to have attacked it successfully. The degree of effectiveness could not, however, be accurately assessed owing to the lack of photographic confirmation. All crews reported that landmarks on the route were easily recognised and the Stirlings, in particular, whose GEE was found to be incorrectly tuned, navigated throughout by H.2.S. The experiences of this operation suggested that a new and valuable aid to both navigation and blind bombing had indeed been acquired.

75. Subsequent operations showed that the value of H.2.S. as a navigational aid was principally to assist in the identification and location of landmarks along the route. Routes were frequently chosen so that there was a suitable H.2.S. subject – in the sense of a feature which would give a good return which could be positively identified – at or near turning points or at the commencement of the run up to the target. The picture returned from the ground immediately below the aircraft was normally too confused for it to be used for the final selection of an aiming point, and bomb or target-indicator release was usually calculated by D.R. from a nearby pinpoint. (*See also* Appendix "B," paras. 30-51.)

The Crew Factor

76. As with all other radar devices, the degree of success likely to be obtained from the use of H.2.S. depended very largely on the skill and experience of each individual operator. Although it was apparently a simple matter to navigate when the towns on or near the route were clearly indicated, in practice it was impossible to tell, without actual experience, just how the response from any particular landmark was going to appear in the cathode ray tube of the H.2.S. equipment. Indeed, the shape or appearance of any one town would vary considerably with the angle or direction from which it was viewed, nor did it necessarily bear any relation to the shape that would be presented to the naked eye. Thus it might normally be difficult to associate the picture as seen on the H.2.S. screen with that given on a map.

77. Coastal features and water were more easily recognized. The difference in presentation between land and sea returns was more uniform and the shapes of lakes, rivers and estuaries were well reproduced. This increased the value of H.2.S. when it was used in coastal areas and some of the most successful attacks made with its assistance were on targets where there were easily identifiable water features. The "Battle of Hamburg" provided a notable example of the results to be obtained from the use of H.2.S.

The Fitting Programme

78. H.2.S. was designed to enable an aircraft to put its bombs on to a built-up area and the original intention was that every bomber should be fitted and thus be able to navigate and bomb independently. However, the first operational employment of

H.2.S. took place only six months after the decision to produce it had been taken, and the equipment came through so slowly that, for the first four months of its life, the average number of H.2.S. aircraft included in any raid was no more than 12. These were used solely as markers and were instructed to drop their target indicators or sky-markers, according to the conditions under which the attack was to be carried out, blindly on H.2.S. alone. This was calculated to eliminate the errors of visual identification and produce a pattern round the selected aiming point which could be more precisely marked by "backers-up." Later, the H.2.S. aircraft dropped flares which enabled the "backers-up" to identify the aiming point visually. (For a fuller discussion of H.2.S. bombing technique *see* Appendix "B," paras. 30-51.)

Early Results

79. This was a period of elimination of teething troubles and the careful investigation of the causes of errors in the accuracy of the equipment. It was found that H.2.S. was satisfactory as a navigational aid, but fell below expectations as a target marker. Attacks on large towns were not as successful as those on smaller ones owing to the difficulties of identifying an aiming point in a town as distinct from the town itself. Although theoretically it should have been possible for backers-up to identify and select the mean aiming point in the marked area, in practice the small number of H.2.S. aircraft available and other limiting factors made this a matter of some difficulty. It was found that the most successful raids were those where the H.2.S. flares enabled the target to be identified visually.

80. The first blind bombing raid of any appreciable size that was made with all H.2.S. aircraft, in accordance with the original intention, was on 17/18th November, 1943, when 83 aircraft of the P.F.F. attacked Mannheim/Ludwigshaven. It was estimated that 60 per cent. of the bombs fell in the target area and 50 per cent. within 1½ miles of the aiming point.

81. By this time the fitting programme had been considerably extended and six P.F.F. and 12 main force squadrons had been equipped. It became evident, however, that the value of H.2.S. was chiefly as an aid to navigation; it was the sole radar aid that was capable of use beyond GEE coverage and it was estimated that track-keeping could be maintained with an accuracy of 4 miles. Since the apparatus was self-contained in the aircraft itself, this was independent of the actual position of the bomber and was governed chiefly by the proximity of suitable H.2.S. landmarks. Bombing accuracy was found to be greater with visual identification following an H.2.S. check than with the blind use of H.2.S. alone.

82. One of the limitations imposed upon the employment of H.2.S. was the comparatively low serviceability rate of the equipment, particularly during the early stages (*see* Appendix "B," para. 35). This was attributable to four main causes:—

(i) The complexity and size of the equipment, which for these reasons made it more subject to failures.

(ii) The high priority of operational requirements which necessitated the introduction of the equipment into aircraft before adequate service trials had been completed.

(iii) Consequent upon this operational urgency, there was insufficient time for aircrews to gain the necessary experience required to handle such complex equipment under operational conditions.

(iv) Also, consequent upon the speed of introduction of the equipment into operational use, there was a serious lack of trained maintenance personnel. This was overcome only by the establishment of the Bomber Command Radar School; but there remained the unavoidable time lag before the mechanics trained in this school reached squadrons.

H.2.S., Mark III

83. In November, 1943, H.2.S., Mark III, was introduced. This worked in the 3-cm. band and was claimed to give much better definition of small towns, lakes and rivers and other features which provided suitable responses. Fitting of this mark, which was in small supply only, began in the P.F.F., and it was used in all major raids during December for marking targets. H.2.S., Mark II, was fitted in Mosquitos of the P.F.F. in February, 1944, and was used by them until the end of the war. Large problems were involved in overcoming the difficulties of fitting such equipment in Mosquitos.

84. Fitting of H.2.S. in the main force increased rapidly in late 1943 and early 1944. In January, 1944, approximately 30 per cent. of all sorties by Bomber Command were made by H.2.S. equipped aircraft, and by July this figure had risen to over 40 per cent. After this date, the changed conditions arising from the invasion and the advance across Western Europe, which made possible the provision of ground navigational aids on the continent, reduced the relative importance of H.2.S. as a navigational aid.

H.2.S. Silence

85. The campaign for signals silence which gained ground in September, 1944, had its effects on H.2.S. As a transmitter, H.2.S. was liable to be homed on and also to be plotted from the ground. It was known that the enemy had an apparatus called Naxos for this purpose, but so long as H.2.S. was the only reliable radar aid to navigation that Bomber Command possessed which could be used beyond GEE range, the risk was accepted, because there was no positive evidence that the homing risk had involved H.2.S. aircraft in additional danger.

86. Nevertheless, when in September, 1944, the enemy lost a great part of his early warning system, his plotting of H.2.S. transmissions proved an invaluable means of obtaining long-range early warning of the approaching bomber stream. Representations that H.2.S. should not be used at least within the areas where the

bombers could not be plotted by other means were rejected at first, because it was found that there were technical difficulties connected with the switching on of H.2.S. at operational heights and in calibrating the equipment in time to obtain any practical value from it. The first of these was quickly overcome. The second was solved by the fact that the point at which H.2.S. ceased to be a potential warning of approach always lay within GEE coverage, so that it was possible for the navigator to run his H.2.S. plot from a GEE fix. Consequently, the point from which H.2.S. was permitted in the main force was laid down for each raid in accordance with the route, the extent of GEE cover along that route and the enemy's early warning range.

LORAN

Introduction of Loran

87. All aircraft of this Command were to have been fitted with Loran, but trials showed the Loran system to possess considerable limitations in comparison with GEE – its value as a homing aid was low, and the working frequency was very susceptible to interference. Consequently, in November, 1944, the decision was amended, and the retrospective fitting of Loran was restricted to all aircraft of Nos. 5 and 8 Groups, together with the heavy aircraft of No. 100 Group.

Operation of Loran

88. In the Loran system, the working frequency of which (2 mc/s) is much lower than the GEE frequencies (above 20 mc/s), ground stations transmit pulse signals which are received by the aircraft equipment. The pulse signals from the master and slave ground stations are synchronised, and the time difference in reception of the pulse signals are measured by the aircraft apparatus. By this means the position of the aircraft can be determined in a similar manner to that employed with the GEE system. With the Loran system, only running fixes can be obtained as against simultaneous fixes with the GEE system.

89. By virtue of the frequency, Loran gives much greater range and wider coverage than the GEE system; at night the range of reception can be increased to approximately 1,400 miles by making use of "sky wave" signals reflected from the ionosphere. In Europe, it was found that the normal ground-wave signals were of very limited operational use, but that the "skywave" (S.S.) signals from the European S.S. Loran chain could be received over Western and Central Europe between 6°E. and 14°E. S.S. Loran was first used on operations on 11/12th November, 1944, against Hamburg, and results suggested that its accuracy as a navigational aid was approximately equal to that of GEE.

90. Loran was, however, very easy to jam; enemy interference commenced in February, 1945, and was reasonably effective. The area of jamming was widespread over Northern and Western Germany. The jamming effects were overcome to some extent by modifications to the aircraft equipment, and were never as severe in heavy aircraft as in Mosquitos. Nevertheless, the practical value of the system was seriously affected.

91. The value of S.S. Loran to Bomber Command can be summarised as follows:—

(*a*) In blind bombing: Its theoretical accuracy of approximately 2 miles was insufficient, except for area bombing of very large targets. Analysis of bombing results by means of S.S. Loran, supported by night photographs, showed that the errors achieved under operational conditions were far greater than the theoretical error, and were quite unacceptable for a blind bombing device.

(*b*) As a navigational aid: As a long range night navigational aid it was of value, but owing to the frequency employed it was very susceptible to enemy jamming and interference, which rendered it difficult to use except by experienced crews.

(*c*) In homing and landing bombers: The coverage and accuracy obtained over this country was so poor that Loran was of little use for homing or landing aircraft.

92. On the other hand, Bomber Command experience with Loran was not extensive, and it is not improbable that many of its disadvantages might have been overcome. This would certainly have been tried had the war lasted longer, as its potential value as a long-range navigational aid was of the highest importance.

RESEARCH AND DEVELOPMENT

93. The successful application of radar aids to blind bombing and navigation has not been accomplished without considerable development work and research into their operational employment. This was done mainly by the Signals Staff and the Operational Research Section at Command Headquarters, assisted by the Bombing Development Unit. Prior to the introduction of a new aid, it has been the normal practice to carry out extensive trials to determine the best way in which it could be used to improve the efficiency of the bomber force.

94. These trials have involved the exploration of various possible operational techniques in order to determine the best; the assessment of the accuracy of the one

selected; and the development of a suitable training scheme. The training results obtained by the squadrons have then been carefully analysed in order to ensure that the desired standard was obtained. Finally, the performance of the device under operational conditions has been continually studied with a view to seeking ways to improve its tactical employment, to determine the causes of inaccuracies and how these can be reduced, and to demonstrate where improvements in design are required.

95. All the radar aids referred to in this appendix have been continually subjected to this close and intensive study, which has undoubtedly been an important factor in ensuring that the best use has been made of them and has led to improvements in the accuracy obtained and enabled requirements for modifications to new marks of equipment to be laid down.

Notes:-
1 (See Part II, para. 13, and Appendix D, paras. 9, 10 and 11.)
2 See Appendix B, para. 63.

APPENDIX B

THE DEVELOPMENT OF BOMBING TECHNIQUES

Night Bombing Techniques before the Introduction of Radar Aids

1. In these days of radar aids to navigation and highly developed marking techniques it is difficult to form an adequate conception of the difficulties which confronted our early attempts at raiding enemy targets at night, when the only aids available to the navigator-cum-bomb-aimer were compass, loop, map and sextant, combined with such visual identification of ground features as he was able to make by starlight, moonlight, or in the light of an occasional unshaded flare. The problem in these days was largely one of navigating to the target area, but, having performed this task, the navigator was then faced with the still more difficult, though vital task of getting a visual fix, either of the target itself or of some clearly identifiable landmark within a few miles of the aiming point from which a D.R. run could be made. This process of searching for the target commonly occupied from 20 to 40 minutes and was sometimes continued for more than an hour, and, bearing in mind these conditions, it is easy to understand the lack of success which attended many of our night raids during this period. Indeed, it is a great tribute to the courage and determination of the crews that the results achieved were as good as they were, for even these dark ages of the Command's history were occasionally lightened by outstanding successes. Thus on the attack on Stettin by a force of about 30 aircraft on the night of 30th September, 1941, 80 per cent. of the operational photographs were subsequently plotted within a radius of 2 miles from the aiming point. Such results as these however were exceptional, and more extensive analyses of photographic evidence indicated that the general level of success prior to March, 1942, was very much lower than this. Analysis of 147 raids between the beginning of August, 1941, and the 7/8th March, 1942, showed that on the average 68 per cent. of the sorties despatched claimed to have attacked the primary target, of which it was estimated that 30 per cent. had actually dropped their bombs within 3 miles of the aiming point. This corresponds to about 20 per cent. of the sorties despatched. Even this figure is likely to be an overestimate since it is based entirely on the plotted positions of night photographs

and, as comparatively few cameras were available in these days there was a strong tendency for the squadrons to allocate these to their best crews, so that the photographic sample is liable to be biassed. In addition the night cameras were at that time operated manually so that it was not always certain that the area photographed did in fact show the approximate position of bomb-fall. The latter difficulty was solved by the introduction of an automatic camera control, but accurate assessment of the success of operations did not become possible until all aircraft in the Command were equipped with night cameras. This was not achieved until the Autumn of 1942.

3. The chief factor influencing the success of night raiding at this period was visibility, particularly the amount of cloud and haze and the phase of the moon, since in general it was only under clear moonlight conditions that there was a reasonable chance of getting visual fixes. In conditions of moderate haze or cloud the success was about half that in clear weather conditions and in poor weather very few aircraft ever got within five miles of the target. Visibility remained an important factor in bombing operations even after the introduction of radar aids, and although as the war progressed our bombing tended to become less and less dependent on weather conditions, the menace of bad weather on night operations was never completely overcome.

4. In addition to weather the type of target also had a marked influence on the success of our raids in 1941 and early 1942, considerably better results being achieved against coastal targets than against inland towns. Most difficult of all was the Ruhr, where the ever-prevalent industrial haze and the absence of distinctive landmarks led to the failure of almost all our attacks on this area at that time.

5. An extensive analysis carried out by the Operational Research Section and covering the period from October to December, 1941, showed clearly the need for navigators to use more than one feature to recognise the target, whenever this was possible. Thus, of the crews who claimed to have identified only a single ground feature it was estimated that 33 per cent. successfully located the target, compared with 47 per cent. for those who used two features, and 82 per cent. for those who used more than two. In addition there was found to be a big difference in the reliability of various ground features for visual fixing, lakes and rivers which were the most popular with crews proving the least reliable and coastal features, especially docks, the most trustworthy. This investigation again emphasised the immense difficulties of visual identification at night and brought to light the need for a general improvement in standards of map-reading and for practical experience of its use in flights at operational heights during the period of training. Unfortunately at this period it was not possible to carry out the latter proposal as, owing to G.A.F. activity over this country training flights had to be carried out below a ceiling of 7,000 ft., and it was not until late in 1942 that this restriction was removed.

6. It was realised from the first that the introduction of radio aids would not provide the complete answer to all the problems of navigation and target finding, particularly on the longer range targets, and it was therefore decided at the end of 1941 to proceed with a more extensive survey of the whole question of the visual identification of

ground features at night, with particular reference to the use of night glasses, the most suitable type of flare for illumination, possible modifications in aircraft design which might assist visual identification, and the desirability of special training in night vision and the lines along which training should be conducted. This line of action was later proved by the course of events to have been completely justified, for although the task of visual identification subsequently became relegated to specialised crews, it remained until the end of the war the basis of most of the marking techniques used on targets beyond the range of OBOE or G.H. The scope of these investigations and the progress made up to the end of 1942 is fully reviewed in O.R.S., Report No. 64.

The use of Gee as a Target Identification and Bombing Device

7. As a result of the experience in night bombing gained in 1941 it was abundantly clear that, except under clear moonlight conditions, little success could be expected with the methods then in use: although the use of binoculars and flares of improved types and increased training in night vision might, in the course of time, bring about some improvement, no marked advance could be made until the introduction of radar aids which would make successful night raiding less dependent on the visual identification of ground features. The first such device to be used in Bomber Command was T.R. 1335, later known as GEE, which was developed by T.R.E. and was first used operationally on the Essen raid of 8/9th March, 1942.

8. The GEE system, which is based on the measurement in the aircraft of the phase difference between signals transmitted from three different ground stations, was primarily designed as an accurate navigational aid, whose object was to enable large numbers of aircraft to navigate with certainty to targets in Germany, particularly the Ruhr area where most of the heavy industries were situated, and which presented the greatest difficulty from the point of view of visual identification.

9. Before GEE actually came into operational use discussions took place on the best method of using the device. Of the two main types of operation, viz:—

(*a*) Operations led by GEE aircraft;

(*b*) Operations carried out by GEE aircraft only (Blind bombing)

it was considered that type (*b*) in view of the limited number of GEE aircraft which would be available at first, should be used principally in poor weather conditions when it was unlikely that unequipped aircraft would be able to find the target, even if assisted by GEE aircraft. With regard to operations of type (*a*), three possible methods by which the GEE aircraft might lead the force on to the target were considered, viz:—

(*a*) The GEE aircraft to act as fire raisers. Non-equipped aircraft to bomb the fires. (Sampson technique).

(*b*) GEE aircraft to drop flares to illuminate the target for the non-equipped aircraft, who would bomb visually. (Shaker technique).

(c) Formation attacks led by GEE aircraft.

Owing to the tactical difficulties associated with formation flying at night method (c) was not thought to be practicable. Methods (a) and (b) however were subsequently adopted and formed the basis of the night bombing techniques used during 1942. In order to develop a method of collaboration between the flare-dropping aircraft equipped with GEE and the follower aircraft not so equipped, it was arranged for an experiment to be carried out over the Isle of Man, and O.R.S. was entrusted with the task of drawing up detailed plans for such an experiment to be known by the code word "CRACKERS."

10. The Isle of Man was chosen as the "target" for such an experiment because the accuracy of the GEE chain in that area was approximately the same as its accuracy over the Ruhr. According to the plan originally put forward, a force of 12 GEE aircraft were to arrive over the target at zero hour and, after dropping one flare each, were to orbit and make a second run, attempting to identify the target visually and, at the same time, dropping another flare. Altogether six such runs were to be made thereby keeping the target illuminated for a period of about 20 minutes. The object of these flares was twofold, namely, to provide a beacon to guide the non-equipped aircraft to the target, and to illuminate the target sufficiently to make visual bombing possible. The plan of the exercise was later extended to include the use of flare sticks for illumination to test the value of coloured flares and searcher flares.

11. The first exercise, which took place on the night of the 13th February, 1942, was rather spoilt by a ground station fault which resulted in the flares being laid in two groups several miles apart, and by an exceptionally high wind. It did however serve to establish that the illumination provided by single flares dropped on GEE at the rate of 12 every three minutes, although satisfactory as a beacon, was quite inadequate to permit visual identification of the target. Sticks of flares consisting of six bundles of three flares spaced at distances of one mile however, gave much better results and it was accordingly decided to organise a further exercise, "CRACKERS II," to test more fully this method of flare dropping and to decide on the best number of flares and stick spacing to use.

12. The railway station at Brynkir (North Wales) was the "target" for this second exercise which took place on the night of the 19/20th February under clear but somewhat hazy conditions. The exercise was fully successful and on the basis of the results, 3 Group were able to submit a detailed plan of attack. GEE aircraft would illuminate the target for a period of 15 minutes, attacking in successive waves and each carrying 12 bundles of three flares to be dropped at 10 second intervals. In the light of these flares an incendiary force would attack between Zero and Zero + 15 minutes, dropping their loads visually and starting conflagrations which would be bombed by the main striking force.

13. The above plan, which formed the basis of the "Shaker" technique, was first put into operation on the night of the 8/9th March, 1942. The target was Essen, and high hopes were held that a really heavy blow could at least be struck at this most important but very difficult target. A force of 211 aircraft was despatched, including 74 equipped with GEE, and weather over the target was good apart from the usual

ground haze. The raid lasted for 2 hours and 10 minutes, but the results were most disappointing, and post raid cover revealed no damage to the main target area. An investigation of the causes of failure showed that although the flare laying was on the whole satisfactory, many of the incendiary force did not arrive until the flares were out and scattered their loads over a wide area mostly short of the target, thereby attracting other aircraft of the main striking force.

14. Within the course of the next three months 11 further major operations using GEE were carried out against Essen, including one of 956 aircraft. On most of these raids the original "Shaker" technique, with minor variations in timing, was employed. The "Sampson" technique was also used on the 10/11th March when the GEE aircraft dropped 250 lb. incendiaries to act as a beacon to the main force. Daylight reconnaissance showed that no major damage had been inflicted, either on Krupp's works or on the town of Essen, and it became clear that the difficulties in attacking this target could not be overcome by the method devised.

15. Although the operational accuracy of GEE in the Ruhr and Rhineland was found to be more than three times worse than that achieved by expert crews over this country, the 50 per cent. zone being about 5 miles in radius, it was clear that this alone was not responsible for the failure to hit Essen, particularly as operations against other cities such as Cologne had achieved considerably greater success. It was concluded that the relative lack of success on Essen was due in large measure to the prevalence of thick industrial haze and the peculiar situation of that target; in particular, the lack of any clearly recognisable landmarks in the near vicinity, and the proximity of many other towns of similar size, made Essen an especially difficult target for any method of attack such as "Shaker" which depended on visual identification, and on at least two occasions the incendiary force attacked the wrong target (viz. Hamborn on 9/10th March and Schwelm on 12/13th April). Moreover, the main striking force who were not equipped with GEE were instructed to bomb on the fires started by the previous aircraft, and this made them very vulnerable to the enemy decoy system. Thus on two of the raids during March, 1942, a large proportion of the force were diverted by the decoy fire sites at Rheinburg, some 20 miles W.N.W. of Essen. The Sampson technique, used on the 10/11th March, was no more successful, as apart from the poor timing of the GEE aircraft the 250 lb. incendiaries which they dropped proved inadequate to prove a beacon for the main striking force. There was clearly a need for a far more distinctive type of marker bomb if operations of this type were to be carried out successfully.

16. Another important cause of failure of the GEE attacks on the Ruhr was the inadequacy of the illumination provided by the Mark III 4·5 in. reconnaissance flare, which was the general type then in use. Whilst satisfactory under perfectly clear conditions, the hazy conditions met with in the Ruhr valley resulted in a very considerable scatter of light from the flare, which reduced the contrast of ground detail, rendering it less easily visible at low levels of illumination. This effect was accentuated by the use of flares in sticks, and many crews reported that the flares were a hindrance rather than a help in seeing the ground.

17. As early as June, 1941, the General Electric Company, working in conjunction

with R.A.E., had collected experimental data on the polar distribution of light from flares and had made measurements of the veiling brightness due to haze scatter, the greater part of which, they suggested, could be eliminated by a cylindrical screen which would cut off the light from the flare over a range of about 40 degrees above and below the horizon. At the instigation of Lord Cherwell this suggestion was taken up and G.E.C., working in close contact with O.R.S. (B.C.), undertook further work which led eventually to the development of the 7 in. hooded flare, which came into general use in 1944 and proved highly satisfactory. G.E.C. later carried out work on the optimum height and spacing for flares of various types in different weather conditions, the results of which found practical application in the Pathfinder Force.

18. Although the effect of GEE on the success of our bombing operations was by no means as spectacular as had been hoped for, an appreciable improvement was discernable under certain conditions of attack. Thus, for raids on Ruhr targets in moderate weather conditions, the percentage of successful photographs showing the target area increased from 11 per cent. over the period June, 1941-February, 1942, to 18 per cent. during the months of March and April, 1942, when GEE was used. In addition there was a marked rise in the percentage of sorties reporting attack on the primary target (68 per cent. to 75 per cent.), an effect which was largely attributable to the introduction of GEE. In general, the effect of GEE was most marked against the shorter range targets under conditions which were unfavourable for visual identification, *i.e.,* cloudy, hazy or moonless nights. Under optimum conditions of bright moonlight and good visibility there was no evidence that GEE had had any significant effect on the success of operations.

19. Enemy interference with the GEE system, the possibility of which had always been borne in mind, was first suspected on the night of 6/7th August, 1942, and was confirmed beyond reasonable doubt on the raid on Osnabruck on the 9/10th August. The effect of the jamming was to reduce the effective range from Daventry from about 400 miles to 250-300 miles, with the result that practically all German targets were beyond the effective coverage. Consequently GEE could no longer be used as an aid to target identification and bombing on German targets, though it was still of considerable use as a navigational aid over the greater part of the route. Although from time to time the situation was temporarily relieved by the introduction of various counter-measures, it became clear that new techniques in night bombing would have to be devised. It was at this stage in the war that the Pathfinder Force was formed.

Early Pathfinding Methods

20. The basis of most of the target-marking techniques used by the Pathfinder Force during the latter part of 1942 was visual marking of the aiming point in the light of flares, or, as at Frankfurt on the 24/25th October, in moonlight. Flares were dropped on GEE on targets where this was still available, but usually other methods, such as timed runs from visually identified landmarks, had to be used by the first aircraft to reach the target. A marked advance in the technique of illumination was made on the

night of the 16/17th September, 1942, when the flare-dropping aircraft were for the first time differentiated into "Finders," whose function was to drop long sticks of flares right across the target area, and "Illuminators," who were detailed to search for the aiming point itself and to illuminate it with much shorter sticks of flares for the benefit of the Visual Markers.

21. Special marker bombs were at this time still under development by M.A.P. and as an interim measure groundmarking was carried out with 30 lb. and 250 lb. incendiaries released in salvo. Experience showed that these were by no means entirely satisfactory, as in the early stages of the raid, when the target was brightly illuminated, they were often difficult to see, and later they became lost amongst the mass of incendiaries and fires. 4,000 lb. gel incendiaries ("Pink Pansies") were also tried on a few raids but with no greater success, for although very distinctive whilst bursting, they failed to leave any permanent mark. Experiments were also carried out on the use of coloured flares for marking either the release point or the extremities of the target. These were an improvement but had the great disadvantage compared to groundmarkers that they were subject to wind drift. Moreover they would be relatively easy for the enemy to copy.

22. The Operational Research Section carried out a detailed investigation into the first 21 attacks led by the Pathfinder Force, which brought to light several points of considerable operational importance. Thus, the complete or partial failure of at least five raids was established as being mainly due to an inadequate number of finder aircraft, of which it was estimated that at least 8 to 12 were required on normal targets, particularly when weather conditions were not expected to be ideal. On the raids already carried out the number of finders had usually been considerably less than this. In addition, it was found that the flare fuze then in use was not functioning satisfactorily, and numerous cases were reported of flares opening too high, thus failing to illuminate the ground properly and at the same time causing considerable dazzle. This difficulty was not finally overcome until the introduction of the barometric fuze.

23. In general it was found that up to the 20th/21st November, 1942, the Pathfinder Force had been successful in carrying out their planned marking technique on one-third of the attacks on Germany which they had led, and partially successful in almost another third. Although these results do not, on the surface, appear very creditable, it must be remembered that target marking methods were at that time still in their infancy and that the Pathfinding Force itself was not as yet composed of experts. Moreover, they were not during this period provided with any special navigational or target finding equipment, and on German targets enemy interference had deprived them even of the use of GEE. Against Italian targets, which were only weakly defended, and where the conditions of visibility were invariably better than over German targets, results were much better and the target marking technique only failed to go according to plan on two out of nine occasions.

24. Although no immediate improvement in the overall results of our night bombing was discernible as a result of the introduction of Pathfinder methods, a very definite advance in technique had in fact been made. In order to appreciate this it is

necessary to make a comparison of the situation with that existing during 1941 and the early part of 1942.

25. Before the introduction of Pathfinding methods it was normally the responsibility of each individual crew to identify and bomb the detailed aiming point. The errors due to mis-identification and, to a lesser extent, bad bomb-aiming, were often very large, but on the whole were distributed in a random manner about the aiming point. Special cases giving rise to a typical bomb pattern did, of course, occur from time to time, as when any considerable proportion of the force was diverted by decoy activity, but usually the result of this type of bombing was a widely dispersed pattern of bombs whose M.P.I. (mean point of impact) was centred on, or close to, the detailed aiming point. The chief problem which faced the Command at the beginning of 1942 was how to reduce the random error of bombing and thus achieve higher densities of the bombing within the target area. The use of Pathfinder methods did in fact largely solve this problem, and was followed by an immediate and very marked improvement in the concentration of bombing, which is well reflected in the increase in the percentage of night photographs plotted within 3 miles of the M.P.I. of the bomb pattern (Table I).

26. At the same time, however, another unforeseen source of error was introduced. As the Main Force were no longer detailed to aim at the aiming point itself, but at marker bombs dropped by the P.F.F., the M.P.I. of the resulting bomb-pattern no longer coincided with the aiming point, but was determined largely by the position of the marker bombs. Any errors in placing the markers were therefore likely to be perpetuated throughout the attack, causing the M.P.I. of the bombing to be displaced from the aiming point. Thus in the seven months prior to the introduction of the Pathfinder Force only about 14 per cent. of all the raids carried out showed any marked displacement of the M.P.I. of bombing from the aiming point, whereas during the following seven months something like 67 per cent. showed an appreciable displacement. The distance between the M.P.I. of bombing and the detailed aiming point is referred to as the overall *Systematic Error,* and the problem of how to reduce this source of error to its lowest limit became one of the most important problems facing the Command at this time. Although much was done during 1943, 1944 and 1945 to reduce the magnitude of this error by improving the accuracy of the marking methods used, the problem of the elimination of the Systematic Error was never completely resolved.

TABLE I.
Effect of Pathfinder Force on Success of Operations

	Period March, 1942, to August, 1942. (Pre-P.F.F.)	Period August, 1942, to March, 1943. (P.F.F.)
Overall percentage of photos plotted within 3 miles of centre of concentration.	35 per cent.	50 per cent.
Overall percentage of photos plotted within 3 miles of aiming point.	32 per cent.	37 per cent.

27. As the figures in the above table show, the considerable increase in concentration achieved as a result of the introduction of the Pathfinder Force was largely offset by the introduction of systematic errors, so that the overall increase in the efficiency of the force was, at this time, comparatively small. As in the case of GEE, the advantages conferred by the P.F.F. were greatest for raids in moderate weather conditions.

28. Up to the end of 1942 the Pathfinder Force had no radar aids to assist them in their task of finding the target and no special marker bombs to enable them to mark the target satisfactorily. Early in 1943 both these handicaps were removed and a new era in the technique of night bombing was initiated. OBOE, Mark I, was first brought into operation for the raid on Dusseldorf on the night of the 31st December, 1942, T.I. groundmarkers on Berlin on the 16/17th January, 1943, and H.2.S. on Hamburg on the 30th/31st January. The introduction of these devices presented the Command with a new series of tactical problems, the nature and solution of which are described in subsequent paragraphs dealing with the operational use of H.2.S. and OBOE.

29. In spite of the early difficulties and failures which seem inevitably to be associated with the introduction of new devices, successful and reliable marking techniques were gradually evolved. The marking techniques used during the early part of 1943 were fluid, often varying widely from night to night, but gradually as experience was gained, undesirable features were eliminated, improvements were introduced, and the methods became more and more stabilised. Sometimes the reasons for the failure or the partial failure of an operation were fairly obvious, but more often a very detailed intensive study of the development of the raid was necessary before any definite conclusion could be reached as to the primary cause of the failure, or suggestions made as to how the same mistake could be avoided in future. In this respect the detailed raid analyses carried out by the Operational Research Section at Headquarters proved of great value and enabled many useful tactical lessons to be learnt which might have otherwise passed unnoticed.

Marking Techniques Employing H.2.S.

30. H.2.S. was essentially different from the other radio-aids used by the Command, in that the whole of the equipment was airborne, so that there were no limitations

imposed by range from the ground stations as in the case of GEE, G.H and OBOE. The equipment was originally designed to enable an aircraft to drop its bombs on a built-up area, but in view of the limited number of sets which would be available at first it was decided, as an interim measure, to employ it as a Pathfinding device. The first production sets of Mark I equipment, which were ready by November, 1942, were therefore allocated to Halifax aircraft of 35 Squadron, and the following month Stirlings of 7 Squadron were also fitted. By January, 1943, two flights of Pathfinder aircraft had been equipped, and on the 30th/31st January the first H.2.S. operation took place, the target being Hamburg. By the end of September, 1943, all the heavy aircraft of the Pathfinder Force had been equipped and H.2.S. was beginning to be introduced into the Main Force. By the end of February, 1944, 23 squadrons of the Main Force were equipped or converting and approximately one-third of all the sorties sent out were H.2.S. aircraft. As soon as a substantial proportion of the Main Force had been fitted the question was raised as to whether H.2.S. should continue to be used as a Pathfinding device, or whether it should be used for blind bombing by the Main Force. In view of the success which was being achieved with the Newhaven technique at this time, however, the weight of argument favoured the view that its primary use should be for target marking, and that the Main Force should use it chiefly as a navigational aid. With the exception of two experimental blind bombing attacks on Ludwigshafen 17/18th November, 1943, and Brunswick 12/13th August, 1944, this was the policy followed by the Command.

31. The average number of H.2.S. equipped aircraft despatched per raid during the first two or three months of its operational career was about 14. Of these about four were detailed to attack at zero hour and the remainder were spread throughout the attack at intervals of 1, 2 or 3 minutes, depending on the length of the raid. In view of the uncertainty of weather conditions over the target, particularly in the amount of haze which would be encountered, each H.2.S. aircraft normally carried reconnaissance flares, T.I. markers, and two-coloured skymarkers (Wanganui flares), and it was left to the discretion of the Captain whether he should illuminate, groundmark or skymark the target. When it was obvious that the weather would not be good enough for visual identification, as on the first H.2.S. operations, illuminating flares were not carried, and the target was to be groundmarked with T.I.s or skymarked with Wanganui flares according to the amount of cloud encountered.

32. It was realised that H.2.S. was not a precise marking device and that a certain scatter of markers was to be expected, though there was at this time little information on how great this scatter was likely to be. In order to overcome this difficulty an averaging technique was used, the Main Force being instructed to aim their bombs not at a particular T.I. marker, but at the M.P.I. of all the markers seen. In order to assist them to identify the M.P.I. and to ensure continuity of marking throughout the raid, a new type of marker aircraft was introduced. These were the Backers-up, later referred to as Visual Centerers, whose function was to estimate the mean point of impact of the T.I.s dropped by the Blind H.2.S. markers and to mark this point with T.I.s of a second colour. Five Backers-up were used on the first H.2.S. operation, but this number was found to be quite inadequate to maintain the necessary concentration

of markers throughout the duration of the raid, and was increased on subsequent attacks to about 20. When conditions were good enough for illumination of the target, the Backers-up were detailed to function as Visual Markers, aiming their markers visually at the aiming point which they would identify in the light of the flares.

33. The above plan of attack, which appeared theoretically sound and which, on paper at least, seemed to be practically foolproof, in practice proved unsatisfactory in many respects. During the first two months after its introduction 15 major operations using H.2.S. were carried out of which only three caused any appreciable damage to the target. In spite of these disappointing results, however, valuable experience was gained and many tactical lessons were learnt which enabled further and more successful techniques to be devised.

34. One of the chief reasons for the lack of success of these early H.2.S. raids was found to be the very small number of primary T.I.s (*i.e.* those dropped blindly on H.2.S.) which were burning at any one time during the raid. Detailed time analyses showed that it was unusual for the early Backers-up on arrival at the target, to find more than one or two groups of primary T.I.s alight on the ground, instead of the five or six expected. It was consequently impossible for them to centre the raid accurately, and it was often possible for any single primary T.I., irrespective of its accuracy, to attract the Backers-up. Many raids were for this reason a long way off centre.

35. Apart from the comparatively few H.2.S. equipped aircraft available at this time and the low serviceability of H.2.S. during the first few months (only 55 per cent. of sorties had serviceable equipment on arrival in the target area), several other factors contributed to this sparseness of primary marking. It was found, for example, that of the crews who arrived in the target area with serviceable equipment rather less than half actually used it for blind marking: the remainder released their T.I.s visually, often simply backing up markers already down and thus defeating the averaging technique. The few aircraft which did use their H.2.S. for blind marking often made large errors, and on the longer range targets the situation was further aggravated by poor timing. The latter was partly due to the fact that the Stirlings, which at this time comprised about half the marker force, had a very small speed range.

36. Steps were immediately taken to put right these defects in the method which had been brought to light by the early H.2.S. raids. In order to get a good concentration of primary markers down early in the raid, the number of Blind Markers was increased and, instead of being spread throughout the raid, these were detailed to attack simultaneously at the beginning of the attack. It was strongly impressed on all Blind Marker crews that they must on no account attempt to bomb visually, neither were they to release their markers if their H.2.S. was not working satisfactorily. In view of the fact that the raids on which visual marking in the light of flares laid by H.2.S. aircraft had been used had proved much more successful than those on which purely blind marking had been employed, it was decided to use this method whenever possible. In addition, instructions were issued that H.2.S. target maps should be revised from the latest air cover in order to guard against mistakes such as occurred at Wilhelmshafen on the 19/20th February, 1943, when the H.2.S. operators mistook

a new suburban area to the north of the town, not marked on the H.2.S. target map, for the target itself.

37. The final outcome of all these changes was the development in April, 1943, of the Newhaven marking technique which proved so successful that, with various minor modifications, it remained the standard H.2.S. marking technique until the end of the war.

38. In the original form of the Newhaven method the attack was opened by a wave of about 15 H.2.S. aircraft, all detailed to attack at the same time, who would blind-mark the target with T.I.s and at the same time illuminate it with sticks of flares. These Blind Marker Illuminators, as they were called, were followed after an interval of about 2 minutes by a smaller number of Visual Markers, whose function was to identify the aiming point visually in the light of the flares and to mark it accurately with T.I.s of a distinctive colour. If they were unable to do this on account of weather or for any other reason, they were to refrain from dropping their markers. Finally came the Backers-up, attacking at the rate of one or two per minute throughout the duration of the raid, who would either back up the Visual Markers' T.I.s or, if these had not been dropped, would centre the attack on the M.P.I. of the Blind Markers' T.I.s. The later Backers-up, arriving after the primary markers had died out, would continue to back up the T.I.s of the previous Backers-up.

39. On the early Newhaven attacks the Visual Markers and the Backers-up both used the same colour T.I. markers, but this proved unsatisfactory, since the Backers-up had no means of telling whether they were in fact backing up the primary marking or were simply aiming at the T.I.s dropped by previous Backers-up. Also the Main Force had no method of distinguishing the more accurate primary T.I.s from the less accurate secondary T.I.s. A three-colour Newhaven, with the Blind Markers using yellow, the Visual Markers red, and the Backers-up green, was therefore devised. This was first tried out on an experimental attack on Munster on the 11/12th June, 1943, and proved very satisfactory. It remained in use throughout 1943, but was eventually abandoned early in 1944 when the hooded flare came into general use, since it was found that these flares when viewed through haze were liable to be mistaken for yellow T.I.s. This was thought to have led to some confusion on the raid on Frankfurt on 20th/21st December, 1943, and the use of yellow T.I.s for marking was subsequently abandoned. The Newhaven colour scheme was then changed to green for blind marking, red, or large salvoes of red and green for visual marking, and green for backing up. This modified colour scheme was first tried out on the Stettin raid on the 5/6th January, 1944, and proved quite satisfactory.

40. A further improvement in the Newhaven technique was introduced at the beginning of August, 1944, when the Blind Marker Illuminator Force was split into two sections. The Blind Illuminators, who opened the attack, carried flares only. They were followed by the Visual Markers who would attempt to identify and mark the aiming point in the light of the flares. Thirdly came the Blind Markers, carrying T.I.s which they would release only in the event of the Visual Markers having failed to mark. The purpose of this modification was to prevent the Visual Markers being dazzled by the light from the Blind Markers' T.I.s as had sometimes occurred with

the older version of the technique.

41. The great virtue of the Newhaven method was that, should the weather over the target prove unsuitable for visual marking of the aiming point, the attack would automatically develop as a Blind Parramatta (Groundmarking) raid. In 1943 over half our Newhaven attacks did, in fact, develop in this manner, but during 1944 and 1945, as the efficiency of the illumination and the skill of the visual markers increased, an ever-increasing proportion of attacks developed as visual Newhavens. This was one of the many factors contributing to the steady improvement in the efficiency of the Command as the war progressed.

42. The difficulty of achieving satisfactory primary marking of the target using H.2.S. was by no means the only problem encountered in developing a satisfactory night-bombing technique. It was found, for example, that even on raids where the primary marking was satisfactorily accomplished, the attack as a whole was very rarely centred on the primary mark, and that as the raid progressed the bombing tended to drift further and further back along the line of approach. In an attack of 25 minutes' duration it was common for the M.P.I. of the bombing to shift by as much as 3 or 4 miles, and much research was carried out to try and discover the reason for this drift. The fundamental cause was undershooting, both by Backers-up and Main Force aircraft, who in many cases were taking aim, not at the M.P.I. of the marker pattern, but at the first group of T.I.s to be encountered on the run in to the target. The undershooting was thus cumulative and the bombing became more and more displaced as the raid progressed. This undershooting was due partly to the relative visibility of the markers, those that were lying short of the target in open country being much more easily seen than the more distant ones on the target itself, which were often partially hidden by buildings or obscured by smoke. An additional factor was the not unnatural desire to bomb as soon as possible.

43. An attempt was made to reduce the drift of the attack by detailing the Backers-up to aim at the far side of the concentration of all the markers seen, and to counteract its effects by choosing the aiming point well towards the far side of the area it was desired to hit. As interim measures both these procedures had a certain amount of success, but drift remained as one of the undesirable features of our raids throughout 1943. The final solution of the problem did not come until 1944, when, by concentrating the aircraft in time and by reducing the size of the forces employed, it became possible for the first time to limit the attack to the duration of the primary marking, thus to a large extent eliminating the necessity for secondary marking and its attendant evils.

H.2.S. Skymarking Attacks

44. Whenever the meteorological forecast showed a chance of considerable cloud over the target, provision had to be made for a skymarking attack as an alternative to visual Newhaven or Blind Parramatta. In attacks of this type the H.2.S. aircraft released skymarking flares, usually red with green stars or green with red stars, and

the main force were instructed to aim their bombs at the estimated centre of all the flares seen. Owing to the drift of the flares in the wind the usual backing-up technique could not be employed on skymarking raids and it was therefore necessary to plan for the H.2.S. aircraft to attack at intervals throughout the duration of the raid if an adequate concentration of flares was to be maintained. These timing requirements were therefore incompatible with those for a Newhaven or Parramatta attack, where it was necessary to plan for the maximum concentration of H.2.S. aircraft at the beginning of the raid, and great difficulty was experienced in devising a satisfactory alternative ground-skymarking method for use on occasions when the weather forecast was doubtful.

45. An attempt to solve this problem was made by dividing the blind marking force into two sections, known respectively as primary and secondary blind markers. The primary blind markers would attack at the beginning of the raid dropping both T.I.s and Wanganui flares, whilst the secondary blind markers would attack at intervals throughout the raid and would drop Wanganui flares only if the cloud conditions were such that T.I.s burning on the ground could not be seen. Unfortunately, the available numbers of blind marker crews severely limited the size of the secondary blind marker force, so that it was rarely possible to obtain an adequate concentration of Wanganui flares, except at the beginning of the raid. For this reason the bombing on most of our skymarking attacks was scattered over a relatively wide area, though on at least one occasion (Leipzig 3rd/4th December, 1943) a good concentration was achieved and enormous damage inflicted on the target.

Attacks on Berlin

46. Berlin, Bomber Command's most important target, proved itself one of the most difficult to attack successfully. The chief source of difficulty was the very large size of the built-up area, which meant that it was not possible to employ the usual H.2.S. "homing" technique, and the absence of sufficiently distinctive H.2.S. landmarks in the near vicinity of the target from which timed runs could be made. All the H.2.S. attacks on this target were blind ground or skymarking attacks, and although the possibility of employing the Newhaven technique was discussed on several occasions, this method was never used against Berlin as it was considered very doubtful if it would be possible to achieve a sufficient concentration of flares to illuminate an aiming point adequately, or, even supposing sufficient illumination was achieved, whether the visual markers would be able to identify their aiming point in such a large built-up area.

47. The first raid on Berlin using H.2.S. was on the 1st/2nd March, 1943, when the direct homing technique was used. Owing to the difficulty referred to above the blind markers dropped their T.I.s on the S.W. suburbs of the city, and although extensive damage was caused in this area, the whole raid was about six miles off centre. On the next attack (29/30th March) a timed run was made from the Muggel See, which was to be illuminated with flares and identified visually. This technique

proved much more satisfactory and most of the early blind markers dropped their T.I.s within three miles of the aiming point. Unfortunately, owing to bad weather on route the main force failed to arrive at the target in time to take advantage of this marking, and by the time they did arrive markers had also been dropped on the SE. suburbs of the city. On the next two large scale attacks an attempt was made to obtain an H.2.S. range and bearing fix on a hooked projection of characteristic shape on the northern edge of the built-up area, but difficulty was found in recognising this on the P.P.I. display. A subsidiary cause of failure on the second of these attacks was an incorrect wind forecast, which upset the timing of the attack and brought the main force into the target area on the wrong track. On the 3rd/4th September, the Muggel See was again used as the starting point for a timed run, whilst other blind marker squadrons attempted to get an H2S fix on Brandenburg. This attack was considerably more successful than the previous two, and although the centre of the city again escaped damage, a large area in the suburbs was destroyed.

48. The main "Battle of Berlin" started in November, 1943, and continued until February, 1944. During this time 15 major attacks were delivered, enormous damage being inflicted on the German capital. Most of these raids were skymarking attacks carried out over 10/10ths cloud, and in the complete absence of night photographic evidence it is not possible to make any definite statement on the success of individual raids. Whilst it is almost certain that some of them went completely astray, it is equally certain, from the extent of the damage revealed by daylight cover, that some of them found their mark. Much of the credit for this must go to the new Mark III (3 cm.) H.2.S., which was first used by the Pathfinder Force in the Battle of Berlin, and to the Ground Position Indicator (G.P.I.). The latter instrument made it possible to carry out accurate timed runs in heavily defended areas.

H.2.S. Mosquito Raids

49. In addition to its use in heavy aircraft H.2.S. Mark II, and later Mark III, was fitted into Mosquito aircraft of 139 Squadron, and throughout 1944 and the early months of 1945 these aircraft were used to lead Bomber Command's light striking force of Mosquito's.

50. These raids, at first planned primarily as nuisance raids or as feint attacks to divert enemy fighters from the main target for the night, were gradually increased in size and eventually played a not insignificant part in our bombing offensive. The tactics used on these operations were very simple, the most usual being blind H.2.S. groundmarking by four to seven Mosquitos dropping either red or green T.I.s, the M.P.I. of which was then bombed by the main force. In cloudy weather T.I. floater or Wanganui flares were used in place of the usual groundmarkers.

51. In spite of the limitations of H.2.S. in the Mosquito the accuracy of marking achieved was very satisfactory, the average radial error of two miles being the same as that achieved with Mark II H.2.S. from heavy aircraft. The accuracy of the main force bombing on the markers corresponded to an average radial error of 1·2 miles

from which it was estimated that for targets other than Berlin about 35 per cent. of the bombs dropped in clear weather raids had fallen on the built-up area of the target (excluding suburban areas). The estimated figure for Mosquito attacks on Berlin, based on a very small amount of data, was 70 per cent.

Night Bombing Techniques Developed by 5 Group

52. During 1942 and 1943 aircraft of 5 Group normally formed part of the main force on the major night operations carried out by the Command, but were in addition entrusted with the carrying out of special attacks such as those on the Schneider works at Le Creusot (17th October, 1942) and the Zeppelin sheds at Friederichshafen (20th/21st June, 1943), which called for a high degree of precision and intensive training. On these special attacks both the bombing and the marking of the target were carried out by 5 Group and the success achieved was so great that, during 1944, 5 Group was allowed to a large extent to operate as an independent unit. As a result they developed their own marking and bombing techniques which were different from those used by the Pathfinders and the rest of the main force. In particular they were responsible for the methods known as offset marking, line bombing, and sector bombing which are briefly described in the following paragraphs. They also originated the master bomber technique, first tried on the Friederichshafen raid, and which was later used by the Pathfinder Force.

Offset Marking

53. In order to overcome the problem of the obscuration of the markers by smoke, which frequently occurred in the later stages of raids, 5 Group experimented in 1943 with a method of indirect bombing making use of a timed run from some well-defined landmark outside the target area, which would be visually identified by all crews. This was first tried out on the 20th/21st June, 1943, on the Friederichshafen raid, but with only limited success. It was again tried at Peenemunde on the 17/18th August, 1943, when aircraft of 5 Group, instead of bombing the markers laid by the Pathfinder Force, bombed on a time and distance run from Rugen Island. On this occasion they obtained reasonably good results, but at Munich on the 2nd/3rd October, 1943, their plan to employ a time and distance run from the northern tip of the Wurm See was frustrated by cloud over the lake. One of the disadvantages of the method was, of course, the difficulty of identifying visually the starting point for the run, and this was overcome by allocating this task to special crews who marked the starting point with T.I.s. This technique was developed to a high pitch of efficiency during the summer of 1944 when 5 Group, in common with the rest of the Command, was engaged in attacks on tactical targets in Northern France and the Low Countries. The earlier 5 Group attacks in this series were carried out using direct marking of the aiming point, but offset marking was introduced on the 11/12th May and in

conjunction with the low level visual marking technique also developed by 5 Group led to an immediate improvement in results, the extent of which is illustrated in the following table:—

TABLE II.

Bombing Accuracy Against Lightly Defended Targets
During the Summer of 1944

Type of Raid.	Overall Systematic Error.	Random Error.
5 Group controlled Visual marking (direct marking of aiming point).	205 yards	370 yards
5 Group controlled Visual marking (offset marking, using low-level technique).	110 yards	265 yards
Controlled OBOE Groundmarking.	230 yards	420 yards

54. In the technique as originally used against tactical targets a single marker was laid by a special crew upwind of the target at a distance of about 400 yards from the aiming point. Its distance and bearing from the aiming point was then estimated by the Master Bomber. Several other aircraft equipped with the A.P.I. would then find winds in the target area and pass them by R.T. to the Master Bomber who would take an average, add a vector to allow for the offset of the marker, and then broadcast the resulting false wind to the Main Force. The Main Force would then set this false wind on their bombsights and take aim at the offset marker in the usual way.

55. The advantages of this technique over ordinary direct bombing were very considerable. Not only did the marker remain clearly visible throughout the attack and was unlikely to be blown out or obscured by the bombing, but by the use of different false wind settings more than one aiming point could be bombed with only a single marking operation. This was in fact done on many of the marshalling yard attacks where, owing to the elongated shape of the target, two, or sometimes three separate aiming points were necessary. The success of the technique is reflected in the very high relative bomb densities obtained by 5 Group in their attacks on tactical targets (Table III).

TABLE III.

*Density of Bombing Achieved on Night Attacks on Tactical Targets
in Occupied Territory*

Technique.	Number of Raids.	Relative Density as Hits per Acre at the A.P. per 1,000 Bombs Dropped.
		Per cent
OBOE Groundmarking	40	2·17
Controlled OEBE Groundmarking	18	1·79
8 Group Visual marking	11	1·41
5 Group Visual (direct marking)	12	2·50
5 Group Visual (offset marking)	14	5·43
1 Group Visual Groundmarking	4	1·62
Total	99	2·50

56. Although the results achieved were highly satisfactory, the method was not without its disadvantages. On several occasions the main force were kept waiting in the target area for 10 or more minutes while the marking was being carried out, and as a result heavy casualties were sometimes sustained. A modified form of the offset marking technique was therefore developed for use against highly defended targets in Germany, which was put into operation in the autumn of 1944.

5 Group Newhaven

57. This was a modified form of the Newhaven technique employing offset marking which was developed by 5 Group for use against German area targets. As in the standard Newhaven method the target was first of all illuminated and blind-marked by a force of H.2.S aircraft. In the light of the flares a force of from five to nine low-level Visual Markers would then mark a clearly identifiable "marking point" 1,000 to 2,000 yards away from the detailed aiming point. Red 1,000 lb. T.I.s fuzed for low bursting were normally used for marking, and any T.I.s which fell wide of the mark would be cancelled by the Master Bomber who would drop a yellow T.I. on top of them. The Main Force were detailed to approach on a definite track and to release their bombs an appropriate number of seconds after the markers were in their bombsight. By allotting to different sections of the Main Force, different lines of approach and different overshoot delays any number of aiming points could be bombed from a single marking point. Thus at Bremerhaven on the 18/19th September, 1944, where the built-up area was very elongated in shape, five separate aiming points were used. A further development of this procedure resulted in line bombing and sector bombing.

Line Bombing

58. In this type of bombing the aircraft of the Main Force were detailed to aim at an offset marker with an overshoot of so many seconds. Each aircraft or group of aircraft was instructed to attack on a different heading, the headings of the whole force being spread evenly over about 30° to 80° of arc, depending on the size of the area it was desired to hit. The result of this was that the bombs were distributed in a Gaussian manner, not about an aiming point, but about an aiming line, which was itself an arc of radius approximately 100 by T yards (where T is the overshoot delay in seconds), centred on the marking point. This technique was used for the very successful attack on Darmstadt on 11/12th September, 1944, where two aiming lines were used, at Munich 17/18th December (five aiming lines) and Munich 26/27th November (nine aiming lines).

Sector Bombing

59. A still further and final development of this type of bombing was where each aircraft was given, not only a separate heading on which to attack, but also a different overshoot time, with the result that the aiming line was replaced by an aiming area whose shape was that of a sector of an annulus. Examples of this type of attack are Brunswick, 14/15th October, 1945, and Heilbronn, 4/5th December, 1944.

Advantages of Sector Bombing

60. The bombfall pattern resulting from the usual type of attack carried out by Bomber Command was circular or elliptical in shape with the highest density of bombing in the centre (M.P.I.), falling away rapidly towards the edge of the distribution. These bombfall distributions approximated closely to the mathematical form known as the Gaussian or Normal Distribution. From the practical point of view their great disadvantage was that, in order to obtain an adequate density of bombing at the edge of the target it was necessary to put down a density far in excess of that required in the centre of the target, and a large proportion of bombs were inevitably wasted through overhitting. In sector bombing, where each aircraft was in effect given a separate aiming point, a statistically uniform distribution of bombs was achieved and the density of bombing was approximately the same in all parts of the target area. A much more economical use of bombs was therefore achieved, and it became possible to devastate large built-up areas with comparatively small forces of bombers, as was in fact done on many of the raids mentioned in the above paragraphs.

61. One of the requirements for successful line and sector bombing attacks is a high degree of precision in the placing of the T.I.s on the marking point. In 5 Group this was achieved by the use of low-level visual marking by Mosquito aircraft. The markers were released at the bottom of a shallow dive at an altitude of from 500 to 1,000 ft., no bombsight being used, and the accuracy achieved on defended targets

in Germany was of the order of 300 yards. This was considerably better than the average error of 1,038 yards for ordinary high-level marking from Lancasters using the Mark XIV bombsight, against targets of similar type.

Marking Techniques Employing OBOE

62. OBOE trials during 1941 and the early months of 1942 had indicated that the system had very great possibilities as a blind bombing device, for although the range was at this time somewhat limited, the accuracy achieved was very great. As a blind bombing device, however, it suffered from the very serious limitation that a pair of ground stations could only control one aircraft at a time, and that aircraft could only be brought on at the rate of one every 10 minutes. In June, 1942, the Operational Research Section put forward a suggestion that OBOE might more profitably be employed for target marking and submitted a detailed plan showing how such an attack might be carried out. This suggestion was adopted and proposals were immediately submitted to the Air Ministry that two ground stations and six aircraft be equipped with OBOE, Mark 1, on the highest priority, and also that the necessary training of personnel should be started immediately. This was done and by December, 1942, the ground stations were ready and six Mosquito aircraft of 109 Squadron had been equipped.

63. The first operation using OBOE was carried out on the 20/21st December, 1942, the target being Lutterade. This was primarily a calibration raid in which only OBOE aircraft took part. Similar small scale blind bombing attacks by OBOE controlled aircraft were made at intervals during December and January, mostly against steel works in the Ruhr, with the primary object of completing the training of OBOE crews and gaining the necessary operational experience. The accuracy achieved on these raids was of the order of 650 yards, though on a few occasions errors of up to 1½ miles were noted.

64. OBOE was first used as a pathfinding device early in 1943. Owing to the bad weather prevailing at that time it was not possible to use it for groundmarking, as had been originally intended, and an alternative skymarking technique was used. Each OBOE aircraft was to mark the release point with four bundles of three flares red with green stars, and the Main Force were detailed to aim their bombs at the flares whilst flying on a definite predetermined height and heading. The Mosquitos also released red or green flares steady several miles short of the release point, to act as a warning to the Main Force. The first operation of this type took place on the last night of 1942, the target being Düsseldorf, and during the first fortnight of 1943 eight further OBOE skymarking attacks were carried out against Essen and Duisburg. Only on one of these was sufficient night photographic evidence obtained to enable an assessment of the attack to be made, viz., Essen 9/10th January. On this attack the main weight of the bombing fell about two miles S.W. of the aiming point, but nevertheless the success achieved was considerably greater than in the case of any previous attack on this target. It was estimated that 60 per cent. of aircraft bombed

within three miles of the aiming point, the highest percentage previously achieved on this target being 20 per cent. The damage caused by these attacks was limited by the relatively small scale of the raids; the small number of OBOE aircraft available at the time and the short burning time of the flares limited the size of the Main Force to between 30 and 70 aircraft.

65. On OBOE groundmarking attacks the OBOE aircraft drop primary T.I. markers, usually red in colour, on the aiming point at the shortest possible intervals throughout the raid. In order to ensure continuity of marking Backers-up are employed to drop secondary markers, green in colour, aiming them visually at the primary markers. The Main Force are instructed to aim their bombs at the OBOE markers if these are visible, otherwise at the centre of the concentration of secondary T.I.s. The first OBOE groundmarking raid was carried out on the 27/28th January, 1943, against Düsseldorf. This however was only a small scale attack and was marred by bad weather. The first large scale OBOE groundmarking attack was against Essen on the 5/6th March, 1943, when 442 aircraft were despatched. This was a highly successful raid and, for the first time, very severe damage was inflicted on Essen and Krupps works, the devastation amounting in all to approximately 680 acres. It seemed that the key to successful night raiding in the Ruhr, which GEE had failed to provide, had at last been found, and this hope was more than justified by subsequent attacks which, by the end of the year had resulted in the virtual destruction of all the major industrial centres.

66. The OBOE raids during the first half of 1943, although far more successful than any which had preceded them, did not invariably go according to plan. The principal cause of such diversions of effort as did occur was gaps in the OBOE marking. During this period only two OBOE channels were available, which meant that OBOE aircraft could only be brought on at the average rate of one every 5 minutes. Moreover the serviceability of the equipment during the early months was low, only 66 per cent. of the OBOE sorties despatched making successful attacks, and in view of this situation the greatest difficulty was experienced in maintaining the primary marking over the 40 to 60 minutes duration of the raid; in fact, absolutely continuity of marking was never achieved during the first five months of OBOE groundmarking. During the gaps in the marking it was found that OBOE raids exhibited the same tendency as H.2.S. raids to drift away from the target, and on occasions this drift was aggravated by the use of decoy T.I. markers by the enemy. The latter, although not particularly good imitations of our own markers, were often effective in the absence of any genuine T.I.s of the same colour.

67. In July, 1943, a third OBOE channel was introduced and resulted in an immediate improvement in our bombing effort. On the first raid on which the three channels were used (Essen 25/26th July, 1943) the OBOE marking was almost continuous over a period of 50 minutes, and on Remscheid 30/31st July, continuous primary marking was achieved for the first time. Both of these attacks were outstandingly successful.

68. In addition to its use in the Ruhr campaign OBOE was also used during March and April, 1943, for attacks on the French Atlantic ports. For these targets, however,

only one pair of ground stations was available and, as a consequence the OBOE marking was so sparse that it was probably without appreciable effect on the results of the operations, which were in any case extremely successful.

69. It is of interest to compare the overall results achieved against area targets in 1943 by OBOE and H.2.S. respectively. The following statistics are based on an analysis of night photographic evidence for all such raids between April, 1943, and April, 1944:—

TABLE IV.

Estimates of Percentage of those Aircraft reporting Attack which Bombed within 3 miles of the Aiming Point for Attacks on Towns between April, 1943 and April, 1944.

Technique.	Location of Target.	Good Weather.	Moderate Weather.
		Per cent.	*Per cent.*
OBOE Groundmarking	Germany	66	59
H.2.S. Newhaven	Germany	62	-
H.2.S. Newhaven	Italy	84	-
H.2.S. Blind Groundmarking	Germany	51	37

70. It will be seen that for raids in good weather on German targets the results produced by OBOE were only slightly better than those of the H.2.S. Newhaven technique. The great disadvantage of the latter technique, however, was that it could only be carried out in good weather. In moderate weather such attacks normally reverted to H.2.S blind groundmarking, the results of which were far inferior to those produced by OBOE groundmarking. The outstanding success of the series of Newhaven attacks on Italian cities during July and August, 1943, is attributable partly to the weak defences of these targets and partly to the fact that the weather conditions prevailing were almost always exceptionally favourable for visual identification of the target.

Bombing Techniques Employing G.H.

71. The division of the bomber force into a highly specialised Pathfinder section and a less specialised Main Force, whilst it proved satisfactory as an interim measure, can only be regarded as an intermediate stage in the evolution of bombing techniques, the ultimate aim of which was to make every aircraft in the force its own Pathfinder, and to provide it with such equipment as would enable it to find and bomb the detailed

aiming point independently of the other aircraft in the force. The development of GEE and H.2.S. had shown how this might be done, but unfortunately the accuracy of both these devices proved insufficient to enable the ideal to be realised. The introduction of G.H. however, the accuracy of which was known to be far greater than that of GEE or H.2.S. and which, at the same time, was free from the serious limitation in the number of aircraft which could operate from a single pair of ground stations, which is a feature of the OBOE system, at last brought the ultimate goal within range of practicability.

72. The great potentialities of the system were well shown by the results of the first blind bombing using G.H. against the Mannesmannrohrenwerke on the northern outskirts of Düsseldorf on 3rd November, 1943. Although this raid was only on a small scale the accuracy achieved was very satisfactory, the 50 per cent. zone of the bombfall distribution being of the order of 750 yards.

73. During April, 1944, five small scale experimental and calibration raids were carried out against the marshalling yards at Chambly and Vilvorde. In June and July of the same year G.H. was used to a limited extent for mine-laying, and, during July and August, for daylight attacks on flying-bomb launching sites in northern France. The latter attacks were carried out by Stirlings of 3 Group using the new technique of G.H. formation bombing. Two G.H. aircraft (leader and deputy) were detailed to lead a formation of eight non-G.H. aircraft flying in pairs line astern with a separation of 200 yards. Each pair of aircraft were to release their bombs on seeing the bombs leave the pair immediately in front of them. The performance of the G.H. aircraft on these attacks was highly satisfactory, the average error of 275 yards being of the same order as that achieved on training runs in this country. The following aircraft, however, obtained very poor results due to extremely bad formation keeping. This was especially marked on the first two attacks, but later showed some improvement, and was clearly due to lack of practice in formation flying.

74. These early G.H. raids were all in the nature of small scale experimental attacks, designed to discover the potentialities of the equipment, and the best methods of using it operationally. By October, 1944, however, a considerable force of 3 Group Lancasters had been equipped, and the middle of the month saw the start of a series of relatively large scale G.H. attacks directed against synthetic oil plants, towns, marshalling yards and similar targets, in N.W. Germany. The total number of aircraft despatched on these raids was normally of the order of 100 to 200, and the attacks were continued at the average rate of three to four per week until the end of the war. The vast majority of these raids were blind bombing formation attacks carried out in daylight, many of them over 10/10th cloud, but on a few occasions G.H. aircraft were used for ground or sky-marking.

75. On these attacks between one-quarter and one-third of the total force sent out was equipped with G.H. The aircraft were detailed to fly in vics of three or five, or in boxes of four, each vic or box being led by a G.H. aircraft. Surplus non-G.H. aircraft, if any, were detailed to fly in a gaggle behind a normal vic. In addition the G.H. aircraft normally dropped T.I. markers, Wanganui flares or coloured smoke puffs for the benefit of stragglers who lost formation and who had to bomb independently.

The G.H. aircraft would release their bombs blindly, and the other aircraft in the formation would release immediately on seeing the leader's bombs fall.

76. Analysis of the G.H. formation attacks between October and the end of 1944 showed that the average error of the bomb distributions achieved was 1,172 yards, with an overall systematic error of 375 yards. In addition there were 23 per cent. of aircraft which made gross errors of 2,500 yards or over. Further analyses showed that by the beginning of 1945 a considerable improvement had taken place, the average radial error having been reduced to about 900 yards and the gross errors to 8 per cent. These improvements were attributed to better handling of the equipment and from the improvements in formation flying which had resulted from continued practice. Nearly all the G.H. formation attacks against German towns were outstandingly successful; in particular heavy damage was inflicted on Bonn, Solingen, Witten and Wesel. Considerable success was also achieved against synthetic oil plants and benzol plants in the Ruhr, but in view of the fact that such targets call for a bomb density of three to four times that required to devastate a built-up area, a second attack was often found to be necessary.

77. G.H. formation attack was certainly one of the most promising bombing techniques for use in daylight which was developed by the Command. Although the average error was slightly greater than that achieved on OBOE groundmarking attacks, the systematic errors were small and, provided that the cloud tops were not higher than 17,000 ft. this type of attack was virtually independent of weather conditions. There is in fact a certain amount of evidence that attacks carried out through 10/10ths cloud cover were somewhat more successful than those in clear weather conditions, possibly as a result of the much weaker flak opposition.

Bombing Techniques used against Tactical Targets

78. During 1944 Bomber Command was called upon to assist with preparations for the invasion of Europe, and during the spring and summer of that year almost the whole of its bombing effort was diverted from the strategic bombing of German cities for attacks on tactical targets in northern France and Belgium. During March and April many attacks were carried out on French marshalling yards and during subsequent months the programme was extended to include gun batteries, airfields, ammunition dumps, road junctions, military camps and troop concentrations, etc. As these were entirely new types of targets for Bomber Command, no special techniques other than those used for night attacks on German cities were at first available. The earlier attacks in this campaign were all carried out at night using straightforward OBOE groundmarking. Later a Master Bomber and a Deputy Master Bomber were introduced to control the attack, their function being to direct the bombing on to the most accurately placed OBOE marker, and, if necessary, themselves to mark the target visually. A further development of the controlled OBOE technique was Musical Newhaven where the OBOE markers were dropped very early and were intended to serve only as a guide to the flare force who would then illuminate the target for the visual markers as on a standard Newhaven attack. On the earlier Musical Newhaven

raids, backers-up were used, but these were found to be unnecessary in view of the sort duration of the attacks and their use was therefore abandoned. The resulting type of attack was known as visual groundmarking (with OBOE proximity marking) to distinguish it from the earlier Musical Newhaven method. In addition to these techniques, 5 Group developed a special visual marking method employing offset bombing and low-level marking which has already been described (paragraph 54). A few targets were also marked by 1 Group who used controlled visual marking with impact bursting T.I.s backed up with spot fires.

79. During the first three months of the campaign against tactical targets all the bombing was by night. In June, 1944, however, 17 per cent. of the effort was by day and this percentage continued to rise until September when day raids accounted for 70 per cent. of all the sorties despatched. The marking techniques used on these day attacks were, in many cases, the same as those employed at night, except that the illumination of the target with flares was, of course, not required. In addition several special techniques were evolved for use in daylight, including Formation G.H. which has already been discussed (paragraph 73), Formation OBOE and visual bombing either without T.I.s or with T.I.s used for proximity marking only. As can be seen from a comparison of Table V (below) with Table III the success achieved on these daylight operations was of the same order as that achieved at night against similar targets, with the exception of raids carried out using the formation OBOE technique, which resulted in an exceptionally high relative density of bombing at the aiming point.

TABLE V.

Density of Bombing achieved on Day Attacks on Tactical Targets in Occupied Territory

Technique.	Number of Raids.	Relative Density as Hits per Acre at the A.P. per 1,000 Bombs Dropped.
		Per cent.
OBOE Groundmarking	4	2·16
Controlled OBOE G.M.	41	2·80
Visual bombing	15	4·18
Visual bombing with OBOE (proximity markers)	13	3·31
Formation G.H.	4	1·73
Formation OBOE	15	7·44
Total	98	3.57

80. In the earlier formation OBOE attacks, OBOE equipped Mosquitos were used to lead formations of Lancasters, flying in pairs line astern, but great difficulty was

experienced owing to the different speeds and heights of attack of the two types of aircraft. Later, all Mosquito formations were used with much greater success. As can be seen from Table V the method is very efficient per ton of bombs dropped, but at the same time suffers from various limitations which prevented more general use of the method. Thus only comparatively small scale attacks are possible, and the number of abortive or partially abortive raids due to failure of the OBOE leaders was of the order of 25 per cent. In addition, when clear conditions were encountered at the target, these small formations proved very vulnerable to flak.

81. Next to formation OBOE, the highest relative densities of bombing on daylight attacks was achieved on raids where visual bombing without the assistance of T.I.s was used. Here again, however, there were serious limitations in this form of attack which prevented its use on a more widespread scale. Owing to the rapid obscuration of the target by smoke and dust from the bombing, it could only be used with success for very small scale attacks. Moreover, in spite of the very high densities achieved on certain occasions, the method was on the whole an unreliable one. It demanded very careful and detailed briefing of crews to ensure that the right target was attacked and was far more susceptible to unfavourable weather conditions than were groundmarking or formation attacks.

Planning of Operations

82. Prior to the beginning of 1944 there was little detailed information on which to base any estimates of the size of the force which would be required to destroy any particular target. For the campaign against tactical targets, however, the Operational Research Station developed methods of forward planning which enabled them to provide information on the effort required to achieve the level of damage desired by the military authorities. These methods were first applied, with considerable success, to the attacks on the French marshalling yards, and were also made use of in planning the operations against gun batteries, German marshalling yards, synthetic oil plants, U-Boat assembly slips and other targets. Towards the end of 1944 the technique of forward planning was further developed to enable estimates to be given for attacks on large targets such as towns. These estimates proved of great value during the summer of 1944, when, owing to the very large number of targets which had to be put out of action within a strictly limited period of time, it was of the utmost importance that the forces at the disposal of the Command should be employed in the most economical manner possible.

Changes in Bombing Accuracy during the War

83. As already explained the bombfall distributions of the majority of Bomber Command attacks approximate closely to the Gaussian type and can be completely defined in terms of the following three parameters:—

(i) The *Standard Deviation,* or some other parameter such as the average error or the probable error which is readily derived from it. This measures the scatter of the bombs about their M.P.I. Alternatively it can be regarded as a measure of the concentration of bombing.

(ii) The *Systematic Error.* – The distance of the M.P.I. of the distribution from the detailed aiming point. This gives a measure of the accuracy with which the attack was centred.

(iii) The proportion of bombs despatched which, because of abortive sorties, gross errors or other causes, do not contribute to the normal bombfall distribution. This is known as the proportion of *ineffectives.*

84. The accurate calculation of these parameters for any given raid is a matter of some difficulty and unfortunately it was only during the last two years of the war that sufficient operational data became available and the necessary statistical technique was developed by the Operational Research Section. It is therefore not possible to make any quantitative statement as to how the magnitude of the three basic parameters has changed throughout the course of the war, though some idea of the increase in the efficiency of the Command can be obtained from other less elaborate parameters. Of these, the only one which is available for raids back as far as 1942 is the *percentage of aircraft despatched which bombed within three miles of the aiming point.* This is a compond parameter which takes into account the standard deviation, the systematic error and the proportion of ineffectives. The choice of a radius of three miles was a purely arbitrary one, and was decided on in 1942, bearing in mind the average concentration of bombing achieved at that time. As the war progressed however and the percentage bombing within three miles approached closer and closer to 100 per cent., this parameter became less and less satisfactory as a measure of bombing accuracy.

85. Graph No. 10 (*See* Part V) shows how the percentage bombing within three miles of the aiming point has increased since 1942. It should be realised that the statistics on which this graph is based are all estimated from night photographic evidence and only apply therefore to those raids on which a reasonable sample of night photographs which could be plotted, either by ground detail or by fire tracks, were returned. Raids in poor weather conditions are therefore excluded owing to lack of evidence. All attacks on precision targets such as individual factories, marshalling yards, gun batteries, etc., and raids on Berlin have also been excluded since the concentration of bombing achieved against these targets was of an entirely different order to that achieved on ordinary night attacks on German cities. In order to eliminate violent fluctuations in the graph which would tend to obscure the general trend, a running average over a period of six months has been used. This means that each point on the curve represents, not the average accuracy for that particular month, but the average over that month and the preceding five months.

86. It will be seen from the curve that during 1942 the average accuracy remained fairly steady at about 25 per cent. of sorties despatched bombing within three miles of the aiming point. The first marked improvement came in the Spring of 1943 and followed closely the introduction of OBOE and H.2.S., the combined result of which was to more than double the efficiency of the Command. There followed a slight

drop at the beginning of 1944, which was probably a seasonal fluctuation due to winter conditions, and thereafter there was a rapid and steady improvement until the end of the war. It is difficult to associate this latter improvement with any particular change in our bombing techniques, since so many factors undoubtedly played a part in bringing it about. Among these may be mentioned the increasing use made of Mark III H.2.S., and the G.P.I. and the introduction of the hooded flare. Most important of all however, was the shortening of the period of attack, both by reducing the average size of the raid and by stepping up the number of aircraft attacking per minute. This change took place gradually over a period of several months at the beginning of 1944 and as pointed out in paragraph 43, it was effective in eliminating the backward drift of the attack which had formed the chief source of wasted effort in 1943.

87. A more precise comparison between the effectiveness of our bombing in 1943 and in 1944-45 can be obtained by comparing the density of bombing at the aiming point, which can be readily calculated from the raid parameters. In Table VI this calculated aiming point density is given for 17 typical raids in 1943, and for a further 17 raids in 1944 and 1945. The density is given in two forms; the absolute density in tons per square mile at the aiming point, which takes into account the scale of the attack, and the relative density in tons per square mile at the aiming point per 1,000 tons dropped, which is independent of the scale of the attack and which strictly measures relative accuracy including both centering and scatter.

88. It will be seen from the tables that in terms of absolute density a rate of 57 tons per square mile was averaged in 1943, with a range from 3·2 to 216 tons per square mile. The corresponding figures for 1944/45 are 219 tons per square mile on the average, with a range from 23·7 to 658 tons per square mile; in other words, about four times as great as in 1943. In terms of relative density the 1943 average is 33 tons per square mile per 1,000 tons dropped and in 1944/45 it shows a five-fold increase to 174. The 1944/45 figures include two daylight raids, in order to be representative, but even excluding these there is an increase in accuracy at night to a value of 122·4 tons/sq. mile/1,000 tons dropped, or 3·7 times the 1943 accuracy.

89. It should be explained that the very low values for certain raids are due mainly to bad centering of the raid, and much higher densities were achieved away from the aiming point. Thus in the Hannover raid of the 27/28th September, 1943, when the rate at the aiming point was only 3·2 tons per square mile, a rate of 120 tons per square mile was achieved at the M.P.I., which was offset nearly four miles from the aiming point.

90. All the above figures relate to large, heavily defended targets in Germany. It is instructive to compare the results achieved with those obtained for lightly defended tactical targets of various types in 1944.

Time of Raid.	Number of Raids Analysed.	Average Relative Density At A.P.		
Night	99	1,597 tons	/sq. mile	/1,000 tons.
Day	98	2,280	/Do.	/do.
Total	197	1,939	/Do.	/do.

91. It will be seen that an altogether higher level of accuracy has been achieved, on the average, on these small targets. This is partly to be explained in terms of the smaller forces despatched, the comparative lightness of the defences and to the fact that the majority of these targets were ideally situated from the aspect of radar marking devices.

TABLE VI.

Density at the Aiming Point – German Cities.
(Calculated from Raid Parameters).

1943			
Target.	Date.	Absolute Density (tons/sq. mile).	Relative Density (per 1,000 tons dropped).
Duisburg	26/27-4-43	8·3	5·9
Duisburg	12/13-5-43	53·4	36·6
Bochum	13/14-5-43	21·0	21·0
Dortmund	23/24-5-43	35·2	16·3
Barmen	29/30-5-43	84·3	46·6
Düsseldorf	11/12-6-43	145·5	72·0
Krefeld	21/22-6-43	86·8	44·6
Cologne	3/4-7-43	72·5	40·3
Mannheim	16/17-4-43	7·5	22·6
Hamburg	24/25-7-43	47·8	20·2
Hamburg	27/28-7-43	7·7	3·3
Nuremberg	27/28-8-43	3·8	2·2
Mannheim	23/24-9-43	28·6	15·4
Hannover	27/28-9-43	3·2	1·4
Kassel	3/4-10-43	39·0	25·1
Hannover	8/9/-10-43	108·9	64·8
Kassel	22/23-10-43	216·1	128·8
Average	-	57·1	33·4

1944 and 1945			
Target.	Date.	Absolute Density (tons/sq. mile).	Relative Density (per 1,000 tons dropped).
Stuttgart	25/26-7-44	159·1	110-2
Hamburg	28/29-7-44	48·9	42·4
Russelsheim	12/13-8-44	23·7	24·5
Bremen	18/19-8-44	108·1	95·6
Russelsheim	25/26-8-44	139·0	89·4
Frankfurt	12/13-9-44	328·2	212·0
Saarbrucken	5/6-10-44	89·8	54·0
Dortmund	6/7-10-44	305·7	184·3
Bochum	9/10-10-44	46·1	31·7
Wilhelmshaven	15/16-10-44	349·8	163·8
Bochum	4/5-10-44	658·4	198·3
Freiburg	27/28-11-44	287·2	169·3
Ludwigshaven	2/3-1-45	182·6	149·5
Magdeburg	16/17-1-45	238·3	223·5
Nuremberg	2/3-1-45	182·7	87·7
Emden	6/9/44 *	463·6	797·5
Munster	12/9/44*	110·5	315·7
Average	-	218·9	73·5
Increase over 1943	-	3·8-fold	5·2-fold

* Day raids.

APPENDIX C

THE PROGRESS OF ARMAMENT

Introduction

The history of Armament in Bomber Command between February, 1942, and May, 1945, is one of increasing striking power and improving technique, though this progress was hampered by an unending series of technical difficulties and failures. Details of many of these are given below, but I must here assert, in the hope that repetition of such occurrences may be avoided in future, that the armament design side, as evidenced by the stores issued to my Command, showed throughout a standard of incompetence which had the most serious repercussions on the efficiency and effectiveness of the Bomber Offensive.

That such shortcomings are not inherent in the difficulties of armament design is in turn evidenced by the outstanding success of weapons designed outside the Air Ministry – M.A.P. organisation. Without exception these proved successful and efficient, *e.g.,* Admiralty mines, the Rose turret, the Wallis "Upkeep" weapon, the Wallis 12,000-lb. and 22,000-lb. bombs and various Service modifications to bad official designs.

I therefore submit that the most drastic overhaul of the design personnel concerned and the organisation responsible is a *sine qua non* of efficiency and of our national safety in future.

2. In the early months of 1942, the Command was in the transition stage, turning over from small bombers carrying comparatively light bomb loads, to the heavy four-engine bombers capable of carrying greatly increased loads. Up to the beginning of 1942, the largest bomb dropped by this Command was a 4,000-pounder, but the size of individual bombs carried increased steadily up to the 22,000-pounder dropped in 1945.

3. Not only did the size of individual bombs increase, but a steady increase was recorded in the bomb weights carried by each type of aircraft. In this connection, the Command relied considerably upon self-help in developing ways and means of increasing the loads carried in the stowage capacity available.

4. The increased numbers and weight of bombs to be handled brought in their train many problems of organisation which had to be overcome to ensure the aircraft being bombed up in time for take-off, and also many problems in the development of handling equipment. Again, although much help was given by the Ministries concerned, the major problems of bomb handling equipment were solved by the Command itself, where new techniques were built up as a result of experience.

5. Frequent shortages of vital equipment seriously complicated the task of the armament staff, while much American equipment, and British equipment which had not been fully developed, had to be brought into emergency use. This lack of standardisation caused serious difficulties in planning and handling loads and bombing up aircraft.

6. As the striking power of Bomber Command increased, so did the efficiency of the German night fighter defences, and although our four-engine bombers carried a four-gun tail turret in place of their predecessors' two-gun turrets, the bomber was never in a position to take on and defeat the enemy night fighter. It is obvious that for night attack the first essential is that the gunner should have a clear and unrestricted view from his turret, and this need led to numerous modifications within the Command to the standard designs of turrets. As the night fighter increased the weight of its armour and armament, the provisioning of guns of heavier calibre than ·303 in. became an urgent matter, but, in spite of numerous representations and reminders from this Command, no ·5-in. gun turret of official design was in action before the end of the war. It was left to the Command itself to develop with a private firm the only ·5-in. turret in use before May, 1945.

7. Radar gun-laying was tried out on a small scale from the autumn of 1944, but, as supplies of the equipment were limited and no satisfactory solution had been found to the problem of air-to-air identification, no really comprehensive trial was possible.

8. In war time, heavy dilution of experienced personnel must take place in all departments, and under the spur of war many articles are accepted for Service use before they are fully developed; many of the Command's difficulties would, however, not have arisen had more designers been available with practical experience in the operational use of armament equipment. This fact emphasises the need for maintaining in peace time a strong team of designers of armament equipment, with practical experience of the conditions under which the equipment for the design of which they are responsible will be used.

9. The subsequent sections of this Appendix deal briefly with the characteristics and behaviour of the major items of armament equipment used in Bomber Command during the period under review, together with reference to the policy governing the use of each item.

LIST OF SECTIONS

Section I.   H.E. Bombs.
Section II.   Incendiary Bombs.

SECTION I – H.E. BOMBS

500-lb. M.C.

At the end of 1941 small supplies became available of 500-lb. M.C. bombs, which contained approximately twice the H.E. content of the G.P. bombs then in use. A number of different Marks of this bomb were produced, and trials were made with these against the reinforced two-storey building at Braid Fell during 1943. On this very resistant target some of these bombs broke up. This caused some doubt as to their performance when dropped with tail delay fuzing against German city targets, with the result that for a short period nose instantaneous fuzing only was employed. Further investigations showed that it was only the Mark I type of bomb which possessed serious weaknesses, and that all the other types were likely to function satisfactorily against German built-up areas when fuzed tail delay. A requirement was put forward, however, by this Command, for supplies of the forged Mark II type bomb for use with long delay fuzes, in order to ensure that these bombs would not break up when subjected to heavy treatment.

1,000-lb. M.C.

2. The 1,000-lb. M.C. bomb which was introduced into the Command in the spring of 1943 proved to be a most valuable and effective weapon. Supplies, however, were always inadequate, and during 1944, in spite of many requests for increased output from this Command, recourse had to be made to American type bombs, to 500-lb. British bombs, and even to 250-lb. bombs. The shortage of 1,000-lb. M.C. bombs at times gave rise to the gravest concern and stocks had to be husbanded with the very greatest care.

4,000-lb. M.C.

3. In January, 1943, small supplies of these bombs became available, and operational trials were made during the next six months. The bombs were originally intended for low level bombing, a type of operation not normally undertaken by Bomber Command at this period. Small numbers of these bombs were dropped on city targets from high altitude, but accurate photographic assessment of the results was never possible, and, as 4,000-lb. H.C. bombs were in good supply, the use of M.C. bombs against this type of target did not appear to be justified. During the autumn of 1944, 4,000-lb. M.C. bombs were used by Mosquito aircraft for high altitude night bombing, as the ballistics of these weapons are much superior to those of the 4,000-lb. H.C. bomb; it was also used with success to breach the dykes on Walcheren Island. Partly because only one could be carried by Lancaster aircraft and none by Halifaxes, however, it never became a widely used store in Bomber Command.

American Bombs

4. During 1944, large quantities of American A.N.M.44, 58 and 64 (500-lb.) and A.N.M.59 and 64 (1,000-lb.) bombs were used. The A.N.M. 58 and 59 were S.A.P.s of about 33 per cent. C.W. ratio, the other types being equivalent to the British M.C. range, but slightly less powerful owing to their 50/50 Amatol or straight T.N.T. filling. These bombs gave good service, and were quicker and easier to fuze and tail than their British counterparts, but the American box type tails seriously reduced the number which could be carried in British aircraft. A design of British type drum tail was therefore prepared, but supplies of these tails never matched up with the supply of bombs; moreover the drum tail slightly reduced the stability of the bombs.

2,000-lb. A.P.

5. A number of these bombs was used against the "Scharnhorst" and "Gneisenau" at Brest in 1942, and subsequently some were used against underground oil storage plants on the west coast of France during 1944. Results were disappointing, and it was subsequently found that a large number of blind bombs resulted through the malfunctioning of the No. 37 fuze; to overcome this, the Mark IV bomb was introduced early in 1944. This type of bomb incorporated a normal pistol detonator combination, but as suitable targets were not available none of these bombs were used.

S.A.P. Bombs

6. Very few S.A.P. bombs were used during the period under review, as suitable targets were seldom available. During the acute shortage of H.E. bombs in the

summer of 1944, the use of S.A.P.s for general bombardment purposes was discussed, and a few were in fact used against flying bomb sites in France.

2,000-lb. H.C.

7. At the beginning of 1942, 2,000-lb. H.C. bombs were used with parachute attachments, which rendered them practically unaimable, and took up considerable storage space. In March, 1942, an urgent requirement was put forward to the Air Ministry for the provision of a ballistic tail, and supplies of these started to come in to the Command at the end of August of the same year. All subsequent deliveries of these bombs were provided with the ballistic tail.

4,000, 8,000 and 12,000-lb. H.C.

8. The 4,000-lb. H.C. bomb was already in supply at the beginning of 1942. This was followed later by the two larger sizes, of which the 12,000-lb. was mainly used for special precision targets. No serious troubles were encountered in the use of these weapons, but the assembly of the larger ones was a somewhat lengthy operation, in spite of the provisioning of special jigs. All these bombs were liable to detonate on a take-off crash, owing to the small margin of safety provided in the nose pistols.

4,000-lb. G.P.

9. On the 28th March, 1942, I asked the Air Ministry to proceed with the development and production of 4,000-lb. G.P. bombs. On the 31st March, 1942, a requirement was placed for 500 of these bombs to cover the next six months. By May, 1942, 4,000-lb. G.P. bombs were coming off production. The bomb, however, did not prove satisfactory in use, as if fuzed with any delay it was liable to break up, and if fuzed instantaneous, for blast effect, it was much inferior to the 4,000-lb. H.C. bomb. Therefore, in November, 1943, I informed the Air Ministry that this Command had no further operational requirements for this type of bomb.

Owing to the restricted life of these bombs, in November, 1943, I instructed Groups to expend their stocks at the rate of three bombs per Group per operation when bomb loads of mixed incendiary and H.E. were ordered.

"Upkeep"

10. This unique weapon, thought out and designed by Mr. Wallis of Vickers Armstrong Ltd., cleared its trials just in time for an attack to be made against the Mohne, Sorpe and Eder Dams with the full head of spring flood water in the lakes. The attack was made by night in the first week of June, 1943, and the Mohne and

Eder Dams were successfully breached. Although the Sorpe Dam was not breached, the enemy was forced to reduce the water level in the lake. The use of this novel weapon caused a direct loss of water to the industrial area of the Ruhr and, in addition, widespread material damage due to flooding.

"Johnnie Walker"

11. This weapon, developed by M.D.1, was a 500-lb. store for the attack of ships in harbour. Development was started in 1942, and a good many difficulties were encountered, but supplies of a bomb, with considerable operational limitations, were forthcoming during the early summer of 1943. No suitable targets were then available, but a few of these weapons were dropped against the "Tirpitz" when lying in the Alten Fjord, during the autumn of 1944, but no reports of their effectiveness were ever received. The bomb required too great a depth of water to be usable except in harbours of unusual depth.

C.S. Bomb

12. Development of this weapon, for the attack of capital ships, was well in hand in the first half of 1942. The first design had a diameter of 45 in., so that it could not be carried on any aircraft then available. Supplies of a modified 38-in. diameter bomb, which could be carried by the big bomb door Lancaster aircraft, became available in the spring of 1943. These bombs, designed by M.D.1, at first incorporated a parachute, which made them practically unaimable from anything other than low altitude, and it was not until later in the year that bombs with normal ballistic tails were available.

A few of these weapons were dropped on Italian harbours, but no results were obtained, and the bomb was not used again.

12,000-lb. and 22,000-lb. M.C.

13. These bombs, designed by Mr. Wallis of Vickers Armstrong Ltd. for the attack of underground targets, marked a major step forward in the matter of bomb design and bomb ballistics.

Small supplies of the 12,000-lb. bomb became available in the early summer of 1944, and the first attacks made with these weapons met with instantaneous success. A variety of targets was attacked, including a number for which the bomb had never been designed, *e.g.,* reinforced concrete structures. Although these bombs did not destroy these targets, they did considerable damage and forced the enemy to increase still further the heavy protection already provided against air attack. During the summer of 1944, the supply of these weapons was of a hand-to-mouth nature, and many targets would have been effectively dealt with at an earlier date had more bombs been available. In the autumn of 1944, three attacks were made with these bombs on the Tirpitz. The second attack crippled this powerful vessel, and the third attack sank her.

As a result of the success of the 12,000-lb. bomb, production of the 22,000-lb. type was started. The first one was dropped against, and wrecked, the Bielefeld viaduct in the spring of 1945. Further bombs were used successfully against U-Boat shelter targets in North-West Germany.

H.E. Fillings

14. In the middle of 1943, improved fillings became available for H.E. bombs, the first of these being R.D.X./T.N.T., which was filled into 500-lb. and 1,000-lb. M.C. bombs from July onwards. At approximately the same time, small quantities of Torpex became available, and this was used in 12,000-lb. H.C. bombs. Towards the end of the year, Minol was filled into 4,000-lb. H.C. bombs, becoming standard for these bombs and also, subsequently, for the smaller M.C. types. No troubles were encountered with any of these fillings and their increased power over Amatol fillings proved of great value.

In 1944 American filled 4,000-lb. H.C. bombs, and a few 500-lb. and 1,000-lb. bombs were received filled with Tritonal. This mixture of T.N.T./A.L. was satisfactory.

SECTION II. – INCENDIARY BOMBS

4-lb. Incendiary Bomb

1. The mainstay of the Command throughout the war was the 4-lb. magnesium I.B. The main (and a very serious) difficulty met with in the use of this weapon was its lack of aimability when dropped from small bomb containers, which resulted in incendiary attacks being widely dispersed and tending to fall downwind from the target with consequent great risk to our own aircraft from showers of loose bombs over the target area. Another major trouble was the susceptibility of the bomb tail to damage in handling, resulting in bad ballistics and increased trail. Although these troubles were overcome in principle with the introduction of clusters in 1944, nevertheless, as will be seen later, these themselves suffered from many defects.

30-lb. Incendiary Bomb

2. Various Marks of this bomb, varying only in detail, were used, and although perhaps not ideal as fire raisers, they were at least aimable. The phosphorus filling had a great morale effect, as had also the flash and bang of the bomb when it

functioned. These bombs are regarded as satisfactory for the work for which they were used.

30-lb. "J" Type Incendiary Bomb

3. As a result of a static test held at Hammersmith on the 8th March, 1943, orders were placed for the 30-lb. Incendiary Bomb, Type "J," and I was informed by the Air Ministry in the middle of April that quantity production was expected in six months or less.

A demonstration was arranged on the 18th August at my Headquarters as a result of which I informed the Air Ministry that although I did not wish to pre-judge the issue, I was not impressed with the design of the "J" bomb, and asked for an assurance that its production would not prejudice the output of the 30-lb. phosphorus bomb which had been giving good results on operations. I again wrote on somewhat similar lines to Air Ministry on the 6th October, 1943, pointing out that deliveries of Pathfinder Force pyrotechnics were being delayed owing to the clash of "J" bomb cluster manufacture with the pyrotechnic clustering programme.

When small quantities of the "J" bomb clusters were received for trial in December, 1943, troubles were encountered owing to the instability of the store with the tail then fitted, and a number of blind bombs caused by parachute failure. These troubles were investigated at the beginning of January, and the supply of new type tails commenced at the end of February, together with bombs with an improved parachute, but supplies were still insufficient for operational trials.

During the period April-August, 1944, ten operational trials were made, and the results indicated that the 30-lb. "J" bomb was only half as effective per ton as the 4-lb. Incendiary.

The sorry story of this bomb points a moral anent enthusiastic protagonists of a theoretical weapon being allowed to override the opinions and advice of the operational user.

SECTION III. – CLUSTER PROJECTILES

1. In May, 1943, at my instigation, an Air Staff requirement was raised for cluster projectiles. These projectiles were required for the economic carriage of small bombs whose terminal velocity was too low for them to be aimed individually by means of the Mark XIV bombsight, to prevent trail back of incendiary attacks, and to protect our own aircraft from showers of small bombs scattered from S.B.C.s. Clusters, it was decided, would also eliminate the slow and laborious task of filling S.B.C.s. On May 15th, 1943, I stressed the importance of these clusters and urged that the development of a 1,000-lb. version should be hastened in order that full use could be made of the 1,000-lb. bomb position in heavy bomber aircraft in use in my Command.

2. The 500-lb. projectile was, however, produced first, on the grounds that it was

capable of being carried by all heavy bomber aircraft. The development of the 1,000-lb. cluster was undertaken in two stages. The first stage was to develop a simple cluster containing 166 bombs which was capable of being carried on all 1,000-lb. bomb carriers (this development was never completed). The second stage of development was the production of a 1,000-lb. cluster containing 220 bombs, this being undertaken as a long term development. The latter projectile was intended to be fitted with a telescopic tail to enable it to fit into existing 1,000-lb. stowages.

3. On 27th May, 1943, I again urged the Air Ministry to take special measures to speed up production and introduction into the Service of the 500-lb. cluster projectile. I also pointed out that there was an urgent need for larger clusters to enable the maximum permissible load to be carried by Lancaster and Halifax aircraft. In June, 1943, I again emphasised that the 1,000-lb. incendiary cluster mock-up should be developed on the highest priority, for although it did not fully meet requirements, it would however allow the maximum permissible weight of bombs to be carried.

4. On 30th May, 1944, I expressed grave concern on the question of damage to our own aircraft from 4-lb. I.B.s released from S.B.C.s and I again urged the Air Ministry to take most energetic action towards production of clustered projectiles. On the 16th May, 1944, a requirement was placed for each cluster to contain 10 per cent. explosive type bombs. Early in August, 1944, information was received that owing to difficulties at the factories in transport and storage of clusters containing explosive bombs, it would be necessary to accept the provision of cluster projectiles loaded with 100 per cent. explosive type bombs, but that, as soon as conditions were suitable, clusters would be filled with overall proportion of 10 per cent. explosive type.

5. On the 8th September, 1944, I informed the Air Ministry that a requirement existed for a 750-lb. I.B. cluster suitable for carriage on No. 12 station on Lancaster aircraft, when a mixed load of 4,000-lb. H.C. bombs and I.B. clusters was carried. I suggested that if the 750-lb. cluster were modified to incorporate a telescopic tail unit similar to the one provided with the No. 16 cluster, and if the suspension lug was located slightly to the rear of its present position, it would meet my requirements. Early in September, 1944, I was informed that a No. 15 cluster projectile was being developed.

In February, 1945, the Air Ministry were asked by me to investigate the possibility of using a cluster projectile of approximately the same dimensions as the 2,000-lb. H.C. bomb, to carry 4-lb. I.B.s and requested that this should be developed as either a nose or tail ejection cluster.

6. Supplies of 500-lb. (No. 14) clusters started to trickle into the Command at the end of 1943, and these were followed by the 750-lb. (No. 15) cluster, in the summer of 1944 and by the M.17 (American) cluster. Deliveries of the 1,000-lb. (No. 16) clusters did not commence until the autumn. The supply position was always precarious and supplies were always behind production forecasts. In addition, insufficient transit cases were available, and such as existed were of unsuitable design, being either cumbersome steel crates, laborious to open, or wooden crates flimsy and non-weatherproof. The clusters themselves were extremely fragile, and once out of

their crates were easily damaged in handling or by moisture. I eventually found it necessary to take over an aircraft hangar on each station to house these easily damaged stores, and to provide an elaborate system of roller conveyor for handling them. I repeatedly represented all these difficulties to the Air Ministry, and was informed that a new type of Nose Ejection cluster, which would prove satisfactory, would soon be available. These, however, were not forthcoming before the end of the war.

Cluster Projectile A.N. M.17

7. In order to supplement supplies of the No. 14 cluster projectile, the production of which was insufficient to meet the Commands full requirements, trials were being arranged in February, 1941, with the American cluster A.N. M.17, in order to determine their suitability for use in this Command. These clusters contained 110 by 4-lb. I.B.s and functioned in a somewhat similar manner to the British version. As a result of these trials, it was found that the wooden boxes and compressed cardboard cylinders used to protect the clusters during transit caused complications at operational stations. In September, 1944, I informed the Air Ministry that, due to the number of operations necessary to prepare this cluster for use, it could only be accepted in this Command in the event of an emergency. A modified form of the M-111 fuze was used in this cluster, the modification consisting of the fitting of a tetryl booster in place of the black powder booster. Early in September 1944, information was received that the M-127 fuze had not been accepted for Service use, but that M.A.P. had designed an adapter booster No. 1, Mark I, to be used in conjunction with the No. 42, Mark IV, fuze which would permit this fuze being used with the M.17 cluster. First consignments of this adaptor booster were placed on trial and gave very unsatisfactory results, five out of six failing to function correctly. At the end of March, 1945, a new consignment of modified adaptors were received. These also failed to give satisfactory results during trials. Indeed, up to the end of the European War no suitable or safe fuze had been designed for this cluster.

On the 3rd February, 1945, this Command informed the Air Ministry that a number of hang-ups were occurring due to the cocking lever thumb piece of the carrier fouling the top of the store, and a special suspension lug adaptor was designed to give the necessary clearance. By May, 1945, a thousand of these adaptors had been produced, but owing to the satisfactory quantities of cluster projectiles of British manufacture then available, I informed the Air Ministry that future developments and production of these adaptors was unnecessary.

8. The story of the development of clustered incendiary projectiles makes sad reading, and there can be no doubt that the failure to produce a satisfactory cluster before the end of the war enormously reduced the efficiency of our incendiary attacks.

SECTION IV. – FUZES AND PISTOLS

No. 30 Pistol

1. This tail pistol which had been used in all medium calibre H.E. bombs through the war was discovered, when used in daylight during the autum of 1944, to be the cause of bombs detonating shortly after leaving the aircraft. The first defect was due to the arming nut binding on the striker spindle and forcing it on to the detonator. Immediate modification action was taken, but this did not entirely stop accidents, and further investigations revealed that under certain circumstances the arming nut could bounce forward on to the striker spindle, and drive it on to the detonator. As a result of this serious state of affairs being investigated by the M.A.P., the design of a pyrotechnic arming stop was prepared, tested, and put into production; but supplies were not available to this Command before the cessation of hostilities.

No. 44 Pistol

2. In the midsummer of 1943, the No. 44 blast-operated nose pistol became available to supersede the normal direct action nose pistol for H.E. bombs. A modification to this pistol, known as the No. 42, was put into immediate use in H.C. bombs, and these, it is thought, gave an appreciable increase in the performance of these weapons. The No. 44 pistol which was being used in 500/1,000-lb. bombs was used on a few occasions against close support targets in 1944, and gave quite satisfactory results.

No. 37 Long Delay Pistol

3. The Mark IV design incorporating an anti-removal device which was introduced into the Command at the beginning of 1943 was still in use up to the end of the war. These pistols possessed several dangerous features which resulted in the loss of the lives of many of our own personnel and the destruction of a number of aircraft.

Despite my many and frequent requests made to the Air Ministry for an improved design of long-delay pistol, this was not forthcoming by the end of the war. Several new designs were promised for delivery from the middle of 1944, but none of these were received, nor were any major improvements made to the No. 37 pistol. The anti-removal device which was the cause of a considerable proportion of the accidents that had been encountered was deleted in the last months of the war. This was done as a result of a trial, made at the request of this Command, which showed that with the anti-removal device in operation, 15 per cent. blind bombs resulted. A previous request in August, 1943, to eliminate the anti-removal device was not accepted by the Air Ministry on operational grounds.

It is true to say that the No. 37 pistol was the most fruitful source of serious armament accidents in this Command, and that although it no doubt caused the enemy annoyance, it could be so easily removed from the bomb, if circumstances warranted such action, that it was probably more of a menace to ourselves than to the enemy. The continued delay in the delivery of improved designs of No. 37 pistol, or of alternative new type pistols, was most disappointing, and at the end of the war my Command still possessed no efficient and safe long-delay pistol.

No. 53 Pistol

4. The No. 53 half-hour delay pistol and the No. 53A one-hour delay pistol were brought into use in the spring of 1944. Both pistols were based on the same principle as the No. 37 L.D. pistol, but they were not provided with an anti-removal device.

I required these pistols for concentrated bombing of precision targets, in order to prevent the target being obscured by smoke during the period of the attack. Considerable quantities of these pistols were used, but supplies were never adequate and stocks had to be carefully husbanded.

Owing to the basic similarity of these pistols, to the No. 37 pistol, accidents occurred, and the design cannot be regarded as in any way safe or satisfactory. Suggestions were put to the Air Ministry for improvements, but none of these were incorporated in issues to any Command before the end of the war.

Fuze No. 845

5. Deliveries of this anti-disturbance pistol, which fitted in the nose of G.P./M.C. bombs, and functioned on disturbance, commenced in the spring of 1942. The fuze functioned electrically, power being drawn from a small battery contained in it.

The design was not satisfactory, as the fuze was difficult to test and was apt to become live when it should have remained safe. This culminated in a serious explosion in a bomb dump in the autumn of 1943, which resulted in my banning the further use of this fuze.

I asked the Air Ministry to produce an improved type of anti-disturbance fuze, but none was ready before the end of the war.

Fuzes Nos. 848 and 849

6. The No. 848 fuze had proved unreliable in the 4·5-in. photographic flash, and it was superseded by the No. 849 fuze in the late spring of 1943. This fuze gave fairly satisfactory results, although its reliability in this store, and also with the 4·5-in. and 7-in, reconnaissance flares, still left room for improvement.

7. The No. 42 fuze, which has a simple pyrotechnic delay, was in service throughout the period under review, both for initiating flares and incendiary bomb clusters. The fuze, although simple in design, gave considerable trouble, owing to its susceptibility to mal-functioning through moisture. In spite of my frequent reports of the failure of this fuze, no improved design had been received in this Command by the end of the war.

8. In the summer of 1942 I asked the Air Ministry for a barometric fuze to function reconnaissance and marker flares and target indicators, at a pre-determined height, irrespective of the height at which the aircraft was flying. Development was already proceeding on an item of this sort, and after successful trials supplies of the No. 860 fuze became available during the spring of 1943.

These fuzes gave fairly satisfactory service, although their accuracy and regularity of functioning left much to be desired, but they were none the less a great improvement on the previous pyrotechnic type fuzes which had to be used until these barometric fuzes came into use.

At the end of 1943 supplies of the No. 867 fuze, which became available for tail fuzed stores, to some extent supplanted the No. 860, which was for nose fuzing only.

9. Early in May, 1943, I pointed out to the Air Ministry the necessity for a fuze giving a sensitive time delay for use with the 4·5-in. photographic flash, and asked for information on the American fuze M.111 which was then on trial at Boscombe Down. This fuze, I hoped, would meet Command requirements. In June, 1943, 100 of these fuzes were issued to this Command for Service trials. On the 2nd June, 1943, owing to the unsatisfactory nature of the present type of fuze then available for photo flashes, I asked Air Ministry to introduce this fuze immediately for operational use, and requested that the 10,000 fuzes then available in this country should be issued without delay. In consequence, a small quantity was issued to my Command for Service trials. The result of these trials showed a great improvement over those obtained from the No. 848 fuze, and in August, 1943, I asked the Air Ministry to take the necessary provisioning action to provide a general issue to all units in my Command. Supplies were, however, still limited, but by December sufficient quantities were available throughout the Command. During January, 1944, an analysis of night photography showed a high proportion of unsuccessful photographs which were attributed to the failures in the M.111 fuze. Tests were conducted resulting in the re-design of the fuzing wire, and an alteration of the lanyard for the tri-cell chute.

SECTION V. – BOMB HANDLING EQUIPMENT

1. Bomb loads, and the variety of weapons in use, continually increased from the beginning of 1942 until the end of the war. Both these factors seriously complicated the whole question of bomb handling and of bomb-handling equipment, the supply of which was almost invariably a stage behind the operational requirements. However, much ingenuity was displayed by various individuals in the Command in improvising handling equipment of all sorts for everything from 4-lb. to 10-ton bombs.

2. The various items of equipment are too numerous to describe in detail, and only major items will be dealt with, but the main lesson is that there should be no gap between the operational use of a store and the introduction of suitable handling equipment. It is also clear that the whole process of bomb handling must be fully mechanised, in order both to save man-power and to obtain quick turn round of the aircraft. The layout of station bomb dumps, which has a very direct bearing on handling problems, always lagged behind operational requirements, resulting in gross overloading of the storage capacity available and increasing the difficulties of "working" the dump.

H.E. Bombs

3. All H.E. bombs, except the large M.C. types, were handled by rolling, except on a few stations where the old 72-ton type dumps, provided with overhead gantries, were available. The bombs were rolled off the bomb lorries into the 200-ton dumps, and from the dumps on to the bomb trolleys. The system worked well, the only difficulties encountered being due to the fact that many of the dumps had only cinder or hard core floors, and wooden battens were always in short supply. Some difficulties, too, arose in handling mines, owing to the necessity for selecting specified types, which might be anywhere in the bay. If a crane was available, and this was frequently not the case, the problem was solved; otherwise recourse had to be made to "juggling" the mines over each other out of the dump on roller conveyor.

The large M.C. bombs were handled by crane alone, the Lorraine proving satisfactory for the 12,000-lb. type. For the 22,000-lb., Bay City and Rapier cranes were used, the former being unsatisfactory until the power-lowering device became available in the late spring of 1945.

Incendiary Bombs

4. At the beginning of 1942, Mark I type S.B.C.s were in use, and these carried either 8 x 39-lb. bombs or three "packs" of 30 x 4-lb. The packs were lifted as units into the S.B.C.s held in a rotatable jig and then inverted on to a transporter. This system was fairly satisfactory except for the flimsy construction of the transporter. In 1943, the Command developed a deeper S.B.C. holding 12 ÷ 30 lb. or 150 x 4-lb. bombs.

The introduction of this equipment necessitated individual transfer of the bombs from the 30 "packs" into the new 50-pack liners in the S.B.C., a laborious operation, but justified by the greatly increased load. The rotatable jig became redundant and a more robust transporter a necessity, but in spite of urgent representations to the Air Ministry, supplies of the latter only trickled into the Command in early 1945. This shortage of transporters, which resulted in much unnecessary damage to S.B.C.s and bomb tails, complicated the whole handling problem. Requests were also made for the bombs to be packed in 50-pack liners, instead of 30, but production considerations ruled this out.

S.B.C.s when filled, were stored on end in Nissen huts. Many ingenious devices were produced for handling these heavy and fragile items of equipment from their storage position on to the bomb trolleys.

Bomb Trolleys

5. At the beginning of 1942 the standard trolley was the Type "B," capable of carrying 4 x 500-lb. bombs, and the Type "D" for 1 x 4,000-lb. H.C. bombs. The Type "B" was gradually replaced by the Type "C," with a maximum load of 6,000 lb., and the Type "F," with a maximum load of 8,000 lb.; of these the "C," Mark III, proved the most useful. At the end of 1943 a Type "E" trolley was introduced for H.C. bombs up to 12,000 lb. in weight, and in 1944 the Type "H" for the large M.C. bombs. Except for the Type "H," all these trolleys possessed the same basic features, namely, a low rectangular chassis, with adjustable chocks to locate the bombs, and small pneumatic tyres. The equipment stood up well to arduous treatment, but there were frequent shortages of spares, notably tyres, tow bars and brake gear.

For two years the Command pressed for the provision of mudguards on trolleys, to protect the loads from mud and water, but it was not until the end of 1944 that trickle supplies became available.

To support the bomb the "H" type trolleys incorporated a cradle which was raised by a winch at each corner, for hoisting the bomb into the aircraft.

Fordson and David Brown tractors were used, the latter being the more satisfactory as a greater reserve of power was available. In 1944 one Finger truck per station became available. These handy little vehicles proved of great value, but could only work on hard ground as they were fitted with small solid rubber tyres.

Bomb Winches

6. Bomb-hoisting winches were developed to handle into the aircraft the various weapons brought into Service. Generally speaking, they functioned very satisfactorily. In the early summer of 1944, a big step forward was made by the provisioning of trolleys fitted with hydraulic motors, attached to the hoisting winches. This powering

of the bomb hoisting operation was a great boon during the intensive operations of 1944, saving much blood, sweat, toil and tears.

SECTION VI. – BOMB-CARRYING EQUIPMENT

Carriage of Medium Calibre H.E. Bombs

1. During the period under review no major changes were made in the general principles of carrying medium calibre H.E. bombs, except that a change over was gradually made from the British system of vertical fuze control links to the American horizontal system. Carriers otherwise remained basically the same, except for minor modifications to ease production and allow an increase in load. An adaptor, produced in the Command, to enable two 500-lb. stores to be carried from one carrier marked a con-siderable step forward in the load-carrying capacity of our heavy bombers.

Heavy Bombs and Mines

2. Heavy bombs, except the two large M.C. bombs, were all carried on release slips fitted into the aircraft bomb cell and attached to the lug on the bomb, the crutches being also built into the bomb cell. Adaptors were produced for carrying two mines, or two 2,000-lb. A.P. bombs from the slips, the introduction of this equipment giving a great increase in the number of these weapons which could be carried. For the large M.C. bombs a different system was used; the bombs were carried on a metal chain girdle attached to the aircraft and joined together by an E.M. release unit at the bottom of the girdle, the crutches again being built into the bomb cell.

All this equipment worked satisfactorily, and no major modifications were necessary except, as will be seen in the ensuing paragraphs, to some types of bomb release slip.

Small Bombs

3. All bombs up to and including 40 lb. in weight were carried in small bomb containers, until the beginning of 1944, and subsequent to this date clustered stowage was available for 4-lb. and 30-lb. "J" incendiary bombs only, the remaining small stores still having to be carried in S.B.C.s.

Small bomb containers proved fragile in use, the release slips were generally unreliable, filling of the S.B.C.s was laborious and supplies of S.B.C.s were normally tight. This equipment was therefore unpopular in the Command, but none the less it remained our only means of carrying small bombs for practically the whole war, and various ways and means had to be devised to alleviate the worst of the difficulties encountered in the use of this equipment.

Single Hook Release Slips

4. Single hook release slips for the carriage of 500/1,000-lb. bombs had given trouble throughout the war and innumerable modifications were introduced during the whole period. In 1944, when an increased proportion of 1,000-lb. bombs was carried, these troubles were accentuated, and several fatal accidents occurred through aircraft landing with a slip which had functioned but had failed to release the bomb. In the spring of 1944 a further modification to the design was got out at R.A.F. Station Oakington, and after much pressure on the Air Ministry, permission was obtained to modify all the slips in the Command. This modification overcame the difficulties, but resistance was encountered from the production side, who were unwilling to introduce this modification, as it would have caused a temporary reduction in output, and supplies were short.

Type "N" Release Slip

5. An improved type of slip, known as the Type "N", was put forward for trial in June, 1943, to overcome the difficulties encountered with previous designs. Numerous modifications were found to be necessary during the trials and quantities for extended tests were not available until the autumn of 1944. When these were received, accidents occurred through the bombs being released when loading on to the aircraft, owing to the depression of the test plunger against the carrier housing. Serious corrosion of the E.M. unit and release lever system was also encountered. Further modifications were necessary, with the result that these release slips were not in general service before the end of the war.

Type "L" Release Slip

6. To overcome the difficulties encountered with release slips on S.B.C.s, a new Type "L" unit became available for trial in March, 1943, and as the result of these trials a recommendation was put forward in April for production of these units, on the grounds that they were superior to the existing type.

Production was urged during the ensuing months, but it was not until the end of the year that quantities of these units became available. Although an improvement on the previous design, the "L" type units gave considerable trouble from icing, corrosion and mechanical weaknesses.

7. The whole problem of stowing and launching pyrotechnic stores was in a state of flux during the whole period of the war. Numerous different types of launching chute were developed, some of these were armoured, in order to provide protection from the dangerous photograph flash bomb, others were small unarmoured chutes for normal pyrotechnics. The installation of these various chutes in the operational aircraft frequently required considerable modifications to the airframe, and there was also a serious time lag between the introduction of a new type of chute and the equipment of operational aircraft.

SECTION VII. – BOMBSIGHTS

1. At the beginning of 1942 the following bombsights were in use in Bomber Command:—

(*a*) Mark IX course setting bombsight.

(*b*) Automatic bombsight.

(*c*) Sperry O.1 bombsight – No. 90 Squadron, Fulbeck. (This sight was only in use for a short time in Fortress aircraft.)

(*d*) Low level (hand held) bombsight, Mark I.

Mark II Course Setting Bombsight

2. This sight was in general use in Bomber Command from the outbreak of hostilities until 1942. It is a pre-set Vector bombsight. In so far as it is pre-set and has open sights, it is suitable for night bombing when darkness prevents the target being seen until the last moment. Its accuracy depends on accurate wind determination. The sight does not lend itself to bombing whilst taking evasive action, and for the correct use of this sight the average distance at which the target must be sighted is 2½/3 miles.

In January, 1942, it was decided that Mark IXA bombsights fitted with the Fourth Vector (moving target attachment) should be provided on a 100 per cent. basis for those squadrons equipped with Halifax, Stirling and Liberator aircraft. Boston and Mosquito aircraft were fitted with C.S.B.S., Mark IXE* (without Fourth Vector attachment), and all other aircraft equipped with C.S.B.S., Mark IXA* (without Fourth Vector attachment).

In March, 1942, I decided to equip four squadrons, Nos. 12, 460, 101 and 115, with the Mark IXA C.S.B.S., for specialist training in "B" bombing.

Low level attachments for the C.S.B.S. were supplied to No. 2 Group in May, 1942, as the C.S.B.S. with a low level attachment gave better results and was more operationally suitable than the low level bombsight (hand-held), Mark I.

Mark XIV Bombsight

3. I came to the conclusion, as the war progressed and the enemy strengthened his defences, that a general purpose bombsight to meet the requirements of my Command should possess two essential features. First, it must reduce to a minimum the length of time at which the aircraft is flown absolutely straight and level during the approach to the target. Secondly, the number of settings required to be made by the bomb aimer during flight should again be a minimum, to enable him to concentrate on releasing the bombs at the correct moment.

The Mark XIV bombsight satisfied both these requirements. At any time during the bombing attack the point on the ground covered by the graticule cross represents the point of impact of a bomb released at that instant. Avoiding action can therefore be taken up to the instant of release and bombs can be released if required while making a correctly banked turn or when gliding or climbing. Unlike previous bombsights, the Mark XIV bombsight has a different computor box for each aircraft type; this led to difficulties and delay in production.

4. In January, 1942, I attached three crews from the Command to A. and A.E.E. to complete interrupted Service trials of the Mark XIV bombsight. The first six sights allotted to my Command for training purposes were hand-made. In March, 1942, trial installations on all types of bomber aircraft were in hand. I decided to equip the Stirling on first priority because this aircraft carried the largest number of 2,000-lb. A. P. bombs. At this time it was found necessary to forward a requirement for an emergency computor for use with the bombsight in the event of the computor box becoming unserviceable. The priorities of issue of Mark XIV bombsights were amended from time to time in the light of operational requirements. On the 17th June, 1942, advice was received from M.A.P. that the static vent data had not been obtained for the Lancaster, nor had the trial installation been completed.

5. In July, 1942, the latest production figures as given by the Air Ministry were as follows:—

July	65 bombsights.
August	50 bombsights.
September	60 bombsights.
October	90 bombsights, rising by June, 1943, to 900 per month, and by December, 1943, to 1,500 per month.

6. In July, 1942, I drew Air Ministry's attention to the following limitations in the operational use of the sight:—

(i) No provision for the bombing of moving targets.

(ii) The terminal velocity setting does not allow for bombs having a terminal velocity of less than 1,000 ft. per second. At this time it was pointed out that it was impossible to carry out accurate bombing with 4-lb. incendiary bombs.

7. With the formation of the Pathfinder Force in August, 1942, the priorities of issue

I reviewed once more, and decided that squadrons of that force should have absolute priority for re-equipment with the Mark XIV bombsight.

8. Some troubles were encountered over the supply of sights for Wellington III aircraft as all Mark XIV bombsights due for early delivery were originally ordered for heavy bomber types. By August, 1942, the trial installation had not been completed in the Wellington III, and sights for this aircraft were not available until mid-December. On the 14th September, 1942, the position in the Command was as follows:—

> No. 35 Squadron – eleven aircraft completely fitted and serviceable, and one aircraft partly fitted.

By October, 1942, some Halifax aircraft were coming off production fitted with the Mark XIV bombsight. In February, 1943, it was decided to fit the Mark XIV sighting head only, in place of the C.S.B.S., Mark IXE, in Boston, Mitchell and Mosquito aircraft of No. 2 Group. I had already decided that the Mosquito aircraft would not be fitted with the full sight until the completion of the heavy bomber programme.

9. The introduction of the T.1 bombsight (American-manufactured, Mark XIV) in March, 1943, for Wellington aircraft meant that all British production could now go to heavy bombers.

10. In May, 1943, I asked the Air Ministry to increase the angle of climb allowed by the Mark XIV bombsight as No. 8 Group had found that the restrictions imposed by the present sight, 5° climb and 20° dive, were affecting the accuracy of marking. The Air Ministry agreed to increase the angle of climb to 11° by decreasing the angle of dive only to 19° and in February, 1944, the first bombsights were delivered to No. 8 Group, incorporating the increased pitch freedom mechanism. In July, 1943, Mark XIV sighting heads replaced the C.S.B.S. in O.T.U. aircraft.

By the middle of January, 1944, the majority of operational heavy bomber aircraft in the Command were fitted with the new sight.

Mark XIVA Bombsight

11. In May, 1943, I requested the Air Ministry to consider increasing the height limitation of the Mark XIV bombsight from 20,000 ft. to 30,000 ft. as Lancaster aircraft were then carrying out operational attacks up to 22,000 ft. The Air Ministry replied that the introduction of the Mark XIVA bombsight in the production line would make it possible to bomb up to 25,000 ft., but retrospective modification to existing sights was not practicable. The possibility of increasing the height range in this type of sight still further up to 30,000 ft. was being examined. In June, 1943, the Air Ministry stated that the Mark XIV bombsight was limited in its use to 25,000 ft. for the following reasons: —

> (*a*) I.C.A.N. laws do not hold in the Tropopause which is frequently in the region of 30,000 ft. or lower.

(*b*) The effect of cross trail, not allowed for on the Mark XIV type of sight, becomes very large at high altitude.

(*c*) Small wind vector errors will cause very large ground errors at high altitude with this type of sight.

In other words, the principle upon which the Mark XIV type of sight is based ceases to apply even approximately at altitudes over 25,000 ft. At heights greater than 25,000 ft. it is necessary to use a bombsight based upon different principles (*i.e.,* revert to the S.A.B.A., Mark IIA).

12. In July, 1943, No. 8 (PFF) Group completed a trial installation of the Mark XIVA bombsight in the nose of a Mosquito aircraft. During subsequent trials by B.D.U. it was found that the suction and pressure supply from the Pesco pumps were insufficient for satisfactory functioning of the sight at high altitude. R.A.E. investigated the problem and reported that sufficient suction up to 30,000 ft. could be obtained by using two electrically operated pumps, similar to those used in American aircraft when the complete T.I. sight is installed. With the two electric T.I. pumps, both the suction and pressure were found to be satisfactory up to an altitude of 30,000 ft.

13. The first Mark XIVA bombsights were provisioned for Mosquitos in August, 1944, and installed in Halifax on production in December, 1944. The Mark XIVA bombsight was a direct development from the Mark XIV with the following main improvements: —

(*a*) Increased height range to 25,000 ft.

(*b*) Instead of a computor peculiar to each aircraft (or group of aircraft) one type only was used and the correction to indicated airspeed for the particular aircraft, at present incorporated in the functioning of the airspeed blade was, on the Mark XIVA, made mechanically in the airspeed tape linkage. The kernel of this mechanism is a small corrector cam peculiar to each aircraft and quickly interchangeable without the need for any re-tuning.

(*c*) The maximum angle of climb for which the computor will compute correctly is increased from 5° to 11°.

(*d*) The follow-up rate of the sighting angle is increased from 2° to 3° per second to 1½° or perhaps 2° per second.

The main disadvantage of the Mark XVIA was that the windspeed limitation in the maximum speed setting on the Mark XIVA bombsight was not acceptable. In October, 1944, instructions for increasing the windspeed range from 77 miles per hour in the Mark XIVA bombsight were received from the Air Ministry. There were disadvantages in this modification. When the maximum wind-speed setting was increased above 65 miles per hour, either or both of the following may occur, dependent on the type of corrector cam fitted: —

(*a*) At low airspeeds with a large head wind, the computation of ground speed may be incorrect, due to the ground speed tape going slack.

(*b*) At high airspeeds with a large tail wind, the ground speed setting will be incorrect, in the case of the Halifax, Stirling and Wellington, assuming that the corrector cam was cut away in order to prevent the tape breaking.

This modification to the Mark XIVA bombsight was unacceptable to me for use in No. 8 (PFF) Group, and the Air Ministry agreed to the following bombsight installation: the increased pitch freedom computor unit (permitting a maximum windspeed setting of 77 miles per hour) suitably modified to incorporate the fast follow-up rate of the Mark XIVA computor unit. This combination caters for greater tactical freedom than the Mark XIVA computor.

T.I. Bombsights

14. The T.I. bombsight is an American-manufactured copy of the British Mark XIV bombsight and is thus identical with the Mark XIV bombsight in principle and differs from it only in minor details in design.

By the end of 1943 all Wellington operational squadrons in the Command were equipped with the T.I. bombsight, and in February, 1944, the first O.T.U. aircraft was fitted with the complete T.I. bombsight, replacing the Mark XIV sighting head installation.

T.I.A Bombsight

15. The T.I.A bombsight is the American version of the Mark XIVA. The two sights are functionally identical and differ in little but the method of construction.

This bombsight was first introduced into the Command in July, 1944, when Canadian-built Lancaster aircraft arrived from North America fitted with the T.I.A. sight.

In January, 1945, T.I.A bomb-sights were installed in Mosquito aircraft in place of the Mark XIVA sights. This was brought about by the shortage of Mark XIVA bombsights as the supply of these sights was being monopolised by the operational heavy bomber groups.

Stabilised Automatic Bombsights.

16. In the spring of 1943, the first stabilised automatic bombsights, Mark II, were installed in aircraft of No. 5 Group, replacing the automatic bombsight Mark II. The stabilised automatic bombsight Mark II is a direct development of the automatic bombsight Mark II. It is a precision sight and is more accurate and easier to use than the unstabilised bombsight. During the early part of the bomb run, when using the

automatic sight, the aircraft follows a curved path. The main disadvantage of the unstabilised sight is that a slight turn must be made for this part of the approach, for if the aircraft banks the bomb aimer sees the graticule move to the right or left of the target. With the stabilised sight, however, a correctly banked turn can be made because the sighting plane remains vertical. If the correct settings are made on the sight, the graticule remains on the target during the bombing run. During flight the attitude of the aircraft changes continuously, the nose continually rising or falling slightly. With the unstabilised bombsight, the bomb aimer may see the graticule move off the target and make the appropriate correction, although the correct setting may already have been made on the sight. This difficulty is not experienced with the stabilised sight as it is stabilised in pitch as well as in roll. The stabilised automatic bombsight is designed to work at an air pressure of 60 lb. per sq. in. With the original auto-control compressor the pressure given at 15,000ft. was only 45 to 50 lb., with a progressive decrease in pressure at higher altitudes. This imposed very grave tactical limitations on the bombsight and great difficulty was encountered in the provision of a compressor capable of producing pressure at high altitudes. It was not until the end of 1943, when the Arrow compressor first became available, that this problem was finally solved.

17. In February, 1943, 100 per cent. of the aircraft in Nos. 97 and 207 squadrons were equipped with this stabilised automatic bombsight, Mark II and Nos. 61, 83 and 106 squadrons each held three of these sights. The stabilised automatic bombsight, Mark II was for use in daylight against moving targets only, the automatic bombsight being the standard equipment for normal operations.

18. In February, 1943, I informed the Air Ministry that I proposed to discontinue the use of the stabilised automatic bombsight in Lancaster aircraft and to use the Mark XIV sight in its place. I had already decided that the Mark XIV bombsight would replace the automatic bombsight in the remainder of No. 5 Group squadrons. Reasons for the change of policy were as follows:—

(*a*) It was found impossible to keep bomb aimers in practice with the stabilised sight owing to operational and other training commitments.

(*b*) With the stabilised automatic bombsight, Mark II, it is necessary for aircraft to fly straight and level for the final approach on to the target.

(*c*) The R.A.E. compressor fitted in the sight was unreliable above 15,000 ft.

On the 26th May, 1943, the Air Ministry agreed to my proposal of withdrawing the stabilised automatic bombsight Mark II from the Command.

19. In August, 1943, I decided to equip No. 617 Squadron with the stabilised automatic bombsight Mark IIA and to train the squadron for precision bombing of selected targets.

The stabilised automatic bombsight, Mark IIA, was a development of the stabilised automatic bombsight, Mark II. Service trials of this bombsight, carried out by 617

Squadron, revealed that given good maintenance and well trained crews, a very high standard of accuracy could be obtained with this bombsight.

In June, 1944, I asked the Air Ministry to investigate a means of bombing off-set targets with this bombsight because against small targets it is frequently necessary to off-set the marker so that it may remain visible and not become obliterated by bomb bursts, smoke and debris. The Air Ministry replied emphasising the fact that the design of this type of sight is not such as to admit incorporation of a device for bombing an off-set target.

In June, 1944, three stabilised automatic bombsights, Mark IIA, were allotted to Nos. 83 and 97 Squadrons. It was proposed to use aircraft equipped with these bombsights to back up initial markers accurately placed by Mosquito aircraft. At the end of September, 1944, it was decided to withdraw the stabilised automatic bombsight Mark IIA from these two squadrons for transfer to No. 617 Squadron. This was largely due to the greatly improved methods of wind-finding which reduced the wind vector error to such an extent that the Mark XIVA bombsight proved sufficiently accurate for backing up markers.

At the time of the cessation of hostilities I had asked the Air Ministry to investigate the possibility of using the stabilised automatic bombsight in conjunction with an American type automatic pilot, and also the incorporation in the sighting head of a system of monocular magnification capable of being selected at will.

As a result of the operational experiences of No. 617 Squadron, various modifications were incorporated in the stabilised automatic bombsight Mark IIA, and by the end of hostilities in Europe it was possible for a well-trained crew to obtain an average error of 80 yards from 20,000 ft. when using this bombsight.

Low-Level (Angular Velocity) Bombsight, Mark III

20. In October, 1942, I informed the Air Ministry that there was a requirement for this sight in the Command. I requested that the development of the low-level bombsight Mark III be undertaken on high priority. The low-level bombsight Mark III was intended for use up to 1,000 ft. and was developed primarily for the bombing of submarines at low level. It was also considered effective for bombing land targets at low altitudes, a large amount of tactical freedom being allowed for by virtue of the fact that the line of sight is stabilised in pitch. On the graticule, which is an oblong piece of glass, are projected an endless series of lines at right angles to the track of the aircraft. The graticule is made to move by means of an electric motor which operates at a speed dependent on the aircraft's height and ground speed. On first viewing the target and moving lines together, the lines appear to be moving faster down the graticule than the target. But as the target's apparent speed increases there is an instant at which it moves at exactly the same rate as the lines and this is the release point.

In May, 1943, the low level bombsight, Mark III, was first installed in Boston aircraft of No. 2 Group.

The only heavy bombers to be equipped with this bombsight were the Lancaster aircraft of No. 617 Squadron. The sight was used successfully on a low level operation carried out by this Squadron in 1944, and this was the first and last occasion on which the low level bombsight Mark III was used operationally in heavy bomber aircraft. Coastal Command had absolute priority on the issue of this sight, though a few were obtained for use by No. 627 Squadron and Mosquito aircraft of No. 8 Group. This sight was little used operationally in the Command during the War, but had it been supplied prior to No. 2 Group's transfer to the Tactical Air Force it would have been of great operational value.

Conclusions.

21. The Mark XIV series bombsights contributed greatly to the improvement in the operational bombing accuracy of the Command during the War. With these sights it is possible for a well trained crew to produce an average error of 150 yards from 20,000 ft. The tactical freedom afforded made this bombsight the most suitable sight for the majority of the operations undertaken by this Command. Though not a precise bombsight like the stabilised automatic bombsight Mark IIA which was used for pinpoint bombing of specially selected targets, the Mark XIV proved to be the best compromise for general use.

The S.A.B.S., Mark IIA, in the hands of a skilled crew, proved itself to be extremely accurate, and invaluable in destroying vital pinpoint targets.

With both the Mark XIV series bombsights, and the stabilised automatic bombsights Mark IIA, design and maintenance troubles were encountered. A number of modifications had to be incorporated, and these, with efficient maintenance and well trained crews, overcame the difficulties and the sights on the whole functioned satisfactorily for the purposes for which they were intended.

SECTION VIII. BOMB DISTRIBUTORS

1. Designed to release bombs in a stick and to enable the bomb aimer to vary the time interval between release of consecutive stores at will, a bomb distributor is a most important item of aircraft bomb release gear.

At the beginning of 1942, two bomb distributors were in general use in the Command.

Hand Operated Bomb Distributor

2. This bomb distributor which was used in Blenheim aircraft, provided for variation of stick spacing by the manual operation of a contact arm moving across a row of

studs, the stick spacing being decided by the rate at which successive studs are contacted.

Automatic Bomb Distributor, Type VI

3. This distributor enables a stick of up to 16 bombs to be dropped at definite intervals to give even crater separation. On the face of the distributor is mounted a contact arm capable of automatic movement over segments numbers one to 16 and a rest position marked "H." In order to permit the release of bombs in any desired sequence and not consecutively, as when using the bomb distributor alone, a pre-selector unit was introduced into the bomb release circuit. The automatic bomb distributor Type VII, was introduced to cater for the release of a stick of up to 32 bombs. This distributor is similar in shape and operation to the Type VI, but has two rows of segments and two contact arms, one moving round after the other.

4. With the above type automatic distributors the maximum stick spacing obtainable was ·5 seconds, and when aiming mixed loads of H.E. and 4 lb. incendiary bombs it was necessary to make allowance for the variations in T.V. by arranging a delay between the time of release. This was catered for by the inclusion of a manual means of arresting the movement of the contact arm on any desired segment. It was then necessary for the air bomber to count the number of seconds delay required before allowing the contact arm to continue its travel over the remaining segments. This delay varied with heights of release and the types of H.E. bombs in the mixed load.

5. In March, 1943, R.A.E. demonstrated a 16-way bomb control unit designed to simplify control for both pilot and bomb aimer and to centralise this in one unit. In this unit automatic operation was used as much as possible to eliminate manipulation errors due to the necessity for a certain degree of avoidable pre-setting, re-setting and selection, especially during flight. This control unit also incorporated an automatic device to simplify the aiming of a mixed load. This was done by a pre-set time delay mechanism. Development proceeded on the new bomb control gear right up to the end of hostilities. In May, 1945, the latest versions of the above gear, namely the 12-24 point bomb distributors, were demonstrated at a meeting at the Ministry of Aircraft Production, where it was decided that after completion of trials at Boscombe Down, the prototype distributor would be given to Bomber Command for Service trials.

6. The automatic distributor, Type VIII, designed for flare release on P.F.F. aircraft, was also widely used in the Command during the War. This distributor provides for the release of a maximum of 14 flares at a spacing of 2, 4, 6 or 8 seconds. It is also possible to release one or two H.E. bombs at any time, independently of the release of the flare stick. Provision is made for the operation of a photo flash and camera time delay, simultaneously with the release of the first flare.

7. Prior to the cessation of hostilities, an automatic time delay unit for use with Types VI and VII distributors was under development at the Ministry of Aircraft Production. This automatic time delay unit has a range from 1-30 seconds and will

A portrait of Air Chief Marshal Sir Arthur Harris, Commander-in-Chief of Royal Air Force Bomber Command, seated at his desk at Bomber Command HQ, High Wycombe, 24 April 1944. (*HMP*)

A painting of Air Marshal Sir Arthur Harris that was completed circa 1943 at the instigation of the Ministry of Information. (*The National Archives*)

Air crew under training in 1939 as part of the expansion of Bomber Command. At the start of the Second World War, Bomber Command faced four problems. The first was lack of size; Bomber Command was not large enough to effectively attack the enemy as a pure, stand-alone strategic force. The second was rules of engagement; at the start of the war, the targets allocated to Bomber Command were not wide enough in scope. The third problem was the Command's lack of technology; specifically radio or radar derived navigational aids to allow accurate target location at night or through cloud. The fourth problem was the limited accuracy of bombing, especially from high level, even when the target could be clearly located by the bomb aimer. (*HMP*)

Ground crew work on a pair of mines in front of 300 (Masovian) Squadron's Vickers Wellington Mk.X, HF598 'BH-E', at RAF Ingham, Lincolnshire. Note the Polish checkerboard on the nose and the fact that the left hand mine has the message "From Polish Airmen" chalked on it. Of the 48,060 air-dropped mines laid off the northern and western coasts of Europe, 47,152 had been laid by Bomber Command – these were termed as *Gardening* sorties. For the loss of around 500 aircraft, these mines sank over 700 enemy-controlled ships (nearly 700,000 tons) and damaged over 550 more. This amounted to some 40% of all German-controlled shipping, more than twice the figure lost to Royal Navy surface and submarine forces (*ww2images*)

A line-up of 408 Squadron Handley Page Hampdens about to be loaded with Mk.I Air Deployable Anti-Ship mines, November 1942. The aircraft in the background of this picture, taken at RAF Leeming, North Yorkshire, is P1166, KE-Q. By the end of the war, Bomber Command had run up an impressive tally through its mine-laying work. Indeed, this could be considered one of the most successful campaigns of the Second World War. Every large, expensive enemy ship lost to mines cost the RAF 0.55 bombers. Compare this to the more well-known Coastal Command strike wings, which suffered 5.28 aircraft lost to every ship sunk while accounting for a smaller figure of 20% of German-controlled shipping losses. (*ww2images*)

A remarkable piece of wartime history, Avro Lancaster B Mk. VII NX611, *Just Jane*, is pictured being "bombed-up" at the Lincolnshire Aviation Heritage Centre at East Kirkby. Part of a batch of 150 B Mk VII Avro Lancasters destined to take part in the war against Japan as part of the RAF's Tiger Force in the Far East, Avro Lancaster B Mk. VII NX611 was built by Austin Motors at Longbridge near Birmingham, in April 1945. (*Courtesy of Gaz West*)

Taken on 2 June 1944, by a photo-reconnaissance aircraft from No.106 (PR) Group, this image shows a small part of Bomber Command's contribution to the D-Day landings. It reveals the severely damaged railway yards and junction (top right) at Saumur, France, after an attack by fifty-eight Avro Lancasters of No.5 Group on the night of 1/2 June 1944. Seven days later, aircraft of 617 Squadron attacked a nearby railway tunnel, dropping the first 12,000lb Tallboy bombs that had been developed by Barnes Wallis. (*HMP*)

Members of RAF ground crew prepare a Short Stirling for its next mission. Designed and built by Short Brothers to an Air Ministry specification from 1936, the Stirling entered service in 1941. It was the first British four-engine heavy bomber of the Second World War. The Stirling had a relatively brief front line operational career as a bomber, being relegated to second line duties from 1943 onwards when other four-engine bombers, such as the Halifax and Lancaster, began being delivered. However, the Stirling provided vital service as a glider tug and resupply aircraft during the D-Day landings and subsequent Allied operations in Europe during 1944-1945. (*HMP*)

Ground crew loading containers filled with propaganda leaflets – "Nickels" – into the bomb bay of a Vickers Wellington. The Nickeling effort reached its peak in August 1942, when some 72,500,000 leaflets were dropped in just four weeks. The increasing strength of Bomber Command was one factor, another was that the leaflets were by then being dropped from containers in bomb bays, making the task much easier. Two months later, Operational Training Units began to supply aircraft for Nickeling, providing crews with valuable operational experience (*HMP*)

One of many. This photograph shows the wreckage of an RAF bomber that was shot down near Hanover, though the exact date, location, and identity of the aircraft and crew is unknown. The picture was received in the UK on 26 August 1940 via the US Clipper news service, having been released for publication a few days earlier by the Germans. (*HMP*)

The Victoria Cross was awarded to no fewer than twenty-three airmen of Bomber Command during the Second World War. This drawing depicts part of the action for which Flight Lieutenant Roderick Learoyd, a pilot with the Handley Page-equipped 49 Squadron, was awarded his. On 12 August 1940, Learoyd was one of the pilots briefed to bomb the Dortmund-Ems Canal. Of the four other Hampdens which had already made the attack that night, two were destroyed and two were badly hit. Flight Lieutenant Learoyd took his aircraft into the target at only 150 feet, in the full glare of the searchlights and anti-aircraft barrage. His Hampden was badly damaged but the bombs were duly dropped and Learoyd managed to get his crippled 'plane back to Britain where he flew round until first light finally landing without causing injury to his crew or further damage to his aircraft. (*HMP*)

One of the many anti-aircraft guns that were deployed to defend the German capital against Allied bombers. This 10.5cm Flak 38 was located on the roof of what was known as the Zoo Flak Tower, a fortified anti-aircraft structure that was constructed in 1941. It was one of several flak towers that protected Berlin, its primary role being to help protect the government building district, as well as provide shelter space for civilians during air raids. (*Bundesarchiv, Bild 183-H27779/CC-BY-SA*)

The ruins of Berlin's Kaiser Wilhelm Memorial Church which is located on the Kurfürstendamm. The church was largely destroyed during an RAF raid on the night of 22/23 November 1943, though the tower, part of the spire and much of the entrance hall survived and are today a monument to the horrors of war. The raid that night was the most effective against Berlin so far undertaken by Bomber Command, which had despatched a force of 764 aircraft (469 Lancaster, 234 Halifaxes, 50 Stirlings and 11 Mosquitoes) to the German capital.

The burnt-out wreckage of a 37 Squadron Vickers Wellington, Mk.Ia P2515 (LF-H), after it was shot-down by flak during a leaflet-dropping, or *Nickel*, raid on the night of 23/24 March 1940. Having taken off from RAF Feltwell, the bomber crashed in flames in a wooded area of the Eifel Mountains in Western Germany. One member of the crew was killed in the crash – the Second Pilot, Sergeant D.W. Wilson – whilst the remainder were taken prisoner. However, the pilot, Flying Officer Paul F. Templeman, had sustained serious burns injuries from which he died on 31 March 1940. (*HMP*)

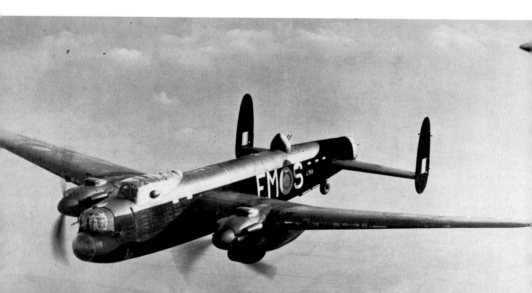

Avro Manchester L7515, 'EM-S', of 207 Squadron pictured during 1941 or 1942. First flying on 25 July 1939, and entering service in November 1940, the Manchester was an operational failure due to its underdeveloped, underpowered, and unreliable engines. However, the aircraft was the forerunner to the successful Avro Lancaster, which would become one of the more capable and famous bombers of the war. (*Courtesy of Mark Hillier*)

Many of Bomber Command's final missions of the Second World War were humanitarian. Operation *Manna*, for example, delivered vital aid to the people of Holland. By the end of the war in Europe large sections of the Dutch population, particularly in the big cities, were starving. By April 1945, for many the daily ration was just "two potatoes (often bad), three slices of bread, a small quantity of meat substitute and a slice of skimmed milk cheese" – barely enough to survive on. This image shows a 150 Squadron Lancaster, 'IQ-Y' (JB613), flying low over the flooded Dutch countryside en route to deliver food aid. (*ww2images*)

Huge quantities of water pour through the breach in the Möhne Dam a few hours after the Dams Raid – an image which clearly shows the depth of water which was lost following the attack. As a result of this breach some 335 million tons of water flooded the West Ruhr valleys. In its path, this flood destroyed 125 factories, made some 3,000 hectares of arable land useless, demolished twenty-five bridges and badly damaged twenty-one more. The attack on the Ruhr dams, Operation *Chastise*, is arguably one of Bomber Command's best known missions of the war. (*HMP*)

Avro Lancaster ED749 pictured during a War Savings Campaign in Manchester during early August 1945. ED749 was one of the last production batch of 620 aircraft completing the final part of contract No.B69247, and was one of 135 Mk.Is from this batch – the remainder were delivered as Mk.IIIs. The first examples reached the RAF in November 1942, the order completed in June 1943 with an average production rate of twenty-five aircraft per week. (*HMP*)

This vivid night photograph shows a Handley Page Halifax of No.4 Group RAF Bomber Command silhouetted against the glare of more incendiary fires, releasing its bomb load through cloud during a successful night raid on Leipzig on 3/4 December 1943. (*HMP*)

B

A

During a raid on Hamburg on the night of 30/31 January 1943, the Pathfinder crews of Nos. 7 and 35 squadrons, from No.8 Group Bomber Command, carried out the first operational use of H2S, the airborne, ground scanning radar system, using the new device to mark the target. Although H2S would later become a more effective device, its use was not successful during this attack, despite the fact that Hamburg, situated by the coast and on a prominent river, was considered an ideal H2S target. Bombing was scattered over a wide area, with most of the bombs falling in the River Elbe or in the surrounding marshes. The image seen here depicts one of the 135 Lancasters involved over the target. The original caption states that the "silhouette of the aircraft was formed by a photographic flash, but owing to prolonged exposure light tracks caused by fires (A) and light flak (B) were superimposed on the detail photographed by the flash". The pilot of the photographing aircraft, Lancaster 'ZN-Y' of 106 Squadron, was Flight Lieutenant D.J. Shannon who, as a member of 617 Squadron, took part in Operation *Chastise* (the "Dams Raid") the following May.

A bomb-damaged street in Hamburg, May 1945. The Battle of Hamburg, *Operation Gomorrah*, was a campaign of air raids that began on 24 July 1943, and lasted for eight days and seven nights. It was at the time the heaviest assault in the history of aerial warfare. The first attack on Hamburg included the first use of *Window*, small metallised strips, like tin foil, which when dropped from RAF bombers produced a gently drifting cloud of metallic strips that created confusing signals on German radar screens and concealed the position of the actual bombers. The results were dramatic. The entire German radar system was disrupted; British crews reported searchlights waving aimlessly, that the anti-aircraft fire was hesitant, and that the night-fighters were unusually ineffective. (*HMP*)

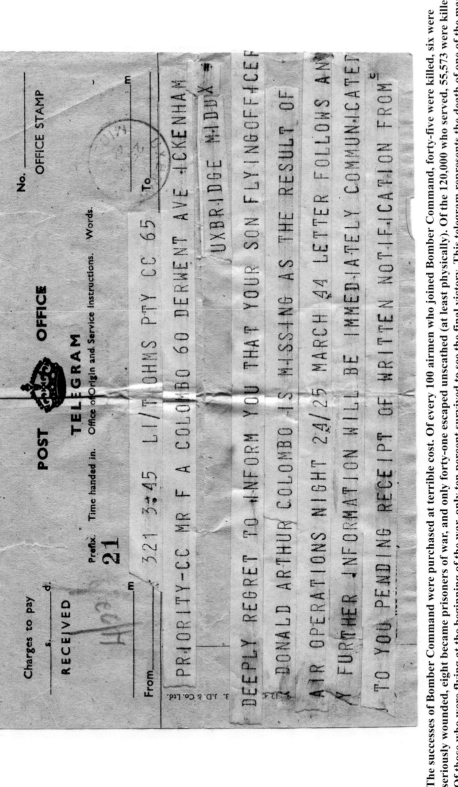

POST OFFICE TELEGRAM

Charges to pay
s.
d.
RECEIVED

Prefix. 21

Time handed in.

Office of Origin and Service Instructions. Words.

No.

OFFICE STAMP

From

To.

321 3.45 LI/T OHMS PTY CC 65

PRIORITY-CC MR F A COLOMBO 60 DERWENT AVE ICKENHAM

UXBRIDGE MIDDX =

DEEPLY REGRET TO INFORM YOU THAT YOUR SON FLYINGOFFICER

DONALD ARTHUR COLOMBO IS MISSING AS THE RESULT OF

AIR OPERATIONS NIGHT 24/25 MARCH 44 LETTER FOLLOWS AN

X FURTHER INFORMATION WILL BE IMMEDIATELY COMMUNICATED

TO YOU PENDING RECEIPT OF WRITTEN NOTIFICATION FROM ⸻

The successes of Bomber Command were purchased at terrible cost. Of every 100 airmen who joined Bomber Command, forty-five were killed, six were seriously wounded, eight became prisoners of war, and only forty-one escaped unscathed (at least physically). Of the 120,000 who served, 55,573 were killed. Of those who were flying at the beginning of the war, only ten percent survived to see the final victory. This telegram represents the death of one of the many aircrew who made the ultimate sacrifice: Lancaster navigator Flying Officer Donald Arthur Colombo. Donald was killed on 25 March 1944, whilst serving with 12 Squadron. The son of Frederick Alfred and Gertrude Louisa Colombo, of Ickenham, Uxbridge, Middlesex, he is buried in Berlin 1939-1945 War

The city of Nuremberg was severely damaged by Allied bombing between 1943 and 1945. On 2 January 1945, the medieval city centre was systematically bombed by the RAF and USAAF, and about ninety percent of it was destroyed in only one hour. The attacks killed 1,800 residents and roughly 100,000 were displaced. In February 1945, additional attacks followed. In total, about 6,000 Nuremberg residents are estimated to have been killed in air raids. (*NARA*)

The devastated German city of Wesel pictured in May 1945, its centre completely destroyed by Allied bombing. Particularly because of the town's strategic position with bridges on the Rhine, Wesel soon found itself a target of the RAF and USAAF. The former, for example, undertook several attacks in February and March 1945. It was reported that 97% of the town was destroyed before it was finally taken by Allied troops and the population had fallen from almost 25,000 in 1939 to 1,900 in May 1945. Following the capture of Wesel, Field Marshal Montgomery stated that "the bombing of Wesel was a masterpiece, and was a decisive factor in making possible our entry into the town before midnight." (*HMP*)

The most controversial attack undertaken by Bomber Command during the war was that on Dresden. In four raids between 13 and 15 February 1945, 722 RAF and 527 USAAF bombers dropped more than 3,900 tons of bombs on the city, which at the time was the seventh largest in Germany and the largest un-bombed built-up area left. The resulting firestorm destroyed fifteen square miles of the city centre; between 22,000 and 25,000 people were killed (an investigation conducted in 2010 on behalf of the Dresden city council stated that a maximum of 25,000 people were killed, of which 20,100 are known by name). Post-war debate of whether or not the attacks were justified has led to the bombing becoming one of the moral *cause célèbres* of the war. (*Courtesy of Deutsche Fotothek*)

A low-level oblique aerial photograph showing the damage caused to Frankfurt during the Second World War. By the time of the German surrender, the once famous medieval city centre (seen here with the Cathedral in the foreground), then the largest in Germany, had been destroyed. After the war, the official assessment of the damage caused to this city by the RAF and USAAF stated that between one and two thousand acres had been devastated. (*HMP*)

Pictured on 11 April 1945, RAF officers inspect an unfinished siege gun in a wrecked building of the Krupps armaments works at Essen, Germany, a principal target for Bomber Command throughout the war. The Krupps AG works at Essen, Germany, was seriously damaged by Bomber Command in 1943, and further wrecked in the daylight raid of 11 March 1945. (*HMP*)

A memorial dedicated to the men of 158 Squadron was unveiled in the village of Lissett, Yorkshire, on 17 May 2009. It depicts a life-size seven-man crew of a Halifax Bomber and has been cast in the same metal as the Angel of the North. The memorial carries the name of each of the 851 men from the squadron who were killed in operations during the Second World War. The squadron, which operated Halifaxes in Bomber Command for most of the war, was stationed at the No.4 Group airfield at Lisset between 28 February 1943 and 17 August 1945. (*HMP*)

The memorial to Marshal of the Royal Air Force Sir Arthur Harris BT, GCB, OBE, AFC, which is located in the Strand, London, outside St Clement Danes, the Central Church of the RAF. It was unveiled in 1992 by the Queen. (*HMP*)

Thousands of Bomber Command veterans and their relatives together with twelve members of the Royal family were present as Her Majesty the Queen unveiled the Bomber Command Memorial in London's Green Park on 28 June 2012. Made from Portland stone, the Memorial, a model of which is seen here, was designed by architect Liam O'Connor.

The human cost of the Allied bombing campaign against targets in Europe was high, with estimates of the number of civilian casualties varying (depending on source) between 600,000 and 1 million. Taken by a British soldier in August 1945, his image shows the last resting place of just a few of the civilian casualties from the Allied attacks on Hamburg. (*HMP*)

The central bronze sculpture, created by Philip Jackson, which, depicting seven airmen, lies at the heart of the Bomber Command Memorial in Green Park. Above them a small section of the Memorial is open to the sky, allowing light to fall directly on the aircrew. For Bomber Command the deaths in action began with the loss of Wellingtons and Blenheims on the night of 3/4 September 1939, and ceased more than five and a half years later, after two Halifaxes from 199 Squadron at North Creake and a Mosquito from 169 Squadron at Great Massingham failed to return on the night of 2/3 May 1945. (www.shutterstock.com)

provide a mechanical means of accurately releasing a mixed stick of high and low terminal velocity stores using the Types VI and VII distributors.

SECTION IX. – PYROTECHNICS

Pathfinder Force – Pyrotechnics

1. With the establishment in August, 1942, of a specialised Pathfinder Force, an entirely new principle was applied to night bombing. The finding and marking of the target became the duty of a number of specially selected and trained crews whose task it was to provide a clearly visible aiming point for the remainder of the bombing force. Throughout the period that followed there was a race between the Development Branches in this country, and those of the enemy, who made every effort to produce imitations of each new pyrotechnic device produced by us, so that he might use decoy markers and divert the weight of bombs from vital targets. In this race, thanks to the Ministry of Aircraft Production, we always had a lead, even if at times only a short one. This lead was an essential to the success of pathfinding technique. Between 1942 and the end of the War over 40 different types of flares and marker bombs, in many different colour variations, were used.

2. In the preliminary stages of the development of this new technique 4·5-in. recce. flares were used in very large quantities with the idea of providing that the whole target area would be so illuminated that the main force could identify the exact aiming point. These flares were carried in a variety of ways until the adoption of the S.B.C. Mark IA, which carried four flares.

3. In order to increase bombing concentration, large quantities of incendiary bombs were dropped as early as possible in an attack to develop large, concentrated fires for following crews to aim at. With this in view, the 4 lb. incendiary was supplemented by the benzol-rubber-phosphorus filled 250 lb. incendiary and later by the "Pink Pansy" – a 4,000 lb. H.C. bomb case filled with the same mixture, but coloured so that the initial flash was of a brilliantly distinctive pink colour. This bomb, owing to the lower density of the filling, weighed only 2,800 lb.

4. For certain types of target which were capable of being attacked by OBOE aircraft, the marking method was supplemented by another technique, that of skymarking, in which case coloured flares, some with stars of contrasting colours, were dropped in various codes. The sky markers were to be so placed that bombs aimed at them by aircraft on a fixed heading would fall in the target area, and although this method could not give accuracy of visual bombing at this stage, it did allow attacks to be made on nights when, owing to cloud cover, visual bombing was absolutely impossible.

5. On the 16th January, 1943, during an attack on Berlin, the first target indicator bombs were dropped. These bombs, later developed in a great variety of forms, formed the basis on which all the ground marking techniques were built up. The T.I.

bomb consists basically of a case of good ballistic properties, from which at a given height above the ground pyrotechnic candles are ejected. These are ignited on ejection and either fall to the ground in a brilliantly luminous cascade and burn out there; or else lie dormant during the cascade-and-burning period, lighting up only when the first candles are going out. The height of burst was controlled by a barometric fuze, which, theoretically, irrespective of the height of release, ejected and ignited the contents of the bomb at the given height above sea level. The contents normally scattered over an area of about 100 yards diameter for each 250 lb. bomb. The difference that this bomb made to the concentration was enormous and together with OBOE it may justly be said to have ensured the overwhelming success of the Battle of the Ruhr the smoke and haze filled valleys of which had hidden so well the vital armaments works they contained.

6. T.I. bombs were used initially in the double role of guides to approaching aircraft and as indicators of the exact aiming point. Functioned at heights up to 9,000 ft. or more, the cascade of burning candles was visible from great distances and this was a feature that the enemy was never entirely successful in simulating, although he later produced some creditable imitations of the candles burning on the ground. In another form, the Spot Fire, which gave a single spot of red or green light of moderate intensity, the bomb was extensively used for route marking, providing the equivalent of a lighthouse to the bomber stream on their long outward and homeward flights over occupied Europe.

Explosive candles were introduced into the bombs to discourage fire fighters and, at different times, various lengths of delay were incorporated in the pyrotechnic candles so that, at the expense of some intensity, the marker could be capable of longer duration.

Yet another form consisted of 25 candles, each with its own parachute, giving a candelabra effect, and was mainly used for skymarking. It was, however, also used on a few occasions for illumination purposes; in that application only the yellow colour proved effective.

7. Outside the range of OBOE visual methods were, however, still needed. As a consequence, a hooded flare was, after many trials and tribulations, developed which succeeded in eliminating most of the upward glare experienced with the old 4·5 in. Recce. flare. At first used singly, a cluster mechanism was quickly developed for these flares which enabled the effective illumination of targets to be enormously increased in spite of a reduction in the total candle-power employed. The clusters had to be assembled and filled with flares at stations and this work imposed a very severe additional strain on armament staffs. Each cluster took some 25 minutes to prepare and as many as ninety clusters were used by a single squadron on one night and the process repeated on following nights as well.

8. As time went on, the enemy's attempts at simulation became more and more effective. The colours red, yellow and green were already in use as marking colours, and blue proved, after a long series of experiments, to be impossible to obtain in sufficient intensity, tending always to be confused with the intense white of the 4 lb. incendiary. The only alternative course therefore was to swamp all such attempts at

"spoofing" by employing markers in such quantity or of such size that no mistake should be possible. Accordingly the 1,000 lb. T.I. bomb was developed in order more economically to fill the Lancaster bomb stowages. This bomb more than trebled the number of candles carried on each bomb station, and promised extremely well. Unfortunately, when with the strengthening of the enemy defences bombing heights increased, it was found that some weapons which had been ballistically stable and accurate from the lower heights were far from satisfactory at the greater heights. The 1,000 lb. T.I. was one of the worst sufferers in this respect.

9. Designed to give operational freedom in height of attack to Pathfinder crews, the barometric fuze, which had up till now been used as a nose fuze, was now developed as a tail fuze with the idea of giving a greater range and greater accuracy of bursting height. This tail version proved to be especially subject to interference from ballistic causes. An oscillating bomb was found to burst completely unpredictably as to height. These defects were partially overcome by the fitting of the now old-fashioned long tail as originally designed for the 1,000 lb. H.E. bombs and the continuation in use of the nose fuze (No. 860). This had the effect, however, of limiting the available load in a Lancaster to 6 x 1,000 lb. T.I.s + 4 x 500 lb. bombs or 4 x 1,000 lb. T.I.s and 4 x 1,000 lb. bombs. As, however, the German decoy efforts became disorganised and sporadic the necessity for "swamping" was less acute.

10. From D Day onwards the need for markers for use by day became of increasing importance and still more new versions of the T.I. bomb came to the fore as a result. In the early stages, smoke fillings, especially yellow smoke, were employed to mark targets and later to serve as cancellation signs to countermand any markers that might fall too close to our own front line troops. A difficulty with these large scale day attacks was the vast clouds of dust and smoke which quickly obscured the whole target area and the markers burning on the ground. To deal with this, and also to assist in blind bombing by day, a pigment-filled marker was produced which also met with very considerable success. These left a puff of coloured dust in the air which was remarkably distinctive and persistent. It could be used as an aiming mark in favourable conditions for over two minutes after functioning. Red, yellow, green and (at last) blue colours were available and were selected according to the nature of the expected background.

11. Yet another version of the T.I. was in constant use by the Mosquito bombing force on their nightly visits to Berlin. This bomb, besides a somewhat reduced number of the usual pyrotechnic candles, also contained a photoflash and some remarkable photographs were obtained by this means from aircraft flying as high as 35,000 ft. These Mosquitos also had their own navigational problems and a special route-marker device was developed for them, consisting of a special Verey pistol cartridge of greater intensity and duration than the normal. This was produced in the usual three colours enabling turning points to be effectively marked without risk of confusion and, more important still, without sacrificing a bomb station.

12. The last marking requirement for a marker was to aid supply-dropping operations. For these, ordinary T.I. bombs were used from which the explosive candles had been removed. It may be noted that on the first of these operations, which

took place before the end of hostilities, there had not been time to remove the explosive candles and one marker fell on the grandstand at The Hague racecourse, which was one of the dropping zones for that day, and to the delight of the local populace burnt it to the ground, complete with the great stores of German equipment it contained. It may also be noted that although on these operations the supplies were dropped from as low as 300 ft., the marking was, for accuracy's sake, done from 30,000 ft.

13. The development and supply of P.F.F. pyrotechnic stores between 1942 and the end of the War was most satisfactory, and contributed in no small degree to the increased effectiveness of the Command. Although these stores were used primarily by No. 8 (P.F.F.) Group many of them were also widely used by all the Main Force Groups.

Photographic Flashes

14. By the beginning of 1942, the standard items of armament equipment used in connection with night photography were:—

(i) The 4·5-in. Photographic Flash, Mark II.
(ii) The No. 848 Fuze.
(iii) The Tri-Cell Chute.

The use of this equipment helped to overcome previous troubles by providing armour-plated protection for the flash and greater reliability of functioning and accuracy of timing in the fuze. The release of the flash was effected through the bomb release wiring system, and until the end of 1942, had been timed so as to obtain a photograph of the bomb bursts. At this time, however, it was decided that night photography should be used to pinpoint the position of the aircraft at the instant of release.

15. The great concentrations of aircraft (each with its photographic flash) and other light sources below the aircraft led to a stated requirement for a more accurate fuze. This would permit a reduction in the "open frame" time of the camera. In the middle of 1943 trials were carried out with the American M-111 (Clockwork) Fuze. As a result it was possible to cut down the "open frame" time from 8 to 4 seconds. This fuze was then in short supply unfortunately, but by the end of 1943 it was available in sufficient quantities to permit full scale introduction.

16. The casing of the 4·5-in. flash, which was identical to that of the 4·5-in. Reconnaissance Flare had very unreliable ballistics. In order to overcome this trouble, a High Terminal Velocity (H.T.V.) Flash was designed and became known as the Mark III. It had a T.V. of 585 f.p.s. as against 270 f.p.s, of the previous marks of flashes. Also, the Mark III flash contained a filling, less vulnerable to flak. M.G. and cannon fire. Unfortunately, this filling lowered the light intensity of the flash itself, but after further experiment, the Mark III* flash was evolved. This had a different filling in the central tube (T.N.T./A1, 70/30) and in trials gave excellent results. By using the H.T.V. flash it was possible to carry out level flight photography as no

camera tilt was necessary in order to allow for the excessive trail of the flash as was previously the case. The introduction of the Mark III* came too late to permit of its use operationally.

17. Another attempt to give better aimability and to permit carriage of a flash on Mosquito (OBOE) aircraft, in which no flash-chute is fitted, was that of placing a photographic flash inside the casing of a 250-lb. T.I. bomb. This was done by removing 20 candles from the T.I. Excellent results were obtained, as it gave a true position of the T.I. candles. This benefit was obtained without sacrifice of H.E. bomb stowage, but a type of combined T.I. and flash of this kind was required only for P.F.F. purposes.

18. The timing of camera operation in relation to flash explosion was one of the major problems in night photography and in order to eliminate the inconsistent time lag between release of flash and operation of camera, two new launching chutes have been designed. These are the Tri-cell, Mark III and the Single Chute, Mark V. Both incorporate a time lag eliminating device which ensures that the operation of the camera cannot commence until the flash has actually left the chute. Neither of these chutes were introduced for Service use before the end of the war.

19. In May, 1944, there was an operational requirement for low level oblique night photography in order to permit photographing of T.I. cascades and ground detail of the area on which they would fall. This requirement was met by using 1½-in. photographic flash cartridges, fired from the photoflash discharger, the latter being fired electrically and controlled through an automatic bomb distributor. Release spacing was normally set at ·8 seconds. The photographic flash cartridge gives a peak illumination of approximately 10,000,000 candle power, which is attained 3 milli-seconds after initiation; 75 per cent. of the light is emitted in a period of 4 milli-seconds.

SECTION X. – AIRCRAFT MINES

1. Aircraft mines were introduced to meet a requirement for the laying of non-contact ground mines, in the vast and important areas where minelaying surface craft could not operate. They are basically similar to mines carried in M.T.B.s but are modified in order to give added protection to the internal mechanism on impact with water at comparatively high striking velocities. To be aimable, a fairly high T.V. is essential, but the stores are equipped with a parachute to keep the striking velocity within practical limits. All aircraft mines have been developed and supplied by Naval sources, and many different firing mechanisms have been produced to defeat the enemy's countermeasures. A total of 45,490 mines was laid by this Command from January, 1942, until the cessation of hostilities in the European theatre, and these played havoc with the enemy's shipping. Lancaster and Stirling aircraft carried loads of up to six 1,500-lb. mines, without any modification to the aircraft.

2. Early in 1942, I decided to concentrate on the 1,000-lb. version for use in Halifax aircraft, as it was uneconomical to use this aircraft for the carriage of 1,500-lb. mines.

Later a modification was designed which enabled this aircraft to carry a load of four of the lighter mines. The carrier used for this modification was a converted No. 3 heavy Handley Page carrier, but owing to its size and weight it caused many complications during loading. During 1944, an adaptor was designed which simplified the carriage of all types of mines in this aircraft.

3. With the introduction of the Mosquito aircraft, a standard mine was adapted by the Armament personnel of this Command, in conjunction with specialist naval officers of H.M.S. "Vernon," the direct result of which was the bottling up of many thousands of tons of enemy shipping in the Kiel Canal prior to "D" Day.[1]

4. The main types of mines used during the European operations were:—

(i) Single Contact Magnetic Ground Mines.
(ii) Double Contact Magnetic Ground Mines.
(iii) Oscillating Mines.
(iv) Acoustic Mines.
(v) Anti-sweep Mines.
(vi) Nose-contact Mines.
(vii) Impact Mines.

5. In order to defeat mine sweeping by the enemy and to guard against counter-mining, a number of devices were produced which could be incorporated in the firing systems. The principal devices used were as follows:—

(a) *Period Delay Mechanism.* – This was used as an anti-sweeping device to ensure that the firing circuit remains inoperative until it has been actuated a required number of times.

(b) *Mechanical Delay.* – This ensures that the firing of the mine is delayed sufficiently to allow of it actuating below the target ship.

(c) *Anti-Counter Mining Switch.* – This switch was used to prevent the mine being actuated should the enemy attempt to destroy the field by counter-mining and to prevent the destruction of the field should a neighbouring mine be functioned.

(d) *Electric Arming Clock.* – This clock renders the mine incapable of actuation until a pre- determined time after laying. The expiration of this period closes the firing circuit and renders the mine "live."

(e) *Sterilizers.* – These are incorporated in the firing systems to limit the life of a mine to a predetermined period.

SECTION XI. – TURRETS, GUNS AND AMMUNITION

Introduction

1. In reviewing the defensive armament of heavy bombers used in Bomber Command between February, 1942, and May, 1945, it is necessary for reasons of clarity to state the operational Groups that were in existence during the period, and the various types of aircraft used on operations. Details of the defensive armament carried by the various types of aircraft are attached at Annexure "B." A summary of operational aircraft is at Annexure "A."

2. The defensive armament of the types of aircraft in use in Bomber Command in 1942 hardly differed from the original specifications laid down in 1936. In the main, the defensive armament of all aircraft in 1942 consisted of a combination of turret-mounted and hand-held guns, all of ·303 in. calibre. An exception was the limited number of American aircraft equipped with ·50 in. guns which were used in No. 2 Group during the period under review. The introduction of the ·5-in. gun with American aircraft was, as events were to prove, the only occasion during the war in Europe in which aircraft carrying ·5 in. armament as standard equipment were supplied for operational use in Bomber Command. Towards the end of the war against Germany, a very limited number of ·5-in. guns, both turret-mounted and hand-held, were in use in British aircraft, but this increase in the calibre of the guns became available to Bomber Command solely through the efforts made by the Command itself as the officially designed turrets were not ready in time.

3. With the arrival of the Lancaster aircraft in Bomber Command in March, 1942, the numbers of four engine aircraft operating against Germany steadily increased. As was expected, the German High Command, to meet this growing bombing offensive, deployed an increased number of both twin and single engine night fighters against our heavy bombers, in addition to increasing their flak defences. The German night fighter was provided with heavy protective armour and carried guns of larger calibre than those fitted to our bombers. As a result, the ·303-in. guns became largely ineffective, since the enemy fighters armour plate could not be penetrated at normal fighting ranges, while at the same time the German fighter, by virtue of carrying larger calibre guns, could outrange our bombers on all occasions.

4. I have always maintained that the defensive armament of our heavy bombers was insufficient. A continuous flow of recommendations (some dating since, 1940), have been submitted to the Air Ministry, covering such aspects as the vital need for improved view from turrets, the provision of four instead of two guns in dorsal and tail positions, and the need for larger calibre guns was continually stressed. By the end of 1942, I had reached the conclusion, that if turrets were to be worth carrying they should possess the following characteristics:—

(*a*) The gunner must be provided with an uninterrupted field of view.

(*b*) Guns mounted in turrets must be of sufficient calibre to penetrate the armour plate fitted to German fighters when engaged at normal fighting ranges.

(*c*) Turrets should be so designed that the gunner could escape in emergency (irrespective of the position in which the turret is installed) without having to depend on power supply from the aircraft engines.

(*d*) Adequate means of heating the turret should be provided in order to prevent the guns and turret components from freezing up, and to keep the gunner reasonably warm and so maintain his efficiency.

5. In August, 1942, the Air Ministry informed me that the provision of four-gun mid-upper turrets for Stirling, Halifax, and Lancaster aircraft was being pushed ahead, but they would not be available for use by Bomber Command before August, 1943. It was also stated that the introduction of two 20 mm. guns into the dorsal turret of Lancaster aircraft was not feasible because of the C.G. consideration. In September, 1942, I again stressed the necessity for the provisioning of tail and dorsal turrets carrying ·5-in. guns and the installation of the Gyro gun sight. This was followed up in January and February, 1943, when I wrote to the Air Ministry expressing disappointment with the lack of attention being paid to visibility from turrets, and urging that turrets carrying heavier calibre guns than ·303-in. should be designed with proper regard to the gunner's field of view. The Air Ministry informed me that the F.N. 20 turret had been extensively modified to improve vision at the expense of 75 per cent. of the armour protection. I was asked to agree to this modification in order that the work could be used as a basis for the design and production of ·5-in. tail turrets. At this time F.N. tail turrets installed in aircraft of Bomber Command were modified under Command instructions to provide a better field of view. This modification involved the removal of a large section of the perspex cupola, thus providing a large direct vision opening in the rear of the turret.

6. In March, 1943, I inspected the first mock-up of a new proposed British ·5-in. tail turret, namely the F.N. 82 and I stated that this design in no way met the requirements of the Command. I said, however, that I would reluctantly accept that design as an interim measure, pending the development of a turret which would meet the requirements of the Command in respect of vision, etc. I requested the Air Ministry to develop such a turret on high priority. Following further representations to the Chief of the Air Staff, a conference was called by the Air Ministry in June, 1943, to investigate turret development policy. As a result of this conference, a desperate attempt was made to improve the rearward and downward view from existing tail turrets by removing the Servo Feed and the two inner guns from the four-gun F.N. 120 turret. The ammunition capacity for the two remaining guns was reduced to 500 rounds per gun, and the turret was renamed the F.N. 220. The calibre of the guns still remained ·303-in. This turret was never put into production, as I stated in October, 1943, that as the F.N. 121, though unsatisfactory, was considered superior, every effort should be made to get this turret into production with the minimum of delay.

7. Owing to the lack of progress in the design of tail turrets with ·5-in. guns, *i.e.,*

the F.N. 82 and the B.P. Type "D," I directly encouraged Messrs. Rose Brothers of Gainsborough, who, with the assistance of Bomber Command personnel, designed and produced a tail turret carrying two ·5-in. guns. This turret possessed novel features in that the controls were of a design which differed from the standard F.N. or B.P. systems, and apart from carrying ·5-in. guns, provided a large field of view, since the rear portion of the cupola was left open as a direct vision opening. Furthermore, escape from this turret was extremely easy, as the direct vision opening was sufficiently large to allow the air gunner to leave the turret via the opening in the cupola. The Rose turret was introduced into operational use in Bomber Command in July, 1944, and at the end of the German War, 180 of these turrets had been built and installed in Lancaster aircraft of No. 1 Group. The design, progressing, and introduction of the Rose turret into Bomber Command was entirely due to the efforts of the Command itself, and in particular of A.O.C. No. 1 Group, although, towards the later stages assistance was provided by the Ministry of Aircraft Production, which arranged for the production of certain component parts by firms other than Messrs. Rose Brothers.

8. As a result of further communications with the Air Ministry during the autumn of 1944, on the whole subject to heavy bomber defensive armament, a meeting was called on the 22nd November, 1944, under the chairmanship of the C.A.S., to review the position. At this meeting it was stated that the introduction of the new type turrets was nine months behind schedule, but that every effort was being made to get this equipment into Bomber Command aircraft with the minimum of delay. The question of rendering assistance to Rose Brothers in the production of the Rose turret was also discussed, together with problems in connection with tail turret heating. A plan was also made for the allocation of the new type turrets to the different types of aircraft.

Under Defence

9. Originally, an under turret known as the F.N. 64 had been provided by the Air Ministry in limited numbers for use in Stirling, Halifax and Lancaster aircraft. The turret was not used on operations for the following reasons:—

(*a*) It proved useless for night work as it employed periscopic sighting.

(*b*) No means were provided for the gunner to determine in which direction his guns were pointing, relative to the direction in which his own aircraft was proceeding. The position originally provided for this under turret was later occupied by various Radar devices.

As an alternative, however, a single ·5-in. gun mounting was designed and introduced into the Command for use in aircraft not carrying special Radar equipment, and this under defence gun was used on operations to a limited extent in Lancaster aircraft of No. 3 Group, and in Halifax aircraft of Nos. 4 and 6 (R.C.A.F.) Groups.

Vulnerability of Turrets

10. Between 1942 and 1945 a careful check was maintained of all incidents in which turrets were damaged either by flak or fire from enemy aircraft. These records were later analysed, and it was proved that turrets operated hydraulically, such as the F.N. 120, were between seven and thirteen times more vulnerable to damage and fire, than turrets operated electro-hydraulically, such as the B.P. turrets fitted to Halifax aircraft. As a result of these findings I recommended to Air Ministry that future designs of turrets should be entirely operated by electrical means.

Heating of Guns and Turrets

11. Soon after the outbreak of the War in 1939, it became apparent that heating of guns and turrets was a necessity in order to maintain the efficiency of the air gunners. Progress concerning introduction of an efficient heating system in turrets was most unsatisfactory. Despite my continued representations, it was not until 1944 that any real progress was made. Briefly, the requirements as regards heating of guns and turrets divided itself into two distinct channels—

(*a*) the provision of electrical gun heaters for fitment to the guns themselves;
(*b*) the provision of heat to the turret as a whole.

Gun heaters became available in quantity in 1944, but they did not solve the problem in so far as Lancaster aircraft were concerned, since this aircraft was equipped with the F.N. tail turret, which in order to afford a reasonable field of view, was used with the rear of the cupola removed. Moreover, the number of electrical gun heaters that could be used in Lancaster aircraft was limited by the power supply. In the case of the Halifax, adequate power supplies were available, and as this aircraft was equipped with the B.P. "E" turret fitted with an adjustable direct vision panel, the problem of keeping the guns warm was simplified.

11A. The supply of heat to turrets as a whole was an involved problem. A British designed turret heater, known as the Gallay, was given extensive trials by the Ministry of Aircraft Production, but it was finally turned down in 1944. Development was eventually undertaken to supply heat to the turrets by ducting heat from the main aircraft engines to the mid-upper and tail positions. The first aircraft with ducted heating fitted was received in Bomber Command in August, 1944, and the number of Lancasters so fitted gradually increased, until at the cessation of hostilities approximately 50 per cent. of the Lancaster aircraft in use at that time were so fitted. Trials were also put in hand to provide turret heating for Halifax aircraft. In this instance, use was made of an American heater known as the Janitrol. It was hoped that if this heater proved successful, it would be fitted to all Halifax aircraft. But as the embodiment of this heater took 200 man hours, it was accordingly decided that no retrospective fitting could be undertaken in respect of Halifax aircraft, Marks VI and VII, although it was agreed that Halifax aircraft should be fitted with the Janitrol heater on the production line. However, as the war against Germany drew to a close, the installation of the heaters in Halifax aircraft was dropped, as it was known that this aircraft would not be used in Bomber Command after the cessation of hostilities.

When the war ended, the situation in regard to heaters was that gun heaters (of limited efficiency) were available; about half the Lancasters were equipped with ducted heating; but Halifax aircraft were still lacking in heating for the tail turret.

A.G.L. (T) (Automatic Gun Laying (Turrets))

12. During night combats, the Fighter invariably has the advantage over the bomber for the following reasons: the fighter having the initiative, can select his line of approach; the bulk of the bomber is at least twice that of the fighter and visual range is about proportional to bulk, with the consequence that the fighter always sees the bomber at three times the range at which the bomber can see the fighter and is then enabled to make a surprise attack. Moreover, the fighter usually approaches from below. He is therefore against a dark background, while the bomber is silhouetted against the sky. In addition, many fighters have A.I. and can approach the bomber without visual contact. Therefore a means of providing early warning to a bomber of a fighter's approach is a requirement of vital importance. Numerous Radar devices which give this warning have been developed by T.R.E. but not with clear definition of the line and range of approach.

During October, 1942, representatives of this Command, during a visit to T.R.E., were shown an experimental backward-looking A.I. device with which, it was hoped, blind firing would be possible. The vital importance of A.G.L. (T) to this Command was immediately apparent, and a letter was at once sent to the Air Ministry stressing the great need for A.G.L. (T). To obtain an early introduction of A.G.L. (T) into the Command, the Air Ministry agreed to a "Crash Programme" of 100 sets of A.G.L. (T) to be fitted in a modified F.N. 120 turret renumbered F.N. 121. Starting early in 1944, this programme was scheduled to begin well before the main A.G.L. (T) installation thus enabling large-scale operational trials to be made.

13. I decided that the crash programme aircraft should go into two main force squadrons, armed with H.2.S. Lancasters. The selected squadrons were No. 460 Squadron, Binbrook and No. 49 Squadron, Fiskerton of Nos. 1 and 5 Groups, respectively; and trainers for them were installed by the R.A.E., Farnborough. In the meantime, the B.D.U., Newmarket, had started intensive trials on the first prototype A.G.L. (T) installation in a Lancaster aircraft. Although a few "teething" problems were encountered by the B.D.U., trials in the first place proved highly satisfactory, although various modifications for tactical and technical reasons were suggested and, in most cases, incorporated.

It was clear, however, that some efficient method of identification between friend and foe was vital. It was expected that far more contacts with friendly bombers would be obtained with A.G.L. (T) than contacts with enemy aircraft, and unless identification was nearly 100 per cent. efficient it appeared certain that the bomber losses would increase rather than decrease with the advent of A.G.L. (T).

14. The identification problem was tackled promptly, but no form of positive identification was found. The alternative, negative identification, where the friend must prove himself friend, increases the necessity for greater efficiency and for some extremely simple and efficient means of identification. The B.D.U. working in conjunction with the R.A.E. and the A.R.L. devised the present Type "Z" equipment. Briefly, these equipments require the whole bomber force to be fitted with I.R. transmitters and for all A.G.L. (T) aircraft to have an I.R. telescope aligned with the sight. Identification was then assured by coded transmission which the gunner in the A.G.L. (T) aircraft was able to read.

15. The first twelve aircraft of the crash programme were fitted A.G.L. (T) at S.I.U. Defford, the remainder by No. 32 M.U. On 16th March, 1944, the first aircraft arrived at Binbrook. By the end of March, 1944, the B.D.U. had not received the vital harmonisation gear for A.G.L. (T). Since considerable unreliability had been experienced with prototype gear in the latter part of the trial, it was agreed to fit two production Type A.G.L. (T) sets to the two B.D.U. aircraft; on the return of these two aircraft with the production type sets, serviceability of A.G.L. (T) fell to a very low level. I issued instructions on 1st April, 1944, that no further aircraft should be fitted with A.G.L. (T) until the troubles experienced by the B.D.U. had been cleared, and Air Ministry were informed of this decision by signal and letter of the 1st and 2nd April, 1944, (BC/S. 30373/Armt refers). It was decided to form a special flight within the B.D.U. so that reliability trials could be completed as quickly as possible on the six production type aircraft, and that, as soon as A.G.L. (T) had been proved, the crash programme would continue. This step was necessary because a rear turret fitted with A.G.L. (T) in an unserviceable state would be rendered thereby practically unserviceable since the gunner's vision would be restricted by the A.G.L. (T) collimator and the Type "Z" equipment, while his downward view would be cut off to an appreciable extent by the scanner.

16. By April 15th, 1944, the B.D.U. trial had shown some improvement in A.G.L. (T) reliability and I agreed that, if the reliability was maintained, the B.D.U. would start training A.G.L. (T) instructors on April 24th. I decided to train the squadrons by flights. The first flight of No. 460 Squadron stood down from the 27th June to the 18th July, 1944, and the second flight started training from the 26th July; initial training was completed by the end of August.

Comprehensive instructions were sent to the groups on the use of A.G.L. (T) and a tactical instruction dated 28th June, 1944, was sent to all Bomber Command Operational Groups. This paper, besides giving the principles of operation and limitations of A.G.L. (T) gave orders for the operational use of the equipment.

17. The equipment was first used operationally by No. 460 Squadron on the 20th/21st July, 1944. Whilst the equipment worked well generally, it was obvious from the first that negative identification required great care and restraint by gunners. To make matters worse, trouble was experienced with I.R. filters fitted to the transmitting lamps, and I therefore decided to operate A.G.L. (T) aircraft only under certain conditions and when other aircraft were not likely to be encountered. In the meantime, aircraft had been arriving at No. 49 Squadron and gunners had been trained

in the equipment. This squadron first operated A.G.L. (T) on the night 11th/12th September. Both the squadrons experienced a considerable amount of unserviceability with A.G.L. (T) and test gear was therefore fitted so that the gunner could try out the equipment during flight. When the equipment was working well, numerous contacts, chiefly friendly, were made. It was apparent, however, that gunners mistrusted the Type "Z" identification and were loath to fire blind at what they thought might be friendly aircraft. As a tail warning device, the equipment was exceptionally good, giving both correct line and range of approaching aircraft.

18. On the 19th October, 1944, Air Ministry agreed that one more squadron could be fitted with A.G.L. (T) before the end of the year. A squadron of No. 8 Group was selected, and a training flight at Warboys to train gunners in the equipment was established. At a meeting held at Headquarters, Bomber Command, on the 9th February, considerable emphasis was laid on the fact that A.G.L. (T) was a definite operational requirement. It was true that this device was being introduced very slowly, but that was because of the practical impossibility of fitting and maintaining the equipment in the face of the acute shortage of trained Radar mechanics.

19. The first squadron to be equipped with A.G.L. (T) in No. 8 Group was No. 635. The A.G.L. (T) aircraft had been taken away from No. 460 Squadron of No. 1 Group and these aircraft were placed at the disposal of No. 8 Group.

By the end of the war, squadrons fitted with A.G.L. (T) were:—

No. 49 Squadron	No. 5 Group.
No. 635 Squadron }	
No. 582 Squadron }	No. 8 Group.
No. 35 Squadron }	

20. To sum up, A.G.L. (T) gave promise of becoming one of the greatest assets to the defence of heavy bombers at night, but unfortunately, no completely successful identification system was found and there was no practical scheme for one by the end of the war. Moreover, it has been found that the present Mark of A.G.L. (T) is most difficult to keep in a serviceable condition, and when unserviceable puts a gunner at a distinct disadvantage owing to the restrictions in view which the extra equipment imposes. A.G.L. (T) Mark III, or, as it is likely to be, Mark IV, should offer very distinct advantages over Mark I as the necessity for continuous search with Mark I is most tiring to the air gunner.

Sighting

21. In 1942 all aircraft in Bomber Command were fitted with the normal type reflector sight, *i.e.,* the Mark IIIA* gunsight. At this time relative speed sighting was taught and gunners used tracer as an aid to aiming.

I had been notified of the development of the Mark IC G.G.S., and when some of these sights became available they were fitted to Blenheim aircraft of Nos. 18 and 114 Squadrons of No. 2 Group for an operational trial. Although such a sight was a requirement for Bomber Command it had been decided that, as it was a prismatic type, it was useless for night operations. The Blenheim aircraft of No. 2 Group were operating by daylight.

In order to clear the view from turrets as much as possible, the Mark IIIA* sight was modified. The hood of the sight was removed and slight internal modifications effected. This sight, the Mark IIIN, was introduced into the Command for all tail turrets on the 17th May, 1944.

The first G.G.S., Mark IIC, sights became available with the A.G.L. (T) crash programme and as it was apparent that the sight would shortly be coming into use in the Command without A.G.L. (T), I decided to carry out operational trials with the sight. Twelve F.N. 121 turrets without A.G.L. (T) were diverted from the A.G.L. (T) crash programme and were sent to No. 460 Squadron at Binbrook for operational trials. These trials, as was expected, proved the sight to be successful for night operations.

On the 14th July, 1944, I wrote to the Air Ministry asking for retrospective fitment of the Mark IIC G.G.S. to F.N.121, B.P. "E," B.P. "A" and Glenn Martin 250CE turrets. On the 1st September the Air Ministry replied pointing out that the proposal was impracticable since 200 man-hours were required to fit the Mark IIC sight into existing turrets. It was unfortunate that arrangements had not been made whereby all turrets could be capable of taking the G.G.S., Mark IIC, as a simple modification, as it had been known for a considerable time that the sights would become available.

22. On the 21st October, 1944, Lancaster aircraft started coming off the production line fitted with the F.N.121 turret and the G.G.S., Mark IIC. No previous warning had been given to me that the sights could be expected at that time and in consequence training of air gunners in the manipulation of the sight was behind-hand. At the beginning of December, 1944, I was informed that there was a surplus of F.N.121 G.G.S. turrets available and arrangements were therefore made to fit these turrets retrospectively to aircraft of No. 3 Group, which was chosen because of its daylight commitments.

At the end of the war, a total of 450 G.G.S. turrets had been supplied, all the remaining aircraft were still equipped with the reflector sight.

Gun Performance

Vickers Gas Operated Gun

23. During the period under review the V.G.O. was used on a limited scale, and although this weapon functioned satisfactorily its use was discontinued because of limited ammunition capacity.

0·303-in. Browning

These guns performed most reliably throughout the war, the main trouble experienced was the freezing of guns at high altitude, but this was overcome to some extent by careful maintenance, the use of special lubricants and electrical gun heaters.

0·5-in. Gun

The 0·5-in. Browning guns mounted in turrets appeared at the very last stages of the war with Germany, and were only used on a very limited scale. Consequently little operational experience was obtained.

20-mm. Hispano

This weapon was used on a very limited scale by Bomber Support squadrons and was fitted to Mosquito aircraft as a fixed gun, and gave satisfactory service.

Summary

24. From the foregoing paragraphs it will be seen that in so far as turrets and guns were concerned, very little had been done between February, 1942, and May, 1945, to improve the defensive armament of heavy bombers and, apart from the Rose turret, no real progress had been made in producing for Bomber Command a turret which possessed the characteristics laid down by this Command in 1942. The Air Ministry had under development the F.N. 82 and B.P. "D" tail turrets, each armed with two 0·5-in. guns, and the Bristol B.17 mid-upper turret with two 20-mm. cannon, but none of these turrets became available for use in Bomber Command during the war against Germany. Throughout, those responsible for turret design and production displayed an extraordinary disregard of the requirements of the Command.

Ammunition 0·303-in.

25. At the beginning of 1942 only 0·303-in. ammunition was used by Bomber Command and consisted of the following types:—

Ball, incendiary, tracer (day), tracer (night), and armour piercing.

Between January, 1942, and May, 1944, the operational sequence for belting 0·303-in. ammunition was as follows:—

7 A.P.,
2 incendiary,
1 tracer (day or night).

On the 26th May, 1944, provision was made to alter the current sequence, should the necessity arise, to enable a quick turn-round of aircraft for day/night operations, to be effected (*see* table below).

Turret.	Gun.	Quantity.	A.P.	Incend.	Tracer (day).	Tracer (night).
Rear	Top Left	All	70	30	-	-
	Top Right	1st 500 rounds	70	30	-	-
		Remainder	50	20	30	-
	Bottom left	All	60	20	-	20
	Bottom	All	60	20	-	20
Mid-upper and front	right	1st 300 rounds	60	20	-	20
	Both	Remainder	60	20	20	-

With ammunition tanks so filled, the following methods were adopted:—

Night Operations
(*a*) In the event of more than 300 rounds being fired from each gun of the rear turret, the top right-hand gun was made "safe" leaving three guns available for combat. It was considered that under reasonably light conditions, the small percentage of day tracer would not interfere with sighting, in which case the top right-hand gun could have been used. It was considered unlikely that more than 300 rounds per gun would be fired from the mid-upper or front turrets.

Day Operations
(*b*) The 300 rounds of night ammunition in the top right-hand gun ammunition tracks were removed before the guns were used operationally. The first 300 rounds of each belt in the mid-upper and front turrets were removed and the tanks replenished with daylight sequence before the turrets were used.

Tracer Ammunition

26. The question as to whether tracer ammunition was of value in sighting had always been debated. To obtain a concensus of opinion I wrote to all Groups on the 14th November, 1944, and stated that as conflicting opinions had been put forward from time to time regarding the effectiveness of tracer ammunition as an aid to sighting, I considered that the time had come when a definite decision should be made as to whether continuance of the use of tracer ammunition for both day and night operations was warranted.

I felt that with the advent of the gyro gunsight Mark 11C the use of tracer would be unnecessary and that it might be a disadvantage. I more than suspected that some gunners did not use their sight at all at night, but merely "hosepiped" tracer in the general direction of the attacking fighter.

Certain trials were carried out, and as a result of these, and a review of the points put forward by the operational groups, instructions were sent out on the 20th February, 1945, to discontinue the use of tracer.

The points in favour of the discontinuance of the use of tracer were summarised as follows:—

(*a*) The very real danger of the gunner "hosepiping" tracer in the direction (approximate) of the fighter, disregarding his sight altogether.

(*b*) In view of the adoption of the zone method of sighting, tracer ammunition only served to indicate line accuracy. In the corkscrew this value was lost.

(*c*) It was considered that the use of tracer ammunition was so distracting that with gyro gunsight Mark IIC the gunner could not properly track a target with the moving graticule.

Thus, on the 20th February, 1945, an argument which had continued from the last war was brought to a final conclusion.

S.A.A. Operational Sequence – April, 1945

27. On the 14th April, 1945, I wrote to all groups and stated that in future 100 per cent. incendiary ammunition would be used. It was pointed out that daylight attacks against heavy bomber aircraft may be carried out by armoured single-seat fighters. At night most attacks would be from armoured twin-engined fighters. The 0·303-in. A.P. bullet was incapable of penetrating the armour protection of either type of fighter and thus the aircraft structure and the fuel constituted the only vulnerable portions of the fighter. Against aircraft structure the incendiary bullet, by virtue of the steel sleeve inside the envelope, is more effective than ball ammunition and is almost as effective as A.P. ammunition. The incendiary bullet possesses, in addition, the power of igniting the fuel either in tanks or in pipelines. This sequence of belting of operational ammunition was in force at the cessation of hostilities.

0·50-in. Ammunition

28. 0·50-in. ammunition was first issued to No. 2 Group for use in American aircraft on the 18th September, 1942. The following types of 0·50-in. ammunition were used:—

A.P., incendiary and tracer (day and night). Made-up belts consisting of 40 per cent. A.P., 40 per cent. incendiary, 20 per cent. tracer were issued to the group in March, 1943.

With the introduction of the Rose turret into No. 1 Group early in 1944, 0·50-in. ammunition belted in the sequence 3 A.P., 1 incendiary, was issued, together with supplies of tracer and A.P.I. for introduction into belts under local arrangements which were:—

(*a*) 17th January, 1944. 3 A.P., 1 incendiary, 1 night tracer.

(*b*) 10th February, 1944. Sequence changed to 1 A.P.I., 2 A.P., 1 incendiary, 1 night tracer.

(*c*) 29th January, 1945. Sequence changed to 4 A.P.I., 1 night tracer.

(*d*) 30th April, 1945. Changed to 100 per cent. A.P.I.

1 See Appendix H, para. 11.

ANNEXURE "A"

BOMBER COMMAND OPERATIONAL AIRCRAFT

1942

1 Group.

January	Operating with Wellington Ic, II and IV.
April	Wellington III began operating.
July	Wellington Ic were taken off operations.
August	Halifax began operating.
November	Halifax and Wellington II were taken off operations and Lancasters began operating.
December	Ended the year operating with Wellington III and IV and Lancasters.

2 Group.

January	Were operating with Blenheim IV.
March	Boston III began operating.
June	Mosquitos began operating.
August	Blenheim IV were taken off operations.
October	Ventura I and II began operating.
December	Operated with Boston III, Mosquitos and Ventura I and II.

3 Group.

January	Operating with Wellington Ic and Stirlings.
March	Wellington III began operating.
May	Wellington Ic were taken off operations.
August	Operating with Wellington III and Stirlings. P.F.F. formed (15th). Path Finding with Wellington III, VI, Stirlings, Halifaxes, Lancasters and Mosquitos.
September	Mosquitos and Wellington VI taken off Path Finding.
December	Mosquitos again Path Finding. Ended year operating with Wellington III and Stirlings and Path Finding with Wellington III, Stirlings, Halifaxes, Lancasters and Mosquitos.

4 Group.

	January	Operating with Wellington II, Whitley V and Halifaxes.
	May	Whitley V and Wellington II taken off operations.
	September	Wellington III began operating.
	December	Ended year operating with Halifax and Wellington III.

5 Group.

	January	Operating with Hampdens and Manchesters.
	March	Lancasters began operating.
	June	Manchesters taken off operations.
	September	End of September Hampdens taken off operations.
	December	Ended year operating with Lancasters.

8 Group.

	January	Operating one Squadron with Fortress I.
	February	Fortresses taken off operations. Group disbanded.

1943

1 Group.

	January	Operating with Wellington III, IV and Lancasters.
	March	Wellington X began operating.
	April	Wellington IV taken off operations.
	December	Ended year operating with Lancasters and Wellingtons.

2 Group.

	January	Operating with Boston II, Mosquitos, Venturas. Began operating with Mitchells.
	March	Mitchells taken off operations. Bendix turrets unserviceable.
	May	Mitchells began operating again. Group transferred to 2nd T.A.F.

3 Group.

	January	Operating with Stirlings and Wellington III. Path Finding with Stirlings, Halifaxes, Lancasters, Mosquitos and Wellington III.
	March	Wellington III taken off operations, Lancaster II began operating.
	September	Lancaster II taken off operations.
	October	Lancaster II put back on operations.
	December	Ended year operating with Stirlings and Lancaster II.

4 Group

	January	Operating with Halifaxes and Wellington III. Wellington X began operating.

	April	Wellington III taken off operations. Operating with Halifax II and V and Wellington X.
	September	Wellingtons taken off operations.
	October	One Halifax III began operating.
	November	The Halifax III taken off operations.
	December	Ended year operating with Halifax II and V.
5 Group.	January	Operating with Lancasters.
	December	Ended year operating with Lancasters. (Have used Lancaster I and III and began Lancaster II in March.)
6 Group.	January	Operating with Halifaxes and Wellington III. Wellington X began operating.
	April	Operating with Halifax II and V and Wellington III and Wellington X.
	August	Lancaster II began operating.
	September	Lancaster II taken off operations.
	October	Lancaster II operating again. Wellingtons taken off operations.
	December	Ended year operating with Halifax II, V and Lancaster II.
8 (PFF) Group.	January	Group formed operating with Stirlings, Halifaxes, Lancasters and Mosquitos.
	June	Operating Lancasters, Stirlings, Halifax II, Mosquito IV and IX.
	August	Stirlings taken off Path Finding.
	October	Halifax III began operating.
	December	Ended year operating with Lancasters, Halifax II and III, Mosquitos IV and IX.

1944

1 Group.	January	Operating Lancaster I/III and Wellingtons.
	March	Wellingtons taken off operations.
	December	Ended year operating with Lancaster I/III.
3 Group.	January	Operating with Stirlings, Lancaster II and I/III.
	September	Stirlings taken off operations.
	October	Lancaster II taken off operations.
	December	Ended year operating Lancaster I/III.
4 Group.	January	Operating Halifax II and V. Halifax III began operating.
	May	Halifax II taken off operations.
	July	Halifax V taken off operations.
	December	Ended year operating Halifax III.

5 Group.

January	Operating with Lancaster I and III.
April	One Squadron of Mosquito IV began operating (target marking).
July	Mosquito XX operating with Mosquito IV.
October	Mosquito XXV operating with Mosquito IV and XX.
December	Ended year operating with Lancaster I/III and one squadron of Mosquito IV/XX/XXV.

6 Group.

January	Operating with Lancaster II, Halifax II and V. Lancaster X and Halifax III began operating.
May	Halifax V taken off operations.
June	Halifax VII began operating.
July	Halifax II taken off operations.
August	Lancaster II taken off operations.
December	Ended year operating Halifax III and VII and Lancaster X.

8 Group.

January	Operating Lancaster I/III, Halifax II and III, Mosquito IV and (PFF) IX. Mosquito XVI and XX began operating.
February	Halifax II taken off operations.
March	Halifax III taken off operations. Lancaster VI began operating.
May	Lancaster VI taken off operations.
September	Mosquito IV taken off operations.
November	Mosquito XXV began operating.
December	Ended year operating with Lancaster I/III, Mosquito IX, X/I, XX and XXV.

100 Group.

February	Group formed. Operating with Mosquito II and IV, Halifax III and Wellingtons.
March	Mosquito VI began operating.
April	Fortresses began operating.
May	Halifax III and Mosquito IV taken off operations.
June	Mosquito XIX and Stirlings began operating.
September	Liberators began operating.
October	Halifax III operating again. Mosquito V began operating.
December	Ended year operating with Mosquito II V, VI, XIX, Halifax III, Stirling, Fortress, Liberator.

1945

1 Group.

January-April	Operating with Lancaster I/III.

3 Group. January-April Operating with Lancaster I/III.

4 Group. January Operating with Halifax III.
February Halifax VI began operating.
April Ended month operating with Halifax III and VI.

5 Group. January-April Operating with Lancaster I/III, Mosquito IV, XX, XXV. Mosquito IX and XVI began operating in January.

6 Group. January Operating with Lancaster X, Halifax III and VII.

February Lancaster I began operating.
March Lancaster III began operating.
April Ended month operating with Lancaster I/III, X, Halifax III and VII.

8 Group. (PFF) January-April Operating with Lancaster I/III, Mosquito IX, XVI, XX, XXV.

100 Group. January-April Operating with Mosquito II, IV, V, VI, XIX, Halifax III, Stirling, Fortress, Liberator. Mosquito V taken off operations in January. Mosquito XXX began operating in January.

ANNEXURE "B"

GUN ARMAMENT OF AIRCRAFT BY TYPES

Blenheim IV　　Fixed gun (1x 0·303-in.) firing forward.
Mid-upper turret – Bristol (2 x 0·303-in.)
Under defence (2 x 0·303-in.) firing downwards and
rearwards, from blister. Operated from navigator's position
(free guns).

Boston　　Mid-upper position (2 x 0·303-in.) mounted on a scarf ring.
Mid-under position (1 V.G.O. free gun).

Ventura　　Upper turret (2 x 0·50-in.).
Under gun position (2 x 0·50-in.).
Nose guns (2 or 4 x 0·303-in.) fixed guns.

Mitchell B.25C　　Mid-upper turret (2 x 0·50-in.).
Under defence (2 x 0·50-in.).
Nose (1 free gun 0·303-in.).
1 fixed gun firing forwards (0·50-in.).

Mitchell B.25D　　Armament as for B.25C, except for one 0·50-in. free gun in
nose instead of one 0·303-in.

Mosquito Bomber　　No defensive armament.

Hampden　　Nose (1 free 0·303-in.).
Mid-upper position (2 x 0·303-in.) Rose mounting.
Mid-under (2 x 0·303-in.).
One fixed gun 0·303-in. firing forward.

Whitley　　Nose turret F.N.16 (1 x 0·303-in.).
Tail turret F.N.4 (4 x 0·303-in.).

Wellington　　At the beginning of 1942 Wellington aircraft were equipped
with the following gun armament:—
Nose turret – F.N.5 (2 x 0·303-in. Brownings).

Tail turret – F.N.20 (4 x 0·303-in. Brownings).
Beam guns – F.N.56 (1 x 0·303-in. Browning on each side).
On 18th May, 1944, Headquarters Bomber Command stated in a letter to the Air Ministry that the F.N.56 mountings were no longer an operational requirement. The only other changes in Wellington gun armament have been fitment of F.N.120 tail turret and removal of front turret at Operational Training Units.

Stirling Nose turret – F.N.5 (2 x 0·303-in. Brownings).
Mid-upper turret – F.N.7 (2 x 0·303-in. Brownings).
Mid-under turret – Provision is made for F.N.64 (2 x 0·303-in. Brownings). This was not used on night operations, but replaced by one hand-held 0·50-in. under gun.
Tail turret – F.N.20 (4 x 0·303-in. Brownings).
Beam guns – F.N.55 (1 x 0·303-in. gun on each side).
Operational Air Gunners were not satisfied with the view from the F.N.20 because of restricted vision. It was urged that the F.N.20 be replaced by the older F.N.4 and this was actually done with some aircraft in No. 7 Squadron. The production of F.N.4 turrets was not sufficient to meet requirements and the F.N. 20 was suitably modified and was adopted as the standard tail turret for Stirling A/C.

Manchester Nose turret – F.N.5 (2 x 0·303-in.).
Mid-upper turret – F.N.7 (2 x 0·303-in.).
Tail turret – F.N.20 (4 x 0·303-in.).
Provision made for mid-under F.N.64 (2 x 0·303-in.).

Halifax Nose turret – B.P. (2 x 0·303-in.). Replaced by hand-held gun and later replaced by the Ideal nose with no forward armament.
Mid-upper B.P. "C" (2 x 0·303-in.), later removed and replaced by B.P. type "A" (4 x 0·303-in.).
Tail turret – B.P. "E" (4 x 0·303-in.).
Under defence mounting (1 x 0·50-in.).

Lancaster Nose turret – F.N.5 (2 x 0·303-in.).
Mid-upper – F.N.50 and 150 (2 x 0·303-in.).
Tail turret – F.N.20 (4 x 0·303-in.), later replaced by the F.N.120 and then F.N.121.
No. 1 Group Lancasters were being fitted with the Rose turret (2 x 0·50-in.) other armament remaining the same.
No. 6 (RCAF) Group aircraft were in some cases fitted with Glenn Martin 250 CE 23A mid-upper turret (2 x 0·50-in.).

APPENDIX D

TACTICS

The tactics developed by Bomber Command in night operations throughout the War were influenced by a number of factors which were constantly changing. The most important of these factors were:—

(*a*) The type and number of aircraft available to the Command.

(*b*) The nature and general disposition of the enemy defences.

(*c*) The changes in the German Night Fighter System.

(*d*) The equipment carried by the enemy fighters.

(*e*) The development of accurate navigational and bombing aids.

(*f*) The introduction of radio countermeasures.

2. On the basis of these factors, the War period, so far as Bomber Command tactics are concerned may be divided roughly into six phases, the salient features of which were as follows:—

Phase 1. September, 1939, to June, 1940, when very small bomber forces were employed and the enemy defences were light.

Phase 2. July, 1940, to February, 1942, when the enemy defences expanded owing to the occupation of France, the searchlight belt was introduced and the G.C.I. system was started.

Phase 3. February, 1942, to July, 1943, when the G.C.I. defences increased very rapidly and the searchlights were removed from the belt and placed in the Gun Defended Areas. The Command was growing in strength and the policy of concentration was introduced.

Phase 4. August, 1943, to February, 1944, when the use of Window caused the enemy to abandon the G.C.I. system. During this phase the use of "feint" attacks was inaugurated.

Phase 5. March, 1944, to August, 1944, when the Command's main effort was diverted against targets in Occupied Territory in preparation for and support of the invasion.

Phase 6. September, 1944, to May, 1945, when "feint" tactics and radio countermeasures were fully exploited and when the enemy defences progressively disintegrated.

Each of these periods will be studied separately. In order to make the narrative intelligible, it is necessary to deal briefly with the period from the outbreak of War to February, 1942.

Phase 1. September, 1939, to June, 1940

3. During this period the Command was chiefly equipped with Battles and Blenheims and possessed only a few medium bombers – Hampdens, Whitleys and Wellingtons. The Command was heavily engaged in the hopeless task of supporting the Allied Armies during the battles which led to the fall of France and the evacuation of the personnel of the British Army from Dunkirk. Most of this was done in daylight. After the fall of France, considerable daylight bombing of the invasion ports was carried out. Night bombing on a very small scale commenced in February, 1940, and by June the total night-bombing effort was 2,349 sorties, the weight of bombs dropped being roughly 1 ton per sortie. The enemy defences at this time were – by present standards – rudimentary, consisting mainly of gun-defended searchlight areas, operated on the basis of sound locators, built around important targets, plus a few free-lance night fighters. No precise navigational aids were available to the bombers, which routed themselves independently to the targets, and only in moonlight and clear weather were they likely to locate their objectives.

Phase 2. July, 1940, to February, 1942

4. The main development in this period concerned the enemy defences. Following the occupation of France and the Low Countries, the enemy started to evolve an elaborate system of night-fighter defence. An early warning Radar system was installed along the coasts of Denmark, Holland, Belgium and France and a belt of G.C.I. stations was built extending through Denmark and Holland down the western frontier of Germany. The latter was backed up by a searchlight belt covering the Ruhr. It is probable that some G.C.I. stations were already functioning in the early part of 1941 and there is no doubt that by the end of the year a large area was covered. Each G.C.I. station controlled one fighter within a "box" of relatively small dimensions and all boxes in the belt were contiguous. When the boxes were manned after receipt of early warning from the coastal Radar stations, the enemy was in a position to attempt interception of any single bomber entering a G.C.I. box, and the greater number of boxes brought into operation by a scattered bomber force the greater were the opportunities presented to him. As this system was built up, the effectiveness of

the German defences steadily increased and the routeing of the bombers to avoid passing through a large number of G.C.I. areas became increasingly important.

5. During this time, the size of the force available to Bomber Command was gradually increasing and the heavy bombers in very small numbers had made their appearance (the Manchester and Stirling in February, 1941, the Halifax in April, 1941, and the Lancaster in April, 1942).[1] Small forces were usually detailed to a number of targets and the selection of routes was left to Groups and Squadrons. The rate of bombing was usually in the region of 40 aircraft per hour. At this stage attacks were achieving little success, and losses were on the increase.

6. This was the situation when, on 23rd February, 1942, I assumed command of the force.

7. The nature of the problem involved in improving the effectiveness of attacks, while keeping losses at a reasonable level, had already been appreciated and the developments, which were under way and which were to make possible the improvements in accuracy to be seen in the next phase, were pressed forward with greater energy. The first of these developments to become available was GEE, the navigational aid which permitted accurate track-keeping for distances of the order of 350 miles from base. GEE became operational early in 1942 and it assisted in making possible the concentrated raid, which a scientific analysis of our bomber losses in November, 1941, had shown to be desirable. The potentialities of GEE as an aid to target location were also fully exploited for raids within the coverage. Selected crews in No. 3 Group were detailed to lay flares over the target blindly by means of the instrument and other selected crews detailed to mark the target with loads of incendiary bombs. While the hoped-for accuracy in bombing was not achieved, owing to the characteristics of the device at the ranges in question, improved results were obtained and the standard of navigation was increased considerably. The flare technique was ultimately used with great success by the Pathfinder Force when improved blind marking devices became available.

8. The first steps in the radio countermeasure warfare were also taken. Crews had reported for some time that the switching on of their I.F.F. caused searchlights to dowse or fall away, but analysis of these reports had yielded no conclusive results. However, examination of enemy equipment captured at Bruneval revealed a possible scientific basis for the effect, and immediate steps were taken to incorporate into the I.F.F. set a modification for use by aircraft picked up by searchlights. The value of this procedure was never proved, but its use was continued in view of its good moral effect. The important point was that the use of radio countermeasures had begun and, as will be seen later, these were to play a most important part in the tactics of the bomber force.

Phase 3. February, 1942, to July, 1943

9. The first concentrated raids, foreshadowed by an attack against Mannheim on the 15/16th December, 1940, in which all available aircraft were used, occurred towards

the beginning of this phase, culminating in the attacks on the Renault Works, Paris, and on Lubeck and Rostock, in which between 200 and 300 aircraft were employed.

10. The tactical aim of Bomber Command in this period can be described in the one word "concentration." The policy of individual routeing to the target was therefore discontinued in June, 1942, and, with the improvements in navigation provided by GEE, a move was made to step-up concentration in time. To demonstrate the effects of saturation of the defences, both in respect of losses and in the infliction of damage to the target, and to prove that large concentrations were practicable, the first 1,000 bomber raid was planned. In planning this raid two important factors had to be taken into consideration, namely, the risk of the loss of aircraft due to collisions and the damage from falling bombs. These factors were investigated and it was found that, for a planned bombing time of one hour and a half, the risk from both causes was small. The project went ahead and the raid was carried out against Cologne on the night 30/31st May, 1942, by 1,047 bombers, including 300 heavies, all following a common route and with a planned time over target of 90 minutes. 900 aircraft in fact bombed within the planned period. The success of the experiment proved that a bombing attack delivered in sufficient weight could be devastating; that a concentrated attack could saturate the enemy flak and A.R.P. defences and that losses could be kept at an economical figure and did not increase in proportion to the size of the force employed.

11. From this time onwards one target, against which practically all available forces were used was selected for each night's operation. Co-ordinated plans for each attack and common routes were laid down at Command Headquarters, in consultation with Groups, and the planned concentration of bombing remained at 10 aircraft per minute until the end of July, 1943.

12. During the whole of the period under consideration the enemy defences, while showing no particular innovations, continued to develop along the lines already indicated and increased in strength and efficiency. In particular the radar control of guns and searchlights improved and the G.C.I. belt was increased in depth and was gradually extended south-westwards from Belgium as far as Paris until, in time, it became almost impossible to penetrate into Germany without crossing it. In addition, free-lance fighters habitually operated in moonlight, particularly if deep penetrations were made. The main searchlight belt was, however, disbanded and the searchlights moved to the heavily gun-defended areas. G.C.I. interceptions subsequently took place without searchlight assistance.

13. Since a successful attack depended on visual identification of targets, it was necessary to operate mainly on clear or moonlight nights, which gave a great advantage to the night fighters, but, even so, great difficulty was experienced owing to the dazzle effect of the enormous number of searchlights concentrated in the target areas. Increased concentration *en route* and in time over the target helped to minimise losses but, due to the rapidly increasing efficiency of the defences, the loss rate continued to rise. It was clearly necessary to increase the accuracy of our attacks and to have the means for carrying out operations on moonless nights, when the enemy defences would be less effective. Methods for countering the enemy radar, on which

his defence was based, were also required. For these purposes, a number of devices under development at T.R.E. were likely to be of value:—

(*a*) H.2.S., a self-contained airborne device with no range limitation, which could be used both as a navigational and blind bombing aid. It was not, however, regarded as a precision bombing device.

(*b*) OBOE, a ground-controlled blind bombing device with a range of the order of 250-280 miles, by means of which target marking and bombing could be carried out blindly with great accuracy.

(*c*) MANDREL and WINDOW, which could be used to jam respectively the FREYAS and WURZBURGS on which the enemy G.C.I. organisation was based.

(*d*) MONICA, a device for providing the bomber with early warning of the approach of another aircraft.

The development and production of all the above devices were pressed for by Bomber Command with the utmost vigour.

14. Prior, however, to the production of the radar bombing and navigational aids referred to above, the Pathfinder Force was formed in August, 1942, in which specially selected crews were placed and which was made responsible for developing the operational use of the equipments when they were produced. The plan was to use OBOE, fitted in a small number of Mosquito aircraft, to mark all those targets which came within its range and to use H.2.S. to assist in marking all other targets. After having equipped all the Pathfinders with H.2.S. it was proposed, in view of its potentialities for improving navigation, to extend it to all other heavy bombers in the Command.

15. H.2.S. became operational in December, 1942. In the first stages the fitted aircraft laid markers blindly by means of the equipment, but it was found that the markers were widely scattered due to inaccuracies in the device and difficulties in interpreting, the indications. Attempts were then made to lay flares blindly over the target by means of the instrument, and selected Pathfinders, known as "visual markers," marked the aiming point visually in the light of the flares, in the same way as previously attempted with GEE. A great improvement was immediately obtained and this technique, with slight modifications and improvements, remained the main method of marking by the Pathfinder force under appropriate weather conditions for the remainder of the War.

16. OBOE became operational in January, 1943, and after a number of preliminary operations involving the use of small forces, during which the device was well tested and essential experience gained, a full-scale attack on Essen was carried out on 5/6th March, 1943. This important target, which had for so long proved almost impossible to locate, was accurately marked and very severely damaged. From then on one target after another in the Ruhr and surrounding area was attacked and destroyed by means of OBOE marking, which was also used with success until the end of the War on all targets within its range.

17. From early 1943 onwards, then, the Pathfinder technique was built on H.2.S. and OBOE. From the tactical point of view the increased freedom of action which these two radar devices gave was all important. Hitherto, successful attacks had depended primarily on clear weather conditions in the target area and on the operations being carried out in moonlight, conditions ideal for the enemy defences. By means of OBOE it was now possible to mark the target regardless of weather conditions or the state of the moon. Thick cloud was still a disadvantage to the main bomber force and completely successful attacks still required conditions in which ground markers could be seen. However, fog and low stratus at the target no longer precluded a successful attack and the accuracy of OBOE was such that sky-markers, bursting above thick cloud, could be dropped in an emergency and thus prevent an attack from becoming entirely abortive due to unforeseen weather conditions. Equally important was the fact that moonlight was no longer essential to a successful operation and, as a result, operations were now carried out mainly during the dark period of the month when the enemy fighters were thereby deprived of their main tactical advantage. The rising loss-rate was halted and the effectiveness of the attacks enormously increased. The large-scale re-equipment of the bomber force with Halifax and Lancaster aircraft which was now well under way was an important contribution to the weight of attack delivered on the target.

18. It is convenient at this stage to describe a typical plan of attack for a major operation during this period, for example, that on Essen already mentioned (5/6th March, 1943). 412 aircraft, including 140 Lancasters, 89 Halifaxes, 52 Stirlings and 131 Wellingtons were detailed, together with a P.F.F. marking force of 8 OBOE Mosquitos and 22 heavies. The route was direct from Egmond, on the Dutch coast, to a point 15 miles north of the target. From this point aircraft started the run up to the target, turning wide left after bombing and returning to Egmond over a point 20 miles N.E. of the target. The planned time over target was 38 minutes, *i.e.,* 11 aircraft per minute. Pathfinder heavies dropped yellow route markers at the turning point, 15 miles short of the target, and the aiming point was marked by the OBOE Mosquitos dropping red T.I.s at three and seven minute intervals alternately. P.F.F. heavies backed up the red T.I.s with greens, dropped at intervals of 1-2 minutes throughout the attack. Thus the target was kept marked throughout the attack by red and green T.I.s, of which the reds were given as the primary point of aim if they could be seen.

19. For targets outside OBOE range, plans of attack were similar, except that target marking was done visually by selected crews of the P.F.F. in the light of flares dropped blindly by means of H.2.S. Markers of a distinctive colour were also dropped blindly by selected crews for use by the main force in case the visual markers were unable to identify the aiming point through unexpected weather conditions.

20. In connection with the drive to increase the accuracy of attacks, crews were now even more closely interrogated than hitherto as to the success of their mission and an elaborate form, known as the "Raid Report," was completed for each sortie. These were all carefully analysed, together with the night photographs taken at bombing. Night photography played a most important part. Cameras, as they became available, were fitted in all aircraft and, when weather conditions were suitable, it

was possible to plot accurately the fall of bombs. The importance of this cannot be over-emphasised for, until this time, crews had no means of checking where their bombs had fallen and the new opportunity of bringing back evidence of good results provided a remarkable stimulus which was undoubtedly beneficial in improving accuracy. It also enabled the progress of the whole raid to be studied and the causes of failure to bomb the target to be investigated. Thus mistakes could be rectified and planning improved.

21. A further aid to accuracy in bombing was the official abandonment of the practice of taking evasive action from flak in the target area. A study of the types of evasive action taken had shown that in many cases it did not decrease, but rather increased, the chances of being hit by flak and that it was having a very harmful effect on bombing accuracy. Straight and level flying also minimised the collision risk in the target area.

22. So long as the planned rate of bombing remained at about 10 aircraft per minute, as it did throughout this period, the bomber streams, while narrow, were relatively long – probably of the order of 100-150 miles for a force of 300-400 aircraft. The importance of accurate track keeping and timing was continually stressed and in view of the improvement obtained it was found desirable in July, 1943, to specify safe height bands in which aircraft forced to return early could fly safely against the stream. The average height flown over enemy territory was normally 18-20,000 ft., although the actual height for any particular operation was left to the discretion of groups.

23. Throughout this stage of the War, therefore, the powerful enemy defences were countered mainly by the policy of concentration, and the slightly increasing losses were more than offset by the greater accuracy and weight of the attacks delivered. Though at the end of 1942 the enemy appeared to be gaining tactical superiority over the attacking bombers, the striking advances made in bombing technique in the first half of 1943 indisputably established the value of the heavy bomber offensive.

24. However, even in this period the enemy defences were directly countered to some extent, both by the defensive tactics of individual bombers and by further slight advances in radio countermeasures, including the use of MANDREL. A new and lethal method of fighter attack was first observed in March, 1942. It consisted of a steep climb to a position under the tail of the bomber, the fighter opening fire at close range and continuing to fire, up to the stall. Subsequently, surprise attacks from below became relatively frequent and, as the searchlight belt disappeared and more enemy fighters were equipped with A.I., the unseen approach, particularly on dark nights, became easy. To counter these tactics the banking search and corkscrew evasive manoeuvre were introduced and formed the basis of individual action taken by Bomber Command crews. Crews were also encouraged to be aggressive and to open fire on all hostile aircraft within range. Radar devices, group warning of the approach of an enemy fighter, had by now been produced and at the end of this phase of operations MONICA I and BOOZER had just come into use.

25. The possibility of confusing ground radar stations by the release from aircraft of metallised strips of suitable length (WINDOW) had long been known and the subject of its exploitation by Bomber Command had been under investigation since late in 1941. The Command pressed for its release, but the fear of enemy retaliation, in view of the susceptibility of our defensive radar, and the unsuitability of the form of the countermeasure, were the arguments put forward against its use. By early 1943, however, a suitable form of WINDOW for jamming the enemy G.C.I., G.L. and A.I. was available and the power of the enemy defences required drastic counteraction. The immediate use of the countermeasure was therefore strongly urged by the Command as there seemed a good chance of thereby reducing bomber losses by about one-third. A scientific study was made to determine the quantity required, the best rate and manner of discharge and the areas over which it should be used.

26. By mid-1943 it was agreed by the Air Ministry that the possibility of retaliation by the enemy was acceptable and the first WINDOW raid was made against Hamburg on the night of 24/25th July, 1943. A new era in Bomber Command tactics was inaugurated and the use of WINDOW in various forms continued thereafter until the end of the War. Its effect was immediate. Crews' reports after the first attack described searchlights waving aimlessly, while the intercepted wireless traffic showed the enemy ground controllers to be hopelessly confused. The enemy's extensive night-fighter defence system, built up over the two previous years, was rendered largely useless, and predicted heavy flak fire had to give way to barrage fire, except against isolated aircraft outside WINDOW cover. An analysis of the first ten WINDOW raids showed a reduction in losses of rather more than one-third by comparison with previous experience of similar targets, a result remarkably near to the estimate. These analyses also showed where improvements in the operational use could be made, and amendments to the rates and areas of discharge were made from time to time. It was later known that, in addition to rendering the ground radar ineffective, WINDOW also interfered seriously with the enemy fighters' A.I.

27. After the first debacle the enemy quickly improvised a fighter defence system, making more use of the Observer Corps to plot the bomber stream and transmitting orders by broadcast running commentary to large numbers of free-lance fighters drawn from all over Germany, some of which were obliged to operate at distances of up to 300 miles from their bases. The commentary gave height and direction of the bomber stream, the areas over which it was passing and the probable or actual target. For the first few weeks, its object was to get the fighters to the target where they could contact the bomber stream and follow it out on the homeward journey, and until the target had been identified or guessed the fighters were held back orbiting special beacons. Interceptions were temporarily confined to the immediate vicinity of targets or the early part of the homeward routes.

28. The use of visual aids in profusion was a characteristic feature of the new enemy technique, searchlights exposing simultaneously in large numbers, either coning aircraft direct or illuminating the cloud base to assist the fighters. In addition, illuminating flares were dropped from the air over targets or laid in lanes at bomber

heights along the in and out routes near the targets. The new enemy defence method was quite soon achieving some success, but investigation showed that it suffered from a serious defect, namely, that the fighters often arrived late in the target area and therefore failed altogether to make contact. This was confirmed by the fact that the aircraft arriving early at the target suffered lower losses and were attacked less frequently than those arriving later.

29. In order to take advantage of this deficiency it was decided to shorten the duration of raids, and therefore the planned rate of bombing was stepped up to 30 aircraft per minute. It was realised that this tactic would increase the losses caused by collisions and strikes from falling bombs, but it was considered that the extra losses suffered from these causes would be much more than compensated by the reduction in losses due to the enemy action.

30. In the early days of Bomber Command's night operations, after large-scale raids had begun but before the formation of the Pathfinder force, it was found advantageous to begin each attack with a wave of bombers with specially experienced crews. This first wave of the attack was expected to find the target and to start conflagrations which should guide the less experienced crews at least to the neighbourhood of the target. In course of time, as the organisation of operations became more centralised, it was found convenient to develop a more complete system of division into waves for every large-scale attack. The various waves of the attack were planned to follow one another, usually without any gaps between them, so that the effect produced was a roughly uniform stream of bombers over the target. The advantage of the division into waves was that each aircraft was briefed to arrive at the target at a definite period of the raid, thus preventing "bunching" over the target, facilitating the handling of aircraft on their return and making possible the specialisation of function of aircraft during the attack itself.

31. The system of attacking in waves, once instituted, was found to be capable of being used and modified for tactical purposes. In the first place, when, in the spring of 1943, the concentration of aircraft over the target area became habitually high, the high-flying Lancasters were usually placed in separate waves from the lower flying Halifaxes, and the Halifaxes in separate waves from the low-flying Stirlings and Wellingtons; in this way the risk to the lower-flying aircraft of being hit by incendiary bombs from the higher-flying aircraft was mitigated. Further, as a defence measure, it was desirable to place the slower Stirlings and Wellingtons between the Lancaster and Halifax waves in time over target. In the second place, the introduction of WINDOW in July, 1943, made it desirable to keep the cross section of the bomber stream, at each point along its length, in as narrow a height band as possible, in order to obtain a high concentration of WINDOW in space. Since the cross section of the stream at any point in general consisted of aircraft belonging to a single wave of the attack the height-spread of such cross sections was kept to a minimum by assigning each wave of the attack to a single type of aircraft.

32. In order to take advantage of the protection afforded by WINDOW in the autumn and winter of 1943, it was considered desirable to modify the existing wave plans, and three complicating factors had to be taken into account. First, the fact that

the original types of WINDOW fell through still air at about 500 ft. per minute made it desirable to arrange that each high-flying wave should be immediately followed by a wave of aircraft flying 2,000-3,000 ft. lower, so that the WINDOW dropped by the earlier wave should be of benefit to the later; thus the waves should for preference attack in the sequence Lancaster-Halifax-Stirling. Second, the varying cruising speeds of the different types of aircraft made it certain that any wave-plan designed to give maximum WINDOW protection at the target would fail to give maximum protection on the outward and homeward route; in particular, the Stirlings, with their lower speed, had to be put in the first half of the attack to avoid the danger of their straggling dangerously far behind the other types on the homeward route. Thirdly, the immediate reply of the German fighters to the introduction of WINDOW was to concentrate their forces for free-lance interception in the target area; in order to make the task of these fighters harder, it was desirable that the height of attack of successive waves of bombers should vary widely and irregularly, so that the fighters should have less chance of either finding or being directed to the height-level at which the bombers at any moment were concentrated. The wave-plans actually used during the autumn of 1943 were a necessary compromise between these various requirements ; a certain amount of variety was used to add to the difficulties of the fighters, but the basic principle of keeping each wave to a moderately narrow height-band was conserved.

33. By the spring of 1944, the Stirling and the Halifax II and V aircraft were no longer employed on deep penetration, and the aircraft of the Command became roughly of equal performance as far as operational heights and speeds were concerned. At the same time the enemy fighters changed over to intercepting the bomber stream en route to the target rather than in the target area. For these two reasons the system of wave-plans lost most of its tactical importance as a defensive measure, although it was retained until the end of hostilities as a convenient method of regulating the flow of bombers over the target.

34. A further innovation introduced in the winter of 1943-44 was the detailing of a number of aircraft of the main force to bomb with H.E. only while the Pathfinders were in the process of marking the target. This tactic was designed to give cover to the Pathfinders by increasing the concentration and WINDOW protection. H.E. bombs only were used, to minimise the risk of starting fires away from the target which might mislead the main force.

35. Following the introduction of WINDOW the enemy quickly established a network of visual and radio beacons over Germany, at which the fighters were assembled and held until the Controllers could direct them to the target, and as early as September, 1943, it became clear that the hesitation and uncertainty of the Controllers in making their decisions could be exploited by erratic routeing and by making diversionary attacks to lead them into confusion. The diversions were at first made mainly by small forces of Mosquitos, which usually followed the main bomber route for most of its way before breaking away. The enemy confusion was also made worse at times by the operation of several enemy Controllers issuing contradictory instructions to the fighter force, though by October the control was becoming more co-ordinated, authority frequently being delegated to a single Controller who deployed the whole available fighter force to cover possible targets.

36. Apart from the increased concentration already mentioned the general plan of Bomber Command attacks during the whole of this period remained the same as that described for the previous period, *i.e.,* the employment of single large forces of mixed heavies on one target. The general standard of navigation was improved by the gradual fitting of H.2.S. throughout the force, but it was still assisted for deep penetrations by route markers dropped by the P.F.F.

37. A combination of radio countermeasures, which had recently been introduced, small diversionary raids and WINDOW, aided the policy of concentration in keeping losses moderate until well into November. The type of opposition remained the same, *i.e.,* it was mostly restricted to targets and homeward routes.

38. In November, 1943, taking advantage of the long nights, a sustained offensive against targets deep in Germany, particularly Berlin, was commenced and shortly afterwards it became apparent, not only that losses were steadily rising, but that the incidence of the opposition had now changed and that it was being encountered mainly on the outward journeys. The greater penetration being made allowed the enemy ample time in which to assemble fighter forces from all over Germany and direct them in good time to the general area likely to be attacked. To counter this, straight routeing was avoided, and routes were chosen which appeared to threaten important targets, turning only at the last moment in the direction of the real target. A final run of 40/50 miles on to the target was considered to be the minimum, as experience had shown that shorter runs prejudiced the accuracy of the bombing. By January, 1944, the enemy Controllers, instead of attempting to predict the target, were directing the fighters from their assembly beacons into the outbound bomber stream, and even out to sea at a very early stage to meet the approaching bombers. Particularly in the coastal areas the enemy was also making much greater use of the Benito system, by which fighters were controlled into the bomber stream instead of on to individual bombers. Losses continued to rise and it became necessary to make further changes in tactics. These changes, which are described in the next section, were gradually introduced as from 20/21st February, 1944.

39. Within the present period the warning devices BOOZER and MONICA, Mark III (replacing MONICA, Mark I), had been in use by large numbers of the bomber force, but had failed to give the hoped for results, although MONICA was shown to be of some value. At a later date (November, 1943), yet another warning device was introduced. This was FISHPOND, an attachment to the navigational aid H.2.S. It gave a visual presentation of the position and range of aircraft in the hemisphere below the bomber and was hoped to be of value in reducing surprise attacks from this direction. It continued in use until the end of the war, though its results were also disappointing. The aggressive action by gunners, encouraged in the previous period, proved to have its dangers with the high concentration of bombers now employed and, in view of the relatively high proportion of damage inflicted by friendly fire, the importance of making positive identification before firing had to be continually stressed. The lack of a warning device with a positive method of identification, which had long been a requirement in this Command, was a serious drawback. Apart from the technical troubles experienced with MONICA, the value of this equipment, and also of FISHPOND, was largely prejudiced by lack of means of identification.

40. The fact that the initiative in combat is held by the fighter, which is able to choose the direction of attack and obtained visual contact at much greater range than is possible for the bomber, emphasises the need for a reliable warning and blind firing device. Such a device, A.G.L.T., finally became available in small numbers in July, 1944. It was designed to provide the rear gunner with information sufficient for him to open fire at ranges beyond his vision. Identification was of even greater importance and in an attempt to overcome the problem the whole of the bomber force was fitted with infra-red identification lamps. The scheme, however, was not satisfactory and the potentialities of A.G.L.T. could not be exploited. It is clear that the comparative failure of all the warning devices used by the Command was largely due to the lack of a reliable and positive identification system. This remains an important outstanding requirement for a night bomber force.[2]

41. Many of the returning bombers attacked by fighters continued to be taken by surprise and it was believed that this also applied to the majority of those shot down. In an endeavour to alleviate the position, improved vision from rear turrets and the fitting of the under-gun position to all aircraft not carrying H.2.S. were palliatives which were tried. The under-gun (which was only fitted to a small number of aircraft) finally came into operational use in May, 1944, but this proved a disappointment owing to the difficulty of downward search and the great discomfort in which the gunner was obliged to work.

42. As has already been mentioned, the introduction of navigational and blind bombing aids gave increased freedom of action to bomber forces in so far as weather conditions, both en route and at the target, were concerned. With the exception of OBOE, however, these aids did not give the necessary accuracy to ensure a successful attack under completely blind conditions and clear weather at targets outside OBOE range was a pre-requisite for a completely successful attack. Nevertheless one major problem, namely that of the weather at bases and over the route, was overcome. Until GEE came into use the necessity for good weather conditions on the return had to be taken into account in planning operations. The magnitude of this problem was greatly reduced by the bombers now being able to return to their bases without difficulty and, in the event of low cloud and/or poor visibility, being able to maintain their position without visual aids until convenient for them to land. Operations could therefore take place in the face of a threat of bad weather at bases, a risk which hitherto could not be taken. For the same reason the routeing of aircraft to and from targets could be planned with a view to making maximum use of bad weather areas where enemy fighters would probably be grounded, and this factor was always taken into account. There is evidence to show that on occasions losses were considerably reduced by the failure of enemy fighters to take off in conditions of fog and low cloud which in no way interfered with the bombers. Weather conditions therefore became a positive factor which not only influenced the decision whether or not to operate but played an important part in the tactical planning.

43. At the beginning of this phase an important step in the training policy of the Command had been taken. This was the opening in August, 1943, of the Bomber Command Tactical School, formed with the object of giving to members of the

H.C.U. instructional staffs, experienced operational squadron personnel, officers appointed as Group tactical officers and other key personnel, up to date information on bomber tactics to be used in the instruction of operational aircrew. In the early years of the war there was little background of experience on which such instruction could have been based, but it was now possible for valuable tactical training to be given to aircrew. At a later date the courses were extended to include Signals Leaders so that wireless operators might have the proper grounding in the enemy defence measures to enable them to make the most efficient use of warning devices.

Phase 5. – March 1944 to August 1944

44. The heavy fighter opposition encountered in January and early February, 1944, caused some uneasiness and several suggestions for alleviating the situation were received from Groups. For example, 5 Group proposed the manoeuvre of "side-stepping" – *i.e.,* the whole bomber force to turn up to 90 degrees at a given time and fly in the new direction for a given number of minutes before resuming course – and 3 Group suggested the use of radio-transmitters to replace visual route-markers. The first of these measures was tried only once, but the second could not be used since there was no suitable apparatus immediately available.

45. In February, 1944, an extensive survey was made of the operations in recent months to determine the reasons for the rising losses and to show where the current tactics could be improved. It was concluded that a single, large bomber stream, making a deep penetration into enemy territory, was easily plotted and its great length considerably eased the problem of timing for the fighters. Consequently the fighters habitually converged on the stream before it had reached the target. Small diversionary Mosquito forces were now having little effect and the enemy was making use of the route markers laid for the guidance of the main force.

46. It was clear that under existing conditions it was necessary to split and confuse the enemy night fighter defences and after careful consideration it was agreed that future tactics should be developed to this end. It was also decided to form the Bomber Command Tactical Planning Committee in order to consider the practicability of all possible tactics and to plan in outline routes and tactics for certain main targets for a variety of conditions. Regular meetings of this Committee were held thereafter.

47. The main features of the new tactics were as follows:—

(*a*) To shorten the length of the bomber stream, either by attacking more than one target or

by sending two smaller forces to the same target by different routes.

(*b*) To carry out two attacks on the same target on the same night, the attacks to be separated by a suitable time interval ensuring that the enemy fighters would be dispersed or grounded when the second bomber force arrived.

(*c*) To employ heavy bombers on a much larger scale than previously for diversions, routed well away from the main force track. (These at first took the form of minelaying operations and diversionary sweeps by aircraft of the O.T.U.s and H.C.U.s across the North Sea. Their object was to hold a substantial part of the fighter force in areas well removed from the real scene of operations and to cause fighters to be airborne for as long as possible before the main operations).

(*d*) To make more frequent use of a southern route into Germany across France, since the enemy plotting system and general night fighter organisation appeared to be much less effective in Southern Germany.

(*e*) To reduce to a minimum, and as soon as possible, abolish the use of route markers. (After a few attempts at off-track route marking it became practicable to dispense altogether with route markers, since navigation, already greatly improved by the use of H.2.S., was still further assisted by "broadcast winds," *i.e.*, the transmission from Groups at regular intervals during an operation of the mean of the wind velocities transmitted back to them by special wind-finding aircraft in the bomber force).

(*f*) To vary tactics continually and to co-ordinate the timing of the more complex operations envisaged for the purpose of putting the greatest possible strain on the night fighter organisation.

48. The new principles were applied gradually commencing on February 20/21st and their effect can be seen from the following figures for percentage losses, which apply to attacks on targets in Germany:—

November, 1943.	December, 1943.	January, 1944.	February, 1944. First 2 Ops.	February, 1944. Last 3 Ops.	March. 5 Ops.	March. 2 Ops.	April.
Per cent. 3·7	Per cent. 4·9	Per cent. 6·4	Per cent. (7·1	Per cent. 3·3)	Per cent. (2·7	Per cent. 10·5)	Per cent. 3·5
			5·1		5·1		

The monthly loss-rates alone show that a substantial reduction in losses was effected immediately, but in March the degree of the general improvement was obscured by heavy casualties suffered in two operations due to abnormal weather conditions.

49. During this period some difficulty was experienced in ensuring accurate time-keeping and proper co-ordination between the Pathfinders and main forces. It was necessary, for example, to prevent such occurrences as the possibility of the marking being carried out punctually and the main force arriving after the markers were extinguished, or vice versa. To some extent the problem was solved by careful and co-ordinated planning of time-wasting tactics. Aircraft set out with a generous allowance of time in hand, and, if necessary, manoeuvred to lose time in accordance with an agreed method, designed to reduce the collision risk to a minimum. The old

habit of periodic orbiting, both for time-wasting and as a defensive manoeuvre, was abolished in July, 1943, and the approved manoeuvre now became a simple, short dog-leg. The adjustable zero-hour was a more positive method for co-ordinating the timing of Pathfinders and main forces. This was designed to be used only on occasions when the forecast winds were likely to be inaccurate. The method incorporated a scheme for obtaining wind values from aircraft specially detailed for the task, and the values sent back were averaged and re-broadcast to all aircraft. If the average differed from the wind value forecast to an extent that aircraft would obviously reach the target considerably earlier or later than expected, a new zero hour would be broadcast. There were however practical difficulties in the application of this plan and the idea was abandoned after one or two trials. Wind broadcasting was, however, continued with success.

50. The tactical principles outlined above continued to form the basis of raid planning to the end of the war. After D-Day, when the large-scale use of radio countermeasures became practicable, operations of the greatest complexity were carried out.

51. The bombing of specialised targets in France and Belgium in support of the invasion of the Continent – railway marshalling yards, gun positions, coastal radar sites, etc. – commenced on a large scale in March, 1944, and this became the major operational role for Bomber Command in the next three months. At the beginning of this period these operations were almost unopposed by fighters, but the vital nature of the targets attacked caused the enemy to make radical changes in his defences. The network of visual and radio beacons, used for the assembly of fighters was extended into France and Belgium, where airfield beacons were probably used as a temporary expedient, until finally the system of beacons extended as far west as the mouth of the Seine and Orleans, with a corresponding redistribution of night fighter bases to cover the same area. The centralised system of night fighter control also gave place to local controls and, though long range fighters continued to operate against such penetrations as were made into Germany proper, those based in France and Belgium confined their activities mainly to the vicinity of their own bases, assisted by medium range control.

52. As a result of this redistribution of his strength, at a time when deep penetrations into Germany could be more or less discounted, the enemy was able to tackle bomber forces making short penetrations into Occupied Territory and he finally succeeded in intercepting those bombing the Channel coast targets, though only when these attacks were of long duration. Consequently, the losses suffered in these areas rose considerably, reaching a maximum in June of 5·0 per cent. of the sorties despatched to inland targets within the fighter defended areas of France and Belgium. It was difficult to find a means for reducing them because the enemy task at this time, and in this area, was comparatively simple. The operational field was small and coincided in the main with a region thickly congested with night fighter airfields, so that on many occasions the markers dropped at the targets must have been within visual range of some of the fighters as they circled their airfield beacons awaiting orders. The light summer nights also made interception extremely easy. In general,

the only method for evading the fighters was to make attacks extremely short. This was done as far as possible by employing small forces simultaneously on a number of targets, the individual Groups, for reasons of practical convenience, tending more and more to operate separately.

53. The fighter-defended area of France never extended west of the Greenwich meridian or south of 47° N., so that the greater part of France was almost undefended. Also, fighter interceptions at targets on the Channel coasts and the flying bomb sites in the Pas de Calais did not occur to any extent until after D-Day.

54. The nature of some of the targets in the Occupied Countries and the desire to avoid civilian casualties demanded extremely close control of marking and bombing. For this purpose the Master Bomber technique, which had been tried from time to time on German targets and by means of which a selected and experienced crew was detailed to assess the accuracy of the marking and instruct the main force accordingly, was introduced. In these attacks OBOE was used to make the approximate position of the target for the benefit of a small force which dropped flares to illuminate the area. The exact aiming point was then marked visually by the light of the flares. The Master Bomber assessed the accuracy of the marking and instructed the main force accordingly, issuing further instructions as necessary throughout the attack. In order to increase the accuracy of the attacks bombing was normally carried out at medium altitudes and in cases at relatively low altitude from below cloud, a policy which was possible in view of the paucity of the flak defences. In this way extremely accurate and successful attacks were made, in which the minimum number of bombs fell outside the specified targets.

55. Three equipments, the details of which were unknown to the Command at the time, were in use by the enemy fighters in the early summer of 1944, and they undoubtedly help to explain their considerable success. Information received from Intelligence sources had suggested the existence of a new type of enemy A.I. – the S.N.2 equipment of unknown frequency – and also of a device known as FLENSBURG, which was then said to be an A.I. of range about 100 miles. The existence of NAXOS, for homing on to H.2.S. transmissions, was also rumoured. By great good fortune, a Ju.88 night fighter of latest type landed undamaged in this country on 13th July, 1944, as the result of a navigational error. It was immediately examined and was found to be equipped with both S.N.2 and FLENSBURG.

56. The S.N.2 proved to be a wide-beamed A.I. working on a frequency of 90 mc/s. WINDOW Type MB, designed originally for use against the enemy Freyas, was known to give a good response in this frequency and it was decided to use the small existing stock of this material as an immediate countermeasure to the A.I. without waiting for trials. This decision was carried into full effect, commencing with the raid on Kiel of 23/24th July and successful results were obtained. After a time the more experienced enemy crews apparently became accustomed to the interference and were able to read through it, though the less accomplished pilots were still in difficulties. Statements made by captured night fighter pilots leave little doubt that the S.N.2 was eventually made useless by interference, but the electrical jammer, DINAH, carried by special aircraft of 100 Group from October onwards, is thought

to have had the bigger effect.

57. Trials with the FLENSBURG against MONICA showed that urgent measures to deny the enemy the use of this device were necessary. Technical modifications designed to this end were made to the MONICA sets and a trial flight was made over this country using the FLENSBURG-equipped Ju.88 against a large force of MONICA-fitted aircraft. The opportunity was also taken to test the effect of the type MB WINDOW on the S.N.2. The results showed that the modification made to MONICA did not interfere seriously with the use of the FLENSBURG, but that type MB WINDOW was a good answer to the S.N.2. In the light of this result and since MONICA-fitted aircraft were sustaining the same loss rate as those not fitted, the device was withdrawn from operational use (12th September, 1944), and the use of WINDOW against S.N.2 was further developed by the production of types more efficient than the heavy type MB which had been used as a stop-gap.

58. Although no sample of a NAXOS equipment became available for examination, some details of it were provided by captured night fighter aircrew. It was also known that the enemy had prepared an elaborate ground organisation for plotting the bomber force by means of the H.2.S. transmission, and serious consideration was given to the desirability of restricting the use of H.2.S. Losses of H.2.S aircraft were, however, no greater than those of aircraft not so fitted and in view of its valuable navigational assistance, no restriction was imposed on the use of H.2.S for the time being.

59. 100 Group was formed at the end of 1943, its task being to combat the enemy defence organisation by means of radio countermeasures and offensive night fighter patrols. For the first six months after its formation, the Group concentrated on the development and use of night fighter forces while the specialised equipment for the R.C.M. aircraft was in process of production and the squadrons to use it were being built up and trained. From December, 1943, up to D-Day, high level patrols by Mosquitos equipped with SERRATE (an equipment for homing on to the enemy fighters A.I. – Lichtenstein) were made in target areas during and after attacks, at the fighter assembly points and on the fringes of the bomber stream. While these patrols at first had some success, the number of SERRATE contacts obtained fell off as the enemy fighters were equipped with the new type of A.I., S.N.2. Nevertheless, the patrols undoubtedly upset the enemy night fighter aircrew, though it is probable that a greater effect on their morale was caused by the low level intruder attacks against airfields which were commenced by 100 Group in April, 1944, and carried out thereafter in conjunction with approximately equal forces of Fighter Command aircraft. These fighter patrols, both high and low level, were continued with a varying degree of success until the end of the war.

Phase 6 – September 1944 to May 1945

60. The situation as it existed until the late summer of 1944 has been described. A new phase of tactics then commenced with the introduction of radio countermeasures

on a large scale.   Attempts to jam the enemy coastal warning equipment and the ground-air communications of the fighters had started as far back as 1942, using both airborne jammers carried by bombers in the main force and, for a short time, a MANDREL screen operated by Defiants. Shortly after WINDOW was introduced, some success had also been achieved in jamming and confusing the running commentaries broadcast by the enemy to his fighters. With the exception of A.B.C. (airborne jamming of V.H.F.) the responsibility for all electronic jamming was now vested in 100 Group and its aim, apart from carrying out constant investigation flights to obtain information on changes in the enemy signals, was supporting the bomber force by cutting down the enemy's early warning and thereby hiding the approach of bomber forces jamming enemy communications; and, in addition, directly attacking the enemy fighters as described above.

61. A screen of airborne MANDREL jammers, patrolling at suitable distance from the enemy coast, was designed for the first of these tasks. It was used first on the night 5/6th June, 1944, in connection with the invasion of Normandy, but for the next ten days it could not be used in direct support of the extensive Bomber Command raids into Northern France, for fear of interference with naval and beachhead equipment. From 16/17th June onwards, however, the MANDREL screen was employed in support of nearly every major night bomber operation to the end of the war. New measures were taken simultaneously for the jamming of enemy communications (FIDGET and JOSTLE).

62. The invasion of Europe being successfully launched, the strategic bombing of targets in Germany was gradually resumed from mid-July. The full effect of the combination of radio counter-measures with the tactical principles previously adopted was then demonstrated, though the reduced operations against targets in Occupied Territory continued to be heavily opposed.

63. An important new development in 100 Group was the formation of a special WINDOW force, consisting of a small number of heavy bombers whose function was to drop large quantities of WINDOW for the purpose of giving the enemy the impression of a large force of heavies. In addition to the new special force, aircraft of the H.C.U.s and O.T.U.s continued to be used in diversionary sweeps, and several targets were attacked on the same night, with Mosquitos in considerable numbers for subsidiary attacks and night fighter patrols. Operations of great complexity were planned, in which the MANDREL screen was used to cover the approach of real or diversionary forces, as required, and the timing and routeing of the various forces employed were co-ordinated with a view to causing the maximum of confusion to the enemy controllers. By keeping a constant watch on the enemy's reactions to these methods and adapting plans accordingly and, finally, by keeping up the pressure in the scale and intensity of operations, Bomber Command succeeded in creating conditions in which the enemy defence could no longer operate efficiently.

64. While the enemy defence organisation at this time was still intact and at full strength the fighter controllers were kept in considerable doubt as to which of the several bomber streams approaching enemy held territory were real and which "feint", and they were accordingly in great difficulty in making the necessary fighter

dispositions. On occasions a large fighter reaction was made to a "feint" attack while the real force was left unchallenged, and the general sensitivity about approaches to Germany proper gave great scope for feint attacks on nights when no heavy bomber raids could be made. WINDOW forces operating alone with the MANDREL screen were often able to simulate an abortive night fighter reaction, and a few mistakes of this kind soon undermined still further the confidence of the controllers and made them loth to commit themselves to decisions. Very often, when the appraisal of the raid situation was correct, the delays engendered by lack of confidence and excessive caution caused the night fighter reaction to be initiated too late to achieve a good result.

65. The deterioration which had set in was soon accelerated. The break-out of the armies from the Cherbourg peninsula was made early in August and the rapid advance through France which followed brought about far-reaching changes. First, the most westerly of the night fighter bases and fighter assembly points started to fall, followed by those in the Paris area, until by the end of the month the Luftwaffe had been practically cleared from France, and its position in Belgium and Holland was precarious. Reorganisation of the enemy fighter defences was required to meet a situation in which all targets for night bombers would be in Germany, some needing only short penetrations, and the creation of a system similar to that used previously in France was expected. Some developments along these lines actually took place and numerous subsidiary beacons and local controls again came into use. A concentration of most of the available fighter strength was also made down the whole of the western front. These measures not only made it difficult for the enemy to deal with bomber forces making deep penetrations when once they had passed through the front line of defence, but they also failed to meet the needs of the new situation for three reasons:—

(*a*) Because the number of bomber streams operating simultaneously, as already described, rarely permitted the Controllers to devote their undivided attention, in the early stages of an attack, to any one threat.

(*b*) Because the ground organisation was largely deprived of early warning, and therefore defensive action had usually to be instituted at short notice.

(*c*) Because individual enemy fighters were deprived of the use of their A.I. and homing equipment.

66. By the end of August the enemy had lost his early-warning installations on most of the Normandy coast and it was already possible for bomber forces to be routed to southern Germany through territory almost entirely under Allied control. The MANDREL screen, which at first was used only to cover approaches to the Continental coast, could be positioned, from October onwards, over France, and it could then be used to cover almost any approach to Germany. With the deterioration of the enemy early warning system, due to the effect of MANDREL and the loss of territory, it became necessary to reconsider the desirability of restricting the use of H.2.S., by means of which he was getting early warning which would otherwise have

been denied. This important point was considered at great length and in view of the fact that very good GEE coverage was now available right up to the front line (it had previously been restricted due to jamming) it was clear that no loss in efficiency would arise from the restriction of H.2.S. up to the front. Some overlap was, of course, necessary and it was decided that H.2.S. was not to be used outside a line 50 miles from enemy-held territory. In view of the extreme importance of early warning to the enemy it was likely that he would use any other transmissions from the bombers and a complete "signals silence" was accordingly imposed over the same area. As far as weather conditions permitted, low flying on outward journeys was also adopted as an additional precaution against detection.[3]

67. The use of MONICA by bomber aircraft was entirely abandoned from the night 11/12th September, 1944, and the enemy fighters were thereby deprived of the use of the FLENSBURG homer which had previously helped them to find the bomber stream.   DINAH, the electrical jammer which came into service in October, added to the interference of their S.N.2 which was already jammed by WINDOW, with the result that the enemy night fighters had to rely mainly on general instructions passed to them from the ground and the visual signals made by other fighters which had succeeded in finding the stream.

68. A further tactic, which was employed with success throughout this phase and which was useful both in evading the fighters and in shaking them off when they had once made contact, was that of making considerable changes in height at various stages of the route. Since fighters were normally expected to make contact at the target it became the practice to lose height rapidly on leaving the target area, a manoeuvre which was most successful on a number of occasions. The planning of height changes *en route* was left to the discretion of groups, except when one bomber force was comprised of aircraft from several groups or when groups, on their way to different targets, followed a common route for any distance.   In these instances co-ordinating of height planning took place at Command Headquarters.

69. By this time the efficiency of the German fighter defence was seriously reduced. In spite of the reduced area which they now had to defend, they were unable, except on rare occasions, to carry out route interception and could only send fighters to target areas at the last minute. There is no doubt that in the last few months they had suffered an additional handicap in a shortage of petrol, which greatly reduced the number of fighter sorties which could be flown. Even so, the short supplies were frequently wasted in making an abortive effort against "feint" attacking forces.

70. The basic tactics employed in the last phase of the War may be briefly summarised as follows:—

(*a*) The simultaneous employment of some or all of the following forces: several small or medium-sized bomber forces against different targets; forces of Mosquito bombers against subsidiary targets; small "feint" attacks dropping WINDOW to simulate larger forces of heavy bombers; small or large forces of minelayers; aircraft of the H.C.U.s and O.T.U.s for diversionary sweeps.

(*b*) The despatch of high and low level night fighter patrols, the former to escort the bomber stream and patrol the areas where enemy fighters were likely to assemble, the latter to attack enemy airfields and destroy fighters taking off or landing.

(*c*) The use of the MANDREL screen to cover the early movements of the bomber and/or diversionary forces.

(*d*) Low flying and Radar silence on outward journeys to prevent detection and plotting by the enemy.

(*e*) Full application of radio countermeasures against the enemy ground Radar, communications and A.I.

(*f*) Exterme concentration of all the bomber forces employed.

No major changes in these tactics were necessary, though a few minor improvements were made. For example, the "feint" attacks by WINDOWers were made more realistic by sending with them Mosquito bombers which, after the feint had turned back, continued on track, to mark and bomb a target. The tactics of the WINDOW force were also varied slightly when penetration had to be made into a limited area in which bomber operations were likely to be anticipated by the enemy, *e.g.,* the Ruhr. The WINDOWers in these circumstances, instead of staging a diversion, were used to fan out in advance of the main force over the whole area of the Ruhr, discharging large quantities of WINDOW, through which it was extremely difficult to pick out the spearhead or track of the bomber force.

71. As an illustration, both of the current tactics and of the enemy reaction to them, a typical night's operation in the closing phase in the war is given below.

On the night 14/15th February, 1945, the following operations took place:—

	Target.	Forces.
First Phase	Rosnitz	224 heavies, 8 Mosquitos.
	Chemnitz	329 heavies.
	Duisberg (feint)	12 Mosquitos.
	Mainz (feint)	19 Mosquitos.
	Berlin	46 Mosquitos.
	Minelaying (Kadet Channel and Sassnitz)	54 heavies.
	Diversionary sweep	95 heavies.
Second Phase	Chemnitz	388 heavies.
	Frankfurt (feint)	8 Mosquitos.
	Nuremberg (feint)	11 Mosquitos.
	Dessau (feint)	14 Mosquitos.
Bomber Support	MANDREL Screen	101 aircraft.
	WINDOW forces	101 aircraft.
	NIGHT FIGHTERS	

72. In the first phase the MANDREL screen was stationed just west of the battle line, extending from approximately opposite Arnhem to near Luxembourg. Minelaying forces flew across Denmark to the Kadet Channel, while the largest force of Mosquitos was on its way across N. Germany to Berlin. At the same time, the approach across France of the two main heavy bomber forces, bound for Rositz and Chemnitz was covered by the MANDREL screen. To the north of them, two small WINDOW forces, accompanied by Mosquitos, first broke cover of the screen and flew respectively towards Duisburg and Mainz. Their purpose was to engage the attention of the fighters based in the Ruhr and N.W. Germany and prevent them from being sent south towards the main forces. The two main forces, following a common track, then broke from the screen heading towards Coblenz. Just north of this city the two forces diverged N.E. and S.E. and later converged towards their targets.

73. As was hoped, the WINDOW diversions were accepted by the enemy in the early stages as a threat to the Ruhr and fighters were moved to this area, though they were soon transferred farther south to a beacon near Cologne from which interception of the main forces was attempted. These were being accurately plotted by the time they reached Coblenz, from which point both routes were plotted until they merged at about 12° E. After this, only the Chemnitz force was followed. It is probable that elements of 10 groups of fighters, including those brought from the Ruhr, were gathered near Cologne to intercept the main forces, but their moves were evidently made too late and though they pursued on towards the target, they did not make contact. Two other groups of fighters were sent from the Berlin area to Chemnitz, but they also appear to have arrived too late, since combats were extremely few, and further units brought from the south towards the return routes were equally unsuccessful. A distinct and entirely separate reaction was made to the minelayers over Denmark, probably by locally-based fighters under medium range control and the diversionary sweep was also plotted and assessed as up to 350 aircraft. Some fighters were assembled at a beacon near Hamburg, probably in response to this threat, but they apparently made no further moves.

74. In the second phase of operations, which took place about three hours later, the MANDREL screen resumed jamming in a position a little farther south. The main force bound for Chemnitz was routed south of Mannheim and a WINDOW force preceded it as it left the screen, and broke away towards the Mainz-Frankfurt area. Plots on the main force began near Liege and were coherent from Kaiserslautern to the target, but again the WINDOW feint caused an initial confusion. Night fighters from ten Gruppen, four of them on second sorties, were up in response to the second phase of operations, and the WINDOW feint having prevented interception near the frontier, some units were sent to a beacon near Erfurt, from which they were vectored towards the bomber stream 80 miles from the target.   Opposition was, however, negligible, and it is presumed that the fighters failed to find the bombers owing to jamming of their A.I. and presence of cloud on part of the route. Little attention was paid to the Mosquito forces and no reaction to them was observed. The total losses for the night were 20 aircraft or 1·3 per cent.

75. As a result of the experience gained in the precision bombing of small targets

in France and Belgium, great advances in bombing technique and accuracy were made in the last phase of the war.

76. OBOE continued to provide the most accurate marking aid available for targets within its coverage and, as new ground stations were established on the Continent, the coverage of OBOE was considerably extended. For targets outside OBOE range, the accuracy of target marking had been greatly assisted by the use of H.2.S., Mark III, which became available, as a replacement to the Mark II, in substantial numbers by mid-1944. By use of this equipment the flare forces were able to find and illuminate the aiming point much more easily and the visual markers were thereby given much better opportunities for accurate marking.[4]

77. A very high standard of efficiency in target marking and accurate bombing was attained by 5 Group, which operated almost entirely as an independent unit from April, 1944, onwards, and developed its own methods. Visual target marking by the Pathfinders was carried out from Lancaster bombers at high and medium level using the Mark XIV bombsight, but the visual markers of 5 Group, flying in Mosquitos, descended almost to ground level to drop their markers entirely by eye. Provision was also made for cancelling any marker which the Master Bomber assessed as having fallen wide.

78. 5 Group also originated and practised the methods of offset marking and sector bombing. The object of off set marking was to prevent the markers from being obscured by smoke or extinguished by bombs early in an attack and before the main force aircraft had completed their task. Sector bombing, a development from off set marking and designed to produce the desired distribution of bombs over a given area, was also employed with success. This technique required that the direction of approach to the markers and the time of overshoot should be specified separately for each squadron or, possibly for each aircraft in order that their bombs should fall as uniformly as possible over an area of given size and shape.

79. A fundamental tactical disadvantage of the 5 Group methods was, however, the time taken to assess the markers and this sometimes meant that the bomber force had to be kept waiting in the target area while this was done. As the technique was developed this defect was improved, but there is no doubt that greater losses were incurred because of it.[5]

80. Although little change had been made in the planned concentration of attacks, which remained generally at about 30 aircraft per minute, the concentration in practice often reached peak values of 40-50 aircraft per minute. This very high concentration of aircraft in the bomber forces became pronounced only after the capture of France. Up to this time, jamming by the enemy had considerably reduced the original range of GEE and before D-Day the maximum GEE cover extended only to a line running roughly down the west of the Zuyder Zee, thence south to the Scheldt and S.W. to approximately Paris. In August, 1944, the position was improved by the capture of large areas of country in which the jamming equipment was sited, and GEE coverage was then extended up to the limits of enemy-held territory. Shortly afterwards, GEE ground stations were erected on the continent and in October the range had extended to Hannover, Frankfurt and Stuttgart, later to Nurnberg and Augsburg. Thus, from

August onwards, navigation to many parts of Germany presented very little difficulty and since a common route was laid down for all aircraft in each attacking force, the concentration of aircraft in the stream became very high.

81. While a high concentration of aircraft in the stream was still desirable from most points of view, the extreme values now frequently reached seriously increased the collision risk. The reports of crews returning from operations mentioned fairly often the observations of a collision and the number of cases of damage by collision to returning aircraft tended to confirm the reports. In any case it was clear that although bomber losses were extremely low a larger proportion of aircraft than formerly were being lost to causes other than enemy action. The whole problem of concentration in relation to current tactics and the state of the enemy defences was therefore reviewed, but it was concluded that any increase in the length of stream was most undesirable under existing conditions. The four possible methods for reducing collision were, however, all tried at the discretion of groups:—

(*a*) Burning navigation lights on the outward journey until near to enemy territory.

(*b*) Increasing the width of the stream by sending out the force for those parts of the route within GEE range, on two or more parallel routes separated by about 5-8 miles.

(*c*) Broadening the height band in which aircraft of any one force were detailed to fly to 4,000 ft. instead of the customary 2,000 ft. A larger height spread could not be recommended for fear of increasing the length of stream due to the differences in their air speed and wind, and in any case this tactic had to be confined to those parts of the route where low flying was not enforced.

(*d*) The necessity of careful search at route turning points where there was a higher collision risk was also emphasised.

82. Mention has already been made of the fact that from about September, 1944, onwards, the individual enemy fighters were almost entirely deprived of the use of their aids to interception. This was most fortunate, since an unorthodox type of offensive armament, designed for use in conjunction with homing devices, is thought to have come into much greater use about this time. Information was received from Intelligence sources in August, 1944, that some of the enemy fighters were equipped with cannon, fitted above or in the fuselage, and fixed to fire upwards at a steep angle to the horizontal. The evidence obtained from examination of bombers previously damaged by fighter attack was re-investigated and the results suggested that the weapon had probably started to come into use in January, 1944, and had subsequently been used probably in 10 per cent. of non-lethal fighter attacks. Considerable apprehension was felt as to the danger of any extended use of this weapon, since MONICA had already been withdrawn and no effective provision against it could be made in the case of aircraft equipped with H.2S., constituting the bulk of the bomber force. These aircraft could not be fitted with downward-firing guns and FISHPOND

was not able to detect fighters at close range. A tactical note was issued recommending the execution of a diving turn following any FISHPOND indication or of a banking search every 5-10 minutes for all non-FISHPOND aircraft and modifications to FISHPOND were put in hand to reduce its minimum range to the order of 300 yards. Trials carried out by B.D.U. showed the corkscrew to be the most effective form of combat manoeuvre against fighters equipped with upward-firing guns and this therefore continued to be the recommended manoeuvre.

83. The proportion of damaged bombers showing strikes from upward-firing armament increased considerably towards the end of 1944 and 1945, and it is probable that, but for the general difficulties of the fighters in effecting interception, the extended use of this weapon might have been much more serious.

84. The great difficulty experienced in contacting the bomber streams over Germany forced the enemy to attempt the interception over this country of bomber forces leaving – or returning to base. It was suspected for some time in advance that such an operation was planned and the necessary arrangements were made for making emergency diversions; for obtaining news from Intelligence sources of when such an attack was imminent; and for informing aircrew by wireless of the presence of intruders. Whenever weather and other conditions permitted, the bombers were routed over the south coast of England and west of London on return. The full scale attempt was made by the enemy on the night 3/4th March, 1945, using approximately 70 night fighters. These had taken no part in the night's defensive activity over Germany, but were engaged solely in the special intruder operation under the control of 3 JD, which broadcast details of the homeward routes of the bombers. The fighter force crossed the English coast in two waves and dispersed to predetermined airfields at which the bombers were expected to land. Including aircraft of the H.C.U.s and O.T.U.s, which had taken part in a diversionary sweep, 786 aircraft of Bomber Command operated on this night and of these 45 were attacked in the air, at or near, their bases. Many had not received the intruder warning and were burning navigation lights. Twenty-seven were damaged, including 19 totally destroyed, and three other aircraft of the Command, engaged on training flights, were also shot down. Six of the intruders were shot down by the home defences.[6]

85. Two similar attempts, although on a smaller scale, were made later in March, the intention in each case apparently being to attack the bombers as they were taking off. Both attempts proved abortive because no bomber sorties were made at the times expected by the enemy and this method of interception was then abandoned. However, further precautions had to be taken to guard against a repetition of the damage inflicted on the 3/4th. Starting on the next night, the current restrictions on the use of H.2S. were extended, and signals silence was imposed over the greater part of homeward routes.

Light Bomber Operations

86. Light bombers were originally employed by only a single group of Bomber

Command, namely No. 2 Group, which operated small forces of various types of light bombers both by day and by night. Up to the middle of 1942 only Blenheim and Boston aircraft made night sorties, carrying out small intruder operations and occasionally bombing attacks in conjunction with the main bomber force.

87. Mosquito bombers made their first appearance on night operations in No. 2 Group, on 25/26th June, 1942, when, together with Blenheims and Bostons of the same Group, four of them were detailed to intrude on enemy airfields in support of the 1,000 bomber raid on Bremen. They made only one other appearance, on the same small scale, before the end of that year.

88. The Pathfinder Group, formed in August, 1942, was equipped with one Mosquito Squadron to operate "OBOE" and this squadron became operational in December, 1942. At the same time, two non-"OBOE" squadrons, having no navigational aid apart from "GEE," had been built up in No. 2 Group for daylight operations. They were switched to night operations on 20/21st April, 1943, when 11 of them were detailed to attack Berlin, each carrying four 500-lb. H.E. bombs. From then to the end of May they made 67 night sorties against a number of targets in Germany, mostly Berlin. They attacked in very small numbers (10 or less) usually from above 20,000 ft. and without the aid of blind-bombing devices. Flares were sometimes dropped to assist in locating a built-up area.

89. The non-"OBOE" Mosquito squadrons were transferred from No. 2 Group to the Pathfinder Force as from 1st June, 1943. One of them was then equipped with "OBOE," while the other formed the basis from which the light, fast bomber force was built up. At the end of the war, this consisted of 10 squadrons of Mosquitos. The build-up, was, however, gradual and at first, the operations of this force consisted merely of nuisance-raiding on a very small scale. No special equipment was carried and aircraft were obliged to bomb on D.R., assisted for short-range targets by "GEE" fixes. For longer-range targets it was sometimes possible to make a timed run from some easily identifiable landmark.

90. After the introduction of WINDOW the Mosquitos were also used for a number of other tasks in support of the main forces. These were:—

(*a*) To mark or bomb diversionary targets.

(*b*) To drop "feint" route markers and fighter flares for the purpose of misleading the enemy fighters.

(*c*) To precede main forces at the target, dropping WINDOW.

(*d*) To increase the anti-morale effect of heavy bomber raids by continuing the bombing at intervals for some time afterwards.

91. The first step made towards the development of a technique for Mosquito attacks was the experimental fitting, in December; 1943, of G.H. in one or two aircraft, which were then in a position to drop markers for the benefit of the rest of the force. This method was not pursued, but from February, 1944, onwards, a few aircraft fitted with H.2.S. were used for targets outside OBOE range, acting as Pathfinders for the remainder of the Mosquito force. For targets within OBOE range, forces of non-

equipped Mosquitos were used, from March, 1944, onwards, as main forces bombing the markers dropped by OBOE aircraft. For example, an attack was made on Essen on 8/9th April, 1944, by a force of 40 Mosquitos, eight of which carried OBOE, and the load dropped included 15 by 4,000-lb. H.E. bombs. The fitting of the Mosquito to carry a 4,000-lb. bomb had started in February, 1944, and this increased the effectiveness of the force.

92. After the invasion of the continent the numerous small operations carried out by this light bomber force aided considerably in increasing the strain put on the enemy ground defence organisation. Many of its attacks were arranged to form part of the general diversionary plan and for the purpose of making "feint" threats more realistic the Mosquito forces frequently travelled with WINDOW forces, continuing on track after the latter had turned back to mark or bomb the diversionary target. The Mosquitos were also able to operate on many nights when heavy bomber sorties could not be made and they thus contributed much towards keeping the enemy defences continually occupied.

93. In their independent operations the main target for light bombers from mid-1944 onwards was Berlin which, particularly towards the end, was attacked with great regularity. For example in March, 1945, the Capital was attacked on 29 of the possible 31 nights in the month with an average of 58 aircraft on each attack. The largest Mosquito raid of the War was also made on Berlin by 106 aircraft on April 15/16th, 1945.

94. Flying normally at an altitude of 25,000-30,000 ft. and at a speed approximately equal to that of the orthodox enemy fighters, the Mosquitos, on the whole, were little troubled by the enemy defences, and, in spite of their lack of defensive armament, suffered very low losses during the whole course of their night operations. From January, 1944, onwards, their monthly loss-rate never reached 1 per cent. and was generally less than 0·5 per cent. Since the forces operating were generally small and scattered, the observations of returning crews rarely gave any indication of the cause of loss of the missing Mosquitos and, apart from the evidence of occasional intensive defence activity against them within limited areas, the relative success of the enemy flak and fighters in combatting Mosquito raids was obscure. It was clear, however, from the damage sustained by returning aircraft, from the intercepted wireless traffic and from other sources, that on occasions considerable efforts were made by both the enemy flak and fighters.[7]

95. For example, in the first six months of 1944, the proportion of Mosquito sorties reporting damage from heavy flak was 2·9 per cent., being 1·7 per cent. for OBOE aircraft and 3·5 per cent. for the non-OBOE. In the first nine nights of July, however, the synthetic oil plant at Scholven-Buer was attacked eight times by Mosquitos, in the course of which 25 per cent. of the OBOE sorties made sustained flak damage. This was evidently due only to the regularity of the attacks and to the fact that the OBOE aircraft were compelled to make their run up to the aiming point on a fixed heading and at a fixed height. The high damage rate was reduced as soon as regular attacks on this target ceased. Starting in September, however, great efforts were made against Mosquitos by the flak defences of Berlin, and 15 per cent. of the sorties made

to the Capital reported damage, the aircraft being coned in searchlights and engaged by accurate predicted "seen" fire. Accurate fire of this kind continued to be experienced at Berlin, and occasionally over other heavily defended areas, when clear weather permitted, until the effects of the enemy shortage of ammunition began to be noticeable in January, 1945.

96. As has already been mentioned, the speed of the Mosquito was approximately equal to that of the German conventional night fighters, and this was their main defence against fighter attack. Efforts were made by the enemy to intercept, however, and jet fighters were used occasionally particularly in defence of Berlin. Towards the end of the War, therefore, routes which hitherto had been direct to and from the target were varied and dog legs were introduced. These measures, combined with irregular changes in height, were successful in preventing serious losses from fighters.

Part II. – Daylight Operations

97. Prior to the invasion of France in June, 1944, the main effort of the Command was employed almost entirely at nights. No attempt was made to employ the Command in a sustained daylight offensive which would have certainly failed, in view of the inadequate defensive armament of the bombers and the absence of suitable fighter cover.

98 During this period, however, it was possible to make occasional surprise attacks, using small and medium forces of heavy aircraft, and this was done. In April, 1942, a small scale attack was made against the M.A.N. Diesel Factory in Augsberg in which 12 Lancasters used low-level tactics attacking the target at dusk. In October, 1942, forces of approximately 100 heavy aircraft flew to Le Creusot and to Milan in daylight and returned in darkness.

99. After the invasion of France, it was possible for the Command to increase its freedom of action and to operate against short range targets, mostly in support of the Army and requiring extreme accuracy, in daylight. This was done using the marking technique which was built up during the operations against French marshalling yards during the previous three to four months, but without attempting formation tactics. As France was progressively overrun and the enemy fighter bases were pushed further back, the range of the attacks was extended and greater numbers of aircraft were used. A loose formation known as a "gaggle," in which aircraft flew in company but not in a fixed formation, was adopted. Long range fighter aircraft became available in small numbers.

100. By November, 1944, large scale attacks, using at times up to 1,000 aircraft, were carried out against German targets in the Ruhr. The total time over target in these attacks was worked out on the basis of 30 aircraft per minute and although peak concentrations sometimes reached a much higher figure it was found that this was the most satisfactory average rate.   For these raids the P.F.F. marking technique and special equipment developed for night operations against similar targets was used.

101. It was about this time that G.H. was introduced in quantity into No. 3 Group.

This was a precision blind-bombing device with an accuracy of the order of 300-500 yards, and could handle up to 80 aircraft at any one time. Until this equipment became available, daylight attacks were ordered only when there was a strong probability of clear weather conditions at the target. G.H. provided a method whereby medium-sized forces could make an accurate attack against precision targets which were obscured by cloud. The device had a range of the order of 200-250 miles and the method normally employed was for aircraft to fly in vics of three, of which the leading aircraft was equipped with G.H. and the wing aircraft released their bombs on a pre-arranged signal. This method increased the freedom of action of the Command and was particularly successful against oil targets in the Ruhr during the winter months when it was necessary to sustain the attacks and the chances of clear weather conditions were small. Because of the success of this method, 3 Group were employed more often than any other Group on daylight operations.

102. As previously stated it was not found possible or desirable to use standard close formations. Although this made the task of the fighter escort more difficult it reduced the losses to flak as compared with the conventional formations adopted by the American Fortresses and Liberators. As the penetrations became deeper, however, it was considered advisable to reduce the length of the stream and as a result the concentration of aircraft over the target was increased, and every effort was made to prevent straggling. The "gaggle" formation, however, remained the standard method throughout.

103. During this period, the Command was called upon from time to time to carry out special operations in support of the Army. In these, the tactics described above were used except that bombing was generally from a low to medium level and special precautions were taken to prevent gross errors in bombing. For this reason, in addition to the Master Bomber who directed the attacks, an experienced captain was detailed to make a special assessment of all markers and drop yellow smoke on any marker which was wide of the aiming point as an indication to the main force that it should be ignored. With this precaution it was found possible, in clear weather conditions, to attack targets of which the aiming point was no more than 3,000 yards from the front line.

104. Although the enemy fighter reaction remained slight, it was known that the bomber forces were accurately plotted as soon as they came within range of his Radar coverage. For this reason, tactics such as signals and Radar silence and the low level approach across Northern France which was used with success at night, were continued. It is probable that had the enemy been given the opportunity to make an early assessment of the composition and nature of the approaching force he would have attempted more frequent interceptions.

Part III. – Conclusion

105. When the enemy realised what strategic bombing would do to him if he was unable to stop it, or at least reduce it to manageable proportions, he concentrated the

vast bulk of his fighters and flak for the defence of the Reich. He had seen from his own failure to carry out successful strategic bombing of this country that an effective defence was possible, and he was determined to use all his resources to achieve such a defence. Our strategic bombing succeeded because we were able to equip the force with radar blind-bombing devices, and because our tactics were sufficiently flexible to enable us to outwit the defences.

106. An immense amount of thought was devoted to tactical questions, and there is no doubt that on the whole, we were able to provide the answer. First it was necessary to think out the major tactics affecting the conception of the whole attack, and the minor attacks affecting the conduct of the crews themselves. This entailed a continuous study of the enemy's defences, and a constant readiness to adapt our methods to meet new circumstances. Finally, great care was taken to train all concerned and to give them the fullest understanding of the problems.   In this way Command Headquarters, Group Headquarters, Stations and aircrews were able to work together as a team and to forge a weapon that even the immense resources of Germany were unable to blunt.

Notes:–

:1 *The Manchester was a failure through lack of engine power. The Stirling was a failure partly through being underpowered, but mainly through bad workmanship.*

2 *See Appendix C, Section XI, paras. 12 to 20.*

3 *See Appendix E, paras. 81, 82 and 83.*

4 *See Appendix B, paras. 62 to 70.*

5 *See Appendix B, paras. 52 to 61.*

6 *See Appendix K, para. 20.*

7 *See Appendix B, paras. 49 to 51.*

APPENDIX E

RADIO COUNTERMEASURES IN BOMBER COMMAND

Introduction

1. The Radio Countermeasures offensive, planned specifically to support Bomber Command operations, was wholly developed during the years 1942-45. The German controlled night-fighter system, against which the greater part of the Bomber Command Radio Countermeasures have been directed, became by 1941 a factor which was clearly destined to become a very serious menace to the night bomber. At the same time, the employment of radar aids to flak control increased the efficiency of that other main weapon of German defence against an attack.

2. At the beginning of 1942, the reality of the threat to our aircraft was well established.   The existence of the night-fighter control system was known and much of its method of operational working had been correctly deduced from "Y" service and other intelligence information. There was still lacking, however, the necessary knowledge about the actual radio and radar apparatus in use by the enemy, without which no technical countermeasures could be devised.

3. During the first six months of 1942 this technical information was gradually acquired.   Aerial photographs and captured documents told of the locations and appearance of enemy radar apparatus. From photographs it was possible to form an opinion about the capabilities and functions of the various radar devices and to supplement the information already obtained from the "Y" service, particularly that part of it which was concerned with monitoring radar transmissions. The Bruneval raid of 27th February, 1942, was successful in its object of capturing a small "Wurzburg" apparatus of the type used for plotting bombers and friendly fighters in a closely controlled interception. By May, 1942, an almost complete and very accurate picture of the enemy methods of G.C.I. fighter control had been built up.

4. At the same time, the rate of losses suffered on bombing operations was steadily rising and it appeared that much of the increase was due to the greater efficiency of the enemy defences following the large-scale introduction of radar-assisted control of both guns and fighters.

5. The position was summarised in a paper by O.R.S. on "The Advantages to be Gained by the Use of Countermeasures against Enemy R.D.F." which was published on 18th August, 1942. The arguments put forward were, briefly, that during the previous two months the overall wastage of bombers had been 5·6 per cent. of sorties and of this total a minimum of 30 per cent. and a maximum of 60 per cent., were due to radar-assisted enemy defences; these losses could be eliminated by complete countermeasures against enemy radar. It was stated that it might reasonably be expected that the use of countermeasures could reduce the loss rate by one-third, which would in effect mean that the scale of bomber effort could be increased in the same proportion. In addition, there could probably be a further increase in the effectiveness of attacks consequent on the reduced efficiency and deterrent effect of enemy defences in target areas. The paper concluded with the recommendation that the highest priority be given to the development of all possible countermeasures against enemy R.D.F.

6. At that time – the summer of 1942 – the possible benefit to be obtained from the use of Radio Countermeasures were well known, and their adoption had been urged not only by Bomber Command but by others who were concerned about the growing losses that the Command was suffering from the improving enemy defences. The development of airborne jamming apparatus had been started in late 1941 and was in progress. WINDOW had been conceived. The competent authorities, however, felt that this country was still too vulnerable to air attack to be able to initiate a jamming war, and on these grounds general permission to use Radio Countermeasures had been withheld.

7. One R.C.M. device was, however, already in use in Bomber Command. It had been claimed by many aircrews in late 1940 and early 1941, that the switching on and off of their I.F.F. sets over enemy territory appeared to affect the efficiency of the searchlights, causing them to become uncertain in their scanning or on many occasions to dowse altogether. Since it was estimated that over half of the losses to flak and one-third of the losses to fighters at this time occurred when a bomber was held in searchlights, any method of reducing the efficiency of these searchlights was bound to have a beneficial effect on the casualty rate. Although the use of the I.F.F. set to bring this about was subsequently found to be not wholly justifiable technically, there is no doubt that many crews gained confidence from its use, particularly during the period when nearly every flight into Germany involved the passage of the great searchlight belt in the "Kammhuber Line." To enable the I.F.F. set to be more easily used in this manner, a special switch had been incorporated in July, 1942.

8. Following the publication of the O.R.S. report referred to above (para. 5), the whole question of R.C.M. was re-opened on the highest level. On 21st August, a letter was sent to Air Ministry requesting the provision of suitable radio countermeasures, as a matter of the utmost importance and urgency. Development of radio countermeasures was already in progress. What was now required was the permission to use them.

9. On 6th October, 1942, a meeting was held at H.Q. Bomber Command to

consider the adoption of radio countermeasures. S.A.S.O. Bomber Command presided and others present included Sir Henry Tizard, D.B.Ops., D. of S., the C.S.O. and representatives of Air Staff and O.R.S. B.C.

10. The organisation of the German night defence system at this time offered four possible targets for attack by radio countermeasures:—

(*a*) The early-warning system, the radar components of which were mostly Freyas, situated around the coastline of Germany and Occupied Europe, supplemented by further Freyas inland and later reinforced in coastal areas by chimneys and hoardings. The Freyas had a range of up to 100 miles and the "chimneys" and "hoardings" provided somewhat greater range and accuracy. All these equipments were then operating on frequencies between 120-130 mc/s.

(*b*) The close control system at G.C.I. stations which was based on the use of two Wurzburgs, one for plotting the bomber and the other for following the friendly fighter. The Wurzburg frequency was around 570 mc/s. At each G.C.I. station there was, in addition, a Freya for "putting on" the Wurzburgs.

(*c*) The channel of communication between ground controllers and night fighters. Instructions were passed by H.F. R/T in the 3-6 mc/s band.

(*d*) Enemy A.I. operating on 490 mc/s.

The First Decisions

11. The meeting of 6th October, 1942, made the following recommendations:—

(*a*) The immediate use of I.F.F. sets modified to operate on the intermediate frequency of enemy Wurzburgs (countermeasure SHIVER).

(*b*) Since only a temporary success could be expected from (*a*), the development of an effective airborne jammer against Wurzburgs.

(*c*) The use of airborne jammers in the 120-130 mc/s band (MANDRELS), at the rate of two aircraft per squadron, against enemy Freyas. Ground MANDREL equipment at Dover and Hastings was to be brought into use to supplement the airborne MANDREL barrage.

12. Following these decisions, Bomber Command were able to introduce SHIVER immediately, and MANDREL was first brought into use in December, 1942.

13. At the same time, steps were taken to destroy the vital communication link between enemy fighters and their ground controllers. This was done by modulating the aircraft transmitters with noise produced through a microphone situated inside the aircraft. Each wireless operator was briefed to search a certain bank of 150 kc/s between 3-6 mc/s and to transmit on the frequency of any German or hostile-sounding R/T which he heard. This countermeasure, which was called TINSEL, was first used early in December, 1942.

14. MANDREL and TINSEL were introduced together and it is difficult to assess the relative effectiveness of either countermeasure. There was an appreciable fall in the loss-rate following their introduction. Probably a part of this fall was seasonable, due to the effects of winter weather on the enemy defences, but there was a considerable mass of evidence obtained from the "Y" service to show that TINSEL at least was causing the enemy fighters much inconvenience. Requests from fighters for repetition of orders, and complaints that orders were not being received, were frequently heard and at its lowest the effect of TINSEL must have been to slow up the process of interception. As the interception had to be successfully completed before the bomber had passed through the "box" in which each fighter operated, anything that delayed or prolonged this process must have brought about the escape of bombers which would otherwise have been shot down.

15. The effect of MANDREL is more difficult to estimate. The object of the MANDREL operation was to reduce, by jamming, the range at which the enemy radar could identify and plot hostile aircraft. The anticipated effect on the enemy Freyas was to reduce their range from 100 miles to approximately 25 miles. The proportional reduction in early warning to fighters operating in their own exclusive "boxes" at distances sometimes 100 miles inland, as they were in the Kammhuber Line, would be much less. Once again, evidence that MANDREL was having its effect was provided by the enemy, who began to increase the frequency range over which his Freyas operated.

16. By the beginning of 1943, countermeasures were being taken against enemy early warning, G.C.I. plotting and ground-air R/T communication. No specific countermeasures were in operation against A.I., although there was some evidence of interference from time to time, possibly caused by SHIVER. Despite this, there was little reason to suppose that SHIVER was achieving any notable success and as it was undoubtedly causing serious interference to our own C.H. stations, it was decided to discontinue its use as from 19th February, 1945.

17. Meanwhile, developments were proceeding in the production of ground jammers to cover the frequency of the enemy A.I., and in April a GROUND GROCER station was opened at Dunwich, on the Suffolk coast. Its function was to find and jam enemy A.I. signals on 490-500 mc/s. The range of the jamming was limited to about 150 miles, but from the Dunwich site the GROCER transmitter could cover parts of the Dutch coast and for some miles inland, and particularly the mouth of the Scheldt where the most efficient night fighter units were then operating.

18. Evidence of the success of GROCER was soon received from the "Y" service, who overheard many complaints by enemy fighters of A.I. interference. This traffic suddenly ceased, due probably to improved signals discipline among the enemy

fighter pilots, who must have been warned that their unguarded references over the R/T to the success of the jamming was giving away valuable information.

Difficulties with MANDREL

19. MANDREL continued to be used, but a number of circumstances combined to limit its effectiveness. The original plan had been to have two aircraft in each squadron always fitted and serviceable to cover the enemy's early warning frequencies between 120-130 mc/s. In addition, a squadron of Defiants of Fighter Command was also equipped and given the task of patrolling 50 miles off the enemy coast.

20. Two factors combined to limit the strength of the MANDREL barrage. First, the loss rate of MANDREL-equipped aircraft in No. 1 Group appeared to be excessive, giving rise to the fear that attempts to home on the MANDREL transmissions were being made by enemy fighters. Subsequently, intelligence sources confirmed that a device known as the Freya-Halbe had been developed for this purpose. To counteract any possible attempts at homing the MANDREL transmissions were interrupted by means of automatic on and off switching, the periodicity being two minutes "on" and two minutes "off." This was considered sufficient precaution to prevent homing, but it halved the effectiveness of the jamming as only an average of one-half of the number of equipped aircraft were transmitting at any one time.

21. Further, the enemy extended the frequency range of his Freyas from 120-130 mc/s to 120-150 mc/s, undoubtedly in an attempt to minimise the effect of the jamming. As each MANDREL was capable of barraging over 10 mc/s only, this meant either that more MANDRELS were required to cover the whole band or that correspondingly fewer would at any time be able to cover any part of it. The total effect was to diminish very materially the intensity of the barrage on any particular part of the Freya frequency range. The calculated requirement in August, 1943, was for 600 aircraft to be fitted with MANDREL. Actually at no time was it possible to have more than 200 fitted, owing to lack of equipment. For all this, although it was never possible to raise the MANDREL barrage to the desired intensity, the enemy was compelled to expend a considerable effort to keep his Freyas clear of jamming and, for this reason alone, MANDREL may be considered to have proved its worth. Bomber Command were naturally more concerned with the saving of their own aircraft, and although the achievement in this direction cannot be measured numerically some substantial benefit must have accrued.

A.I. Warning Receiver

23. BOOZER should not, strictly speaking, be included under R.C.M., because it was not an R.C.M. device in the sense that it did not attack any of the signals or radar

aids to the enemy defences. It was intended, however, to play a vital part in the technical war against enemy radar, particularly against Wurzburgs and A.I. to which, at that time, no effective countermeasure had yet become available.

24. BOOZER was simply a receiver which provided a visual indication that a bomber was being held in a radar beam of a type known to be used for following aircraft, and it was intended that a BOOZER warning should indicate that the individual aircraft was at that time being plotted by ground or airborne radar. The action to be taken on receipt of such warning was purely tactical.

25. BOOZER was developed in late 1942 and fitted in a few Stirlings of No. 7 Squadron. More extensive fitting took place in 1943 when a triple-channel BOOZER, which gave different types of warning for G.L., G.C.I. and A.I. beams, was developed. It was planned to make BOOZER a universal fitting in bomber aircraft. In April, 1943, a request for equipment on this scale was made, but for various reasons this target was never within sight of realization. Technical difficulties, arising chiefly from an insufficient knowledge of the details of the enemy equipment, interference with other airborne radar equipment, such as Monica and later Carpet, and production shortcomings all restricted the number of BOOZERS available.

26. The BOOZER idea was undoubtedly a very sound one, the more so because the apparatus did not itself radiate and so was immune from the homing danger, but the practical obstacles were too great for it to be really effective and there is no evidence that it ever achieved the success that was hoped for it. It was finally discontinued in September, 1944.

Introduction of Enemy V.H.F. R/T

27. Since the advent of TINSEL there had been so much evidence of its success and of the trouble which it was causing to enemy fighter communications that it was no surprise when the "Y" service reported, on 3/4th April, 1943, that fighter traffic had been heard on V.H.F. This was one of the possibilities which had been foreseen at Bomber Command but, as so frequently occurred in the conduct of the R.C.M. war, it was not until detailed information of any new development was available that practical countermeasures could be devised.

28. The new communication channel in use by enemy fighters was V.H.F. R/T on frequencies between 38-42 mc/s. "Y" service evidence confirmed that more and more victories were being claimed by fighters using V.H.F., although reception from only a limited area was possible in this country. On 7th April, 1943, the Air Ministry was asked to advise on measures which could be taken to meet this emergency.

29. The first steps were the provision of a ground transmitter, which was set up at Sizewell on the Suffolk coast, to operate a jamming barrage over the whole 38-42 mc/s band. This countermeasure, GROUND CIGAR, first came into operation on July 30th/31st, 1943.

30. It was not immediately possible to assess the results of GROUND CIGAR because it had the effect of destroying the main source of evidence, which was the

"Y" service, who found that their V.H.F. traffic was being completely obliterated. It also raised an energetic complaint from the Admiralty whose own "Y" service, listening to "E" boat traffic on the same frequency band, also experienced the same difficulties.

31. This latter point illustrates a problem which was constantly occurring during the R.C.M. campaign – the conflict between various interested parties for the unrestricted use of some part of the frequency band. R.C.M. jamming was liable to interfere also with our own and other service communications and with "Y" service listening, which proved throughout the war an invaluable source of intelligence information. Every incident was normally dealt with on its merits, but the general principles applied to each case were, first, that nothing must be done to interrupt Bomber Command's own communications, and secondly, that other complaining parties must establish that their loss was greater than the estimated gain to Bomber Command from the continued use of the offending countermeasure. Since during most of the time when R.C.M. was in operation the Germans were on the defensive and Bomber Command were suffering higher casualties than any other branch of the services, the various arguments were usually settled in favour of Bomber Command and the countermeasures continued to be used.

32. This is what happened with GROUND CIGAR. The transmitters remained in operation during the period of Bomber Command attacks but, like all ground R.C.M. on the higher frequencies, suffered from lack of range. The effective coverage of GROUND CIGAR was not expected to be more than 140 miles from the ground station, and much of the area within the coverage was over the North Sea. The real answer to the use by the enemy of V.H.F. communications was felt to be airborne jammers and a detailed requirement for their provision was made to Air Ministry on 6th May.

Use of Airborne V.H.F. Jammers

33. The demand was for the development of an airborne jammer, to be fitted to aircraft of one bomber squadron which could undertake the R.C.M. role in addition to its normal function as part of the bomber force.

34. On 7th/8th October, AIRBORNE CIGAR, later to be generally known as A.B.C., was first used operationally. Lancasters of No. 101 Squadron were fitted with a panoramic receiver and three transmitters, and carried a specially trained German-speaking A.B.C. operator in addition to the normal crew. The operator listened for German fighter control communications, in the nature of which he had already been trained by the use of gramophone recordings of enemy night fighter control traffic, and applied the jamming to any transmissions which he heard.

35. Originally, the A.B.C. operators received some assistance from the "Y" service listening station at West Kingsdown, who passed them details of active frequencies by means of coded references. The "Y" service in this country still suffered from limitations of range and was not able to pick up V.H.F. traffic from the whole of the

area over which the bombers operated. Hence, it was soon decided that the A.B.C. operators should find and jam frequencies independently of any ground control.

36. A.B.C. aircraft were placed at intervals along the bomber stream in order to give complete protection to all aircraft taking part in the raid, and each operator was normally expected to hear and jam V.H.F. transmissions in his own vicinity. In addition, they carried out their normal bombing functions subject only to a limitation in the bomb load due to the extra weight of equipment and the special operator. This weight limitation was of the order of 1,000 lb. A.B.C. was continued in this form by No. 101 Squadron till April, 1945, and gave extremely good results, the enemy being in effect deprived of the use of R/T in his V.H.F. band.

Jamming by WINDOW

37. The outstanding event in the development of R.C.M. in the year 1943 was the introduction of WINDOW. WINDOW was not a new conception. It had long been realised that the use of some mechanical means to produce false echoes on radar apparatus was likely to be the most successful method of limiting their effectiveness. The need for WINDOW had frequently been used by Bomber Command but, for various reasons, permission to use it had always been withheld. Among the causes for the ban on WINDOW were difficulties of production, particularly in the priority of allotment of the quantities of aluminium needed, and the shortage of suitable plant for its manufacture, but, more especially, the overriding fear of retaliation in kind at a time when our own radar defences could have been obliterated by the enemy use of WINDOW. It is now known that the Germans themselves were also influenced by this same fear.

First Use of WINDOW

38. WINDOW was first used on 24th/25th July, 1943, on the occasion of the first attack in the "Battle of Hamburg." Its success in limiting casualties and reducing the general efficiency of the German defences, with the consequent increase in the accuracy of bombing attacks, is well known. From that date until the end of the war, WINDOW in various forms was employed against all known types and variations of enemy radar, and no really effective antidote to it was ever produced. The German fear of WINDOW was proved to have been well founded.

39. The first types of WINDOW used were designed to cripple the German radar on the 53-cm. band. That is the Wurzburgs, which were used for G.C.I. control and for gun-laying. The elaborate and very efficient system of G.C.I. control, which had now been built up into a network covering nearly the whole of Western Germany and Occupied Europe, was immediately thrown into confusion, and hurried expedients had to be devised in an attempt to find some substitute method.

Mass Control of Fighters

40. The first development which followed from the enemy was the introduction of mass control of fighters, in an endeavour to direct as many as possible to the estimated target area.   There they were to attempt interception with the aid of searchlights, which already formed part of the ground defences. To this end, instructions were issued on H.F. (3-6 mc/s) R/T from a central control. Interception along routes was left to the old G.C.I. controls, working as well as they were able through the interference caused by WINDOW. The immediate answer to this new procedure was to attempt to cut the vital ground-air communication link.   TINSEL was already in operation against H.F. R/T, but now instead of each bomber being especially occupied with the one of many frequencies which happened to be in action in its own neighbourhood, there were fewer frequencies active and each one concerned the force as a whole. It became necessary to devise some means of directing the TINSEL effort on to the dangerous frequencies, and at the same time increasing the strength of the jamming. This was done by means of SPECIAL TINSEL.

41. A proportion of all bombers operating in any one force was briefed to use SPECIAL TINSEL. Frequencies in use for running commentary control of fighters were found by the "Y" service (West Kingsdown) and passed out to aircraft in the half-hourly Group Operational broadcasts. On receipt of this information all aircraft which had been briefed to operate SPECIAL TINSEL, originally two-thirds of the aircraft from any one GROUP, immediately began jamming on that frequency.

42. SPECIAL TINSEL was instantly effective, but could be overcome without much difficulty by increasing the number of channels on which the running commentary instructions were passed. This was soon done and was replied to in turn by dividing the SPECIAL TINSEL effort between groups, each one operating on a different frequency.   Every such division of the SPECIAL TINSEL barrage necessarily reduced the intensity of the jamming on any one frequency, but it also forced the enemy fighters to spend valuable time searching for a frequency that was unjammed. Ultimately, of course, it would always be possible for the enemy to radiate on a greater number of frequencies than we could reasonably expect to jam with sufficient power, but in practice this very rarely occurred.

Countermeasures against Running Commentary – CORONA

43. To add to the jamming potential in the 3-6 mc/s band, high-power ground transmitters normally used by the G.P.O. for overseas radio-telegraphy were pressed into service. The objections to ground R.C.M. previously mentioned (para. 32) do not apply in the H.F. band where propagation conditions are different and ranges of 300-600 miles are easily attainable by night.

44. Four of these stations were made available and arrangements were completed to have them controlled by West Kingsdown, who would pass the frequencies to which the transmitters should be tuned, and also modulate them. The preliminary organisation of this countermeasure, which was known as CORONA, involved

negotiations with the G.P.O. and B.B.C., some modifications to the transmitters, and the building of new wideband aerials.   Nevertheless, these details were completed and CORONA was first operated by 22nd/23rd October.

45. A new departure in countermeasure technique was now considered. Previously all R.C.M. had been straight jamming. With the CORONA transmitters it was possible to issue false instructions. The traffic to be jammed was mainly in German plain language, and its nature was well understood by the CORONA operators at West Kingsdown. Typical messages included instructions to proceed to certain known rallying points or, alternatively, information about the movements, height, course, speed of our bombers. It should have been a simple matter to issue conflicting orders to the enemy fighters. It was realised, however, that while the enemy aircrews themselves could be misled, the ground controllers would be provided with a valuable source of information, as they, too, would hear the CORONA traffic and could make appropriate deductions from any false messages they heard. Consequently, it was decided that it would be too dangerous to attempt any deception over the routeing and targets of the bombers, and the CORONA traffic was confined to instructions to land, tuning transmissions, and warnings about unserviceability of bases – all of which were calculated to distract the crews, shake their confidence in their own controllers, and delay their reactions to genuine orders.

46. Once again the evidence of the success of CORONA was supplied by the enemy himself, through the "Y" service. Fighter controllers showed signs of frayed tempers. Various devices, such as prefixing messages with code numbers or using male or female voices to pass instructions, were employed to emphasise the authenticity of the running commentary orders. All of these were replied to in kind, and, as a measure of relief, the commentary would occasionally be interrupted by a suitable recorded extract from one of Hitler's speeches. This wordy warfare could not, however, be continued indefinitely, and was eventually superseded by straight jamming produced from recordings of several genuine lines of traffic superimposed on one another.

47. Further evidence of the difficulties which were being caused by SPECIAL TINSEL and CORONA became apparent in the duplication of running commentaries, first on the M.F. band and later on V.H.F.

Dartboard

48. On 3/4th November, 1943, the high-powered broadcast station at Stuttgart was heard passing instructions to fighters. The simple answer to this was to use a similar transmitter in this country and to jam the traffic, but the problem, at the ranges involved, was to find a transmitter of sufficient power. Fortunately, one was available, and, after negotiations with the Foreign Office, the B.B.C. transmitter at Crowborough, the most powerful station in Europe, was brought into action, for countermeasure DARTBOARD. DARTBOARD commenced on the night 6/7th December, 1943.

49. Further confirmation of the difficulties which the enemy fighter controllers were experiencing in maintaining their communications through the R.C.M. jamming was provided by the very nature of the transmissions on M.F. R/T. Originally, the method used was to interrupt the normal programme momentarily to enable brief instructions to be interpolated. Later, it was suspected that the programme itself was also being used as a means of conveying information and, after some considerable investigation and study of the programme items in conjunction with the known movements of our bomber force, it was discovered that a comprehensive musical code was being employed. Distinctive types of music or musical instruments were played to indicate the progress of a raid, some being used to direct the fighters to certain target areas, others to announce the various stages of the raid, whether the target had been attacked, if the bombers were returning and when the fighters could land. The adoption of such an elementary and haphazard system was conclusive proof of the success of R.C.M., particularly the CORONA campaign.

50. The answer to this new type of activity was already available, in DARTBOARD, and the M.F. control transmission from broadcast stations soon ceased, after a comparatively short life.

Birth of No. 100 Group

51. The other important R.C.M. development of 1943 was the formation of No. 100 Group, on 1st December. No. 100 Group was brought into being as the unit responsible for the operational application and co-ordination of all R.C.M. efforts, ground and airborne.

52. The advisability of having a separate unit, under Bomber Command, to fulfil these functions, arose from the following considerations:—

(*a*) The growing complexity of R.C.M. activities.

(*b*) The need to operate specialist R.C.M. aircraft which had not also to perform a normal bombing role, on account of the size and weight of the special equipment now required or because they might be required to operate away from the main force.

(*c*) Fitting and servicing problems, which were becoming increasingly complicated, could more easily be resolved under centralised control. The need for general installation of R.C.M. equipment in bombing squadrons could be eliminated.

(*d*) The desirability of specialist direction in developing new R.C.M. techniques.

The functions of a specialist R.C.M. unit, which ultimately appeared as No. 100 (Special Duties) Group, was suggested by Bomber Command in June, 1943, approved by Air Ministry on 29th September and completed on 1st December. It was not until

June, 1944, however, that the Group began to function operationally in the role originally conceived for it and its story rightly belongs to that year.

Development during 1944

53. By the beginning of 1944, the following countermeasures were being employed operationally by Bomber Command:—

(*a*) MANDREL, against the early warning system.

(*b*) WINDOW, against G.C.I. plotting.

(*c*) GROUND CIGAR, AIRBORNE CIGAR, TINSEL, SPECIAL TINSEL, CORONA and DARTBOARD against ground-air communications.

(*d*) GROUND GROCER and WINDOW against A.I.

(*e*) BOOZER.

54. A careful watch was always kept for enemy attempts to avoid the effects of any of these countermeasures. The "Y" service could usually be relied on to give immediate notice of such new developments as changes of frequency, particularly of the enemy ground-air communications. During the early part of 1944, the following variations were observed:—

(*a*) *In ground-air communications for fighter control.*
(i) H.F. W/T running commentaries.
(ii) V.H.F. R/T on 31·2 mc/s.
(iii) M.F. navigational radio beacons, which were normally used as rendezvous points for fighters, were also passing executive instructions.
(iv) V.H.F. W/T.

(*b*) *In the early warning system.*
(i) The gradual spreading of frequencies until the band extended from 70-200 mc/s as against the 120-130 mc/s originally used.
(ii) The use of our own I.F.F. transmissions for tracking bombers.

(*c*) *In control of fighters.*
(i) The adoption of the Benito system.
(ii) The use of a S.B.A. type beam to assist fighter navigation.

(*d*) *In A.I.*

Gradual disuse of 490 mc/s (Lichtenstein B.C.).

W/T Jamming

55. The introduction of W/T as a means of passing instructions to fighters provided

another significant indication of the effectiveness of the communications jamming. Whereas any R/T instructions, which were normally passed in plain language or in an elementary self-evident code, could be received by the fighter pilot, W/T instructions had to be passed in code, received and decoded by the W/T operator and then passed to the pilot. All this would involve additional delays in executing the orders and further add to the burden of the wireless operator, who would normally be occupied chiefly with the airborne radar. It is quite evident that this system would not have been adopted while there was any hope of reliable working on R/T, but when used, it was likely to prove more difficult to counteract.

Drumstick

56. W/T transmissions cannot be jammed as easily as R/T, as a moderately competent operator can work through a very considerable degree of interference. A jamming signal must be stronger than the signal to be jammed, which it must also resemble in tone and keying speed. Nevertheless, a counter-measure was devised, operating in a manner similar to CORONA. The monitoring of enemy W/T transmissions was done at the Cheadle "Y" station, and it was arranged that immediate notice of the use of any W/T frequency in the 3-6 mc/s band should be given. A Bomber Command medium-power transmitter was then brought into action on that frequency, operated by an automatic key, radiating a series of meaningless dots and dashes at variable speeds. This countermeasure, which became known as DRUMSTICK, was in operation on 21/22nd January, within a week of the first use of H.F. W/T by the enemy. One consequence of its use was an increase in the number of H.F. W/T frequencies employed, and ultimately some 10 or 12 DRUMSTICK transmitters, including some placed at the disposal of Bomber Command by No. 26 Group, were available. There were occasions when even these were insufficient to attack all the fighter control channels which were active at any one time, but this can be adduced as evidence of the success of the countermeasure. Even though one or more of the many frequencies in use in the various bands may have been unjammed from time to time, the enemy fighter was still faced with the problem of seeking and finding a clear channel.

57. V.H.F. R/T on 31·2 mc/s had a comparatively brief life. It was answered by modifying three A.B.C. transmitters to jam on this frequency. The A.B.C. receiver did not cover the frequency so "blind" jamming was undertaken – not so much in the hope of obliterating any traffic that there might have been as to indicate to the enemy our readiness to engage him if he continued his developments in that direction. This tactic may have been successful, for traffic on this frequency was heard for only a short while afterwards.

Benito Working

58. The Benito system of control, which depended on the reception and retransmission of an audio tone by each individual fighter, was also attacked by means of a modified A.B.C. transmitter. A suitable modulator was designed to radiate, on the Benito frequency, an audio note as near as possible to the pitch of the Benito tone. It was hoped thus to confuse the Benito ranging by the production of spurious signals. There is now evidence that this scheme was very much more successful than it was expected to be.

Fidget

59. The use of M.F. beacons for passing plots to fighters was first noticed on April 22/23rd, 1944. There was an almost ready-made countermeasure for this activity, because No. 80 Wing had already been in action earlier in the war against beacons of the same type when they were used by enemy bombers on operations against this country. It only needed Cheadle to identify the active frequencies and pass the information to H.Q., No. 80 Wing, who used their own transmitters to radiate a jamming signal. This countermeasure, FIDGET, was first used on 27/28th April.

60. Two effects of the MANDREL jamming on the enemy early warning system were apparent at this time, early 1944. It has already been mentioned that the first reaction to MANDREL was the spreading of the frequency range on which the early warning Freyas operated. Originally confined to 120-130 mc/s it had been expanded, in 1943, to cover a range of 120-150 mc/s, with a consequent reduction in the intensity of MANDREL jamming which could be brought to bear on any part of the Freya band. Now there was evidence of an even greater expansion, and radar signals of a type which might be associated with aircraft plotting were heard on frequencies from 70-200 mc/s. There were comparatively few signals received from outside the 120-150 mc/s range and their nature was not sufficiently evident for definite steps to be taken against them, but here was a sign of a further attempt to evade the restrictions imposed by our R.C.M.

I.F.F. Tracking

61. As a further indication of the value which the enemy placed upon the early plotting of our bombers it was also discovered that he was using our I.F.F. radiation for long-range tracking. At this time, I.F.F. were normally switched on until the bombers were 50 miles out from the English coast, after which they were ordered to be switched off until within 100 miles of the coast on the homeward journey. If any sets were accidentally left switched on at other times, then the enemy "Y" service could listen to them responding to the interrogation of our own C.H. stations, or could trigger them off themselves and so provide a valuable source of plotting information.

62. The simplest method of avoiding this new danger was to switch off I.F.F. sets

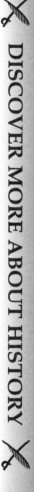

Pen & Sword Books

FREEPOST SF5

47 Church Street

BARNSLEY

South Yorkshire

S70 2BR

in aircraft altogether. Before this could be done, agreement with Fighter Command had to be reached, but that did not present any obstacle. It was a matter of much greater difficulty to persuade crews that it was in their interests to ensure that their I.F.F. sets were switched off and it was only by sealing the switches and prohibiting the use of I.F.F. except in emergency that a satisfactory result could be obtained. It is known with certainty that this prohibition was successful in denying to the enemy a very valuable source of information about the movements of our bombers and one on which he placed so much reliance that he continued assiduously throughout the rest of the war to keep watch for the occasional lapses which occurred from time to time. The restriction on I.F.F. was first imposed on 5th January. 1944.

Enemy A.I. Development

63. Against the enemy A.I. (Lichtenstein B.C.) which operated on 490 mc/s, we had in operation GROUND GROCER, which covered a small area of Holland and Belgium, and Serrate. Serrate, which is not strictly an R.C.M. device, was fitted in night fighters of No. 100 Group to enable them to home on to A.I. transmissions and consequently on to enemy night fighters. It was first operated by Fighter Command in support of Bomber operations in June, 1943, and the squadrons were later incorporated in No. 100 Group. It was noticeable in early 1944 that these fighters were obtaining fewer Serrate contacts and at the same time the GROCER monitoring watch also reported less indication of A.I. activity in 490 mc/s. The inference to be deduced from these facts was that the old type of A.I., against which countermeasures had been devised, was no longer in use to any appreciable extent. Intelligence sources also advised of a new development in A.I. but beyond the fact that it was known as S.N.2, little information about it could be obtained. The "Y" service and No. 192 Squadron both sought energetically for any new radar signals that might be associated with A.I., but without success.

64. It is now known that the enemy had the successful and unrestricted use of S.N.2 for over six months from October, 1943, and even then the solution to the problem of S.N.2 was only obtained by sheer chance. The only clues which had been obtained to the nature of the new apparatus were a few radar signals around 160 mc/s which might have emanated from it, and a photograph, taken by the camera gun in an American fighter, of a novel type of aerial array on an enemy night fighter on the ground, which could have been used for A.I. 167 mc/s was the frequency of the enemy tail-warning device which could possibly have been modified for use as A.I.; the dimensions of the aerial array as seen in a poor-quality photograph suggested a frequency in the neighbourhood of 100 mc/s, which was thought to be too low to produce reliable results. On the strength of the assumption that 160 mc/s would be the new A.I. frequency, a quantity of WINDOW, Type Y, was produced in readiness. This anticipation proved to be incorrect and the special WINDOW was never actually used, for on 12/13th July, 1944, all these problems were solved by the accidental

landing in this country of a Ju.88, undamaged and with S.N.2 fitted and in working condition.

65. Examination of the equipment of this Ju.88 showed that the S.N.2 worked on a frequency around 90 mc/s and, fortunately, a remedy was immediately available. WINDOW, Type MB, had been devised for use against enemy early-warning in connection with the D-Day landings and was designed to cover all frequencies between 70 and 200 mc/s. Good stocks were still in hand, and on 23/24th July this type of WINDOW was used on a normal operation. Its effect was not immediately noticeable, although our losses on that night, in operations against Kiel, were very low. Two nights later in a raid on Stuttgart, our "Y" service intercepts suggested that the enemy fighter controller had successfully followed the movements of our bombers and organised an efficient defence, yet our losses were again surprisingly low. We now know that this was largely, if not entirely, due to WINDOW, Type MB, interfering with the enemy A.I. From that time one or other of the "M" types of WINDOW was regularly used, later in conjunction with electrical jamming, and the enemy was satisfactorily denied the full use of an aid to interception which he had found very valuable up till then.

Electrical Jamming of Wurzburg – Carpet

66. One of the recommendations of the meeting of 6th October, 1942, when the decision to use R.C.M. in support of bomber operations was first taken (para. 11 above), was the development of an effective airborne jammer against Wurzburgs. WINDOW proved to be a very satisfactory counter-measure to Wurzburgs, but one which operated only when bombers were present in the required concentration; it was of little value to stragglers and did not provide adequate protection to bombers at the head of the stream. CARPET was designed to jam Wurzburgs electrically and so close any gaps that might appear in the WINDOW protection.

67. CARPET consisted of an automatic search receiver and jammer operating in the Wurzburg frequency band of 530-580 mc/s. As soon as the receiver picked up a Wurzburg signal the jamming was applied on that frequency for a period of two minutes, after which the receiver continued to search. Any signals received were presumably from Wurzburgs which were actually following that particular bomber, so that CARPET was especially designed for the protection of the aircraft in which it was carried.

68. It was originally intended to fit CARPET first in the Pathfinder Force, whose normal station at the head of the bomber stream placed them outside the protection of the main WINDOW cloud, and fitting had begun by March, 1944.

69. The first effects of CARPET were most satisfactory. The loss rate of fitted aircraft was lower than for the bomber force as a whole and the flak damage, in particular, was very much less than average. However, these benefits did not last long, for the enemy took steps to overcome the CARPET jamming by widening the frequency band in which his Wurzburgs operated and by modifying the equipment

to allow for vertical or horizontal polarisation. At the same time, the number of CARPETS which became available for use in the Command fell very short of expectations.

70. CARPET was used extensively and successfully by the U.S.A.A.F. and it was probably this which caused the enemy to take such vigorous action to counter it. When once this action was taken, Bomber Command was never able to recover the lost ground. Neither the number of CARPETS necessary to cover the extended frequency band nor the aerials to give simultaneous horizontal and vertical polarisation were ever available in more than a fraction of the quantities needed. Theoretically CARPET should have been a cheaper and simpler substitute for WINDOW. It undoubtedly caused the Germans some inconvenience and made them expend some effort in finding the answer to it, but on the whole it must rank among the least successful of the countermeasures attempted by the Command.

R.C.M. for D-Day

71. In the three months before D-Day, June 6th, 1944, much of the R.C.M. development in Bomber Command was concentrated on the part which R.C.M. was planned to play in support of the landings in Normandy. Bomber Command's R.C.M. participation in the Overlord operation involved:—

(*a*) In conjunction with the Navy, the simulation of two convoys approaching the French Coast at two points between Cap Gris Nez and Le Havre (operations TAXABLE and GLIMMER).

(*b*) A Mandrel Barrage and Screen to jam the enemy early warning in the Assault Area.

(*c*) A.B.C. jamming to protect the forces engaged in TAXABLE and GLIMMER and Airborne Forces.

(*d*) Simulation of attacks by Airborne Forces (operations TITANIC I, II and IV).

72. With the exception of A.B.C., each of these operations involved the development of a new technique in R.C.M.

73. In operations TAXABLE and GLIMMER the convoy simulation was produced by new types of WINDOW specially designed to react against the enemy's early warning and coast-watching radar and was discharged at such heights as to produce apparent "big ship" echoes.   The problem of creating just the right effect was principally one of navigation because the "convoy" had to be made to appear to approach at a speed of seven knots and this necessitated the WINDOW-dropping aircraft making a series of very accurate overlapping orbits for a period of up to five hours. The technique was developed by No. 617 Squadron, who carried out tests against our Type 11 radar, and the two operations were actually undertaken by No. 617 and 218 Squadrons respectively.

74. A MANDREL SCREEN had for long been considered a desirable addition to the R.C.M. armoury, but it was not until its creation was given the overriding priority which attached to all projects connected with the D-Day operations that Bomber Command was able to obtain it. The function of the Screen during the landings was to cover the assault forces by jamming all the coastal radar in the Channel area. The frequency band to be covered was from 90-200 mc/s and it was hoped, by the jamming, to limit the range of the early-warning radar to a range of about 30 miles. The task was undertaken by Stirlings of No. 199 Squadron reinforced by Fortresses of No. 803 (American) Squadron. Owing to limitations of power supply, it was never possible to equip one Stirling to cover the whole of the band and these aircraft normally operated in pairs, two to each station. The stations were so selected that no beam from any known coastal radar installation could penetrate the gap between any two of them. No. 803 Squadron, on the right wing of the attack was given the task of jamming the long-range radar in the Cherbourg Peninsula, operating on a frequency of 120-130 mc/s and one aircraft per station sufficed to do this.

75. The A.B.C. aircraft were expected to protect all the airborne forces and aircraft concerned in the OVERLORD operation, by patrolling across the expected line of approach of enemy fighters and jamming their V.H.F. communications. In the event, the effects of this part of the operation far exceeded what was planned for it.

76. The TITANIC operations consisted of the dropping of dummy parachutists, as a diversion to the real airborne landings, by Stirlings of 3 Group using WINDOW to increase the apparent size of the forces employed.

77. These R.C.M. operations contributed very materially to the tactical surprise effected by the landings and were wholly responsible for delay on the part of the enemy in bringing some of his strategic reserves into the battle area. Operation GLIMMER, the convoy simulation in the direction of Boulogne, receiving rather unexpected support from the A.B.C. patrols, which were mistaken as the protection for air forces in the same area, completely deceived the enemy and convinced him that the actual assault was to be made in the Pas de Calais.

78. In addition to the part actually played in the landings, the R.C.M. preparations for operation OVERLORD left Bomber Command with several very valuable new weapons, which were now available for use in support of normal bombing operations. From that time onward the MANDREL SCREEN could be used either in covering the bomber approach, or in unnecessarily alerting the enemy defences. When there were main force operations, the MANDREL SCREEN was active, denying the enemy early warning of the approach of the bomber force or, frequently in conjunction with a small diversionary force of WINDOW-dropping aircraft, distracting his attention elsewhere. During the summer months, when targets in Southern Germany were being attacked and it was impossible to disguise the presence of a large force of

bombers travelling long distances over occupied territory on their way to their targets, the MANDREL SCREEN, operating off the Dutch Coast, frequently prevented or delayed the movement of fighter reinforcements from Holland and Belgium to the bomber routes.

79. The second important development from the D-Day operations was the WINDOW diversion. A small number of aircraft dropping "Freya" type WINDOW – MB MC or any of the M series – could be made to appear several times larger than it really was in the eyes of the enemy's early warning radar. This enabled feint diversions to be staged in support of bomber operations or alone to cause unnecessary activity and wastage among enemy defences.

80. The MANDREL SCREEN and WINDOW DIVERSION were used with telling effect against the enemy's system of mass-controlled night fighters. The reduction in early warning caused by the MANDREL SCREEN gave the fighter controllers so much less time to appreciate genuine and feint raids and make their dispositions accordingly. It was not surprising therefore that they were found to be using other expedients to obtain accurate tracks of the bomber forces.

The "Silence" Policy

81. The use of our I.F.F. radiations by the enemy has already been mentioned. The JU.88 which landed at Woodbridge on July 12/13th was fitted with Flensburg, which was found to be a homing device working on the frequency of Monica. From the crew of this same JU.88 were obtained details of Naxos, which was said to be a homer on H.2.S. Flight trials were carried out by the JU.88 against a force of heavy bombers simulating a genuine raid and operating in the same degree of concentration as would normally be attained on a bombing operation and it was found that:—

(*a*) WINDOW type MB was completely effective against S.N.2.

(*b*) Using Flensburg, it was possible to home into the bomber stream from at least 45 miles and then to select an individual aircraft and complete the interception.

82. It was now quite definite that any radar transmission made from a bomber was a potential source of danger not only to that bomber itself but to the whole of the force accompanying it. MONICA had been installed in bombers purely in the interests of aircraft safety. Experiments proved, however, that it was not the benefit that had been hoped. The concentration achieved by a typical bomber force in mid-1944 was such that any one aircraft equipped with MONICA would receive a large number of warnings from the proximity of other bombers. This number could be reduced by limiting the range of MONICA, in the absence of any device by which friendly aircraft could be recognised, but it was found that then it was not possible to jam the enemy's S.N.2 down to such a range. It was also proved that there was no significant difference between the loss rates of bombers fitted with MONICA and those not so fitted. This established that MONICA was not saving any aircraft and, while there

was no evidence arising from this investigation to suggest that it was responsible for the loss of MONICA-equipped aircraft, the Flensburg experiments had clearly shown the danger to the force as a whole. Consequently, it was decided that MONICA should no longer be used. Partial restrictions were imposed in mid-August when the nature of the Flensburg apparatus was first understood, and a complete ban was placed on its use a month later.

83. The next radar device to come under consideration in the campaign for Signals silence was H.2.S. This presented quite a different problem. Apart from technical difficulties which were soon resolved, arising from the switching on of H.2.S at high altitudes, H.2.S was not, like MONICA, a safety device, but was an aid to navigation on which the success or failure of any attack might depend. Within the area of Gee coverage, however, H.2.S was not needed as a navigational aid and was used there chiefly in order that crews might obtain some additional training. It was fully realised that any suggestion likely to shake crews' confidence in H.2.S or hint at possible danger in its use was likely to lead to the loss of the full value from H.2.S as a navigational and blind-bombing aid. At the same time, the whole of the R.C.M. effort directed against the enemy's early warning system could be rendered useless by a few H.2.S transmissions from bombers. It was finally recommended that H.2.S should remain switched off until the bomber force was within 40 miles of enemy territory, and this was adopted in principle. The actual areas in which radar silence was to be observed were decided as part of the planning of each separate attack, and gradually extended across Western Europe in the wake of the advancing armies.

High-Power Airborne Jamming

84. The possibility of using specialist R.C.M. aircraft fitted with high-power equipment, as support for the bomber force had been suggested in May, 1943. Later in the year, the idea was adopted and the squadrons eventually began forming in 1944, under the control of No. 100 Group. The first specialist R.C.M. heavy aircraft were not used operationally until after they had taken part in the Overlord operation.

85. The aircraft used as specialist R.C.M. aircraft in bomber support were Fortresses. The reasons for the adoption of this type were threefold:—

(*a*) The aircraft had to be large enough to carry the special equipment and provide the power required for its operation.

(*b*) It might be necessary to fly above the main bomber stream out of the WINDOW protection and this, added to the risk of fighters homing on the R.C.M. transmissions, called for a type of aircraft with the speed and ceiling that would enable it to defend itself.

(*c*) No operational type of aircraft could be spared for the purpose.

86. It was decided that the bomber support aircraft should be fitted to jam enemy ground-air communications; A.I., G.L./G.C.I. and Freyas in that order of priority.

Jostle

87. The high-power apparatus developed for airborne jamming of ground-air communications was JOSTLE, which was first used operationally in July, 1944. JOSTLE could jam on any frequency in both the H.F. and V.H.F. bands used by the enemy for ground control of fighters. Two different methods of application were adopted. For V.H.F. jamming it was possible to cover the whole of the enemy's frequency band with a barrage, and this was normally done. Against H.F. controls it was necessary to jam spot frequencies. These were monitored by listening stations in this country and passed by them to the JOSTLE-equipped aircraft. A special operator was required for JOSTLE; he was carried in addition to the normal crew of the Fortress, but he was not called upon to search for active frequencies as was the A.B.C. operator.

Airborne Grocer for A.I. Jamming

88. For engaging the enemy's A.I. it was proposed to develop an airborne jammer known as AIRBORNE GROCER. This was to operate on the Lichtenstein B.C. frequency and be carried in aircraft which would fly above the bomber stream, which they would cover in the downward cone of radiation of the jammer.

89. AIRBORNE GROCER was not ready to be used operationally until June, 1944. It was then withheld for fear of its being used as a homing beacon on summer nights, and later, when it was established that the Lichtenstein B.C. was no longer used by enemy fighters, it was dropped altogether. Thus AIRBORNE GROCER was never used operationally.

90. Electrical jamming of enemy A.I. This time the Lichtenstein S.N.2 was ultimately carried out by PIPERACK. This was a modified form of DINA, which was an American jammer originally designed to reinforce MANDREL. PIPERACK was carried in the special Fortresses of No. 100 Group and, in conjunction with M type WINDOW used by the whole of the main force, was responsible for limiting the effectiveness of enemy A.I. By the end of the War the special R.C.M. aircraft of No. 214 Squadron were equipped with JOSTLE, CARPET, PIPERACK and DINA.

Enemy Loss of Early Warning

91. A climacteric in the history of R.C.M. was reached with the occupation of the greater part of France and Belgium in September, 1944. No other single occurrence in the whole war was responsible for such a great reduction in bomber casualties. This was brought about by the loss by the enemy of all his elaborate system of early-warning just at the time when the technique of the MANDREL SCREEN and WINDOW diversion was being perfected.   From that time until the end of the War, these two R.C.M. instruments were chiefly responsible for reducing the enemy night defensive system to a state of impotence, from which it never recovered.

92. Apart from radar stations on the coast of Holland, which could normally be avoided by routeing bombers out of their range over liberated areas of France, the enemy then had no early warning facilities west of the frontiers of Germany itself. Consequently, it was possible for bombers to approach to within 100 miles of the frontier, and frequently to within less than one hour's flying time of their intended target, before being plotted. The MANDREL SCREEN, placed across the line of approach at a distance usually about 60 miles from the frontier, could further reduce this time to a limit below which the enemy fighters could not operate effectively. The night fighters which were also forced to operate from unfamiliar airfields and without much of the elaborate communication and control facilities which they had enjoyed in France and Belgium, needed at least 40 minutes' warning of an impending raid if they were to put up any effective opposition. This the MANDREL SCREEN was successful in denying them. In addition to this handicap, the defences not only had inadequate time in which to mount any opposition to a threatened attack, but they were faced also with the problem of deciding very rapidly which, if any, of several approaching bomber forces were about to carry out genuine attacks and which were only WINDOW feints. Sometimes they were successful, but more often than not they failed.

93. From September, 1944, until the end of the War in Europe there were no major technical innovations in R.C.M. Every radar and signals aid to the defence of Germany which was considered to be of any substantial value to the enemy was being attacked and during that period no new devices that called for countermeasures were produced. It is possible that had the War lasted a few months longer the enemy would have come forward with something new – either in the field of centimetric radar or infra-red – but, in the event, there were no developments that required any answer from Bomber Command. The principles of R.C.M. were well established and the instruments to put them into operation were available. There was, however, considerable scope for development in their tactical use and the story of R.C.M. during the last months of the War is chiefly one of the tactical employment of R.C.M., particularly the MANDREL SCREEN and WINDOW feints. A very keen watch was kept on all enemy reactions to bombing raids and close liaison maintained with Air Ministry (A.I.4 (f)) and No. 100 Group, who were particularly concerned in studying and analysing these reactions.

Conclusion

94. The primary object of all R.C.M. in Bomber Command was to protect bombers and save them from destruction by enemy ground and air defences. It is not possible to make any accurate quantitative assessment of the degree of success attained. No attempt can be made to state figures of the number of bombers saved. It is, however, indisputable that a very considerable success was in fact achieved. A study of the losses suffered by Bomber Command in night attacks on Germany shows an increasing trend until September, 1944, with a succession of setbacks which coincide

with the adoption of various countermeasures.   The introduction of TINSEL and MANDREL, WINDOW and CORONA, all brought about sharp declines in the loss rate. Between these times there was a rise which indicated the enemy's recovery as he in time developed an antidote to our R.C.M. In September, 1944, the gradual disintegration of the enemy defences following the advance of the armies across France and Belgium coincided with the full development of the R.C.M. offensive and the two combined to deal the enemy defences a blow from which they never recovered.

95. A graph showing the loss rate on German targets by night is at Graph No. 5A, Part V.

APPENDIX F

EXPANSION AND RE-EQUIPMENT
CONTENTS

Annexures:
- A. – Number of Serviceable Airfields by Groups, 1942-1945.
- B. – Strength of Command in terms of Aircraft Operational and Training, 1942-1945.
- C. – Expansion of Training Units, 1942-1945.
- D. – Percentage Strength of Command Non-operational owing to Formation or Re-equipment of Squadrons. Monthly, 1942-1945.

APPENDIX F

EXPANSION AND RE-EQUIPMENT

Introduction

1. The re-equipment of Bomber Command main force squadrons with the four-engine types of aircraft which were destined to play so great a part in bringing the War against Germany to a successful conclusion, was almost wholly achieved in the space of two years – 1942/1943.   Expansion in the front-line strength of the Command, after making some progress prior to 1942, actually lost ground during that year owing to the transfer of Squadrons to Coastal Command from the Middle East. It did not go ahead again until the beginning of 1943, when priorities, which had hitherto favoured in turn Fighter Command, Coastal Command and the Middle East as far as the Royal Air Force were concerned, were at last transferred to Bomber Command.

2. The purpose of this Appendix is to set out briefly the history of Bomber Command re-equipment and expansion in so far as it occurred between February, 1942, and the end of the War in Europe, to describe the progressive reorganisation at all levels which became necessary as a result, and to enumerate some of the more important problems encountered and the methods by which each was overcome.

Bomber Command Prior to 1942

3. In order to present a clear picture of subsequent events, a brief description of the composition and activities of Bomber Command during the period between the outbreak of War and the end of 1941 is necessary. At the beginning of this period, Bomber Command consisted of approximately forty operational squadrons equipped with various types of light and medium bombers, including Battles, Blenheims, Hampdens, Whitleys and Wellingtons.   These were divided amongst four operational groups, Nos. 2, 3, 4 and 5. It was not until the beginning of 1941 that No. 1 Group commenced re-forming in Bomber Command.

4. During the early months of the War, Bomber Command activities were limited to spasmodic attacks on enemy shipping and on certain naval installations and no

strategic bombing of German targets took place. At this time it became apparent that the types of aircraft available were unsuited to daylight operations, so that this period was occupied in intensive night-flying training, and in laying the foundations of a training organisation adequate to meet the very heavy requirements for replacement crews which would soon arise to cover future expansion and operational wastage. As practically all instructors had to be found from the operational units, it became necessary to withdraw a number of squadrons from the front line and to employ them on the operational training of aircrews. These squadrons were eventually disbanded and their establishment of aircraft and personnel used for the formation of operational training units. This fact, combined with the relatively low priority which Bomber Command received at this period of the War, was reflected in the small amount of front-line expansion achieved up to the end of 1940. Progress in 1941, accounted for in part by the re-forming of No. 1 Group in Bomber Command, showed considerable improvement, but even so only some forty squadrons were actually available for operations at the beginning of 1942, although further squadrons were in process of either forming or re-equipping at this stage.

Historical Review – February, 1942, to the End of the War

5. At the beginning of 1942 Bomber Command comprised six operational groups, Nos. 1, 2, 3, 4, 5 and 8, and two operational training groups, Nos. 6 and 7. Of the former category, No. 8 Group did not become operational at this stage and was eliminated entirely in May, 1942, when its stations were transferred to the U.S.A.A.F. No. 2 Group's role was principally tactical, whereas the primary function of the Command as a whole was, and remained throughout the war, the strategic bombing of German targets. For this reason, and taking into consideration the fact that No. 2 Group was transferred to the control of the Tactical Air Force in May, 1943, and consequently had very little bearing on the expansion and re-equipment of Bomber Command, it is proposed to omit No. 2 Group entirely from the present review, and No. 8 Group also until this was resuscitated in January, 1943, to become No. 8 (Pathfinder) Group.

6. For the purposes of this Appendix, therefore, the Bomber Command set-up in February, 1942, comprised the following operational Groups and squadrons. Both here, and throughout the Appendix, squadrons are shown in terms of their equivalent in two flights:— (see Fig.a)

7. Of this total of 55 squadrons, 11 were equipped, or were in process of re-equipping, with four-engine types of aircraft. The length of time taken by squadrons forming or re-equipping to become operational at this stage of the war is reflected in the fact that almost one-third of the total frontline strength of the Command was non-operational.

8. During the year 1942 priorities still eluded Bomber Command. The total number of squadrons actually showed a decrease from 55 to 50½, accounted for by the transfer of five squadrons to Coastal Command and a similar number to the Middle

	Hampden		Whitley		Wellington		Manchester		Stirling		Halifax		Lancaster		Total	
	Op.	Non-Op.	Op.	Non-Op.	Op.	Non-Op.	Op.	Non-Op.	Op.	Non-Op.	Op.	Non-Op.	Op.	Non-Op.	Op.	Non-Op.
No. 1 Group					8½	2									8½	2
No. 3 Group					5	7			2	2					7	9
No. 4 Group			5½		2						2	3			9½	3
No. 5 Group	10						2	2						2	12	4
Total	10		5½		15½	9	2	2	2	2	2	3		2	37	18

Fig a.

East. In spite of this, and the posting overseas of substantial numbers of ground personnel just at a time when they were becoming proficient on the four-engine types, good progress was made in the long-term aim. 1942 saw the foundation of the heavy-bomber force well and truly laid (the number of four-engine squadrons, including those forming and re-equipping, increased from 11 to 33) and the elimination from operations of three types of aircraft, Hampden, Whitley and Manchester, which no longer conformed to operational requirements.

9. The following events worthy of note took place during this year:—

May	Nos. 6 and 7 (O.T.U.) Groups were re-numbered 91 and 92 (O.T.U.) Groups. The first detachment of the U.S. Bomber Force arrived in the U.K. No. 8 Group was disbanded and stations in this area used for the reception of the U.S.A.A.F.
June	A third O.T.U. Group, No. 93, was formed in Bomber Command.
July	The Bomber Development Unit was formed at Gransden Lodge.
August	The Pathfinder Force was formed as an element under the control of No. 3 Group Headquarters. This consisted initially of four heavy squadrons, one drawn from, and supported by, each of the main force groups.
October	The heavy conversion flights, which had hitherto been established alongside heavy squadrons, were re-organised into heavy conversion units on separate airfields. The nucleus R.C.A.F. Group Headquarters commenced forming.

10. At the end of 1942 Bomber Command operational strength was as follows:—

	Wellington		Stirling		Halifax		Lancaster		Mosquito		Total.	
	Op.	Non-Op.	Op.	Non-Op.	Op.	Non-Op.	Op.	Non-Op.	Op.	Non-Op.	Op.	Non-Op.
No. 1 Group	2½	1			3	1					5½	2
No. 3 Group	1	1	4	1							5	2
No. 4 Group	2	8			6½	4½					8½	12½
No. 5 Group							9	1			9	1
P.F.F. Element	1	½	1		1		1		½		4½	½
Total	6½	10½	5	1	10½	5½	10	1	½		32½	18

11. The large number of squadrons non-operational at this stage was in some part due to the formation of no less than eight Wellington Squadrons in No. 4 Group during the last few weeks of the year. These were to form the basis of the R.C.A.F. Group.

12. 1943 was a most eventful year. The strength of the Command in terms of front line aircraft rose approximately 50 per cent. and even more rapidly in terms of striking power, with an increase of 245 per cent. over the 1942 total of bombs dropped. 1943 saw the Wellington, the only remaining medium bomber, relegated to a training role, the Lancaster emerge as the predominant heavy bomber of the war, and the development of the Mosquito in a number of useful roles.

13. Other important events which took place during this year, and which had their effect on the expansion and re-equipment of the Command, were the following:—

January   R.C.A.F. Squadrons, and the stations on which these were accommodated, were transferred from the operational control of No. 4 to that of No. 6 (R.C.A.F.) Group.
The Pathfinder Force which had, up to now, remained an element under the control of No. 3 Group Headquarters, achieved its separate entity, becoming No. 8 (P.F.F.) Group.

March   The "Base" organisation was introduced.

April   The establishment of initial reserve aircraft on heavy bomber squadrons was increased from two to four, bringing the establishments up to 16 I.E. plus 4 I.R. Aircrew establishments were also increased from 10 to 11 per flight.

June   No. 2 Group was transferred to the control of Fighter Command, together with existing stations and squadrons.

November   The first emergency runway, Woodbridge, became available for operational use. Heavy conversion training was re-organised to provide for the use of Stirlings and Halifaxes as pre-Lancaster training aircraft.

December   No. 100 (S.D.) Group Headquarters formed.

14. At the end of 1943, Bomber Command comprised the following operational units:—

	Wellington		Stirling		Halifax		Lancaster		Mosquito		Total.	
	Op.	Non-Op.	Op.	Non-Op.	Op.	Non-Op.	Op.	Non-Op.	Op.	Non-Op.	Op.	Non-Op.
No. 1 Group	½						11½	½			12	½
No. 3 Group			7				3	2			10	2
No. 4 Group					10	1½					10	1½
No. 5 Group							12	1			12	1
No. 6 (R.C.A.F.) Group					6	4	3				9	4
No. 8 (P.F.F.) Group					1½		6½		4	½	12	½
Total	½		7		17½	5½	36	3½	4	½	65	9½

Improved methods of re-equipment were largely responsible for the steady decline in loss of operational effort, as indicated by the lower proportion of squadrons non-operational.

15. 1944 was a year of even greater achievement. The strength of operational aircraft once again rose by approximately 50 per cent., but the striking power of the Command, as illustrated by the weight of bombs dropped, showed an increase of no less than 236 per cent. on the 1943 total and in doing so topped the half million ton mark. The early months of 1944 saw the rapid development of No. 100 (Bomber Support) Group with its heavy aircraft equipped for radio countermeasures role and its long range fighter aircraft. The operations of this group undoubtedly resulted in a reduction of the main force wastage rate and thus directly assisted expansion.

16. The Stirling was eliminated completely as a front line aircraft during the early months of this year and the Halifax II/V was progressively replaced by the more powerful Halifax III. Repeated requests by Bomber Command Headquarters for the diversion of as much production effort as possible to Lancasters began to take effect and the last four months of 1944 showed an increase of no less than 13 Lancaster squadrons, whereas the number of Halifax squadrons commenced to decline. The Canadian-built Lancaster X began to arrive in substantial numbers. The Mosquito Bomber Force also showed a rapid rise in strength and was able to maintain the nuisance raids on Berlin in addition to many other commitments.

17. Other events worthy of note which occurred during 1944 were:—

January.   Increase in squadron aircrew establishment from 11 to 14 crews per flight of 8 I.E. plus 2 I.R. aircraft.

April.   Manston and Carnaby opened up as emergency runways.

July.   Administration and technical functions were centralised on station level.

September.   The formation of No. 7 (Heavy Conversion) Group.

Worthy of mention, also, was the great improvement in re-equipping technique which took place during 1944, and which resulted in a substantial reduction in the time taken by squadrons to become operational. The closing months of 1944 saw the re-instatement of Lancasters in a training role.

18. At the end of 1944 Bomber Command operational resources were disposed as follows:—

	Halifax		Lancaster		Mosquito		Bomber Support Heavy		Bomber Support Mosquito		Total.	
	Op.	Non-Op.	Op.	Non-Op.	Op.	Non-Op.	Op.	Non-Op.	Op.	Non-Op.	Op.	Non-Op.
No. 1 Group			16½								16½	
No. 3 Group			12½	1							12½	1
No. 4 Group	15½										15½	
No. 5 Group			17		1						18	
No. 6 (R.C.A.F.) Group	9		4	1							13	1
No. 8 (P.F.F.) Group			6		10						16	
No. 100 Group							6		7		13	
Total	24½		56	2	11		6		7		104½	2

19. The chief trend during the last few months of the war was the continued re-equipment of Halifax Squadrons with Lancasters, principally in No. 6 (R.C.A.F.) Group. Man-power considerations precluded any further expansion of the Command, and slight increases in No. 100 Group R.C.M. squadrons and in the Mosquito Bomber Force, both at the expense of No. 4 Group Halifaxes, were the only other significant changes. Reduced aircrew wastage enabled No. 93 (O.T.U.) Group to be disbanded in February. The operational strength of the Command at the end of the war in Europe was as follows:—Factors Limiting Expansion

	Halifax		Lancaster		Mosquito		Bomber Support Heavy		Bomber Support Mosquito		Total.	
	Op.	Non-Op.	Op.	Non-Op.	Op.	Non-Op.	Op.	Non-Op.	Op.	Non-Op.	Op.	Non-Op.
No. 1 Group			16½								16½	
No. 3 Group			14½								14½	
No. 4 Group	12										12	
No. 5 Group			17½		1						18½	
No. 6 (R.C.A.F.) Group	5		8	1							13	1
No. 8 (P.F.F.) Group			6		11						17	
No. 100 Group							6½		7		13½	
Total	17		62½	1	12		6½		7		105	1

20. Throughout the war a number of factors have tended in greater or lesser degree to limit the expansion of Bomber Command front line strength. The more important of such factors were the following:—

(*a*) The introduction of the heavy bomber.

(*b*) Shortage of airfields (and transfer of airfields to the U.S.A.A.F.).

(*c*) Shortage of aircraft.

(*d*) Shortage of man-power.

(*e*) Constantly increasing operational intensity.

21. The four-engined bomber, whilst it undoubtedly revolutionized the destructive capacity of strategic bombing, needed an increased maintenance establishment, and gave rise, also, to a number of problems, the chief of which were as follows:—

(*a*) Airfields had to be enlarged.

(*b*) Aircrews had to be converted to heavy types.

(*c*) The crew composition had to be increased.

(*d*) Practically all ground handling equipment became out of date.

(*e*) The scale of workshop, power plant and other technical accommodation became totally inadequate.

(*f*) The scales of bomb storage and handling equipment also became inadequate.

These points are dealt with in detail in later paragraphs, except for the increase in the size of the heavy bomber crew as compared with that required for the medium types which it replaced. The addition of Flight Engineers in particular, the majority of whom were found from the ranks of Fitter trades, involved a considerable and unforeseen demand upon man-power at a time when such skilled tradesmen were at a premium.

22. The shortage of airfields, aircraft and man-power (both aircrews and ground personnel) each in turn tended to become the predominant limiting factor. One of the greatest problems which faced Bomber Command during the period under review was to keep these three factors in correct phase, a task further complicated by the fact that estimates of airfield completion were frequently most inaccurate (in at least one case the Air Ministry Monthly Aerodrome Report showed an airfield as being ready for operational use a full year before it could finally accept a squadron), and by the complete lack of reliable estimates of aircraft production until the closing months of 1943, when Air Ministry introduced a monthly short-term forecast covering the succeeding two months. Even so, aircraft production estimates were constantly upset by the need to incorporate new modifications on the production line, and by labour troubles. The task of planning aircrew output in phase with airfield availability and aircraft production was not simplified by the comparatively long period covered

by operational training, which required no less than five months from the commencement of the O.T.U. stage to the completion of heavy-bomber conversion training.

23. Shortage of airfields was greatly aggravated by radical changes in layout necessary to make these suitable for the operation of heavy bombers. The need for runways of adequate length was not quickly appreciated, except by those responsible for the actual handling of heavy bombers. Although the policy which laid down the dimensions of the normal bomber airfield as it exists to-day was finally agreed by the Air Ministry in October, 1941, more than a year elapsed before this policy was fully implemented. At the beginning of 1942, also, there still remained a considerable number of grass airfields which had to be runwayed before they could be used for heavy aircraft.

24. During the first half of 1942, just at the time when lack of airfields was causing the greatest difficulty, a very considerable number of those scheduled for Bomber Command use were transferred to the U.S.A.A.F. During the second half of the same year, further airfields had to be diverted to meet the needs of H.C.U. training. Details of the actual number of serviceable airfields available to Bomber Command during the period under review are shown at Annexure "A."

25. Even when runways were complete, accommodation was inadequate for the requirements of two heavy squadrons, so that in order to continue expansion in spite of the shortage of airfields, it became necessary to introduce the three-flight squadrons established at 24 I.E. plus 3 I.R. aircraft, as an interim measure, and in this way to make the fullest use of available accommodation. It was found also that, within certain limits, more immediate results were obtained, and economies were effected, by increasing the establishment, and thereby stepping up the operational effort of existing squadrons, rather than by employing all available aircraft to form new squadrons, with the resultant time lag in becoming operational. This policy was given effect, first by increasing, during April, 1943, the aircraft establishment of squadrons from 16 I.E. plus 2 I.R. to 16 I.E. plus 4 I.R., accompanied by an adjustment in the aircrew establishment from 10 to 11 per flight, then in January, 1944, by a further increase in the aircrew establishment up to 14 per flight (this latter device was adopted partially to offset the fatigue factor which had hitherto prevented squadrons from operating on more than two successive nights) and finally by a slight overbearing of aircraft in all main force squadrons. This last practice naturally resulted in an increased strain on the servicing personnel, but as operational opportunities were limited by the weather and other factors, and as periods constantly occurred during which operations were curtailed for several days at a time, it was found to be acceptable to the extent of one or even two aircraft per squadron. Serviceability might suffer temporarily after a concentrated period of operations, but recovery was rapid and the average serviceability showed a steady increase during the last two and a half years of the war.

26. In this manner, planned rates of effort were constantly exceeded in spite of more than one increase in the planned rates. There is no doubt that this increased intensity achieved its primary object of enabling more bombs to be dropped on the

enemy and at the same time overcame, as far as was possible, the limitations imposed by shortage of airfields and by shortage of ground personnel.

Wastage Trends and Their Effect

27. In planning long term expansion, the number of aircraft available for all purposes is determined by the amount of production capacity allocated and can be estimated more or less accurately. The number of aircraft required for training will depend on aircrew requirements which, in turn, can be related to the number of aircraft available for operations. A completely unknown factor is aircraft wastage rate, expressed as a percentage of operational sorties, and on this will ultimately depend requirements for accommodation and ground personnel. Assuming that the size of squadrons is limited by accommodation scales and other factors and that all squadrons operate at a maximum capacity, the extent of expansion obviously depends on the proportion of available aircraft which are absorbed against wastage. As production of aircraft during the period covered by this Appendix was planned to increase progressively and did, in fact, do so apart from periodic set-backs due to switch-over to different types or to labour troubles, and as wastage, except for a few brief periods, was not so high as to absorb the whole production, expansion naturally followed. The following paragraphs describe briefly wastage trends experienced, and the effect these had on expansion.

28. The year 1942 showed a reduction in the operational strength of the Command, accounted for mainly by the transfer of squadrons to other Commands, but also by re-equipment with four-engine types. It is proposed, therefore, to confine consideration to the years 1943/1944. The loss rate fluctuated considerably during this period. In the first quarter of 1943 aircraft lost on operations amounted to little more than 3 per cent. of the total despatched. The second quarter of the year showed an increase to over 5 per cent., accounted for largely by the high loss-rate of the Stirling and Halifax II/V, which by this time was becoming unsuitable for raids involving deep penetration. The introduction of "Window" in July was mainly responsible for the reduced loss-rate during the third quarter of 1943, which came down to 4 per cent. and remained at that level until the end of November. In December the rate again rose to over 5 per cent. and showed a further increase during January, 1944. This higher rate was due to the fact that a substantial proportion of the effort was directed against Berlin, combined with a considerable number of crashes in the United Kingdom owing to bad weather at base. February, 1944, saw a reduction in the loss rate to approximately 4 per cent., and from then on the rate declined steadily until September, when it reached a level of less than 1 per cent., at which it remained practically constant until the end of the war.

29. To assess the effect of wastage on expansion, loss rates must, of course, be considered in conjunction with scale of effort. Throughout the war it has normally been possible to operate during the summer months at approximately 50 per cent. greater intensity than in the winter and as the loss rate has not been greatly affected by change of season, the greater part of the expansion has taken place during the winter months. Although an extremely low percentage loss was experienced during

the summer of 1944, this was accompanied by an enormous increase in effort, so much so that from June to September the number of sorties completed was approximately three times that of the equivalent period in 1943. In consequence the number of aircraft absorbed against wastage actually increased on the previous year.

30. Owing to this seasonal increase in intensity, little or no expansion took place between May and September in either of the years under review. The most rapid expansion was effected in the months of October and November when effort, and consequently wastage, dropped steeply. Expansion slowed down about the end of November as the number of new squadrons formed became operational and themselves incurred wastage, and from then on continued steadily throughout the winter months.

31. It will be seen from para. 28 above that during two comparatively brief periods the loss rate exceeded 5 per cent. of the total number of operational sorties completed by the Command. The first such period, in the second quarter of 1943, was offset by low operational intensity, in that the average effort in April, May and June barely exceeded that achieved in February. In consequence a small amount of expansion took place in spite of the high loss rate, although the total increase in operational strength from mid-April to mid-September of this year was limited to about ten aircraft. The second period during which a high loss rate was experienced, December, 1943/January, 1944, was also accompanied by low operational intensity, but here again, although this coincided with the season when expansion was normal, an increase of only ten aircraft was achieved between mid-November, 1943, and mid-February, 1944. It becomes apparent, therefore, that had a loss rate of 5 per cent. continued for any length of time, combined with anything approaching the actual intensity achieved, the front line strength of the Command would have contracted instead of expanded, because production would have been insufficient to replace wastage in existing squadrons, let alone to form new ones.

32. It should be noted that the percentage loss rate quoted includes all operational types in the Command. The Mosquito bomber rate, which fluctuated very little and which stabilised at approximately 1 per cent. of sorties, had the effect of reducing the overall rate substantially below the level which pertained in the heavy squadrons.

33. During 1943 there was a marked discrepancy between the loss-rate incurred on Lancasters and Halifaxes. This was particularly noticeable in the second and third quarters of the year when the respective rates, expressed in terms of operational sorties completed per gross wastage, were 15·25 and 18·59 for the Lancaster, and 11·25 and 14·43 for the Halifax. This tended to slow up Halifax expansion as opposed to that of the Lancaster although the effect was counterbalanced to some extent by the lower operational intensity achieved by the Halifax squadrons. During 1944 the percentage wastage rate of these two types became approximately equal, and in fact the Lancaster loss rate actually exceeded that of the Halifax for part of the time owing to the use of the former on raids involving deeper penetration into Germany. The higher operational intensity of the Lancaster was, however, maintained right up to the end of the war in Europe.

34. Whilst paras. 35-42 are mainly in amplification of events noted in the "Historical Review," the details are considered to be of interest.

35. In February, 1942, Bomber Command operational groups occupied the following areas. These remained static throughout the War, apart from some minor re-allocation of stations between groups:—

No. 1 Group. –	South Yorkshire and North Lincolnshire. Headquarters at Bawtry.
No. 3 Group. –	Centred around the Cambridge/Huntingdon area. Headquarters at Exning, near Newmarket.
No. 4 Group. –	North and West Riding of Yorkshire. Headquarters at Heslington, York.
No. 5 Group. –	South Lincolnshire and Nottinghamshire. Headquarters at Grantham (subsequently transferred to Moreton Hall, near Swinderby).

36. No. 2 Group, which has been omitted from consideration in this appendix for reasons given in para. 5, had its airfields in the Norfolk area. The headquarters of this Group was located at Huntingdon at the beginning of the period, but subsequently transferred to Bylaugh Hall, near Dereham, in Norfolk.

37. As the Command contracted rather than expanded during 1942, the only new Groups to form this year were the third O.T.U. Group, No. 93, which formed in June with headquarters at Burton-on-Trent, and No. 6 (R.C.A.F.) Group with headquarters at Allerton Park, near Knaresborough, which formed in December and which, on 1st January, 1943, took over control from No. 4 Group of the airfields in the North Riding of Yorkshire together with R.C.A.F. Squadrons which had previously been formed, and which were already in their correct locations. Some adjustment of airfields between Nos. 1 and 4 Groups, to compensate the latter for those transferred to No. 6 (R.C.A.F.) Group, became necessary as a result.

38. On the 25th January, 1943, the Pathfinder Force, which had existed as an element in No. 3 Group since August of the previous year, achieved its separate entity with headquarters at Huntingdon. At the date of its formation as a self-contained Group, No. 8 (P.F.F.) Group comprised three stations and five squadrons (one accommodated at Oakington in No. 3 Group on a lodger basis), but rapidly expanded, until by the end of 1943 it controlled the equivalent of eight heavy-bomber squadrons, four Mosquito squadrons and its own Navigation and Mosquito Training Units, requiring, in all, eight airfields.

39. At the beginning of 1944, No. 100 (Counter Measures) Group was formed in Norfolk, taking over airfields which had previously been occupied by No. 2 Group units. This Group, which had its headquarters at Bylaugh Hall, was given a variety of functions, including the maintenance of a counter radio offensive, for which purpose squadrons were equipped with four-engine aircraft, and the harassing of the German night-fighter force, which was achieved by means of a number of long range

night-fighter squadrons equipped with Mosquitos. The Group was subsequently renamed No. 100 (Bomber Support) Group.

40. During 1944 the number of main force squadrons expanded rapidly, and it became necessary either to form an additional group or to increase the number of operational airfields in the existing groups. It was finally decided to adopt the latter expedient, and at the same time to relieve operational groups of the responsibility for H.C.U. training, by forming a Heavy Conversion Group. As a result No. 7 (H.C.U.) Group was formed with effect from the 20th September, 1944, with headquarters at Grantham, and the Heavy Conversion Bases, which, with the exception of No. 31 Base, remained in their existing locations, were transferred to the control of the new headquarters. This enabled the three stations in No. 31 Base to become operational stations in No. 3 Group and these, together with the inclusion in No. 5 Group of stations which had up to now been on loan to the U.S.A.A.F. Troop Carrier Command and a slight re-allocation of stations between No. 5 and No. 1 Groups, provided space for the new squadrons within the existing operational set-up.

41. With the end of the War in sight, and with casualties falling considerably below planned rates, the early months of 1945 saw a progressive reduction in the number of Bomber O.T.U.s, to an extent which made it possible to concentrate these into two O.T.U.s and ultimately to dispense with No. 93 (O.T.U.) Group Headquarters.

42. Thus, during the greater part of the period under review, Bomber Command controlled Nos. 1, 3, 4, 5, 6 (R.C.A.F.) Main Force Groups, No. 8 (P.F.F.) Group, No. 100 (B.S.) Group and Nos. 91, 92 and 93 (O.T.U.) Groups, or a total of 10 groups, with the addition of No. 7 (H.C.U.) Group in the final stages. Control, both administrative and, to some extent, operational, was necessarily decentralised from Command to Group Headquarters, having regard to the considerable distances involved and the intricacy of communications required. Bomber Command, however, still retained direct supervision of the various Services; and Staffs of the Services, although nominally established at Group Headquarters level, remained under the direct supervision of the relevant Command branches throughout the War.

Bomber Groups

43. Prior to the War, Bomber Command Groups comprised an unspecified number of stations, each of which was designed to accommodate two medium (at this time these were considered as heavy) bomber squadrons, with a combined establishment of 32 I.E. aircraft. Each station was normally provided with a satellite airfield, which at this stage was little more than an advanced landing-ground.

44. To meet the demands of large-scale expansion it was decided that satellites should be brought up to full operational standards, and that, wherever possible, each parent station should be provided with two satellites. After a number of changes during the first two years of the war, policy had more or less crystallized by the middle of 1942, when it was planned that each main-force bomber group should control a total of 15 airfields, of which 12 would be operational and the remaining three allocated to meet the requirements of heavy conversion training. Five of the 15

airfields were to be constructed to parent station standards, whilst the remainder were to be given sufficient facilities to accommodate and to operate the equivalent of two heavy-bomber squadrons at 16 I.E., but were to be under the control of the Station Commander of the parent station and dependent on the latter for their communications and certain supplies and technical facilities.

45. The 12 operational airfields were thus required theoretically to accommodate a total of 24 heavy squadrons. As a result of the number of ancillary units in each Group, however, and the need for providing spare airfields, this total was subsequently reduced to 20 squadrons. Owing to congested flying conditions and other causes (described more fully in paras. 86 to 88), the number of squadrons which it was found practicable to operate in any one Group fell short of this figure.

46. Satellite airfields, when built up to the accommodation standards necessary to operate two heavy squadrons, only differed from parent stations in minor details, and were, in fact, considerably larger in all respects than was the pre-war parent station. It was accordingly decided that the term "satellite" should disappear as far as Bomber Command Operational Groups were concerned and that all operational airfields should be termed "stations" and should be commanded by an officer established in the rank of Group Captain.

47. Towards the end of 1942 it became obvious that it would be impracticable to control efficiently as many as 15 stations from a single Group headquarters, and that some intermediate link was necessary. This question was the subject of considerable discussion and experiment until approval was finally obtained in the spring of 1943 to the introduction of the "Base" system as being the most effective and economical form of organisation for the control, administration and servicing of six heavy-bomber squadrons (or three heavy conversion units) accommodated on three separate but associated airfields. The Base headquarters, commanded by an Air Commodore, assisted by two principal staff officers (Air Staff and Administrative) and by the heads of the Base Services, was located on the parent or "Base" station. This system permitted the centralisation of many specialist and administrative activities previously undertaken on an individual station basis, thereby adding to the efficiency and at the same time enabling the Group Commander and his staff to limit their normal contacts to five instead of 15 lower formations. The system also helped to overcome limitations imposed by the fact that landline communications were only provided from Group Headquarters to Base Stations, and only through these to the remaining stations in the group.

48. Owing to the diversity in function of units in the specialised groups and consequent need for direct operational control from the Group Headquarters, the Base system was not introduced into either No. 8 (P.F.F.) or No. 100 (B.S.) Group, in both of which stations were organised on an independent basis, although a form of centralised Major Servicing was introduced for each type of aircraft. This independent organisation was acceptable by reason of the fact that neither of these groups controlled more than eight operational stations and that, apart from certain specialised training, which occupied only one airfield in each case, all operational training of aircrew replacements was carried out in the main force groups in the case of No. 8

(P.F.F.) Group and No. 100 Group heavy squadrons, and by Fighter Command O.T.U.s on behalf of the Bomber Support Mosquito Squadrons.

49. Little or no change in organisation took place in the O.T.U. Groups during the period under review. The normal bomber O.T.U. was accommodated on two airfields which retained the nomenclature "Parent" and "Satellite." Owing to shortage of airfields, a special scale of accommodation was constructed on certain ones which enabled these to work to a capacity equal to three-quarters of a normal Bomber O.T.U., but this system was not generally adopted, principally because of the limited number of circuits and landings which could be carried out on one airfield in a given time.

50. Apart from the grouping of the Heavy Conversion Bases under the control of No. 7 (H.C.U.) Group Headquarters during 1944, no major re-organisation in the main force bomber groups was found necessary from the introduction of the Base System until the end of the War, except for the centralisation of administrative functions on station level, which is referred to in succeeding paragraphs.

Bomber Airfields

51. As most of the policy decisions affecting the layout of airfields were reached prior to the period covered by this Appendix, it is proposed to describe briefly the basic changes which became necessary as a result of Bomber Command expansion and the re-equipment of squadrons with heavy types of aircraft.

52. At the outbreak of War, the total number of airfields in the Command was 27, all of which were grass-surfaced. Peak requirements in the closing months of 1944 called for the employment of no less than 67 airfields in the operational groups and 61 in training, making a total of 128 airfields, all but two of which were runwayed.

53. Construction of runways was first authorised in December, 1940, when the scale laid down consisted of a main runway of 1,400 yards length and two subsidiary runways each of 1,100 yards. This scale was amended in February, 1941, by an increase in length of the main runway up to 1,600 yards. It was not until October, 1941, that approval was finally given for a layout suitable for the operation of heavy bomber aircraft, with main runway 2,000 yards in length and the two subsidiary runways each of 1,400 yards. In consequence it was not until well into 1943 that airfields constructed to the new scale began to become available in adequate numbers.

54. It will be appreciated that this slowness in facing up to what was required, involving successive changes in policy, not only tended to complicate the letting of contracts and thereby delayed the construction of airfields, but also resulted in many alterations to dispersal schemes, in the construction of much redundant perimeter track and in the need to re-site a considerable number of buildings. Scales of accommodation, also, underwent successive changes, as a direct result of the large increase of establishments following the introduction of four-engine aircraft. It is interesting to note that between the beginning of 1942 and the end of 1944 the cost of a bomber airfield practically doubled, and that at the end of this period the average cost was approximately £1,000,000.

55. Amongst other requirements which resulted from the increasing complexity of aircraft and ever-increasing flying congestion, was the installation of a standard night-landing lighting system on all airfields in the Command. After more than one change in design consequent on experience gained, the Mark II system was introduced which included, in addition to the normal landing strip lights, outer circuit lights, funnel lights, Totem Poles, Glim and flood lights, such refinements as fog funnels, angle of approach indicators, taxying track lights, dispersal signs, portable Glim lights, etc., the whole system being controlled from the Watch Office with dimming provided on all circuits. This system was very effective in reducing the time taken to land heavy-bomber aircraft by night and thus increased the number of aircraft which it was possible to operate from one airfield.

56. Technical accommodation remained inadequate long after reconstruction following the above-mentioned changes in layout was complete. Prior to 1943, policy as regards hangars had been to site four on parent stations and two on satellites, and to build two and one respectively. This was quite inadequate, particularly as far as the satellite was concerned (many of the parent stations were of pre-war construction and as such already had four or five hangars) and no steps had been taken to construct even one hangar on the majority of these by the early months of 1943, a delay which resulted in great hardships for servicing personnel who were required to work long hours in the open during the winter months. Power plant, workshop, and much other necessary technical accommodation was far short of even minimum requirements up to the later stages of 1943.

Bomber Stations

57. The major changes in station organisation which took place between February, 1942, and the end of the war in Europe, were:—

(*a*) The introduction of the Base system, and upgrading of all operational airfields to Station status.

(*b*) The centralisation of aircraft servicing in a Servicing Wing.

(*c*) The centralisation of administrative functions on a Station basis.

58. The first of these, which was introduced in March, 1943, and is described in detail in para. 48, affected stations chiefly in so far as all personnel were posted to the Base instead of to the station, and a number of Services which had previously come under the control of the Station Commander, were centralised in the Base Headquarters.

59. The second change, which became effective in November, 1943, consisted of the centralisation of all aircraft servicing in a Servicing Wing composed of:—

(*a*) Servicing Wing Headquarters.

(*b*) Daily Servicing Squadron.

(*c*) Repair and Inspection Squadron.

The Chief Technical Officer assumed executive command of the Servicing Wing, under the Station Commander, and was assisted by a number of specialist officers.

The senior specialist officer of the Signals and Armament Branches remained responsible for the technical efficiency of work carried out in the Servicing Wing by personnel of his own branch, although all such work was co-ordinated and controlled by the C.T.O.

60. This re-organisation affected the squadron as much as the station in that it limited the servicing personnel established in the former to those required for daily servicing, *e.g.,* daily inspections, re-fuelling, re-arming, etc. Such personnel went to make up the Daily Servicing Squadron, which was established in the Servicing Wing only as a Squadron Headquarters. This system allowed of greatly improved supervision and increased flexibility, in that servicing personnel could be transferred as necessary between the R. and I. Squadron and the Daily Servicing Squadron, and the best possible use made of all servicing equipment.

61. The last of these organisational changes took place in July, 1944. This was the centralisation of administrative functions on station level, as a result of which the station was organised in three wings – flying, administrative and technical (or servicing). All personnel not directly connected with flying were taken off the squadron establishment and re-established in either the administrative or servicing wing, and thus came under the station for all purposes. The squadron was virtually reduced to a "flying echelon" consisting of operational commanders and aircrews plus a minimum of specialist and administrative personnel, and thus became incapable of undertaking independent operations when separated from the station organisation, a state which, in fact, existed even when squadrons were fully established with administrative and servicing personnel. This last change had the effect of continuing the centralisation of servicing to its logical conclusion in that it brought establishments into line with actual practice.

Bomber Squadrons

62. The progressive reorganisation of squadron establishments, and the reasons which made this necessary, have already been discussed in para. 25. The three-flight squadron, introduced to tide over the lag in provision of domestic and technical accommodation, was subsequently preserved throughout the war in certain groups, although the original reason for its adoption had disappeared.

63. The effect of increased centralisation on station level, discussed in para. 61, was to increase squadron mobility, always provided that the fundamental idea that a heavy bomber squadron could only operate intensively with the backing of an adequate station organisation, including correct spares and ground handling equipment, was accepted.

Training Units

64. The development of the Bomber Command operational training organisation forms the subject of a separate Appendix. It is not proposed, therefore, to touch on

this question beyond a few notes on the organisational and accommodation aspects in so far as these affect the expansion and re-equipment of operational squadrons.

65. The transition from peace to war wastage-rates necessitated an expansion of many times the peacetime operational training capacity to back a given number of squadrons. Such expansion had to become effective before any expansion in the front line could commence, and involved airfields, aircraft and manpower. Much of this preliminary expansion was, of course, put into effect prior to the War.

66. In Bomber Command the position was complicated by the introduction of four-engine aircraft, which necessitated a completely new stage in operational training, and also by the enormous strides made in radar devices, which constantly required the establishment of new specialised training units, as the initial shortage of newly-introduced equipment made it impracticable to include training on such equipment in the standard O.T.U. or H.C.U. syllabus as soon as it was incorporated in the production line.

67. It was originally hoped that the conversion training of aircrews could be satisfactorily achieved by the provision of a small training flight on the basis of four aircraft attached to each operational squadron. This proved to be quite inadequate, however, and requirements steadily increased until at the peak no less than 20 Heavy Conversion Units and Finishing Schools, with an aggregate establishment of more than 700 heavy aircraft and 1,720 officers and 25,520 other ranks, involving the use of 20 fully equipped airfields, had to be provided out of Bomber Command operational resources. Thus almost one-third of the total available heavy bomber aircraft had to be diverted into a training role, nor was there any compensating reduction in O.T.U. strength.

68. The difficulty of maintaining a proper balance between operations and training has been stressed in the training review referred to above. When it is realised that the operational training capacity required to maintain heavy squadrons alone in Bomber Command, in addition to the H.C.U. stage (which was an unplanned commitment), involved approximately 1,200 medium aircraft in O.T.U.s and 150 light aircraft in fighter affiliation, etc., the immensity of the problem will be appreciated. The need for aircrew schools as a "buffer" between the O.T.U. and H.C.U. stages of training, which arose owing to the difference in summer and winter intake rates, also raised accommodation requirements which at one time necessitated no less than four airfields being allocated for the purpose.

69. The employment of the Halifax and, more particularly, the Stirling as pre-Lancaster training aircraft, which became necessary partly because of shortage of Lancasters in the front line squadrons and partly in order to make use of Stirlings, which at this time had to be withdrawn from operations owing to the high loss rate sustained, was uneconomical both in airfields and aircraft, as three Lancaster finishing schools were required over and above normal H.C.U. capacity. It, however, achieved its object in that it enabled the offensive to be maintained at a more economical loss rate.

70. Bomber Command training capacity reached its peak by the end of 1944 and commenced to contract during the early months of 1945, by which time expansion in the front line had ceased and operational losses fell considerably below planned

rates. The contraction became effective first in O.T.U. capacity, and finally, but not until after the end of the period under review, in heavy conversion training.

71. Events have proved beyond question that the decision to concentrate on four-engine aircraft, as far as equipment of main force squadrons in Bomber Command was concerned, was a wise one. This decision necessarily dated from pre-war days, and has been the subject of considerable controversy. The dominating factor which has emerged is that heavy bomber aircraft carry nearly three times the bomb load of the medium types and yet only require one pilot. It is more than doubtful whether the resources of the Empire Training Scheme could have produced sufficient pilots to enable a similar weight of bombs to be dropped by medium or light bomber types, and it is certain that a similar degree of concentration could not have been obtained by means other than the heavy bomber.

72. Detailed comparison between the three main types of heavy bomber, Lancaster, Halifax and Stirling, is beyond the scope of this Appendix. Suffice it to say that the Lancaster, measured in no matter what terms, was, and still is, incomparably the most efficient. In range, bomb carrying capacity, ease of handling, freedom from accident and particularly in casualty rate it far surpassed the other heavy types. Hence the constant pressure brought by Bomber Command Headquarters for concentration on Lancaster production at the expense of other types and hence the policy to employ every available Lancaster in the front line, even at the expense of an uneconomical training set-up.

73. At the beginning of 1942, of the four Bomber Command main force groups only No. 1 Group, whose squadrons were equipped with Wellingtons, was restricted to a single type of aircraft. At that time No. 3 Group, although primarily a Wellington Group, was beginning to re-equip with Stirlings. No. 4 Group had Whitleys, Wellingtons and Halifaxes. No. 5 Group had Hampdens and Manchesters and was in process of forming the first Lancaster Squadrons. The importance of keeping Groups "pure" on one type of aircraft was fully appreciated and was already the accepted policy of the Command, but the diversity of types which Bomber Command was called upon to operate, combined with the slow introduction and many teething troubles of the heavies, made it quite impossible to put this in practice. Furthermore, it was important that all groups should be given experience of heavy aircraft at an early date, which was only possible by operating a minimum of two types one heavy and one medium, per group as an interim measure.

74. Good progress towards a more rational allocation of types was made during 1942. In the first place Hampdens and Manchesters were eliminated, enabling No. 5 Group to become "pure" on Lancasters. No. 3 Group had, by the end of the year, practically completed their re-equipment with Stirlings. No. 4 Group already had the two-flight equivalent of 13 Halifax Squadrons; the fact that they also had ten Wellington Squadrons was largely due to the decision to form No. 6 (R.C.A.F.) Group and to re-equip R.C.A.F. Squadrons returning from overseas with Wellingtons as an interim measure, pending availability of heavy bombers.

75. During 1943 the Lancaster II, with the Hercules engine, was introduced. The Wellington was progressively replaced in the front line by heavy types, and the task of restricting groups to one type of aircraft proceeded apace. The year 1943 saw the rise and fall of the Stirling, which in the later months was used as a basic four-engine trainer in order to release every possible Lancaster for the front line.

76. At this stage Nos. 1, 5 and 8 (P.F.F.) Groups were fully equipped with Lancaster I/IIIs except for one squadron in the latter Group which still had Halifax IIIs, No. 4 Group was "pure" on Halifaxes, although the introduction of the Halifax III with its Bristol engine tended to complicate the issue as far as the engineer and equipment branches were concerned. No. 6 (R.C.A.F.) Group was basically Halifax, and No. 3 Group was rapidly re-equipping from Stirlings to Lancaster I/IIIs, although these Groups each had three Lancaster II squadrons as an interim measure.

77. Production of the Mosquito bomber rose rapidly during 1943. The development of the Mosquito bomber force was entrusted to the newly-formed Pathfinder Group, in which Mosquitos were already employed in a target marking role.

78. The year 1944 saw the culmination of the Command policy. All the main force Groups became "pure" on one type except for No. 6 (R.C.A.F.) Group, which still retained the Halifax but which was progressively re-equipping with the Canadian-built Lancaster X, and No. 5 Group to which was allotted one Mosquito Squadron for experimental target marking purposes. The remaining Lancaster II aircraft were relegated to training. No. 8 (P.F.F.) Group controlled a mixed force of Lancasters and Mosquitos. No. 100 (Bomber Support) R.C.M. element included Fortresses, Liberators and Stirlings at this stage, but was re-equipped progressively with Halifax IIIs during the last few months of the war. Its (Bomber Support) fighter units still included several different marks of Mosquitos, but were gradually becoming standardised with Mosquito 30s equipped with Mark X A.I.

79. From the beginning of 1945 to the end of the war a steady increase in the re-equipment of squadrons with Lancaster aircraft, combined with the progressive decline of the Halifax, took place, principally in No. 6 (R.C.A.F.) Group, but there was no change in the allocation of types as between groups.

Re-equipment of Squadrons

80. The formidable re-equipment programme with which Bomber Command had to contend within the space of three years, amounting in aggregate to no less than 129 squadrons, gave rise to a number of problems, not the least of which was the loss of operational effort involved. The question of time taken to complete re-equipment became one of vital importance. Whilst a week lost on the re-equipment of one squadron might not appear appreciable, a week lost on fifty squadrons at peak rates of effort would have resulted in nearly 10,000 tons less bombs being dropped on the enemy. Throughout the period under review, therefore, constant efforts were made to reduce this source of loss. How well these succeeded is shown by the steadily declining number of squadrons non-operational in relation to the numbers forming or re-equipping in any one month, in the tables in Annexure "D."

81. When a medium squadron re-equipped with heavy aircraft, it became necessary for all crews to undergo a comprehensive conversion training course, involving anything up to forty hours flying and a considerable ground training commitment. The new aircraft had to be modified to Command standards, involving some 400 manhours, before these could be used operationally. Ground personnel had to become accustomed to the new type before a reasonable standard of serviceability could be expected.

82. When squadrons were re-equipped with aircraft with a type of engine similar to that in use, the problem was simplified, in that engine handling characteristics were already known and ground personnel were at least partially experienced. Sometimes it was possible to arrange this, as for instance when Whitley squadrons were re-equipped with Halifax IIs, Wellington Xs with Halifax IIIs, etc. In such cases not only was re-equipment more rapid, but the squadron serviceability was found to be higher during the first month or two of operations than with squadrons re-equipping with a different type of engine.

83. Usually, however, changes in the mark of aircraft or other considerations made this impossible. A case in point is that of the re-equipment of No. 4 Group Halifax II/V squadrons with Halifax IIIs. Faulty engine handling gave rise to taxying difficulties which in turn resulted in loss of brake pressure and other defects. This was reflected in loss of serviceability, and it was some time before increasing experience enabled such difficulties to be overcome.

84. Re-equipment invariably resulted in problems for the Engineer and Equipment branches apart from normal changeover of spares, the re-equipment of a medium squadron with heavy aircraft necessitated completely new scales of ground handling equipment. Even standard equipment, such as inspection platforms, became out of date owing to the increased size of aircraft, and technical accommodation of all kinds became inadequate owing to the increased number of engines.

85. Much was done to avoid these and other causes of delay by the establishment of equipment pools well in advance of planned re-equipment, by the modification of aircraft on the Base system, the rapid conversion of aircrews in Heavy Conversion Units, the provision of experienced key ground personnel by diluting existing squadrons of similar type, and the detachment of a proportion of ground personnel to similarly equipped squadrons in order to gain experience. Loss of effort was also reduced by the withdrawal of one flight at a time, the remainder of the squadron remaining operational on the old type until their own turn came to re-equip.

Problems Arising Out of Expansion

86. *Operational.* – From an operational point of view the chief problem, once expansion began to take effect, was one of flying congestion. Not every area was suitable for the construction of airfields to the dimensions, and with the flying approaches, necessary for heavy bomber aircraft, and in consequence bomber airfields were concentrated in certain areas, notably in South Yorkshire, Lincolnshire, Huntingdonshire, Cambridgeshire and Norfolk. Secondly, shortage of airfields,

combined with the steady improvement in serviceability, involved an increasing number of aircraft operating from each airfield. The advances made in Flying Control, the installation of the Mark II airfield lighting system, the provision of emergency runways at Woodbridge, Manston and Carnaby, and the steady improvements in Radar Navigation devices, all helped to overcome these difficulties, and by the end of 1943 it became normal to operate in weather conditions which would have been considered impossible, or at any rate extremely risky, in the early stages of the War. The introduction of "F.I.D.O." on certain bomber airfields provided an added degree of insurance, although this system could cater only for limited numbers of aircraft.[1]

87. Airfield congestion, combined with the increased flying circuit of heavy aircraft, resulted in airfield circuits overlapping in a number of cases, and it became necessary in consequence to relegate some such airfields to a training or non-flying role.

88. A point which has aroused considerable controversy and about which opinions still differ, is the maximum number of heavy bomber aircraft which can be operated by night from any one airfield without loss of operational efficiency. Assuming that concentration in time is required over the target, the limiting factor to the number of aircraft operating from one airfield is the speed with which these can be landed. Latterly, average serviceability has remained constant at over 80 per cent. of the unit establishment so that where two heavy squadrons are accommodated on the same airfield, the normal operational effort is approximately 32 aircraft and even this number is exceeded after periods of enforced inactivity. Allowing an average landing time of three minutes each, 32 aircraft take more than one and a half hours to land, so that on the more distant targets some reduction in bomb load has to be accepted to compensate for the increased reserve of fuel which must be carried. In consequence it is open to consideration whether a three-flight squadron, consisting of 30 U.E. aircraft, operating normally up to 24 aircraft on one night, is not the maximum number of heavy bomber aircraft which can be accommodated on one airfield without loss of efficiency. During the period under review, of course, lack of accommodation left no option to the location of two squadrons on most airfields, but this necessity should not arise in the post-war period. It should be noted here that artificial restriction of operational effort by so-called "planned flying" was unacceptable in Bomber Command, as it would have reduced the overall effort owing to the fact that operational activity is normally governed by "opportunity" and by weather, neither of which are susceptible to long-term forecasting.

89. *Organisation.* – Problems under this heading are basically those which result from lack of accommodation, lack of manpower and lack of equipment. All the major organisational changes which took place in Bomber Command from February, 1942, were made in order to compensate for one or other of these factors, and in order to make the best of available facilities.

90. *Accommodation,* both domestic and technical, fell consistently short of requirements during the whole period from February, 1942, until the end of the War in Europe. Existing scales of accommodation became obsolete with the introduction of the four-engine aircraft with its increased all-round establishments, and in spite

of the additional accommodation provided, overcrowding remained rife right up to the end of the War, particularly in Officers' and senior N.C.O.s' messes. Increased commissioning also had its effect, particularly in the case of R.C.A.F. stations, both operational and O.T.U. When the casualty rate dropped during the later months of 1944, the strength of aircrew on all squadrons exceeded establishments by a considerable margin, and thus prolonged accommodation difficulties even after all planned construction was complete.

91. Works. – The expansion and re-equipment of Bomber Command resulted in many problems for the Works Directorate, itself suffering from lack of experience and of supervisory personnel, due to its rapid expansion in the early stages of the War. Policy governing dimensions and scales of accommodation of bomber airfields changed progressively and the provision of runways and initial increases in accommodation were often only partially completed when further alterations and extensions became necessary.

92. Amongst specific problems with which the Works Directorate were faced were the following:—

(*a*) Alterations in airfield layout and dispersal schemes.

(*b*) Disintegration of runways and perimeter tracks.

(*c*) Shortage of labour.

93. As a result of changes in airfield layout, details of which were given in para. 53, complete sections of perimeter track and large numbers of dispersal standings became redundant, necessitating the preparation of new plans and the letting of new contracts. Approximately 2,600 schemes for aircraft dispersal alone were prepared by the Command.

94. An enormous amount of repair work to runways and perimeter tracks became necessary. Apart from the strain imposed by the intensive operation of heavy bomber aircraft, other factors which contributed to the disintegration of runways were the constant pressure to speed up the construction of airfields and the methods by which both contractors and labour were paid. The former of these led to continuation of work during unsuitable weather conditions, such as frost or heavy rain, and the latter, with its emphasis on haste, combined with lack of proper supervision, often resulted in the mix of cement falling short of the standard laid down. Many runways and perimeter tracks showed signs of disintegration after only brief use and in consequence airfields had to be closed down for repair just at a time when shortage of these was already a cause of concern. Airfields required a degree of maintenance, also, which had not been foreseen and for which no adequate provision had been made.

95. Station Contractors were invariably short of labour, resulting in a hand-to-mouth repair programme. Heavy Conversion Units, in particular, which by reason of the large number of landings imposed a severe strain on runways, worked under a grave disadvantage, and in more than one instance a unit was compelled to carry out its flying programme with only one runway serviceable.

96. The large number of contracts which had to be let led to the employment of financially unsound, or incompetent, or inadequately equipped, contractors, several

of whom went into liquidation before their contracts were completed. In the case of Station Contractors this state of affairs was particularly prevalent and resulted in serious delays before essential repairs could be put in hand.

97. In spite of all these difficulties, however, the Works Directorate managed to keep the vast majority of airfields serviceable and, as a result of improvisation and by methods described elsewhere in the Appendix, the operational effort of the Command suffered little. Bomber Command staff was instrumental in developing, amongst other advances in technique, the "loop" or "spectacle" type of aircraft dispersal standing, which provided ease of access and manoeuvrability of aircraft, combined with considerable economy in labour and material.

98. *Engineering and Equipment.* – Para. 56 referred to the serious lack of technical accommodation and equipment which persisted almost until the end of the War in Europe.   The principal shortages which had to be overcome can be summed up as follows:—

(a) Hangars – not finally overcome until 1944 – resulted in work being carried out in the open under all weather conditions.

(b) Workshop accommodation.

(c) Maintenance Platforms for Heavy Aircraft. – Types F, G and K, which were originally provided, proved to be unsatisfactory. These were finally replaced during 1943 by new types designed in Bomber Command.

(d) Lifting Tackle. – With the steadily increasing weight of components this became extremely serious. No overhead tackle was provided in T.2 hangars and that in the "C" and "J" types was quite inadequate to deal with heavy bombers.

(e) Mobile Cranes. – This shortage affected equipment and armament branches equally with engineering.

(f) Hoses for Refuelling. – Replaced to some extent by booms designed in Bomber Command.

(g) Heavy tractors and other specialised motor transport.

99. Great strides in efficiency were made in the Command, and considerable economies effected, by the centralisation of such specialist sections as plug cleaning, tyre repair and fitting, battery charging and power plant assembly. Servicing work on lower levels was simplified by the fact that all policy matters were covered by Bomber Command Engineer Staff Instructions, enabling new units forming to obtain up-to-date information without recourse to policy letters issued prior to their date of formation.

100. Progressive centralisation did more than anything else to overcome shortages of technical equipment and to increase servicing efficiency, and to make possible the steady increase in operational serviceability which took place from 1943 onwards.

101. Problems to which the attention of the Air Ministry has been directed on more

than one occasion during the period under review, and which had their effect on operational efficiency, if not the actual expansion of the Command, were:—

(*a*) The time taken for Category "B" aircraft to be reissued after works repair.

(*b*) The standard to which engines were repaired.

The average time taken for Lancaster aircraft to be reissued was approximately six months, by which time the aircraft was completely out of date as far as modification standard went and unsuitable for operational use without an immense expenditure of labour. Statistics have proved also that repaired Merlin engines have been just twice as unreliable as new engines, which seems to point to the fact that the repair policy did not cover all items which needed replacement. This last factor resulted in an enormous wastage of man hours due to the need for more frequent engine changes.

102. Apart from those referred to above, most of which concerned Engineering rather than Equipment Branch, the most serious equipment deficiencies were radio valves during 1943, and tyre covers, which rose to a pitch in 1944 when all unserviceable aircraft in Heavy Conversion Units had to be jacked up and the tyres removed to keep serviceable aircraft in the air. For a period tyres were literally collected from the factory and fitted direct to aircraft. Every effort was made to prolong the life of tyres and to avoid bursts, by constant sweeping of runways to remove loose stones, but it is considered that this problem could have been overcome completely, and considerable economy effected, by the provision of treaded tyres.

103. *Personnel.* – Reference has already been made to manpower shortage as one of the factors which tended to limit the expansion of Bomber Command. It is not proposed to attempt a full appreciation of the effect on expansion and re-equipment of deficiencies in various personnel categories, but two shortages, both of which caused concern throughout the period under review, are worthy of special mention:—

(*a*) *Radar Mechanics.*
(*b*) *Armourer Assistants.*

The first of these shortages was due as much to the introduction of the many new radar devices, as to the expansion and re-equipment of the Command. In spite of constant efforts to train personnel to make good the deficiencies, the position remained acute up to the end of the War.

104. The second was due to the fact that no special trade of bomb handling personnel existed, with the result that many airmen were posted almost as soon as they became proficient, and the failure of establishments to keep pace with requirements, owing to the steadily increasing "all-up" weight of the Lancaster and the amazing bomb-carrying capacity of this aircraft. It was due only to the long hours worked in the open in all weathers, to the tireless efforts and splendid morale of Bomber Command ground personnel of all branches and trades (since recognised by the award of the Defence Medal) that no restriction was placed on operational effort by inability to bomb-up aircraft in time for operations.

105. A great deal of loose talk in favour of the general adoption of so-called "planned flying" has been produced during the latter stages of the War, and the present review of Bomber Command expansion and re-equipment from February, 1942, until the end of the War in Europe would be incomplete without some further reference to this subject.

106. "Planned flying," which in its true sense merely means "organised flying," aims to produce a given number of serviceable aircraft at any specified time, and so to stagger the servicing task that all established personnel are kept employed to the fullest possible extent.   This is excellent in its intention and entirely logical (in fact ordinary common sense) as applied to Training Units or to "constant task" squadrons such as long-range reconnaissance squadrons in Coastal Command. In Bomber Command, however, the general application of "planned flying" to the Main Force Squadrons would have meant nothing less than an artificial restriction of effort, since the opportunities provided by the weather, both at base and *en route* to the target, was for a long time the most important factor in heavy bomber operations. The ultimate effect of "planned flying" if applied to Bomber Command as a whole might have been a somewhat accelerated expansion, but this would have increased the shortage of airfields, etc., and have certainly been accompanied by a considerable reduction in the weight of bombs dropped on the enemy. This, in turn, would have led to a prolongation of the War.

107. The aim throughout has been to complete the expansion and re-equipment of the Command with a minimum loss of operational efficiency. Perhaps the truest criterion by which such efficiency can be judged is the scale of effort maintained, and when it is realised that the average intensity of Bomber Command main force squadrons during the summer of 1944 remained consistent at approximately 200 sorties per month per 20 U.E. aircraft and actually rose to an average of 229 sorties in August of that year, the degree of achievement will be appreciated. Unfortunately, no reasonable basis of comparison between the various operational Commands exists, in that the number of engine hours per servicing man is affected by such factors as refuelling, rearming (including bombing up) and repair of enemy damage, but it is felt that, measured on whatever basis, the standards reached in Bomber Command during the last two years of the War would be difficult to surpass.

108. The purpose of this Appendix has been to describe in very general terms how the task of expansion and re-equipment was tackled, to record some of the problems encountered, and the changes in organisation which resulted. Neither lack of precedent nor lack of facilities were allowed to stand in the way of progress. Whether the best use was made of opportunities offered, only history can decide, but the fact remains that the heterogeneous collection of aircraft, many of them semi-obsolete types, which went to make up the pre-1942 Bomber Command, were replaced with modern bomber aircraft, and that these were successfully welded into the vast and efficient machine which achieved the virtual destruction of the German War potential within the space of little more than three years.

Note:–
1 See Appendix K, paras. 26 and 27.

APPENDIX F

BOMBER COMMAND AIRFIELDS IN USE

	1 Group	3 Group	4 Group	5 Group	6 Group	8 Group	100 Group	91 Group	92 Group	93 Group	7 Group	Total.
February, 1942	8	15	10	11	-	1	-	22	12	-	-	79
January, 1943	11	13	12	14	6	4	-	17	17	11	-	105
January, 1944	14	15	14	15	11	8	4	18	16	13	-	128
January, 1945	12	12	11	12	7	9	8	13	14	1	22	121
May, 1945	10	10	9	12	8	9	8	14	14	-	17	111

ANNEXURE "B"
STRENGTH OF COMMAND IN TERMS OF AIRCRAFT OPERATIONAL AND TRAINING

	Operational			Training			Miscellaneous Established Types Medium, Light and Fighter	Grand Total
	Heavy	Light or Medium	Total	Heavy	Light or Medium	Total		
February, 1942	224	702	926	291	1,091	1,382	449	3,078
January, 1943	654	313	1,247	583	1,277	1,860	479	3,804
January, 1944	1,298	167	1,465	531	970	1,501	617	4,362
January, 1945	1,873	371	2,244	468	915	1,383	585	4,384
May, 1945	1,994	422	2,416					

ANNEXURE "C"
EXPANSION OF TRAINING UNITS

	O.T.U.s.			H.C.U.s.			Miscellaneous Training Units			Totals		
	O.T.U.s	Aircraft	Airfields	H.C.U.s.	Aircraft	Airfields	Units	Aircraft	Airfields	Units	Aircraft Strength-	Airfields
February, 1942	15	-	30	3 HCU 12 HCF1	-	3	-	-	-	30	-	33
June, 1942	17	917	35	4 HCU 23 HCF1	210	4	-	-	-	44	1,127	39
January, 1943	19	1,094	39	10 HCU	292	10	-	-	-	29	1,386	49
June, 1943	21	1,145	41	14 HCU 2 HCF	489	16	2	34	3	39	1,668	602
January, 1944	22	1,256	46	15 HCU 2 HCF 3 LFS	583	20	3	45	3	45	1,884	693
June, 1944	22	1,232	40	15 HCU 3 LFS	716	18	4	70	1	44	2,018	594
January, 1945	19	884	31	16 HCU 2 LFS	508	18	6	85	2	43	1,477	515
May, 1945	17	803	28	12 HCU	418	12	6	92	2	35	1,313	426

Key

1. These flights accommodated on airfields occupied by operational squadrons.
2. Misc units inc: 1655 M.T.U., P.F.N.T.U.
3. 1692 Flt., P.F.N.T.U., 1655 T.U.
4. 1655 M.T.U., P.F.N.T.U., 1699, (F) TF, 1692, (B.S.) Flt.
5. 1692 (B.S.) Flt., 1699 (F) T.F., P.F.N.T.U., 1323 Flt., B.C.I.S., G.H. Trg Flt.
6. 1692 (B.S.) Flt., 1699 (F) T.F., P.F.N.T.U., 1323 Flt., B.C.I.S., G.H. Trg Flt.
7. 1692 (B.S.) Flt., 1699 (F) T.F., P.F.N.T.U., 1323 Flt., B.C.I.S., G.H. Trg Flt.

APPENDIX F

PERCENTAGE STRENGTH OF COMMAND NON-OPERATIONAL OWING TO FORMATION OR RE-EQUIPMENT OF SQUADRONS. (MONTHLY)

	No. of Sqdns. Estab.	Sqdns. Non-Op. for Re-equipping.	Est. Sqdns. Non-Op. for Re-equipping.	Squadrons Forming.	Est. Sqdns. Forming.
1942			per cent		per cent
February	51	14	27·4	1	2·0
March	44½	6	13·4	-	-
April	40½	7	17·3	-	-
May	37	9	24·3	-	-
June	33	6	18·5	-	-
July	37	4	10·8	1	2·7
August	39	6	16·0	4	10·2
September	38	5	13·1	2	5·2
October	43	6	14·0	3	7·0
November	47	6	12·7	6	12·7
December	52	6½	12·5	10	20·0
1943					
January	54	1	2·0	3	5·4
February	55	1½	2·8	1	1·9
March	62	½	·8	1	1·6
April	59½	½	·9	1	1·8
May	62½	-	-	1	1·6
June	64½	2	3·1	1	1·5
July	66	4	6·0	1	1·5
August	66½	4	6·0	-	-
September	67	3	4·4	2	3·0
October	70	2	2·8	2½	3·5

November	72½	1	1·4	3	4·1
December	74½	7	9·4	1½	2·0

1944

January	74½	6	8·0	-	-
February	82	6	7·3	1	1·2
March	83	3	3·7	2½	3·0
April	83	1	1·2	½	·6
May	86½	5	5·8	½	·5
June	88½	2	2·2	-	-
July	90½	½	·5	1	1·1
August	93	½	·5	3	3·2
September	95½	½	·5	2½	2·6
October	103½	½	·48	3½	3·4
November	105	-	-	1	·9
December	107	1½	1·4	½	·5

1945

January	107	1	·9	½	·45
February	107½	-	-	½	·45
March	108	1	·9	½	·45
April	107	1	.9	-	-

Note. –

Numbers of squadrons are expressed in terms of standard 2-flight squadrons of 16 + 2, 16 + 4 and later 20 U.E. aircraft.

APPENDIX G

A REVIEW OF TRAINING

Introduction

The purpose of this Appendix is to place on record the progress made in training the thousands of aircrews required to operate in Bomber Command Squadrons during the period between February, 1942, and the end of the war in Europe; to outline the difficulties and the methods employed to overcome them; and to show the steps taken to meet the changing requirements of operational squadrons consequent upon large-scale expansion and continuous development of aircraft, equipment, weapons and tactics. To achieve this object it is necessary to survey the history of crew-training from the first stage in Operational Training Units to the last stage of heavy conversion, together with all the specialist training in armament, navigation, etc., and also to show how these units were developed and the new measures that were introduced to meet the ever-changing needs consequent upon natural technological evolution and upon the development and strengthening of the enemy's defences.

2. In order to show clearly the position in February, 1942, it is necessary to give a brief review of what had occurred since the beginning of the war. When war broke out there was a general shortage in Bomber Command, both of front line squadrons, and of training units. In addition, the types of aircraft which were being, and were about to be, produced, did not admit of a quick transition from the Hart/Audax type of aircraft to the larger aircraft, which required from one to four extra members of the crew. This difficulty was further accentuated later when, with the introduction of four-engined aircraft, a further step in the stages of training had to be introduced.

3. It is an unfortunate fact that, in order to provide training units with instructors of the desired degree of efficiency, it is necessary to select the most experienced pilots and other aircrew available. As these will normally only be found in the front line, this in turn leads to a reduction in operational efficiency. Such reduction might be accepted in peace-time in view of the subsequent assured increase of numbers and efficiency in the front line later, but the small front-line air force existing at the

beginning of the war was already hard pressed to carry out all the operations required of it, and could ill afford to be robbed of its most efficient crews.

4. The solution, so far as Bomber Command was concerned, was the conversion of certain front-line squadrons at the beginning of the war to the role of training units to train others which were carrying out operations. Although at first these squadrons were kept in pairs on one station, by April, 1940, the squadron numbers had been deleted, and the squadrons on each station were united to form one Operational Training Unit, which was given an O.T.U. number.

5. At this time there were five Operational Groups, consisting primarily of Battles, Blenheims, Wellingtons, Whitleys and Hampdens, respectively, and to meet the wastage in those squadrons, a total of eight O.T.U.s were formed, consisting of one Battle, two Blenheim, three Wellington, one Whitley and one Hampden O.T.U. The number of O.T.U.s constantly expanded and ultimately reached its peak in December, 1943, when a total of 22½ O.T.U.s were receiving inputs, and armed primarily with Wellingtons, although a few Whitley O.T.U.s still survived. The Battle and Hampden had disappeared from Bomber Command long before this date, and the Blenheims of No. 2 Group had been handed over, together with one of the O.T.U.s to Fighter Command, later to join 2nd Tactical Air Force.

6. The O.T.U.s were originally concentrated in No. 6 Group, which was subsequently re-numbered 91 Group. When the number of O.T.U.s exceeded the number that could be conveniently dealt with by one Group, a second Group, No. 7, subsequently re-numbered 92, was formed, and took over some of the 91 Group O.T.U.s and opened others. Later a third O.T.U. Group was added (No. 93) which mainly opened new O.T.U.s, but also took over one or two existing O.T.U.s, which were more conveniently placed geographically for 93 Group. Of these, 91 Group had the Oxford and Cotswold area, and two O.T.U.s in the North of Scotland. No. 92 Group was mainly in the Buckinghamshire and Leicestershire areas, and No. 93 Group stretched from Shropshire, across the centre of England, through Derbyshire and Nottinghamshire, with the most northerly O.T.U. at Finningley.

The New Training Policy

7. Until March, 1942, the Wellington and Whitley O.T.U.s were training crews consisting of two pilots, a navigator (B) and two WO/AGs, one of whom manned the rear turret. At first the two pilots were intended to be trained equally, so as to be able to take over from each other in the air. Consequently, only half the time of each course could be given to the training of each pilot, and without a complete double course it was impossible fully to train two pilots. To remedy this, both pilots were given circuits and landings by day and night, after which one pilot was nominated as First Pilot, and did further cross-country, etc., training. This proved most unsatisfactory, and it was clear that, if the pilot was to be trained to the standard required for heavy bombers, one pilot only per aircraft could be provided. In addition, the navigator was fully engaged on his own work and could not successfully be employed as bomb-

aimer in addition. Apart from other difficulties his work as navigator prevented him from getting his eyes "night-conditioned" before attempting to identify the aiming point. In March, 1942, decisions were taken which fundamentally altered the O.T.U. training. These were:—

(*a*) Only one pilot per crew was to be trained.

(*b*) An air bomber was to be introduced into the crew, allowing the navigator to concentrate on navigation. The air bomber was also to be the front gunner, as at that time all night bombers carried front guns.

(*c*) Only one WO/AG was to be carried, the other being replaced by a straight air gunner with no wireless training. Later the WO/AG was replaced by a WO/Air, *i.e.,* a wireless operator who had no gunnery training.

These changes made it possible to give each member of the crew a full course on his own subjects, and, particularly in the case of the pilot, enabled a very much better course to be given, as it was no longer necessary to give a double number of circuits and bumps to each crew. This in turn relieved both the strain on the pilot instructors and the congestion around the O.T.U. airfields. It was further decided that one other member of the crew should have a small amount of training both on the Link Trainer and at the controls of aircraft. At first this training was given to the air bombers; later, for all heavy bombers, to the flight engineers. Once the O.T.U.s began to train for heavy bombers, a second air gunner was added to the crew at the O.T.U. stage, one air gunner being primarily trained for the rear turret, and the other ultimately for the mid-upper turret of the heavy.

8. From the time that the single pilot and the other alterations to the constitution of the crew were accepted, the O.T.U. course settled down to a total of 80 hours, from which it did not deviate during the war. At times the pressure on training very nearly led to a reduction in the length of the course, but, happily, it was always possible to avoid this undesirable consequence. Although the syllabus of the course was constantly improved and altered to fit changing conditions in the front line, fundamentally it remained the same, and culminated always in a succession of long night cross-country flights.

9. There is always in war a conflict between quality and quantity. It is in the first place desirable to provide crews for all the squadrons for which the aircraft, equipment and ground staff can be found. Consequently, if training cannot keep pace with expansion, there is pressure to cut the training hours, and to hope that the less well-trained product will still be able to carry out the operations required without undue casualties, which, it should be remembered, may be due to accidents, weather and other natural hazards, in addition to those imposed by enemy action. It is always difficult to assess whether sufficient training has been given for the task in hand, or whether further training, even at the expense of a lower crew output, will lead to higher operational efficiency, and thereby actually contribute more to the winning of the war. It must also be remembered that in mass production of crews, it is necessary to strike an average, which shall become the standard course. An endeavour must

then be made, by a process of weeding-out in each aircrew category in the early stages, to ensure that once the final stages of training begin, the average crew is likely to complete the course successfully within the time allotted.

Difficulties of Expanding Training

10. One of the biggest difficulties over the whole period until the last few months was to find a sufficient number of competent potential instructors, and to give them training adequate to ensure their efficiency. It was quickly found that only aircrew with operational experience could successfully train crews from the O.T.U. stage onwards; but owing to the constant expansion of the front line, and the rate of casualties at the height of the war, which did not allow of a large number of tour-experienced aircrew becoming available as instructors, there was always a lag in the number of pilot instructors, until the last year of the war. For a considerable period there was also a deficiency in the number of navigators and air bombers, although the position was not so acute in regard to wireless operators and air gunners. Partly because the earlier crews all had two WO/AGs and partly because the later heavy crews had two air gunners, more individuals in these categories completed a tour of operations. In consequence of this, until well into 1944, training units had to struggle along with their strength of instructors almost invariably below establishment. Moreover, individual instructors, having once started to instruct, were kept in the training units very much longer than was originally intended, owing to the difficulty of finding the capacity to train new instructors when in the course of time they became available. The work done by some of the long-term instructors was tremendous. They formed the backbone of all the training units, and gallantly stuck to their work in many cases for well over two years at a time when any relaxation of effort would have had most serious results. This situation was greatly aggravated by the necessity of training a large number of medium crews for overseas, mainly the Mediterranean Allied Air Forces, and to meet the considerable demand for heavy crews for special duty and other squadrons overseas. This demand was originally met by posting crews from any O.T.U. as required, or even by taking them away from operational squadrons, but in April, 1942, the overseas O.T.U. training was concentrated into two special O.T.U.s, and to each of these was attached a ferry training unit in which crews received the actual aircraft which they were to fly out, and also carried out the necessary consumption tests before proceeding to the despatch station. Special attention was given during the training to overseas Intelligence and other matters which would be useful to the crews in their own operational theatre, but otherwise training did not differ from that given at an O.T.U. supplying U.K. squadrons. The heavy crews required were almost entirely Halifax crews (some for subsequent conversion to Liberators overseas), but this drain was never large compared with the call for Wellington trained crews, which at the maximum reached a total of more than 50 crews per month. A further cause of trouble was the difficulty of getting tour-expired crews returned from the Middle East for duty in O.T.U.s and H.C.U.s. For a

long time little or nothing was done to avoid this waste of irreplaceable personnel, but eventually arrangements were made to return them to this country. Finally, Wellington O.T.U.s were formed in the Middle East, mainly in Palestine, and the demand for Bomber Command trained crews diminished and finally died out, enabling the O.T.U.s to devote themselves exclusively to training for U.K. squadrons.

11. Soon after the decision to change the composition of the crew from two pilots to one pilot, and to introduce the Air Bomber, a re-organisation of the staff of Bomber Command took place, by which training was placed under an Air Officer who was on the same level as the Senior Air Staff Officer and the Air Officer Administration. Formerly, training had been a branch of the Air Staff directly under the S.A.S.O., but it was obvious that the expansion of Bomber Command, both on the operational and on the training sides, had led to an immense amount of work which could not be successfully dealt with by a single S.A.S.O. and, by this change, attention could be given to the requirements of training on a high level. It was the responsibility of the Air Officer Training, not only to deal with the day-to-day training matters concerning the O.T.U. and H.C.U. syllabi, but also, in conjunction with the organisation, and planning staffs, to look well ahead to ensure that sufficient training units would be formed in time to meet future expansion of the operational strength of the Command. In this connection it must be remembered that the normal time which was taken by a crew to reach a Squadron properly trained for operations was not less than five months from the date of entering an O.T.U., and it was therefore necessary to look well ahead in the planning of trained units to make sure that this big time lag was not overlooked. The Air Officer Training was also responsible for keeping close liaison with the "P" Staff section concerned with aircrew postings, in order to ensure that no instructors or crews were lost to Bomber Command when they were required for training or operational duties to meet current requirements or future expansion.

Crew Training

12. One of the first problems with which the O.T.U.s were faced was that of welding a number of individuals into a team or crew. Up to their arrival for O.T.U. training, aircrew had received basic training individually, and although a considerable amount of individual instruction for each category has to be retained right through to the time when the crew reaches the squadron, it was important to give great attention to the welding of individuals into a crew. At this stage the captain of a crew, who is invariably the pilot, is charged with the responsibility for the discipline of his crew on the ground and in the air, and this normal development was severely hampered by the fact that the pilot was not always commissioned, usually had officers in his crew, and even if commissioned, was not necessarily the senior officer. In spite of repeated attempts to improve this situation, practically nothing was done up to the end of the war to increase the status of captains, and to ensure that the captain of each crew would be the senior officer in the crew, or if not commissioned, would have no officers under him. Towards the latter part of the war, every endeavour was made at

O.T.U.s to avoid putting officers into crews where the pilot was an N.C.O., as once the crew had started their O.T.U. training, it is undesirable for many reasons to break the crew again until the completion of its tour of operations, other than through the occurrence of unavoidable casualties. As a result, due to the fact that captains of aircraft have not been invariably senior to other members of the crew, the general discipline of aircrew has been unsatisfactory in many instances.

Operational Activities of O.T.U.s

13. It would not be right to leave the subject of O.T.U.s without a short mention of their operational activities. They undertook at all times on a large scale the task of dropping propaganda leaflets over France, thereby relieving operational squadrons of this commitment, and at the same time gaining valuable experience of flying over enemy-occupied country, including the risk of being shot at by flak, or attacked by enemy fighters. But, apart from this, the great event in the life of the O.T.U.s was when they were detailed to take part in the great 1,000-bomber attacks which took place on 30/31st May and 1/2nd June, 1942, and to augment the main force on a few subsequent operations. During the latter part of the war, when Bomber Command consisted entirely of heavy bombers, and the increase in the German night fighter defence made it undesirable to risk Wellington and Whitley aircraft in large numbers over or towards Germany, the final exercises of the O.T.U. crews consisted of a "Bullseye." This was a large-scale exercise carried out within the confines of the British Isles and the adjacent seas, during which the crews attacked targets at which large numbers of searchlights were deployed, at some of which a flashlight target was provided. An important feature of these exercises was that during them crews were liable to be "attacked" by U.K.-based fighters working under operational conditions.

Heavy Conversion Units

14. To turn now to the training of crews for heavy bombers. This was at first considered to involve not much more than the conversion of a crew to a different type of aircraft, and, in fact, the name Conversion Unit has still been retained to describe the unit where heavy bomber crews are trained. It was quickly realised, however, that with this conversion, a definite stage of training was reached which required the highest class of trained instructors, and was, in fact, comparable in importance to O.T.U. training. In the first place heavy aircraft were used only to re-equip front-line squadrons, but as the need for some form of conversion training was recognised, four training aircraft per heavy squadron were allotted, both for this purpose, when a squadron was initially re-equipped, and to meet subsequent wastage. Later small heavy conversion flights were formed in each of the Groups re-equipping with heavies, and finally all these small units and the training flights of squadrons

were amalgamated into units of 32 aircraft, sufficient being formed to cover the conversion of all the crews required in squadrons that were re-equipping, as well as to meet wastage of the whole force.

15. The H.C.U. course, although shorter than that of the O.T.U.s, was conducted on very much the same lines. The mid-upper gunner was introduced for the first time to a mid-upper turret, and the O.T.U. crew was joined by a Flight Engineer. The whole crew required intensive preparation in drills of all kinds, and the giving of day and night dual instruction was a job that called for the most skilful instructors available. As in the case of the O.T.U.s, there was for a long time an insufficiency of instructors to meet establishments, and very hard work, long hours and long periods as instructors were put in by a small number of personnel.

16. In the beginning there were Stirling and Halifax H.C.U.s backing Stirling and Halifax Squadrons, but the arrival of the Lancaster, which was incomparably the best of the three heavies, introduced a new problem. As it was necessary to employ every available Lancaster in front-line squadrons, H.C.U.s backing Lancaster Squadrons were at first equipped with 50 per cent. Halifax, on which day dual and solo was given, and 50 per cent. Lancaster on which crews were finished off by day, and also did all their night flying. At the end of 1943, however, there was a still greater urge to increase the number of Lancasters in the front line at the expense of Stirlings and Halifaxes, and the decision was taken that Lancasters should be removed altogether from heavy conversion units, where in future crews would receive only Stirling or Halifax training. Concurrently Lancaster Finishing Schools were formed at which the crews posted to Lancaster Squadrons would receive a short conversion course to these aircraft. This system continued for approximately a year, after which the improved supply of Lancasters, combined with a reduction in the number of casualties, allowed the re-equipment with Lancasters of all H.C.U.s backing Lancaster squadrons. By this time the Stirling had entirely disappeared from Bomber Command, but there remained a few Halifax H.C.U.s backing Halifax squadrons in Nos. 4 and 6 (R.C.A.F.) Groups.

17. At first the H.C.U.s were established in the Operational Groups, and each Group formed up to a total of three H.C.U.s, or 15 in all. As, however, the Groups further expanded, and more Squadrons were formed, two further H.C.U.s were required over and above the three per Group. Moreover, the attention of the Operational Groups became increasingly absorbed in operations, and this made their training responsibility a serious burden. It was therefore decided in the autumn of 1944 that an H.C.U. Group should be formed (No. 7 Group) into which all H.C.U.s should be placed. This was done, and the Group opened in November, 1944, with the full 17 H.C.U.s, which the size of the Bomber Force now required. The course at the H.C.U. has been throughout based on a syllabus of 40 hours, but as it has been the practice to ensure that crews before leaving the H.C.U. reached a certain definite standard, training time given exceeded 45 hours in many cases. As this extra flying was not allowed for on the maintenance side, it was acccomplished only by excessively hard work for long hours on the part of the maintenance personnel concerned.

Climatic Factors

18. One of the main difficulties to be overcome in training arose from the considerable difference experienced in weather in summer and winter in this country, a factor which vitally affects the number of crews that can be trained by a given unit in different months of the year. It had been supposed at the beginning of the war that, owing to bad weather, night operations would be severely restricted during the winter months, and wastage on operations in consequence would be less in winter than in summer. However, as the war progressed, improvements in aids to navigation, homing, blind bombing and F.I.D.O. enabled aircraft to operate fairly consistently throughout the winter in large numbers. It was therefore necessary to use training units to the maximum capacity during the summer, and then to accept a lower output during the winter, when the difficulties imposed by bad weather were such that they could not normally be surmounted by inexperienced crews still under training. Consequently it was necessary to increase output during the summer, and at the beginning of the winter, to "bank-up" crews, both those who had completed H.C.U. training and had reached squadrons, and also those who, although they had completed O.T.U. training under the summer programme could not immediately be absorbed into H.C.U.s on the winter programme. It was to deal with the latter, that aircrew schools were formed, to serve as holding units for crews who were awaiting entry into H.C.U.s. During the height of the winter, some of these crews had to wait as long as 8/10 weeks before beginning H.C.U. training. Nevertheless, in spite of the disadvantages of this break in training, it was found that, in fact, there was very little loss of efficiency, the crews during this interval being kept usefully busy on ground instruction, including physical fitness exercises, escape procedure, etc. With regard to H.C.U. output, it was planned that as far as possible squadrons should be "banked-up" with crews to the highest possible extent at the beginning of the winter, and by this means it was found that it was just possible to get through to the spring without unduly lowering the number of crews in squadrons. The month of April when operations very often reached a very high intensity, although O.T.U.s and H.C.U.s were not in full summer production, was always a tricky month. The spring of 1943 was the most difficult of all to deal with, for the full implications of summer and winter training and operations had not by then been fully recognised; by spring, 1944, however, the difficulty was successfully overcome, and crew availability allowed for a very large scale of operations in April and May prior to "D" Day. Similarly, the spring of 1945 would also have been weathered successfully, even if operations had not practically ceased in April, with the end of the war only a week away.

Mosquito Training

19. The number of Mosquito light bomber squadrons which at first was small, gradually increased, to provide ultimately a force of 12 squadrons. At first the training was met by the formation of a small Mosquito Training Unit in No. 8 Group. In order to reduce the training of Mosquito crews to a minimum at a time when Mosquitos

were scarce, and as many as possible were required for front-line squadrons, crews were selected as far as possible from pilots and navigators of considerable experience, either of night bombers or of other types of operational flying. With the rapid increase of Mosquito squadrons towards the end of 1944 and the beginning of 1945, it was necessary to enlarge the Mosquito training to such an extent that a complete O.T.U. (No. 16) was turned over from Wellington to Mosquito training, absorbing on its formation the bulk of the Mosquito Training Unit. Owing to the obvious approach of the end of the war, the final two Mosquito squadrons which had been planned were not formed.

Instructors Schools

20. By the spring of 1944, when operations were largely transferred to targets in France in preparation for D-Day, and subsequent to D-Day, when the German night defence organisation was progressively overrun and dislocated, the casualties were rapidly reduced. This, coupled with a very high rate of operations, which made tour-expired aircrew more quickly available, enabled all deficiencies in training units to be made good as to numbers, if not altogether as to quality. During all this time, however, Groups had organised small instructor schools within their own resources, but it was not until November, 1944, that it was possible to form a Bomber Command Instructors School as a single unit to undertake the training of instructors of all aircrew categories.

21. It has always been clear that in order to raise the standard of instructors, and so improve training and reduce accidents, it was necessary to specialize the training of pilots and other aircrew categories on a particular type of aircraft, namely, Wellingtons, heavy bombers, and Mosquitos. It is vain to suppose that a pilot, trained to instruct on Oxfords, will, by the fact of his having operated on a medium or heavy bomber, be automatically qualified to be a good instructor on those types. The formation of an Instructor School on a sufficiently large scale, however, involved in the first place the removal from training units of a considerable number of experienced instructors to become the instructors at the Bomber Command School. Also a large number of pupils would have had to be found from those who were already urgently required to instruct in units. The continual shortage of pilot instructors did not permit the school to be formed until the autumn of 1944, and in fact the first pupils were not taken till January, 1945. Until then, as already mentioned, the Training Groups did the best they could by running short courses in small Group Schools, in addition to valuable assistance given by Flying Training Command in the training of non-pilot categories as instructors, first at North Luffenham and later at Brize Norton. When, in the summer of 1944, the situation in regard to the supply of instructors improved rapidly, it became apparent that the long-awaited Bomber Command Instructor School could at last be formed, although its formation was delayed for some weeks by the difficulty of finding a suitable home. It was hoped for some time that Cottesmore would be released by the Americans, but after waiting

some time for this station, it became apparent that it would not be given up soon enough to be of use. Fortunately, the reduction in number of O.T.U.s which took place from November, 1944, enabled the School to start at one of the stations thus vacated, Finningley, a pre-war station. The School now trains instructors on Wellingtons, Lancasters (formerly on Halifaxes too), and latterly, on Mosquitos; and in addition all non-pilot categories are given a good course which enables them to instruct in O.T.U.s and H.C.U.s and pays particular attention to making efficient use of the large number of synthetic training devices.

Synthetic Training

22. These ingenious synthetic training devices, which were evolved during the war to assist in training, deserve full mention. The object of synthetic devices is not so much to shorten the time spent on training in the air, as a minimum amount of actual flying must always be accepted, but rather to ensure that by careful preparation on the ground the maximum possible use will be made of the air time available, thus reducing the number of repeat exercises or failures likely to result in accidents and other troubles. The pre-war synthetic trainers consisted mainly of the A.M. Bombing Teacher and the Link Trainer, which was just coming into full use at the beginning of the war. Apart from the necessary turret-training set-ups and various forms of screens for projecting the target aircraft, which to a large extent consisted in the erection of existing equipment, perhaps the most elaborate and ingenious synthetic training device was the Grope, or Ground Operational Exercise. This, by enabling a crew to be practised together in conditions equivalent to a long cross-country, undoubtedly contributed greatly to the preparation of crews for actual cross country flying. As new devices, particularly radar devices, were introduced, so ground training had to keep pace, and one of the most successful ground trainers produced was that for H.2.S., which gives a most realistic presentation on the cathode ray tube of a target as seen on actual operations. The D.R.I. was a most successful trainer for navigators, and mention must be made of the Gee Box which, apart from anything else, enables crews to home with greater accuracy than had ever been achieved before. Lastly, in the prevention of accidents and the saving of life, perhaps the greatest contribution was the development of the Airmanship Halls. In these were installed fuselages and, where available, Silloth Trainers; and in these, also, all forms of cockpit, dinghy, escape, crash, etc., drills were taught so as to eliminate, as far as possible, accidents due to faulty procedure and lack of knowledge of drills. Nearly all synthetic devices started life in holes and corners which could be found existing in O.T.U.s, but when, gradually, the necessity for all these devices was recognised, all the later O.T.U.s were provided with a most successful centralized Ground Training Centre in which, as far as possible, suitable buildings were specially erected to house the various types of synthetic training equipment.

23. In addition to the straightforward training in O.T.U.s and H.C.U.s the introduction of new devices and equipment in the front line, with the necessity for such equipment being used immediately on operations, led to the necessity to form small training units in order that specialized training in this new equipment should be given. Examples of this have been radar-controlled gun turrets, and the G.H. navigational aid, for training on both of which special flights were formed outside the normal training units. Another example of special training was that carried out in a unit called the Navigation Training Unit, which was established in No. 8 Group to receive the crews posted to Pathfinder Squadrons from other Groups. A special course on Pathfinder navigation technique and target marking was given to these crews before they were allowed to operate in the P.F.F. role. Latterly, the scope of this unit was expanded to include the special training of the marker crews posted to those selected Mosquito squadrons which operate OBOE and H.2.S. The equipment of two squadrons in No. 100 Group with Liberators and Fortresses for R.C.M. duties make it necessary to establish a special training flight for the conversion of crews who had received their initial four-engined training at one of the standard H.C.U.s. It has always been necessary in war that new equipment should be made available in the front line as quickly as possible, and only as it becomes more plentiful, to introduce training in the use of it into the normal courses at those H.C.U.s and O.T.U.s where the type of aircraft operated allows of the special equipments being fitted. Early on, GEE became a normal fitting in all training aircraft, and latterly H.2.S. was fitted to a large proportion of the heavy training aircraft (Wellingtons were not able to take this equipment). On the whole, the training of crews in the special devices has approximately met requirements, but it has inevitably meant that although it should not be their normal function in war time, Operational Squadrons have had to spend considerable hours in such training.

24. With the intensification of the enemy night-fighter defence of Germany and occupied countries, it became most important that the air gunners should have the most realistic training possible before going on operations. For this purpose, fighter aircraft were established in all Operational Groups so that crews could keep in practice during their operational tour, and also in all Training Units, so that crews, and particularly the air gunners, could have practice both by day and night in taking evasive action, in turret manipulation, and in aiming and firing. An organization was set up for the rapid assessment of films made in these exercises, so that all gunners could have their mistakes explained to them as soon as possible after landing. To ensure that the greatest instructional benefit was obtained, great stress was also paid to briefing of the bomber crew and the fighter pilot before the affiliation exercise, and to their subsequent interrogation after landing. Acknowledgment is made here to Fighter Command for their ready assistance in providing a supply of fighter pilots who were most enthusiastic in carrying out this rather dull routine training.

25. There is no doubt that the safety of the crew on night operations depended largely on the ability of the air gunners to see enemy aircraft before they themselves were spotted, or, at any rate, before the enemy fighter could get into position to fire.

Various aids, such as Monica, Fishpond and A.G.L. (T), were devised as early warning devices, and in the case of A.G.L. (T), for automatic firing; but nevertheless the main responsibility rested on the air gunner's powers of observation and recognition.

26. In order to aid the air gunner's night vision, and also to improve when possible the air bomber's skill in target recognition at night, training in night vision was developed by the formation of a Central Night Vision School, in addition to a number of Night Vision Schools, which were usually attached to H.C.U.s where the main night vision training was given. This night vision training was constantly developed, and there is no doubt that it contributed considerably towards raising the standard of night vision in air gunners and air bombers, as well as teaching them the elements of the use of the eyes at night, and improving recognition of enemy aircraft.

27. Amongst other small schools that were formed was the Bombing Analysis School, the object of which was to teach instructors how to compute bombing results, in order to raise the standard of training of air bombers by explaining to them, and also to pilots and navigators, the cause of bombing errors. Another school was the Engine Control Demonstration Unit which, by means of sectioned engines and suitable aircraft fitted with flowmeters, was able to demonstrate to the pilot the correct running of engines to obtain increased range and reduced petrol consumption. The introduction of more complicated engines had made it necessary to pay considerable attention to the correct running of these engines to avoid excessive petrol consumption leading to disasters due to running out of fuel.

Dominion and Allied Aircrews

28. Mention must also be made of the Dominion and Allied aircrew which were trained in Bomber Command Training Units. The R.C.A.F. and also the Australians were allotted special O.T.U.s, which were manned by R.A.F. ground personnel, although a large proportion of the instructors were of the same Dominion nationality as the crews under training. The New Zealanders, whose requirements were smaller, were allotted a portion of an R.A.F. O.T.U., to the staff of which they contributed a proportion of the instructors. So far as Allied personnel are concerned, there has been for a very long time a Polish element, first at Bramcote, then at Finningley, and later at Abingdon. French crews have been trained at Lossiemouth, and for a time Czechs were trained for one Czech squadron in Bomber Command, until its transference to Coastal Command. With the exception of the Czechs, all these were subsequently trained for heavy bombers, to which Polish and French squadrons, and all Dominion squadrons, were eventually converted. The language difficulty, although not prohibitive, was apparent in ground training, in teaching drills, and sometimes during air instruction; but the number of accidents directly due to language difficulties were few.

Aircraft Wastage Rates during Training

29. The wastage rate suffered in the course of training was kept reasonably low; in fact, throughout the period in both Operational and Training Units it was progressively reduced, as will be seen from the following figures showing the annual aircraft damage rate (not attributable to enemy action) per 10,000 flying hours:—

1942	44
1943	23
1944	15
1945	8

These figures reveal the overall effectiveness of the many improvements in training, equipment and general organisation during the period. The reduction is the result of great attention paid to all factors that affected safety, and reflects the increasing standard of flying discipline maintained.

In spite of the stress and increasing complexity of operations, the quality of the crews steadily improved. In fact the crews arriving in squadrons, in the last few months of the war, were on average better than at any previous time, and there was no sign that there was likely to be any reduction in quality had the war continued.

Conclusion

30. In conclusion, it can justly be asserted that the success of the Bomber Offensive depended ultimately on the standard of training which could be maintained. It would have been easy to improve training at the expense of the front line by increasing the length of the courses given; by training Lancaster crews on Lancasters only; by ensuring that all the best aircrew were taken off operations early in order to fill the pressing need for instructor posts, and by introducing new equipment into training units first, so that crews could have been provided fully trained in all new devices. However, if this course had been taken, the length of the war would have been increased owing to the consequent diminution in the size of the front line and the reduction of bombing effort. It is believed that the balance struck between operational and training requirements was approximately correct, and that the best all-round result was obtained. No doubt, in the exacting conditions under which training was carried out, certain aircrew had to be turned down who would ultimately have made good had it been possible to pay more attention to their individual instruction, and to give them a longer period of training. It was not possible, however, to persevere with the slow learners when there was no guarantee that they would ultimately become efficient. Moreover, it is probable that some crews, who were somewhat below average, became involved in serious accidents because they were pressed a little beyond their capacity. But the general proof that training methods were satisfactory

must rest on the fact that the intensive operations of Bomber Command were carried out successfully with the crews which Training provided.

31. The task of training would have been made much easier and the deficiencies of aircrew in operational units would have been overcome much earlier, if a proper record had been kept in the Air Ministry of the whereabouts of all O.T.U. trained personnel, and if arrangements had been made to ensure that these valuable men were always properly employed. As it was, great surpluses of aircrew personnel, trained in Bomber Command O.T.U.s, were allowed to arise in the Middle East and elsewhere. At one time, hundreds of such aircrew personnel were in idleness or misemployed overseas, while the operational squadrons and the O.T.U.s in Bomber Command were deficient of hundreds of aircrews and instructor pilots. As the result of great efforts made by the Command, supported by the Inspector-General, the situation was gradually put right, but the lesson should be noted that, in war-time, trained aircrew personnel are, in the long run, the limiting factor of both expansion and operational activity, and the greatest care should be taken to ensure that they are always used to the fullest advantage.

APPENDIX H

SEA-MINING OPERATIONS AND ATTACKS ON NAVAL TARGETS

Sea-Mining

1. In order that the offensive already carried out with such success against the German Navy and mercantile marine could be intensified on occasions when the bomber force could not be fully employed on the main task of bombing Germany, I decided to equip all medium and heavy bombers for minelaying.

This extension of the minelaying programme involved an immediate increase in the production of mines for aircraft, and an unofficial agreement was reached with the Admiralty for the production of 1,200 mines per month, envisaging a monthly lay of 1,000 mines. This monthly quota has at times been considerably exceeded, and the average for the period reviewed, February, 1942, to May, 1945, is 1,113 mines per month.

Certain technical difficulties were encountered in the carrying of mines by certain types of aircraft, but these were soon overcome by the armament staffs concerned.

Staff Organization

2. The minelaying operations carried out between 1940 and 1942, although insignificant when compared with the effort which was expended in the years 1942-1943, had demonstrated the necessity for a close degree of co-operation between the Royal Navy and Royal Air Force at all stages of such operations. With the expansion of minelaying potential in 1942, brought about by the gradual equipment of all bomber groups with stocks of mines and components, it was decided to increase the number of Naval Staff Officers at Headquarters Bomber Command from two to four officers. Their duties were the planning of operations, supply and distribution of mines to R.A.F. stations, compiling of comprehensive statistics of operations, maintenance of a careful watch on the enemy's reaction to minelaying operations as

shown by intelligence available from Admiralty and reconnaissance sources, and liaison between the relevant R.A.F. and Naval Technical branches. The importance and scope of these duties fully justified this increase in staff.

3. At the same time the Admiralty agreed to appoint a Naval Staff Officer to the staff of each Group Commander. A naval officer had originally been appointed to No. 5 Group, and had proved his value in that immediate information on both planning and technical matters was available to the A.O.C. when he wished. Similarly, these appointments were of great value in later years when Group Commanders were called on to carry out heavy bombing and minelaying programmes concurrently. A further advantage was that the naval officers at Groups, being in close contact with Group staffs and aircrews, were able through the Naval Staff Officer at Headquarters to keep the Admiralty informed on all the tactical and technical problems and developments concerned with minelaying. It may be noted here that on occasions when naval targets and shipping were being bombed, the Naval Staff Officers at Groups were also in a position to supply any intelligence made available by Admiralty through the Naval Staff Officer at Headquarters Bomber Command on such subjects.

Scale of Effort and Objectives of the Minelaying Campaign

4. From 1st February, 1942, to 8th May, 1945, 45,428 mines were laid, involving 16,240 aircraft sorties resulting in 491 known ships sunk, and 410 ships damaged. This effort represented 4·8 per cent. of the total bomber effort for the period and required an average of 416 sorties per month.

The rate of sinking represents a vessel sunk or damaged for every 50 mines laid.

Operations were carried out according to the broad directif laid down by the Director of Minelaying Operations in the Admiralty. A brief summary of the main objectives of the minelaying programme during the period follows.

Anti-U-Boat Operations

5. Throughout the period a steady harassing effect on the coming and going of operational U-Boats using the Biscay bases was maintained. In spite of the limited nature of the mineable waters on that coast, much embarrassment was caused and heavy sweeping demands were imposed on the enemy, in the attempt to provide a safe passage for his U-Boats. Two outstanding periods of operations in this area call for special mention. First, the heavy minelaying effort in November, 1942, which aided in neutralising the large numbers of U-Boats being held in West Coast of France bases, when the North African landings were imminent and large convoys were moving from the United Kingdom to Gibraltar. Secondly, the effort expended immediately after the invasion of Normandy, when mines laid in the immediate approaches to the same bases helped to disorganize enemy attempts to use the U-

Boat against our cross-Channel build-up, and finally impeded the evacuation of the remaining serviceable U-Boats to Norway.

As a supplement to the campaign against operational submarines, every opportunity was seized for laying mines in their known exercising grounds in the Baltic. Considerable success is known to have been achieved by these lays, and mining is to be numbered as one of the causes of delay in the appearance of the new pre-fabricated U-Boats in operational service.

Offensive against the German Merchant Navy

6. Certain special objectives in the German mercantile marine, which in itself was the main target for our mines, should be mentioned. From 1942 onwards particular attention was paid to the traffic in iron ore from Scandinavia to the Ruhr, via Rotterdam, and from Bilbao to Bayonne, as it was clear that the denial of raw material supplies by dislocation and sinking would be complementary to the bombing effort then being directed against the industries of the Ruhr. This offensive was carried on until Rotterdam ceased to function as a port of any importance. The heavy risks to shipping occasioned by minelaying and bombing are known to have eventually forced the Swedes to withdraw the large amount of tonnage on charter to Germany at a very critical moment.

Another objective was the transport of military stores and personnel from Western to Eastern Baltic ports in support of the Eastern Front. This shipping passed through mineable water on practically the whole of the voyage from Kiel to Konigsberg. Train ferry communication between Sweden, Denmark and Germany also proved a vulnerable target.

The Invasion of the Continent

7. Immediately prior to the invasion of Europe, mines were laid in the areas of the English Channel and Dutch and Belgian coasts, with a view to reducing the movement of enemy light surface craft to a minimum, and for the protection of cross-Channel convoys from such craft during the actual invasion operation. These operations were in addition to the main strategic plans for minelaying, which ran concurrently with them.

Immediately after the invasion of France, intensive minelaying in the Kattegat and South Norwegian area was commenced, in order to hamper the flow of German troops withdrawing from Norway to reinforce the enemy's Western Front. The dislocation of the traffic was widespread and at times complete, the German authorities being hard put to find alternative railhead ports from which to embark troops, as their customary Norwegian ports were efficiently closed by mining.

Enemy Main Units

8. Another special aspect of minelaying worthy of mention is the employment of the weapon against enemy surface units, the most notable being the lay by Hampdens ahead of the movement of "Scharnhorst" and "Gneisenau" through the Straits of Dover, when each ship sustained damage from mines. In fact, on any occasion when German main units were known to be likely to pass through mineable waters within range of Bomber Command aircraft, mines were laid ahead of them with a view to causing delay and damage to such ships.

Operations of Special Interest

9. Outstanding operations include the first laying of acoustic mines in September, 1942, when 346 of these mines were laid from Bordeaux to Danzig, the laying of mines by Lancasters in the Konigsberg Sea Canal and the laying of over 1,000 mines of a new type in 48 hours in all important shipping lanes between Bordeaux and Danzig. The operation in the Kiel Canal, Kiel Bay and Heligoland Bight just prior to D-Day in Europe is estimated to have cost the enemy 2¾ million tons of overseas trade.

Tactics Employed

10. During 1942 mines were usually laid from a height of 600 to 800 ft., the aircraft themselves establishing their position by making landfall over some prominent landmark on the enemy coast and executing a timed run from this point to the laying position. By the end of 1942 the enemy had so increased his flak and light defences in the neighbourhood of various minefields that, in spite of the most careful planning, it became apparent that a new technique must be adopted. Whilst new methods were being sought in view of the increased casualty rate for aircraft, minelaying operations for the time being were directed against more open and less dangerous areas.

The first main difficulty to be overcome was the inability of the mine to withstand the shock of impact with the water when dropped from a height greater than 1,000 ft. This necessitated an improvement in the packing material which encased the delicate mine assembly.

This problem was submitted to the Superintendent of Mines Design and by March, 1943, as an interim measure the mine was cleared for dropping up to 3,000 ft.

The problem of maintaining the accuracy of laying had yet to be solved, but experiments were made in laying mines on "GEE" fixes in late 1942 in open waters in view of possible inaccuracies by this method. Towards the end of 1943, after much patient experiment, the Bomber Development Unit proved that Mark I-IV mines, in spite of the parachute drogue, had a consistent T.V. of 275 ft. p.s. and could be aimed from a height with reasonable accuracy by using Mark XIV bombsights. Meanwhile, Superintendent of Mines Design had produced a mine fit for dropping from 15,000 ft. Parallel with the improvements made in the mine packing R.A.F. authorities improved the parachute in order to stand the increased vibration when dropped from over 1,000 ft.

The eventual result of this research by Bomber Development Unit and Superintendent of Mines Design was the issue of a comprehensive instruction by Bomber Command giving various methods of minelaying by visual and H.2.S. methods.

During 1943 individual aircraft used H.2.S. whilst minelaying and in autumn, 1943, a Pathfinding technique for minelaying was worked out and put into practice. Halifax II and V aircraft, equipped with H.2.S., acted as Pathfinders for the remaining Halifaxes and Stirlings when such aircraft were not required for bombing operations.

With the intensification of enemy night fighter defences generally it became obvious that on almost all occasions it would be necessary to detail H.2.S. aircraft only, as light conditions over such areas as the Baltic would be impossible for minelaying aircraft. The gradual equipment of all aircraft with H.2.S. made this practicable and the accuracy of minelaying was increased steadily by such means, the usual heights of drop being 12-15,000 ft.

On occasions after the invasion of the Continent mines were laid in inshore waters in heavily-defended areas from a high altitude, the risk of a high percentage of obsolescent mines used on such occasions going ashore being accepted in view of increased dislocation effect likely to occur.

Development and Improvement of Mines

11. The history of the gradual development of the weapon during the period under review again proves the close co-operation between Naval and R.A.F. technical branches. The first straight magnetic mine had several faults which had to be corrected before absolute safety could be guaranteed when in transit, testing, etc., and it is interesting to note that although there had been two unfortunate explosions on airfields due to inadequate safety devices in 1940/41, no trouble of this nature was experienced during the period 1942/45.

In 1942 the double contact magnetic mine was followed by the first airborne British acoustic mine and subsequent types of mines were developed on the lines of plain acoustic and plain magnetic, together with both methods mixed in varying proportions in individual types of mine.

The use of period delay mechanisms and arming clocks was practised throughout the campaign. Special anti-minesweeper mines were designed to counter all efforts of the enemy to sweep our minefields. In 1943 a limited production of approximately 200 special mines per month was arranged in order to present the enemy with fresh sweeping problems at frequent intervals. These mines, which were adaptations of main production types, were produced by a small "factory" manned principally by members of the W.R.N.S. Whenever it was known through Intelligence sources that the enemy was adopting some new sweeping technique or mastering our older types of mine, the production of this factory enabled Bomber Command minelayers to give the appropriate answer with greater rapidity than could have been achieved by the normal methods of production.

The mines principally used throughout the period were the A. Mark I-VI 1,500 lbs. and 1,850 lbs, with a few A. Mark V and Mark VII 1,000 lbs.

An example of the speed with which a considerable technical problem can be solved when the situation demands it was given when, to meet an urgent requirement, 1,000 lb. mines were modified for carriage in Mosquito aircraft within three weeks. Briefly, a team of R.A.F. armament officers co-operating with specialist officers of H.M.S. "Vernon" in a Portsmouth workshop, produced a "mock-up" mine converted from standard types, and drawings for modifications to bomb carriers and electrical gear within one week. Within three weeks, by this joint effort, aircraft successfully laid the mines in the Kiel Canal.

Many suggestions for improvements to parachutes, fusing arrangements and other components have been put forward by R.A.F. Armament Officers, and have been incorporated in design.

No statement on the technical aspect of mines would be complete without reference to the two Naval Petty Officers stationed in each group. These ratings, under the direction of the Station Armament Officers, carried out the supervision of all mines and their loading and testing for operations. The expert knowledge of these ratings proved a useful standby when large mining operations were in progress from several stations, and R.A.F. electrical personnel, always under strength and over-worked, were hard pressed to complete the complicated tests prior to the operation. In the capacity of instructors on new mines, etc., their help was invaluable.

Supply and Distribution of Mines

12. In spite of the difficulties involved, supply and distribution of mines worked smoothly. The fact that no squadrons could be employed exclusively in minelaying necessitated the planning of supply to Maintenance Units on a monthly basis. As at one time approximately 35-40 different types of mine were in use – a selection of such types being necessary at each R.A.F. station – considerable ingenuity had to be exercised to ensure correct distribution. This involved monthly planning in conjunction with the Director of Minelaying Operations Division by the Naval Staff Officer at Headquarters Bomber Command, who in turn co-operated with the Naval Director of Armament and Supply, R.A.F. Master Provision Officer and the Naval Staff Officers at Groups. Only by such monthly plans, anticipating squadron moves, and changes in bombing and minelaying policy was it possible to maintain a representative selection of mines where they were most likely to be needed.

On a few occasions this monthly forecast was defeated by unforeseen circumstances, but the ensuing difficulties were usually quickly solved by co-operation of all concerned, and a technique was worked out for the rapid transfer of several hundreds of mines from one Group to another when necessary.

No set quotas of mines were laid down for holding at stations, it being left to Group Staff decision as to whether available stocks should be built up at stations or be drawn from maintenance units as required.

Results of the Offensive

13. It has not yet been possible to obtain a full list of ships sunk and damaged by mining, but known results so far comprise 491 ships sunk and 410 ships damaged by mines laid by Bomber Command during the period February, 1942, to May, 1945.

Casualties have been inflicted upon all classes of shipping, including naval units, U-Boats, trooping liners, depot ships, train ferries, general cargo vessels, tankers, etc. Considerable damage was also inflicted upon the enemy minesweeping force.

In addition to casualties caused to shipping, the enormous delays imposed by mining affected the enemy shipping programme to an increasing extent during the later years of the War. Operations such as the mining of the Kiel Canal and Heligoland Bight particularly proved their worth in the considerable amounts of cargo held up by such operations in shipping arteries vital to the enemy's war effort.

The effectiveness of our minelaying in the Baltic Sea is emphasised in the following extracts from reports rendered to the German Admiralty by the Naval Liaison Officer at the G.A.F. Operations Division (Kapitain-zur-See Mössel); in April, 1943, he drew attention to the shortage of escort, forces which only permitted the escorting of troop transports, tankers, hospital ships and warships in those waters where the greatest danger was mines, and where all ships required individual escort.

In February, 1944, Kapitain-zur-See Mössel expressed his conclusions as follows: "It is evident that the enemy intends to interrupt, if not destroy, our supply shipping to Norway by relatively heavy use of mines. It is now being decided whether night fighter forces in the Jutland area can be reinforced." Later, in April, 1944, the same writer commented on counter-minelaying measures by night fighters as follows: "I have the impression that this desirable countermeasure may succeed in interfering with the minelaying but cannot prevent it." After reference to our successful Pathfinder methods of laying new types of mines he stated that an increase of such enemy activity over a wider area would bring German shipping in the Baltic to a standstill.

By September, 1944, the situation had deteriorated to such an extent that, in his own words, "Without training in the Baltic, and safe escort through coastal waters and the routes to and from operations in mid-ocean, there can be no U-Boat war. Without seaborne supplies, it is impossible to hold Norway. Without freedom of movement in the Baltic, we cannot use transport in German coastal waters" ... "But already we no longer command the sea routes within our own sphere of influence, as is shown by the day and week long blocking of shipping routes in the Baltic approaches."

BOMBING OPERATIONS AGAINST NAVAL UNITS, U-BOAT BASES, AND NAVAL WAR PRODUCTION

14. Throughout the period under review the contribution made by Bomber Command to the destruction of targets of naval importance has been very great. In all, 33,363 tons of H.E. and incendiaries have been dropped on these targets. The naval objectives against which this effort was expended can be summarised in three groups: U-Boats; enemy main warships; and miscellaneous targets. The course of operations against Naval Targets is therefore recorded below under these headings.

U-Boats

15. Sinkings of allied shipping by U-Boats were reaching their peak in the summer of 1942, and Bomber Command lent valuable aid by bombing U-Boat building yards. The yards at Emden, Wilhelmshaven, Bremen, Vegasack, Hamburg, Kiel, Flensburg, Lubeck, Danzig and Rostock were all attacked and useful damage was caused to the yards in most cases. But the attacks on U-Boat yards are by no means the sole measure of the contribution of bombing to the war against the U-Boat. In the 12-month period ended March, 1943, 23 factories engaged in the manufacture of U-Boat component parts were shown by reconnaissance to have been damaged. This represented nearly 20 per cent. of all the known component factories available to the enemy. One of the most important of these factories, the M.A.N. works at Augsburg which supplied a large proportion of Germany's U-Boat engines was temporarily disabled in the Lancaster daylight raid on 17th April, 1942.

16. In July, 1942, No. 61 Squadron was placed temporarily under the operational control of Coastal Command for anti U-Boat patrol work in the Bay of Biscay; and the sinking of a U-Boat was credited to this Squadron on the first day of operations. One month later in August, 1942, Whitleys of No. 10 O.T.U. replaced the Lancasters and continued a steady effort for 12 months. After a slight reduction in sinkings of allied shipping in December, 1942, due partly to increased efficiency of our own air and surface convoy escorts and partly to the bad weather which prevailed in the Atlantic during that month, the casualties among allied merchant shipping again increased in the early months of 1943. With the object of disorganising the amenities of the supply and servicing bases during January and February, 1943, nine attacks were made on Lorient and three on St. Nazaire, which completely devastated the built-up areas of both towns. The heavily protected U-Boat pens were not, however, seriously damaged, nor was their working much interfered with since at that time no bombs were available which could deal with them. During the same month attacks were made on Hamburg and Wilhelmshaven and Mosquitos of No. 2 Group effectively attacked the diesel engine workshops of Burmeister and Wain at Copenhagen.

17. During July and August, 1943, Hamburg was subjected to a series of four very heavy attacks, which resulted in the destruction of a large part of the town. Official

German reports show that U-Boat production at Blohm and Voss yards between July, 1943, and June, 1944, was halved, owing to bomb damage. The same yard in June, 1944, turned over to the assembly of the pre-fabricated type of U-Boat with a programme of 13 boats per month. Of these an average of only five was achieved. This failure to attain the programme figure was due to bombing, which caused direct damage to slips, loss of man-hours in air raid alarms, and damage to sub-contractors' works building U-Boat components sections in other parts of Germany. Amongst such component firms was the Humbold Deutz (U-Boat accumulator) factory at Cologne which on 3/4th July, 1943, was very heavily damaged. Later in the same year 23/24th September the U-Boat engine works at Mannheim also suffered severely, and consequent upon the Battle of the Ruhr, supplies from this area for U-Boat construction could not be maintained. It was, however, in February, 1944, during the attack on Augsburg that the best example was given of crippling damage to a component factory brought about in the course of destroying an industrial centre. The M.A.N. works had all its buildings damaged and some of its largest machine shops completely gutted; a result far surpassing that of the direct attack on the factory in daylight in April, 1942.

18. August, 1944, saw the beginning of the evacuation of the U-Boat bases on the West Coast of France. Successful attacks with 12,000-lb. bombs on U-Boat pens and protected oil storage at Brest, Lorient, La Pallice and Bordeaux were made by No. 617 and 9 Squadrons. It is known that these attacks added considerably to the difficulties encountered by the Germans in sailing their U-Boats to Norway. With a view to disrupting the assembly of pre-fabricated U-Boats the yards at Kiel, Bremen and Bremerhaven were again subjected to heavy attacks in July, August and September, and as Norwegian U-Boat bases now assumed an added importance, on account of the expected appearance of the pre-fabricated U-Boats in operational service, the base at Bergen was twice attacked, damage being caused to U-Boats and constructional works at the pens. The offensive against Norwegian bases was continued with attacks in January and February, 1945, on Horten, an important working-up base for the new U-Boats, and again on Bergen. The former was completely devastated.

During the final six months of the War, attacks were made on U-Boat yards at Hamburg and Farge, and also on the midget U-Boat base at Poortershaven which was completely destroyed.

19. It is very difficult to estimate the full effect of bombing on the German U-Boat campaign. The final assessment must await the detailed reports of the British Bombing Research Unit and other similar organisations, but it can be said with certainty that the effect was very great. The known result at Hamburg was, in itself, an immense contribution to the battle of the Atlantic and it may well be, when all is known, that we shall find that strategic bombing was as decisive in this as in its effect on the equipment of the German army and air force.

20. It is worth recalling the history of the two battle cruisers, "Scharnhorst" and "Gneisenau," which in March, 1941, put into Brest for refuelling, after a most successful sortie in the Atlantic, in the course of which they had sunk 22 allied ships. They were immediately and continuously attacked by Bomber Command, and damaged to such an extent that they were unable to carry out further operations in the Atlantic. Although as they spent all their time in dry-dock, it was impossible to sink them, they were so much harassed that they patched themselves up and, making use of very bad weather with low cloud and nil visibility, dashed through the Channel on 12th February, 1942. They were both damaged by mines laid by Bomber Command in daylight ahead of their position. Shortly after their arrival in Kiel a further attack by Bomber Command damaged the "Gneisenau" to such an extent that she was towed to Gydnia and eventually dismantled. It took some 12 months to get the "Scharnhorst" ready for sea again.

21. On 15th September, 1944, the battleship "Tirpitz" whilst lying in Alten Fjord was attacked from a Russian base by 25 Lancasters. Subsequent investigation has shown that during the attack the ship was hit and severely damaged in the bows. In this damaged condition she was removed to Tromso, where another attack was made on her but, owing to unfavourable weather conditions, it was not successful. In November, however, while still at Tromso the "Tirpitz" was again attacked by Lancasters, and sunk. Two direct hits by 12,000-lb. bombs and some near misses caused her to capsize. In December, 1944, the cruiser "Köln" was attacked and damaged off Horten necessitating her docking at Wilhelmshaven where she was later sunk by Eighth U.S. Bomber Force. As a result of an attack on Kiel in April, 1945, the "Admiral Scheer" was capsized at the quayside. The "Admiral Hipper" was also wrecked by direct hits from three bombs whilst in dry dock during the same raid. The pocket battleship "Lützow" was attacked during the same month and sank in the canal at Swinemunde.

22. The results of attacks by Bomber Command on enemy warships may be summarised as

Follows[1]:—

"Tirpitz"	Sunk.
"Schlesien"	Mined and beached.
"Scheer"	Sunk.
"Lützow"	Sunk.
"Gneisenau"	Held up in Brest from March, 1941 to February, 1942; mined; bombed; partially gutted; finally dismantled.
"Köln"	Damaged by bombs in Oslo Fjord; sunk by Eighth U.S.A.A.F. in Wilhelmshaven to which she had been forced to return for repairs.

"Hipper"	Three direct hits while in dry dock at Kiel; rendered completely unseaworthy for the remainder of the War.
"Scharnhorst"	Kept out of action at Brest by bomb damage for 11 months. Mined on return to Kiel. Later sunk by Royal Navy.
"Eugen"	Damaged by bombs. Kept out of action for nearly a year.
"Emden"	Damaged by bombs at Kiel; beached and burnt out.

Miscellaneous Targets

23. In addition to the above targets Bomber Command attacked a variety of other objectives connected with naval warfare.

On the 14th and 14/15th June, shortly after the invasion of Normandy, a heavy and outstandingly successful attack was delivered against enemy light surface craft lying in Le Havre. On the following day an attack was made on similar units at Boulogne. These two attacks sank 88 war vessels including three torpedo boats, four armed trawlers and 20 E/R boats, and robbed the enemy of the use of these craft against our cross-Channel shipping.

In a very successful attack made in the E-Boat pens at Ijmuiden 12,000-lb. bombs demolished a large portion of the buildings.

During August, 1944, in order to prevent the enemy's blocking the harbour at Brest, five potential blockships – comprising a tanker, two naval hulks and two sperrbrechers – were sunk before they could be placed in position.

Finally, a number of depot ships and much valuable harbour equipment, such as floating docks, have been sunk and damaged during attacks on Hamburg, Stettin, Kiel, Danzig, Sassnitz, etc., and individual attacks on raiders and blockade runners have been carried out when called for in emergency with favourable results.

Note:–
1. "Eugen and Nuremberg" would undoubtedly have been sunk at Copenhagen during the last week of the war but the aircraft were recalled on representations made by the Admiralty. No explanation was given. Copenhagen suffered heavy bombardment by these ships the next day.

APPENDIX J

METEOROLOGY IN BOMBER COMMAND

1. This appendix puts on record a statement of the weather-forecasting procedure employed at Bomber Command from February, 1942, to the end of the War with Germany. A brief mention of earlier history and organisation is also recorded so that the growth and development of the service may be appreciated.

2. In general the function of the Meteorological Service in Bomber Command was to obtain and collate data in order to advise the A.O.C.-in-C. as to the state of weather at bases, *en route* and in target areas, and to provide a weather forecast picture of enemy and enemy-occupied territory, sufficiently clear, accurate, and comprehensive to enable operations to be planned with reasonable confidence. During the first two years of the period covered by the Appendix, the fact that the Service had a civilian status limited close liaison with the various branches of the staff, but towards the end of 1944 this was remedied. Thereafter, militarisation was complete in all operational Groups, and the Meteorological Service was fully integrated with the appropriate Air Force personnel at all levels.

3. The scope and magnitude of the tasks of the Meteorological Service are dealt with below under suitable headings.

Staff and Organisation

4. By August, 1939, in accordance with plan, minor meteorological centres had been provided at the six Bomber Group Headquarters, and subsidiary meteorological stations at the existing bomber airfields (20 to 25 in number). A meteorological teleprinter network connected stations to Groups and Groups to the Central Forecast Station, which was also connected by teleprinter to Paris to enable British and French reports to be rapidly exchanged. Immediately before the outbreak of War, a forecast centre was provided at Command Headquarters. Whereas in peace, meteorological service was not normally required (or provided) continuously on a 24-hour basis, such provision had to be made in war at Command, Groups and Stations. To this end,

and in anticipation of the expansion of Bomber (and other) Commands, an intensive training programme for new entrants both R.A.F.V.R. and Civilian, was instituted in the Meteorological Office, in implementation of earlier plans. With untiring efforts on the part of pre-war staff and with increased numbers, as new entrants completed their training, the needs of the Command were met. Only towards the end of the War, however, did numbers approach, without quite reaching, 100 per cent. of establishment.

5. During the War, there was a very gradual change in the organisation of the meteorological service in the Command from a civilian to a military basis. The first stage occurred late in 1941, when many civilian assistant staff were called up for military service and replaced by W.A.A.F. assistant staff. On the 1st April, 1943, forecasting staff at Command, Groups and Stations were commissioned in the R.A.F.V.R. (Meteorological Branch), except Senior Meteorological Officers at Command Groups, who still remained civilians. Towards the end of 1944, these Senior Officers also were commissioned and the militarisation was made almost complete throughout the Command, the only exceptions being the Senior Meteorological Officers in the Training Groups.

Meteorological Conferences

6. In the early days of the War, operations were largely decentralised to Groups and decisions on the suitability of weather conditions were generally made by Group Commanders acting on the advice of their respective Senior Meteorological Officers. As operational planning became complicated by the need to co-ordinate the attacks of aircraft from two or more Groups, these decisions were made increasingly by Air Staff at Command Headquarters, consulting with Group Commanders. Decisions, however, relating to take-off and climb remained primarily a Group responsibility throughout the War. Thus the stage was reached where an operation was planned partly on meteorological advice given at Command and partly on advice given at Groups, the Meteorological Officers at Command and Groups acting independently. In order that the meteorological work should be co-ordinated and the best possible results obtained, telephone Conferences with Command and all operational Groups linked together simultaneously, commenced in December, 1940, and continued to the end of the War. (For this use the Meteorological Staff had priority in the use of operational telephone lines.) Routine conferences were held daily in the afternoon in summer and both at mid-day and in the afternoon in winter. Additional conferences were called as necessary.

7. At each conference, the "Chairman of the Day" (who was a Senior Meteorological Officer from an operational Group or Command) summarised the results of the discussion and obtained agreement on the summary. This summary then formed the basis for advice given to Air Staff at Command and Groups. Meteorological Officers at O.T.U. Groups were included in these conferences from January, 1942, in order that their opinion about their own bases, in discussions relating

to diversions, might be obtained. From February, 1942, a representative from the Staff of the Central Forecasting Station at Dunstable was also included, in order that Bomber Command should have the benefit of the advice of the team of Senior Forecasters at that establishment, and of any data received at Dunstable too late for broadcasting to Groups.

Advising air Staff and Crews

8. Initial planning for a night operation was normally made on meteorological advice given to the Commander-in-Chief in the Operations Room at 0900 hours. The meteorological situation was reviewed again by Air Staff at Command and Groups following each meteorological conference and plans revised as necessary on later information. Meteorological Officers at stations were advised by their Senior Officers at Groups for every operation. Within this framework and in the light of the synoptic charts prepared at stations, crews were briefed on weather. At the briefing the usual practice was for the Station Meteorological Officer to display the latest synoptic charts and a pictorial cross-section of the weather conditions expected *en route* and to answer any queries which were raised on the forecasts. Written statements giving the weather and winds expected *en route* and at bases were prepared on a standard form which was carried by each aircraft.

Advising Flying Control[1]

9. Early in 1942 a Central Flying Control organisation was formed at Command Headquarters. A close liaison was maintained between it and the Meteorological Section. The forecast at time of take-off, for bases at time of return from an operation, was often such that diversion of aircraft outside the Groups to which they belonged was expected. Provisional diversions would then be arranged before aircraft took off. Final decisions for diversion could be made, however, after aircraft had taken off. In practice, the final decision as to the number of its returning aircraft which could be accepted in any Group, was made by Air Staff of that Group on advice given by the Group Forecaster, who had expert knowledge of local conditions. Arrangements for diversion of the remainder were the responsibility of Central Flying Control on advice given by the Forecaster at Command. For this purpose, hourly charts of observations received from a close network of stations over the British Isles were maintained in the Meteorological Section at Command. By careful examination of these charts and of the general synoptic situation the Forecaster, consulting as necessary with Meteorological Officers at Groups, determined the best areas or airfields for diversion until the last aircraft had landed. Diversion from one airfield to another within a Group was arranged by the Group Flying Control Officer acting on the advice of the Group Meteorological Officer.

10. Diversions for aircraft of other Commands in the British Isles were also

arranged by Central Flying Control. This gave an added responsibility to Forecasters at Command Headquarters.

11. Wholehearted co-operation was received in these matters at all times from Meteorological Officers serving with the American Forces in this country.

Navigational Winds

12. An outstanding feature of the growth of Bomber Command meteorological services was the development of upper wind forecasting, culminating in the formation at Command Headquarters in December, 1943, of a special Upper Air Section. This Section, together with Navigation Branch, played an important part in the successful application of the Pathfinder methods and the special technique of concentrated bombing which necessitated accurate time-keeping, concentration of aircraft and correct timing over target.

13. In operations with deep penetration into enemy territory, values of wind direction and velocity were determined by selected aircrews and transmitted back to Group Headquarters. These "found" winds were telephoned to Command Headquarters and to the Central Forecasting Station at Dunstable. They were plotted and examined by Upper Air Forecasters at Command and at the Central Forecasting Station, who also discussed the results by telephone in the light of their upper air charts. In this way, forecast values of wind for the level of the aircraft on later stages of the route were obtained with considerable accuracy and were transmitted by W/T from Command to the aircraft at pre-arranged intervals. In some operations, when penetration into enemy territory was too shallow to permit of "found" winds being used to amend the forecast winds for further stages of the route, the broadcast technique was applied to determining the bombing wind only. For this purpose the selected crews would determine the wind over a pre-arranged period such as the period from 45 minutes to 25 minutes before reaching target. These values, transmitted back by W/T, were examined, sometimes at Groups only but more often by the Upper Air Forecaster at Command as well, and a revised bombing wind sent to the aircrews.

Weather Reconnaissance of Enemy Territory

14. It was foreseen before the War that there would be a lack of weather information from enemy territory, and aircrews were accordingly trained to make and record observations in flight. This proved to be a very valuable source of information and meteorological interrogations by Meteorologist Officers at Stations became an established part of the interrogation of aircrews. Information so obtained, regarding weather conditions over enemy territory was, however, by no means sufficient and an increasing need was felt for a meteorological reconnaissance of such territory.

This led to the formation in January, 1942, at Bircham Newton, of the No. 1409 ("Pampa") Flight. The Flight was transferred to Pathfinder Group in April, 1943.

15. "Pampa" aircraft were used in two ways, firstly to obtain a broad survey of meteorological conditions over enemy territory in terms of cloud distribution prior to the selection of targets and secondly to survey conditions over those areas of enemy territory which would assist the Meteorologist most in forecasting cloud on routes and at targets after their selection had been made. In the latter case, weather reconnaissance by "Pampa" was normally made "up-wind" from the geographical positions to which the forecast would apply. Each reconnaissance route proposed was examined by Air Staff and compromise made as necessary between what was best meteorologically and what was desirable to avoid the most heavily defended areas and to ensure that the proposed target was not made obvious to the enemy. Towards the end of the War "Pampa" aircraft carried thermometers and made vertical temperature soundings at specified points, but their main purpose was to report on cloud structure and distribution. This often entailed flying through a layer of turbulent and icing cloud to measure the level of its upper and lower surfaces. Crews were also required occasionally to descend to comparatively low levels over enemy territory to measure the base of low cloud.

16. No praise is too high for the work done by "Pampa" crews. Flights were made in every kind of weather if a take-off from base were possible and a reasonable expectation of finding an airfield fit for landing, existed. No effort was spared by these crews to determine the height of the top or base of any cloud over enemy territory when required, and a very high standard of accuracy and descriptive ability was achieved.

Weather at Target

17. In the early days of bombing the first essential for success was that the target should be visual from the level of the aircraft. Consequently targets were selected in areas where the expectation of clear skies was high. The general meteorological conditions favourable to clear skies are also favourable to the development of a broken or continuous layer of strato-cumulus cloud, and the necessary detailed information to enable the forecaster to distinguish the two cases was often not available. With West to Northwest winds the tendency for strato-cumulus clouds to clear at night is much less in Germany than in Eastern England, and in general the winds which give the best weather over the bases tend to produce clouds in Germany. In some meteorological situations, however, skies free from cloud can be virtually guaranteed, though many of these situations are characterised by ground haze or haze layers at higher levels. Forecasting the degree of obscurity resulting from haze, when bombing from high levels, could only be undertaken in vague terms except when the haze was known to be so thick that no possibility of seeing ground details existed. From these causes, many failures were inevitable so long as visual conditions were required for success.

18. With the development of aids to navigation and Pathfinder technique the stage was gradually reached when success in bombing operations could be achieved without identifying the target visually. While this relieved the Meteorologist of some difficulties, he was still required to give as detailed a picture as possible of cloud conditions in the target area. With Pathfinder technique, which depended on the use of flares for marking, it was necessary for Air Staff to know whether the cloud was so thick as to prevent any light from ground-markers being seen from above the cloud or, alternatively, whether a lane free from cloud would exist at the level of the aircraft, of sufficient depth to permit sky-markers being used instead. Obviously, the number of confident forecasts of conditions in which ground-markers or sky-markers could be seen was much greater than the number of confident forecasts for visual targets. Information brought back by "Pampa" aircraft was invaluable in this connection, although the observations were necessarily made some four hours or more before time of attack. On some occasions the meteorologist could be reasonably confident that those cloud conditions found "up-wind" from the target would prevail over it at the time of attack. If so, an accurate forecast depended on knowing the direction and speed of movement of the air at cloud level. Generally this was known with sufficient accuracy for success. On most occasions, however, advection of cloud without change of structure could not be used as a basis for forecasting and normally development had to be taken into consideration. When the only development to be considered was diurnal variation arising from heating by day and cooling by night fair success could be achieved, but when changes arising from development in the isobaric field had to be super-imposed, the forecast was often given with less confidence.

19. The spread of medium cloud sometimes presented difficulties. The forward boundary of high and medium clouds tends to dissolve as it advances, but in some cases there is a very rapid advance in a strong upper current, without dissolution. Some medium cloud systems grow thicker when they reach the Continent, with a lifting of the upper surface.

20. Many cold fronts advancing across Europe have a narrow belt with little cloud and good visibility close behind the frontal zone. Advantage of this situation was frequently taken to obtain a target with good visibility and little cloud. The danger in the situation was the necessity for great accuracy in timing the rate of advance of these fronts. If the front advanced more slowly than expected, or unforeseen wave development took place on it, the worst possible conditions might occur at the target, *i.e.,* thick cloud to great heights instead of clear skies. "Pampa" aircraft were used until the last possible moment consistent with final planning before take-off as an aid to determining the rate of movement of such fronts as well as to detect evidence of wave development on them and any changes in cloud in the fair weather belt behind the fronts.

21. Fitness of bases for take-off and return presented the Forecaster with two major problems – height of cloud base and visibility.

(a) *Height of Cloud Base.* – The need for accuracy increased with any threat of cloud below 1,000 ft. Fortunately, in many cases of very low cloud, the threat was confined to part of the country only. For instance, the spread of low stratus cloud with a draft of air from the North Sea was usually limited to the east of the country, and then airfields free from low stratus could be found in the west. The number of aircraft employed in an operation could then be limited to a figure appropriate to the number of airfields expected to be free from stratus at the time of return. Again, since the formation of low stratus normally increases as the night advances, it was sometimes possible to give a "safe" time limit for operations so far as bases were concerned. In these cases the duration of the operation might be limited by selecting a comparatively short range target to correspond with the period of safety at bases. All aspects of the problem of forecasting low stratus were difficult and Air Staff were usually advised to allow a margin for possible error in the forecasts both in area covered and in time of onset. In order to obtain the most useful data for forecasting low stratus with air from the North Sea, a meteorological reconnaissance aircraft was made available at short notice at Bircham Newton to make ascents over the North Sea as required. The temperature and humidity of the air were carefully measured at vertical intervals of 25 mb. of pressure (approximately 700 ft.)

Another situation full of grave problems for the meteorologist when forecasting cloud conditions at home bases, was that of a front with a wide belt of bad weather (cloud bases well below 1,000ft. and rain or snow) approaching bases. Since fronts usually approach from the west, great assistance in detecting them and in timing their rate of advance was obtained from routine meteorological reconnaissance flights over the Atlantic. These flights were gradually increased in number and in range during the war until, in the last year of war, an excellent network of observations was being obtained. However, with the best possible network of observational data, the rate of advance of fronts and developments on them are often complicated and difficult to forecast. Perhaps the most difficult situation for the forecaster in Bomber Command was the one with potentialities for a sudden extension of the bad weather area eastwards. If an operation were being planned with time of return such that landing would be made just beyond the eastern edge of the bad weather area, the position might be critical but the potentialities of the situation were always fully explained to and taken into consideration by Air Staff in their planning.

(b) *Visibility.* – Fog inland is caused by radiative cooling at night and therefore reaches maximum frequency and intensity in the late night and early morning. In winter it may persist all day. In some situations it may form soon after dusk. These characteristics made fog a serious hazard for night bombing operations. More often than not the problem for the forecaster was to estimate its time of onset in each area of the country. Considerable success was achieved. This success was partly due to fundamental research into the problem by meteorologists at the Central Forecasting Station at Dunstable and partly to close study of local conditions in relation to fog formation by meteorologists at Groups and Stations. It cannot be claimed that a confident forecast of the time of commencement of fog to the nearest hour could always be given, but a reliable forecast in terms of the nearest hour or two was possible more often than not. Smoke spreading over the country from industrial centres caused an earlier onset of fog at night than would otherwise have been the case and sometimes caused fog in air which was otherwise too dry for fog formation. It is interesting to note that but for the amount of industrial smoke in this country the bombing effort against the enemy would have been greater than it was.

In the last winter of the war, the installation at a few operational airfields of a heating system for fog dispersal reduced the hazard to bomber aircraft somewhat but the number of installations was too few to permit of a large force being landed simultaneously in fog. Consequently, so far as the Meteorologist in Bomber Command was concerned, forecasting fog remained one of his primary responsibilities throughout the war.

Weather on Route

22. (*a*) *Climb and Descent.* – The ideal condition for climb and descent is clear sky. If cloud is present and its icing index is high, passage through it becomes dangerous. Collision risk rendered a long flight through non-icing cloud undesirable. The forecaster had therefore to study cloud distribution and icing index carefully in any area where a climb or descent might be made. Thick frontal cloud and heavy convection cloud presented the greatest risk from icing and occasionally an operation was prohibited by the dangers of the climb, but generally speaking it was possible for an area to be found away from the worst icing conditions where a climb or descent could be made without the aircraft being unduly hampered.

(*b*) *At Level of Flight.* – A route relatively free from cloud at level of flight was best: a route threatened by thick icing cloud was normally regarded by Air Staff as prohibitive. Generally speaking, thick icing cloud about 20,000 ft. is found only in the more active frontal zones or in other conditions of instability. In the weaker frontal zones a lane or lanes free from cloud can usually be found at the higher levels. Pampa aircraft were used extensively for determining the structure of the cloud in areas where there was any doubt about the existence of a passage free from thick fog. A feature of instability cloud, when not associated with fronts, is its irregular distribution. Thus in autumn and winter thick convection cloud to great heights arising from instability might prevail over the North Sea, making this route prohibitive, but be absent over East England, North-east France and South Germany. Alternatively, in summer, thunderstorms may be active over land while at the same time there is little cloud over the North Sea. In these circumstances targets could sometimes be reached be a devious route when cloud conditions on the direct route were prohibitive

23. Winds at the level of flight also required careful consideration. Wind averaging 100 m.p.h. at 20,000 ft. between this country and Central Germany is not unknown. A particularly dangerous situation for unexpectedly strong upper winds is that with a warm front approaching the British Isles from the west and with deep polar air to the east, more particularly if cyclonic development is taking place at the same time in the neighbourhood of Denmark.

Weather and Tactics

24. A direct route to a target was the exception rather than the rule. Deviations from the direct route were made for various tactical reasons but sometimes weather influenced the decision. For instance, a devious route might give maximum protection from searchlights and fighters, owing to prevalence of fog or low cloud along it. A defended area might be included in the route in the knowledge that protection by cloud would be a maximum over it and in the belief that the enemy would expect such an area to be entered only if it contained the target.

25. To suggest that weather was in the main an aid to tactics would be misleading. When, for instance, the selection of a target was decided by tactical consideration of a purely military character, the opportunity for attack might have to wait for favourable weather, and tactical value thereby be lost. It was in fact comparatively rare for tactical advantage to be gained from weather; much more often it was lost.

Mine-Laying Operations

26. Mine-laying operations differed from bombing operations in two respects, firstly, the operations were largely controlled by Air Staff at Groups so that special responsibility rested on the shoulders of forecasters at groups, and secondly, the level from which mines were dropped was lower than the level for a bombing operation. In the early days of the war, when mines were laid by visual observation and aircraft could descend to a low level in the mining area, the incidence of poor visibility or low stratus was the primary problem. Later with the development of radar devices to aid navigation and an intensification of enemy defences, the operations were usually carried out between 10,000 and 15,000 ft., often above cloud or in lanes between cloud. Thus the meteorological requirements for mine-laying operations eventually approximated closely to those for bombing operations. Winds at the level from which

the mines were dropped, and also between that level and the surface, were required with as great an accuracy as possible. A routine meteorological reconnaissance flight over the North Sea, from which a temperature sounding at 6° E. was obtained, assisted greatly in this connection. Pampa aircraft were also employed to make wind measurements and observations of cloud when necessary.

High Level Sorties by Mosquitos

27. In the last two years of the war, a considerable force of Mosquito bombers was operating. This force had its own type of weather problems for two reasons (*a*) the level of flight was between 25,000 ft. and 35,000 ft. compared with a ceiling of some 20,000 ft. for the main force, and (*b*) the high speed of flight permitted any particular operation to be completed in much less time than was required by the Main Force.

28. The high level of flight gave the advantage that icing cloud, with tops between 20,000 ft. and 35,000 ft. could be surmounted by the Mosquito force but not by the Main Force. These cloud conditions quite often prevailed.

29. The relatively short period of time required for an operation meant that advantage could be taken of short intervals of favourable weather at bases. For instance it has already been mentioned that the frequency of fog increases progressively at night. Thus it is often possible for the Meteorologist to state confidently that all or many airfields will be free from fog some three to four hours after sunset while few or no airfields will be free an hour or two later.

30. These requirements entailed forecasting the levels of any icing cloud which extended to great heights, as well as the time of onset of adverse weather at bases, with great precision if full advantage were to be taken of every opportunity. It can be claimed that high success was achieved. The forecasting work for these operations was done mainly by the forecasting staff at Group Headquarters.

Bomber Support

31. No. 100 Group was formed in December, 1943, with the specific aim of supporting the bombers by confusing and destroying the German night fighter defences, both air and ground.

32. Low and high level intruding by specially equipped Mosquito aircraft was carried out against enemy night fighter airfields and German night fighters operating near to and in the main bomber stream. In planning these operations the greatest consideration was given to the weather conditions at enemy night fighter airfields and beacons in order to effect the maximum attrition.

33. In addition, to disrupt the German night fighter ground organisation, feint attacks which simulated major bomber operations were carried out by squadrons of heavy aircraft equipped with special devices. In order to allow the night fighter defences, both air and ground, the least possible respite, these feint attacks were

carried out on every possible occasion irrespective of whether or not there was a major bombing operation. Consequently, careful consideration had to be paid to the weather at the targets selected for feint operations so that the German Meteorological Service would not deem a major raid impossible. As continuity of effort was required, provided a limited number of airfields anywhere in this country could be guaranteed for any particular time of return during the night, such feint attacks were normally made.

34. Choice of type of aircraft used for any particular operation was often determined by expected weather conditions.

35. Most of the forecasting work for these operations was done by the Forecasting Officers at the Group.

Daylight Bombing

36. Before the invasion of the Continent some daylight bombing without fighter cover was practised. The aircraft relied on cloud cover for protection and normally required the cover to be continuous over enemy territory. Obviously, cloud which caused icing on aircraft could not be used in this way. There remained available, above freezing level, cloud too tenuous for icing, and below freezing level, sheets of strato-cumulus, or frontal cloud.

37. Tenuous cloud above freezing level, if continuous, is normally found on the fringe of a frontal zone. Such cloud becomes denser, thus gaining icing properties, towards the front. It was always difficult to forecast precisely the areas in which aircraft would be free from icing in this type of cloud.

38. The continuity of strato-cumulus cloud is frequently difficult to forecast. Frontal cloud below freezing level is reliable for continuity and its location can be forecast with fair accuracy, but it is rarely suitable as a medium in which to fly because of its turbulence; furthermore the base of frontal cloud is usually too low to permit of safe descent underneath it for bombing. For these reasons, forecasting for operations depending on cloud cover was extremely difficult.

39. With the invasion of the Continent, bombing by day with cover from fighter aircraft, was practised extensively. Most of what has been said previously about night bombing applies equally to daylight bombing with fighter cover but one or two new features were introduced for the Meteorologist. For instance, at the point of rendezvous between bombers and fighters, clear air above any cloud that may be present was required in order that the fighters might see the bomber force. Reports by "Pampa" usually provided the information required about cloud structure and extent for advising Air Staff to decide on the height and position of the rendezvous.

40. In the autumn of 1944, a special Radar Bombing Technique known as "G.H" was adopted in No. 3 Group. This technique allowed cloud covered targets to be attacked with great precision. In order that damage to aircraft from anti-aircraft fire should be kept to a minimum, cloud covered routes and targets were now desired, irrespective of cloud thickness, provided there was a clearance of a few thousand feet

between the aircraft and the top of the cloud immediately below. The conditions required were often obtained in the early part of 1945.

Meteorological Developments during the War

41. This account of meteorology in Bomber Command would be incomplete without a short note on the general meteorological organisation and some of the developments, organisational and technical, which were made during the war.

42. Mention has been made above of the inauguration of meteorological reconnaissance flights over the Atlantic, North Sea and over enemy territory. Mention must also be made of other developments in the British Meteorological Service which benefited all meteorologists in the country whatever the application of their work.

43. Before the war, the number of meteorological reporting stations in the British Isles was relatively few and distribution of data could be made by wireless telephony, wireless telegraphy or by teleprinter. With the outbreak of war, wireless telephony was discontinued for reasons of security and any transmissions by wireless telegraphy had to be made in cypher. With a rapidly expanding Air Force, the number of stations requiring observational data and providing their own observations for distribution quickly increased. This provided a more detailed and up-to-date weather survey over the country but also entailed an expanding network of teleprinters and an ever-increasing amount of data for transmission. Eventually, second teleprinter channels from the Central Forecast Station to Group Headquarters proved necessary and, towards the end of the war, a third channel had been installed to Headquarters Bomber Command.

44. The whole meteorological communication system was centred at the Central Forecast Station at Dunstable where all data were received, sorted and broadcast over the teleprinter network to Commands, Groups and Stations. The meteorological teleprinter network extended to Shetland in the north and, until the fall of France, to Paris, Rheims and Advanced Air Striking Force, in the south. After the invasion in 1944 the system again extended to France and Belgium and eventually to Germany. The channels conveyed not only raw data but also the results of computation and analysis made at the Central Forecast Station.

45. At the majority of R.A.F. stations in this country an observation of weather was made and transmitted every hour. In addition, as a further safeguard for aircraft, messages were originated when a deterioration to what may broadly be called "unfit" weather occurred and again when "unfit" became "fit." These messages were given priority transmission by teleprinter and were of vital importance in the work of advising Flying Control Officers. W.A.A.F. assistants proved to be very suitable for this observational and reporting routine.

46. Since weather systems affecting this country and Western Europe come most often from the Atlantic with a speed not infrequently 40 to 50 miles per hour, it was imperative to know what was happening over the sea to the west of the country when planning operations in Bomber Command. Before the war, transatlantic ships

supplied observations. The imposition of wireless silence at sea for these ships during the war stopped the observations. In addition to the routine meteorological reconnaissance flights over the Atlantic to which reference has already been made, ships specially equipped for making and transmitting meteorological observations were stationed in the Atlantic so far as was possible. Losses on these ships were inflicted by the enemy.

47. Before the war, observations of conditions in the upper atmosphere were obtained from pilot balloon ascents and from ascents made by aircraft. Pilot balloons suffer from the limitation that their movement has to be observed by theodolite from the ground and therefore no values of wind can be computed in or beyond a layer of cloud. Special aircraft ascents were made for the determination of temperature and humidity: routine ascents were limited to two stations in the British Isles, however, and in height, to some 20,000 ft.

48. A radio technique was developed shortly before and during the war by which both winds and temperatures to levels beyond the troposphere were determined independent of cloud. This not only gave the meteorologist new and fairly plentiful data to great heights but also threw light on the general structure and circulation of the atmosphere. Perhaps one of the most striking early results was that wind velocities well over 200 miles per hour could exist at high levels.

49. Brief mention may be made here of some advance in the science of meteorology during the war. An advance in the forecasting of fog has already been mentioned. The biggest step forward however, came from the enhanced knowledge of the circulation of the upper atmosphere derived from a study of the new observational data obtained from high levels. This information enabled a great advance to be made in the technique of analysis of the atmosphere which not only resulted in an increase of accuracy in forecasting upper winds but also led to an advance in the principles of general forecasting.

50. Additional knowledge, too, was gained about cloud structure from the numerous reports from aircraft. For instance, it became established that thick icing cloud could extend frequently to heights of 30,000 ft. and above and at temperatures well below 10° F. Yet another feature of cloud structure which was brought to light was the frequency with which multi-layered cloud exists, especially in association with weak frontal zones or with fronts which are decreasing in activity.

51. Another advance was made during the war with the development of instruments for the accurate location of atmospherics. This had direct application to operations in Bomber Command. Atmospherics of moderate and heavy intensity are associated with thick icing cloud, usually to great heights. Instantaneous location of areas with such cloud kept the forecaster up-to-date when advising Air Staff of these danger zones. There is also the broader application to general forecasting. The pattern of atmospherics, when plotted on a map, often reveals the position of a front or of increasing frontal activity which could not be detected otherwise.

52. A theoretical investigation of formation of fog and low stratus over the sea enabled forecasts of these phenomena to be made with a greater degree of confidence.

53. Investigation into the formation of condensation trails by aircraft at high levels

resulted in a completer understanding of the physical processes involved. This knowledge was applied to forecasting the level above which condensation trails would form.

NOTE:
1. See appendix K, paras, 12 to 21.

APPENDIX K

FLYING CONTROL AND THE BOMBER OFFENSIVE

Introduction

1. The tactical necessity to achieve a large concentration of heavy bombers over the target had as one of its corollaries the technical problem of getting the bomber force safely on to the ground again on its return. This problem presented two main aspects. The force which was envisaged would create a density of air traffic in the night sky around the base areas far in excess of anything previously experienced, and the safe landing of such a considerable number of aircraft, returning virtually simultaneously to their closely-packed airfields *(see* Appendix F, para. 87) in the dark, with only a narrow margin of petrol endurance, was in itself a problem of the first magnitude; but it was further complicated by the fact that weather conditions frequently rendered many of these airfields unfit for landing thus necessitating the diversion of considerable numbers of aircraft to airfields in other parts of the country where better weather prevailed. It was a problem which could only be solved by bringing the movements of these swarms of aircraft under the orderly control and co-ordination of a ground organisation of a command-wide nature with a comprehensive network of communications, and so it became the concern of the Flying Control organisation which, having been designed primarily as an all-command network to assist aircraft in distress, already possessed the necessary structure and facilities at the beginning of 1942.

2. To deal with the first aspect of the problem Flying Control staffs established at every airfield in Bomber Command took over the control of the local air traffic at these airfields and co-ordinated the movements of the landing bombers in such a way as to ensure a steady and orderly flow of aircraft from air to ground; but the diversion of large numbers of aircraft from their bases to a multitude of other airfields called for co-ordination on a much larger scale and this was the primary function of Central Flying Control, which was established at Bomber Command Headquarters. Flying Control staffs at the various Group Headquarters acted as intermediaries between Central Flying Control and their airfields, and as the co-ordinating authorities for

internal diversions between airfields within their own Group. Provision was thus made for the orderly manoeuvring of comparatively large numbers of aircraft about the country to meet weather conditions, and for their orderly reception at any airfield where they might land.

3. From 1942 onwards, the work of the Flying Control organization, in so far as it had a direct bearing on the bomber offensive, can be divided into three main functions, viz.—

(*a*) the local control of air traffic at airfields and, in particular, the control of the take-off and landing of the operational squadrons;

(*b*) the planning and control of the diverting of aircraft to other airfields; and

(*c*) the original function of assisting aircraft in distress.

No true separation of these three functions can be made, all over-lapping and all being implied in the general principle laid down in the Introduction to A. P. 3024 ("Flying Control in the Royal Air Force") that "the Flying Control organization is responsible for the control and safety of aircraft and crews during the period between the departure of the aircraft from dispersal or hangars until their return to either"; but their development will be more readily followed if a formal separation of them is made.

THE LOCAL CONTROL OF AIR TRAFFIC

4. The problem of the local control of air traffic at airfields was one which was only beginning to be fully appreciated in February, 1942. In the early months of the war, such control as existed was of a minimum and negative character, consisting mainly of the refusal of permission to individual aircraft to land if danger threatened; but the change from day to night bombing during 1940, involving operating from dimly-lit airfields during the hours of darkness, necessitated a further measure of control to prevent collisions in mid-air and on the airfield. This was a problem which presented itself acutely at first only to Station and Squadron Commanders, and, as it was the responsibility of no one section, and anything resembling a clear directive from higher levels was entirely lacking, the result was the inevitable multiplicity of improvisations all designed to achieve the same end, with the equally inevitable confusion and crop of accidents whenever aircraft landed at strange airfields.

5. Prior to 1942, Flying Control Officers were officially "distress specialists" who had nothing to do with the normal air traffic of the airfields where they were stationed, coming into action only when aircraft were in difficulties, but they had all been trained, as no one else had, in various methods of controlling the approach and landing of aircraft, so that many of them soon found themselves in control of the landing of the returning squadrons, and from this it was only a short step to the general control of all local air traffic. This somewhat irregular development, although not by any means universal, tended to focus the attention of the Groups on the problem and

gave it an outlet to higher levels through the Flying Control organisation, with the result that by the end of 1941 several of the Groups, realising the dangerous inadequacy of the existing arrangements, had produced their own standardized landing procedures. The basic principle in all of these was the same one of establishing orbits at different heights for waiting aircraft, but there were still wide differences in detail which were a constant source of trouble when aircraft of one Group landed at the airfields of another, an occurrence of increasing frequency, and the question of responsibility for the control of traffic on the airfields was still unsettled.

6. In March, 1942, the high wastage of aircraft and crews in airfield accidents drew the attention of Air Ministry to the pressing urgency of the whole question, and, as the result of a conference of all flying commands, the full control of local aircraft traffic at airfields was placed firmly in the hands of the Flying Control Officers, and, at the same time, detailed regulations for local air traffic and a standardized landing procedure, based on the best points of the various Group schemes, were evolved, and promulgated in June, 1942.

7. While this standardization was welcomed in principle, the need for it being obvious, such a wide generalization could never fully satisfy all users and for the rest of the war years it was subject to frequent deviations to meet local requirements, and to amendments suggested by local initiative, but it did provide the broad working bases for handling the landing of the bomber force with a degree of safety and efficiency which could never have been attained without it, and paved the way for a further development of considerable importance.

8. The degree of concentration of aircraft over the target and the weight of bombs they could deliver were both closely associated with the questions of the speed with which they could be despatched and, even more important, the speed with which they could be landed on their return, and the problem was accentuated by the growing necessity to operate two squadrons from each airfield (*see* Appendix F, para. 90). At the beginning of 1942 the average rate of landing lay between eight and 12 aircraft per hour, or approximately one aircraft per six minutes, so that the landing of two entire squadrons would have occupied between three and four hours. This was in part due to the improvised nature of the many landing schemes, but was more directly the result of a primary emphasis on safety, combined with the inefficient nature of existing means of R/T communications with pilots and the primitive nature of airfield lighting. Safety remained a primary consideration in the many quick-landing schemes which were evolved and tried out, but, nevertheless, with the assistance of greatly improved R/T communication and airfield lighting, the landing time per aircraft was ultimately reduced to under two minutes, and the operation of two squadrons from each airfield became a practical proposition. Faster speeds were possible (on one occasion, in July, 1944, a squadron of 14 Lancasters landed in ten minutes, giving an average of 43 seconds per aircraft) but they were considered to involve too great an element of danger to be justified as a general practice; even a consistent average of two minutes per aircraft was only made possible by good team-work and mutual confidence between pilots and Control Officers.

9. Airfield lighting, and communication with the pilots have been mentioned above as two factors of considerable importance in the development of local control, and as they were, in fact, the key to the problem their development is worth recording briefly. A primitive form of flare-path, composed of small, battery-fed electric lamps laid out on the grass by hand, and supplemented in poor visibility by paraffin flares of the road-mender variety and a massive and clumsy floodlight, constituted the only lighting system at most airfields in the first year of the war, and the means of communication with aircraft were on the same level, consisting of an R/T set of very early design, and totally unsatisfactory performance, known as the T.R.9, an Aldis morse signalling lamp, Verey cartridges, a scanty supply of rockets, and a vicious signal mortar. W/T, although primarily intended for longer range communication, was sometimes used, but was rather too slow in its operation for the general requirements of local control. (The few Regional Control Centres were equipped in addition with S.B.A., radio beams and a form of built-in electric flare-path in conjunction with it which was known as contact lighting, designed to assist aircraft to land in conditions of really poor visibility, but as this system called for a high degree of skill and alertness on the part of the pilot which could be achieved only by constant practice, it was not entirely suitable for general use in war-time conditions.) In both of these respects the equipment underwent immense improvements during the war. The battery flare-path gave way to a much more comprehensive system of mains-powered, built-in, variable lighting on and around the airfield, controlled centrally from the control tower, and known as airfield lighting, Mark II (*see* Appendix F, para. 56); the paraffin flares were superseded by a similarly controlled system of sodium lighting of high intensity and penetrating power; and cones of searchlights over the airfields ("Sandra") rendered mortar, rockets and floodlight largely redundant. By May, 1944, 95 per cent. of all Bomber Command airfields were equipped with airfield lighting, Mark II, 75 per cent. with sodium funnels, 71 per cent. with Sandra searchlight, 52 per cent. with sodium flarepaths, and 45 per cent. with S.B.A. and contact lighting. A modern R/T set, the T.R.1196, relegated the T.R.9 to the scrap heap, only to be replaced in turn by the still more efficient VHF/RT which had been used so successfully in Fighter Command, and which has since played an important part in a new development in local control, which was still in the experimental stage at the end of the European war.

10. One of the fundamental problems of any scheme of landing control, particularly where high traffic speed is a requirement, is the spacing of aircraft at safe distances from each other, and to achieve this the Control Officer requires as clear a picture as possible of the positions of the aircraft at any given moment. No account of the development of local control would be complete without some reference to the experimental use of radar equipment for this purpose. Towards the end of 1943, T.R.E. at Malvern were approached on the subject and produced the plan position indicator, a set which, after its early teething troubles had been overcome, gave a very satisfactory representation of the aircraft orbiting an airfield, regardless of visibility conditions, and promised to be of great value to Control Officers. Its principal limitation lay in the question of identifying individual aircraft, but a method

of linking the P.P.I. with a cathode ray VHF/DF set working on the R/T from the aircraft was already well advanced by July, 1945, and there is every reason to believe that radar equipment will play a large part in the future control of local air traffic.

11. There is no doubt that without an efficient system of local control at airfields, the bomber offensive could never have achieved the scale it did. From February, 1942, to May, 1945, some 330,000 operational sorties came under the local control of the Flying Control organization for take-off and landing; traffic density in February, 1945, showed an increase of 1,170 per cent. over that of February, 1942 (*see* Part V, Graph No. 12); and the speed of local traffic control was increased 300 per cent., all with a marked and steady decrease in the accident rate. The annual aircraft damage rate (not attributable to enemy action) per 10,000 hours flying, fell from 44 in 1942, to 23 in 1943, to 15 in 1944, and during the four months of 1945 to 8.

THE DIVERSION OF AIRCRAFT[1]

12. The fickle nature of British weather is notorious. The situation of the British Isles in the no-man's land between the tropical and the polar air masses subjects them to successive waves of low cloud, rain, sleet and snow, which sweep in off the Atlantic in a most disconcerting and erratic manner, and the bomber offensive could never have been sustained without adequate measures to overcome these meteorological hazards.

13. Before the outbreak of war, the inability of a pilot to land at his own base was one of the principal dangers of flying and was regarded as a form of distress; so much so that the facilities offered by the limited Regional Control distress organization consisted almost entirely of means of assisting individual aircraft to survive difficult weather conditions. This attitude persisted well into the second year of the war, operational sorties not being undertaken unless there was a good prospect of the aircraft returning to their own bases. The diversion of aircraft to airfields other than their bases was a last-minute arrangement made locally by each airfield for such of its own aircraft as could not possibly be landed there; but by February, 1942, the restrictive effect of this attitude was already beginning to be recognised, and diversion, from being a state of distress, was rapidly coming to be accepted as a normal necessity if full use was to be made of the bomber force.

14. One of the primary causes of the original reluctance to divert aircraft was the absence of any really adequate organization to exercise a co-ordinating control of the process, and the main reason for the change in attitude lay in the development of the Regional Control organization for this purpose (the name being changed in the process from Regional Control to Flying Control). The need for co-ordination had been recognized as early as 1940 when it was decided to establish Regional Control staffs at every operational airfield with a co-ordinating Regional Centre at every Group Headquarters. It soon became obvious, however, that co-ordination on a wider scale and at a higher level was necessary, and in November, 1941, Central Flying Control was created as an inter-command nerve centre to exercise the unified

planning and general overriding control which was essential if dangerous confusion was to be avoided. Bomber Command was already showing signs of being the main user of the organization, so Bomber Command Headquarters, which already possessed most of the necessary tie-line communications and meteorological and other ancillary services, was chosen as the location for Central Flying Control, a decision which had important consequences for the later bomber offensive.

15. By February, 1942, therefore, the necessary machinery for the orderly diversion of aircraft on a large scale was already in existence, consisting of a complete network of fast tied tie-line communications linking the Flying Control Officers at practically every airfield in the country to the Flying Control staff at their respective Group Headquarters, and these in turn to Central Flying Control and to each other. One further step was necessary, however, before the way was really open for the flexible manoeuvring of the bomber force to alternative landing airfields. The original reluctance to divert aircraft from their bases was due in part to the complete absence of standardization in procedures for the local control of aircraft and the consequent dangers of confusion at strange airfields. This difficulty, as we have seen in paras. 6 and 7 above, was overcome by the introduction of the Bomber Command Standard Landing Procedure and the standardization of airfield procedures generally from 1942 onwards, with the result that diversions, from being hazardous enterprises to be avoided if at all possible, rapidly came to be looked upon as the normal means of overcoming otherwise awkward situations. This attitude was finally symbolized in the production, in 1944, of the "Bomber Command Diversion Schedule," a printed publication carried in every aircraft, giving the relevant particulars of all airfields in this country suitable for heavy bombers and allocating a code number to each, so that diversions could be instituted easily and simply by reference to a single number, without the need for transmitting information of a cumbersome nature and of assistance to the enemy.

16. One of the first signs of the changing attitude and of the value of the Flying Control organization was the rapid growth, from 1942 onwards, of the tendency to request provisional diversion arrangements for aircraft before their return to base in cases where any doubt of the weather existed, instead of waiting, as previously, until landing had become impossible and diversion essential. This enabled much less hurried and therefore more orderly and careful arrangements to be made, and the practice was gradually extended to the complete pre-planning of provisional diversion arrangements, for the entire bomber force if necessary, before take-off, with the highly desirable result that the crews could be briefed beforehand on the arrangements made. With this development, the decisive factor in laying on operations ceased to be weather conditions at base on return, and became the question of available diversions; and since satisfactory diversions were frequently available when base conditions were forecast as prohibitive, the percentage of nights on which the Command could operate was thus greatly increased. Subject to other limitations, the bomber force could now strike whenever it was possible to land the aircraft anywhere in the country within range of their petrol endurance.

17. It was in this respect that the location of the Central Flying Control staff in the

Operations Room at Bomber Command Headquarters proved invaluable. When the target and the strength of the force to be employed had been decided at the 0900 hours conference a forecast of the weather conditions over the base areas for that night was obtained from the Command Meteorological Section, and if it was then apparent that diversions would be required, the most suitable areas as regards weather conditions, available airfields and petrol endurance were provisionally selected, subject to confirmation or adjustment after the 1200 hours Meteorological conference with the Groups had produced a clearer picture of the weather outlook.[2] The available diversion airfields were then allocated to the various Groups on request, priority of allocation between Groups being graded according to the severity of the weather threat to each Group area and the percentage of their aircraft likely to require diversion. The airfields in the reception areas were forewarned through their Group Headquarters and given as much indication as possible of the degree of probability of the diversions taking place, in order to allow them to make the necessary arrangements with the minimum dislocation of their own flying commitments.

18. This highly organized system of diverting the bomber force in whole or in part made two further contributions of note to the bomber offensive, the one increasing its scope and the other counteracting an enemy threat.

19. The eastern coastal areas of England were the nearest direct striking point for Germany, but after the liberation of France it became possible to gain an added security and an extra element of tactical surprise by routeing the attacking force out over the south coast of this country and across France at comparatively low levels, thus keeping the aircraft out of sight of the enemy's radar early warning system until close to the target, and a return by the same way brought them over friendly territory soon after leaving the target area, thus avoiding the strong belt of defences between Germany and the North Sea as well as the hazards of the North Sea crossing. The one disadvantage in this procedure was the resultant lengthening of the total distance flown, necessitating a sacrifice of bomb-weight to petrol-weight and putting some of the deeper targets beyond economic range. This was largely overcome by the institution of what came to be known as "petrol diversions," whereby the aircraft, instead of returning all the way from the south coast of England to their bases on the east coast, were landed by pre-arrangement at airfields in the southern area and re-fuelled sufficiently to allow them to continue to base. These petrol diversions were arranged in the same way as ordinary weather diversions through the Flying Control organization.

20. During 1944 Intelligence reports gave strong grounds for believing that the enemy was planning to employ a night-fighter intruder force of some strength against our returning bombers while these were landing at their bases and therefore at their most vulnerable; one medium-scale attack and several smaller-scale ones were, in fact, carried out during the winter of 1944/45. Diversion was again the means employed to overcome this threat. A plan was prepared for the systematic diversion of the aircraft from any threatened bases to other airfields to the west and south-west, crews being pre-briefed each day and the whole plan being brought into force by the simple operative code word "Scram." This arrangement was again made through the

Flying Control organization and, airfields in the west of the country being by no means so plentiful as in the east, Central Flying Control had no easy task, particularly in adverse weather conditions, in finding alternative airfields for up to 1,500 aircraft on every night on which the bomber force operated, especially as "petrol" or "weather" diversions might be required at the same time for six or seven hundred aircraft.[3]

21. For statistics of diversions planned and carried out through the Flying Control organisation *see* Part V, Tables 12 and 12A, from which the immense growth of this work, and its close correlation with the growth of the bomber offensive, will be appreciated. During the period under review provisional diversion arrangements were made for approximately 29 per cent. of all bomber operational sorties undertaken, and actual diversions represented 6 per cent. It is safe to assume that possibly as much as 20 per cent. of all sorties would not have been undertaken had no such facilities been available, a contribution of no mean order to the assault on Germany. In all, provisional diversion arrangements were made for some 95,000 operational bomber aircraft, and approximately 20,000 were actually diverted.

THE ASSISTANCE OF AIRCRAFT IN DISTRESS

22. The Flying Control organisation, as it had evolved from the pre-war Regional Control organisation by February, 1942, was primarily an inter-command organisation for the assistance of aircraft in distress, and the technique of employing every available means to this end was already well developed and understood. The extension of the responsibilities of the organisation to include the general control of air traffic in no way altered this original function and Flying Control Officers continued to be the primary authorities responsible for the co-ordination of all endeavours to assist aircraft in difficulties or distress. There is not sufficiently accurate information available to allow of a mathematical assessment of the contribution in this respect to Bomber Command in particular, but there is ample evidence that many thousands of aircraft were assisted to make safe landings which would not otherwise have done so.

23. The very large measure of success achieved was due primarily to the wide inter-command nature and thorough integration of the organisation and to the very close co-operation which was established with other organisations such as the Royal Observer Corps, the searchlight units of A.A. Command, Police, Home Guard, Coastguards, National Fire Service and Ambulance units throughout the country, all of whom contributed in one way or another to the ultimate outcome.

24. The advances made in airfield lighting, ground/air communications, local control and diversion procedure all rendered the task of assisting distressed aircraft more effective, but perhaps the most notable developments during the period 1942 to 1945 were (*a*) the establishment of Flying Control Liaison Officers in the Filter Rooms of the Fighter Group Headquarters; (*b*) the creation of the Emergency Runways at Woodbridge, Carnaby and Manston; (*c*) the development of F.I.D.O.

F.C.L.O.s

25. The decentralisation of Fighter Command's aircraft plotting system to Filter Rooms at Fighter Group Headquarters during 1941 created centres of accurate information about the movements of aircraft which could obviously have an immense value to the Flying Control organisation, and the establishment of Flying Control Liaison Officers there during 1942 introduced the necessary machinery for their use. The facilities and information available to these F.C.L.O.s put them in the strongest possible position to assist distressed aircraft and rendered them invaluable to the Flying Control Officers of Bomber Command in particular, in locating and assisting distressed aircraft by night.

Emergency Runways

26. Practically every Bomber operation produced its crop of damaged aircraft and injured crews struggling back across the North Sea, and the Emergency Runways, born of a suggestion originating in 5 Group in 1941, were special airfields established on the east coast at Carnaby, Woodbridge and Manston, staffed by selected Flying Control Officers, and equipped with every conceivable facility to assist such aircraft to as safe a landing as possible. This had the added advantage of drawing off these "lame ducks" from the base airfields and so avoiding the obstruction of runways during the landing of the bomber force. The Emergency Runways came into operation during the winter of 1943/44, and their value is shown most strikingly by the fact that in 18 months they were used by a total of 11,250 aircraft, all in some form of distress.

F.I.D.O.

27. Fog has always been one of the worst enemies of aviation and the development, during 1943, of the Fog Dispersal Installations was one which cannot be over-estimated in its value both to the Flying Control organisation in assisting aircraft in distress, and to the bomber offensive, allowing operations to be carried out although it was certain that fog would cover the airfields before the aircraft returned. F.I.D.O. was eventually installed at 15 airfields in this country, 11 of which were in Bomber Command, and from the first operational landing with the aid of F.I.D.O. on 19th November, 1943, until the end of the War in Europe, a total of 2,500 successful landings were carried out by this means which would have been impossible or highly dangerous otherwise.

V. Conclusion

28. The part played by the Flying Control organisation in the bomber offensive can

best be summed up by saying that its development as an organisation for the control of the traffic of the air created conditions which were essential to a sustained offensive of any magnitude. When the war with Germany ended in May, 1945, there were Flying Control Officers and staffs at every airfield, base and group in Bomber Command, a total of some 2,700 personnel. Between them, during the period under review, they controlled the taking-off and landing of bomber aircraft on some 330,000 operational sorties; arranged diversion facilities for just under 95,000 operational bomber aircraft; organised the actual diversion of approximately 21 per cent. of that number; and rendered assistance directly and co-ordinated the efforts of others in rendering assistance to almost every bomber aircraft in distress over and around this country, thereby saving an incalculable number of lives and aircraft. The growth of the offensive was reflected in the 1,170 per cent. increase in the density of the air traffic which they controlled, and such a growth would have been impracticable without the accompanying 300 per cent. increase in the speed of control. Perhaps the most remarkable feature of all is that these achievements were accompanied by a marked and steady decrease in the accident rate; not only was a much greater volume of traffic handled at much greater speed than ever before, but it was handled much more safely. The magnitude of the contribution to the success of the bomber offensive is one which cannot be assessed directly, but nothing is more certain than that without the Flying Control organisation to get the bomber force safely on to the ground again on its return, the massive scale of the offensive could never have been achieved.

NOTES:
1. See Appendix J, para. 9, para. 21.
2. See Appendix J, paras 6, 11.
3. See Appendix D, para, 84.

APPENDIX L

SUMMARY OF PRINCIPAL AIR MINISTRY AND S.H.A.E.F. DIRECTIVE LETTERS AND SIGNALS
23rd February, 1942-8th May, 1945
(Excluding those referring only to operations of No. 2 Group.)

1. *File Ref.:* 62A-III. *See also* 46A. (*Note.* – Bomber Command file references are for File BC/S. 23746 unless otherwise stated.)

    Date: 25th October, 1941.

    Air Min. Ref.: S.46368/11. D.C.A.S. (elaboration of letter of same reference dated 29th September, 1941).

    Primary: *See* Object.

    Object: Destruction of targets by incendiary attacks. (Investigation by A.W.A.S.) and preliminary marking of targets by fire-raising,

    Method: (i) Saturation of fire defences in shortest possible time.
    (ii) To raise fires of size that could not be simulated by decoys.
    (iii) Additional H.E. to (*a*) crack water mains, (*b*) encourage fire by passage of air through holes and broken windows, (*c*) generally complicate fire fighting.
    (iv) Fire-raisers to leave target 45 mins. before Main Force arrive – to allow time for fires to develop.
    (v) Incendiaries in salvos, H.E. in sticks.

    Notes: Includes outline plan for incendiary attacks. Forecast figures for Force with 100 per cent. incendiary loads. Surplus available stowage to be used for 500 or 250 A.P.

2. *File Ref.:* 83A and 84A-III.

    Date: 10th January, 1942.

Air Min. Ref.: A.M. x 355 and 46368/11 D.C.A.S.

Primary: Enemy capital ships.

Object: To neutralise enemy capital ships. Japanese success at Pearl Harbour had increased their importance.

Notes: "Scharnhorst" and "Gneisenau" then at Brest. "Tirpitz" at Trondheim. Plans to be prepared for daylight attack on them.

3. *File Ref.:* 103A-III

Date: 27th January, 1942.

Air Min. Ref.: S.50128 D.C.A.S.

On Demand: The "Tirpitz" at Trondheim.

Object: Destruction of battleship "Tirpitz," in moon period.

Method: Aircraft fitted T.R. 1335 not to be used. (Co-operation by carrier borne naval aircraft – if approved by Navy.)

Notes: To be attacked on 29/30th January. (Executed on that date, and subsequently in March and April.)

4. *File Ref.:* 107A-III. *See also* 113A, 124A (and 118A from B.C.).

Date: 5th February, 1942.

Air Min. Ref.: 46368 D.C.A.S.

Primary: Factories in Occupied France (3 in Paris Area – 1 Villacoublay). *Priority over all other commitments,* as soon as weather permits. First attack to be on Renault factory, Billancourt.

Object: (i) To destroy factories working for the enemy.
(ii) To discourage French labour from contributing to the German war effort.
(iii) To demonstrate to the French people the offensive power of our Bomber Force, while avoiding as far as possible casualties to French civilians.

Method: Only H.E. to be used in view of non-inflammable structure of buildings and contents. Low altitude attacks. No limit to number of aircraft and crews of high standard of training.

Notes: (i) Night bombing of these targets now permitted.
(ii) Full scale trial of flare-force to be used; reduction of striking power acceptable to allow for this (113A).
(iii) After introduction of T.R. 1335 (if this operational before

attacks completed) attacks only to be carried out when weather suitable for this type of attack, and less suitable for bombing of other targets in directive.

(iv) Attacks to follow one another quickly on the various targets.

5.	*File Ref.:*	119A and B.
	Date:	14th February, 1942.
	Air Min. Ref.:	S.46368/111. D.C.A.S.
	Primary:	Primary industrial areas within range of T.R. 1335 – 350 miles from Mildenhall. (*Central Ruhr Area*) *Essen* to be first target attacked. (Attacked 8/9th March.) *Later* when effectiveness of T.R. 1335 proved, precise targets (listed) to be attacked. *Still later,* targets (listed) in Alternative (ii).
	Alternative if	(i) Other industrial areas within range of T.R. 1335 (Northern Coastal *weather suitable* Area).
	– but unsuitable for Primary.	(ii) Other industrial areas beyond range of T.R. 1335 (Northern, Central and Southern Germany). Berlin included in (ii) (*see* Method).
		Primary of No. 4 above (Billancourt) to be alternative if attack not already carried out. (Attacked on 3/4th March.)
	On Demand:	Support for Combined Operations. (*See also* Periodic below.)
	Periodic:	Occasional diversion on to objectives of immediate strategic importance, *e.g.,* naval units, S/M building yards and bases – if, by doing so, good opportunities of attacking Primary not missed.
	Object:	(i) To focus attacks on morale of enemy civil population, in particular of industrial workers. (*See also* Notes.) In the case of Berlin, harassing attacks to maintain fear of raids and impose A.R.P. measures. *See* Notes.
	Method:	(i) Attacks to be made on T.R. 1335. Marking with incendiaries by early attackers to be employed, owing to small proportion of force equipped with T.R. 1335. (*See* 62A, No. 1 above.)
		(ii) *Scale of Attack.* – An appendix to 119A forecasts weight of attack estimated necessary to cause decisive damage to Essen (1,600 tons), Duisburg, Düsseldorf and Cologne on the basis of 50 per cent. efficiency and 1 ton per 800 population; or 7 tons per sq. mile (1,000 tons).
		(iii) *Berlin.* – Attack to be at high altitude to reduce casualties, even at expense of lower bomb load.

Notes: (i) This is modification of directive made at time of year regarded as best for getting maximum effect from incendiary attacks. (*See* 62A, No. 1 above).

(ii) Resumption of bomber offensive on heavy scale would hearten the Russians while maintaining their counter offensive, and depress the Germans.

(iii) Need to make maximum use of T.R. 1335 during next few months while security of it likely to remain and enemy unlikely to develop effective counter measures.

(iv) Maximum effort required in view of (i)-(iii) above.

(v) Great faith expressed in effectiveness of T.R. 1335 to ensure hitherto impossible concentration.

(vi) Concentration required on one target until scale estimated for its des-struction achieved. *See* Method (ii).

6. *File Ref.:* 1A-IV Ref. 62A-111 (No. 1 above).

    Date: 21st March, 1942.

    Air Min. Ref.: S.46368/111 D.C.A.S.

    Primary: Ruhr as at present in force – 119A, No. 5 above. (*See* Method)

    Object: To make concentrated incendiary attacks (such as the enemy had made on us with good effect).

    Method: To stage separate incendiary operations (Ref. 62A, No. 1) using 4 lb. or the 30 and 250 lb., I.B. to determine relative effectiveness of many smaller or fewer larger I.B.s. Latter has greater spread of incendiary material.

7. *File Ref.:* 16A-III.

    Date: 16th April, 1942.

    Air Min. Ref.: S.46368/111 V.C.A.S. *See* D/O, 23rd March, to A/C/M. Freeman.

    Periodic: S.O.E. Ops.

    Object: Co-ordination of political subversive and air offensive action.

8. *File Ref.:* 19A-III.

    Date: 18th April, 1942.

    Air Min. Ref.: S.46368/111 D.C.A.S.

    Primary: Le Creusot Works.

    Method: Daylight attack.

      Notes: My suggestion to attack Le Creusot approved.

9.   *File Ref.:* 23746-IV. 20A-IV. *See* 23A-IV (2 Group).

      Date: 18th April, 1942.

  Air Min. Ref.: S.46368/111 D.C.A.S.

    Primary: Pilsen (Skoda Works).

    Object: To cover highly-organised extensive sabotage attack against German lines of communication with Russian front, and to boost Czech morale while increasing R.A.F. prestige at expense of German propaganda.

    Method: Six heavy bombers (Min. 22).

    Notes: Specific date 23/24th April.

10.   *File Ref.:* 24A-IV.

      Date: 5th May, 1942.

  Air Min. Ref.: S.46368/111 D.C.A.S.

    Primary: Confirms 119A but priorities of Alternatives amended. (*See* Object.)

  Alternative, if: Bremen, Kassel, Frankfurt, Stuttgart under Annex B. 1st Priority GZ. *weather suitable* 2805, GB. 3280. List of other towns with aircraft factories given.

– but unsuitable

  for Primary.

    Object: To reduce output of enemy aircraft, especially fighters, in order to assist Russian and projected Combined Operations.

11.   *File Ref.:* 26A-IV.

      Date: 12th May, 1942.

  Air Min. Ref.: CS. 11078 D.C.A.S.

    Primary: *See* Method.

    Method: Use of explosive 4 lb. incendiaries to hamper and deter fire fighting.

12.   *File Ref.:* 30A-IV. *See* 107A-III and 41A/IV (No. 4 above).

	Date:	25th May, 1942.
	Air Min. Ref.:	S.46368/111 D.B. Ops.
	Primary:	Industrial Plants used by enemy in Occupied Countries additional to France. As soon as opportunity permits. (Extension of No. 4 above.)

Object: (i) To destroy factories working for the enemy.
(ii) To discourage French labour from contributing to the German war effort.
(iii) To demonstrate to the French people the offensive power of our Bomber Force, while avoiding as far as possible casualties to French civilians.

Method: Only H.E. to be used in view of non-inflammable structure of buildings and contents. Low altitude attacks. No limit to number of aircraft and crews of high standard of training.

Notes: (i) Attacks only to be made in favourable weather conditions.
(ii) Experienced crews only.
(iii) Bombing only of target clearly identified on bombing run.

13. *File Ref.:* 32A-IV. *See* 35A and 37A (2 Group).

Date: 28th May, 1942.

Air Min. Ref. 51359 D.B. Ops.

Primary: Le Mans Marshalling Yard.

Object: Experimental attack to determine effect of attack on m/yards as data to assess effect for planning future operations in support of invasion.

Method: No incendiaries. Illumination by flares.

Notes: I suggested in reply, m/yards in Germany. This was not accepted, as post-raid information not so easy to obtain.

14. *File Ref.:* 37B-IV.

Date: 1st June, 1942.

Air Min. Ref.: CS. 14479 D.B. Ops.

Notes: S.O.E. Operations, Bombing of French targets by 138 and 161 Squadrons.

15. *File Ref.:* 47A-IV and 47B.

Date:	18th June, 1942.
Air Min. Ref.:	5988/D.O. D.B. Ops.
Primary:	*See* Method.

Method: Attached paper discussing weight of attack and benefit of concentration. Summary of attacks on Cologne, November, 1940-30/31st May, 1942 (1,000 Raid). Comparison of effort and results.

Notes: Suggested increase of Bomber Command, *i.e.,* Heavy and Medium to 750 to obtain a sustained effort of 250 sorties.

16.   *File Ref.:* 58A/IV, Ref. 73A/III.

Date: 18th July, 1942.

Air Min. Ref.: S.46368/111 A.C.A.S. Ops.

Primary: *See* Method.

Method: Suggestions regarding spacing/length of incendiary sticks. Attached paper discussing incendiary technique.

Notes: Technique of incendiary attack discussed after analysis of G.A.F. raids on Exeter and elsewhere.

17.   *File Ref.:* 60A/IV Ref. 107A/111 (No. 4 above).

Date: 20th July, 1942.

Air Min. Ref.: S.46368/111 A.C.A.S. Ops.

Primary: (i) Schneider works, Le Creusot. }   Revision of
priorities following
(ii) Citroen Works, Paris. } successful attacks under
(iii) Gien Ordnance Depot. } Direction No. 4 above.

Method: Risk of political embarrassment in view of adjacent built-up areas requires three conditions: (i) only reliable and experienced crews to be used; (ii) attacks to be made only in favourable weather; (iii) bombs to be released only if target positions identified on bombing run.

Notes: *See* 107A/III (No. 4 above). Ref. attacks on factories in enemy occupied territory. Apart from armament factory at Le Creusot, French A.F.V. and M.T. industry now have highest priority.

18.   *File Ref.:* 67A/IV. *See* 86A/IV (2 Group).

Date:	30th July, 1942. (7th October, 1942).
Air Min. Ref.:	S.3319/A.C.A.S. Ops.
Primary:	Transportation and Switching and Transformer Stations.
Alternative if:	*By day* goods trains only. *By night* all trains *(see* Notes). Water
weather suitable:	transportation important as complementary to rail transport.
Periodic:	Whenever opportunity permits. S.O.E. Squadron and 2 Group.
Object:	To exploit German transportation difficulties by attacking rolling stock, marshalling yards and other transportation targets in France (Belgium and Holland and barge traffic in latter included by S.3319 A.C.A.S. Ops., 7th October, 1942).
Notes:	*(67A/IV).* Eighty per cent. to 90 per cent. of night traffic in Occupied France is goods traffic: civilians prohibited from travelling at night. Therefore, night attacks now authorised on all trains moving or stationary.

19.	*File Ref.:*	73A/IV.
	Date:	4th September, 1942.
	Air Min. Ref.:	S.46344 A.C.A.S. Ops.
	Primary:	*See* Method.
	Object:	To provide cover for agricultural sabotage.
	Method:	Incendiary leaves to be dropped in harvest season during normal bombing operations.

20.	*File Ref.:*	74A/IV.
	Date:	3rd September, 1942.
	Air Min. Ref.:	S.46368/111 A.C.A.S. Ops.
	Primary:	Poelitz Synthetic Oil Plant.
	Object:	To disorganise enemy's oil supply plans.
	Notes:	Believed output of this plant exceeds that of any other synthetic oil plant in world, and that Germany draws from it large part of fuel need to meet requirements for Russian offensive.

21.	*File Ref.:*	90A/IV.
	Date:	29th October, 1942.

      Air Min. Ref.: C.S. 15803/A.S.P. 1.

      Primary: *See* Notes.

      Method: Bombardment of targets in Enemy Occupied territory restricted to identified military objectives, and only made when conditions obviate risk of undue loss of civilian life. Power stations in Holland, destruction of which would cause extensive flooding, not to be attacked.

      Notes: General (Combined) Bombardment Policy (i) enemy Occupied territory; (ii) German, Italian and Japanese territory.

22.   *File Ref.:* 97A/IV.

      Date: 19th November, 1942.

      Air Min. Ref.: Cypher Signal A.M. Whitehall, A.X.2.

      Primary: Submarine bases at Lorient, St. Nazaire, Brest and La Pallice. Presence of 60 U-Boats in pens at these ports, and remainder with servicing facilities form vulnerable targets.

      Method: On first fine moonlight night, maximum effort; precise attacks on as many of these submarine bases as can be dealt with in one operation. Accuracy essential to avoid undue civilian casualties.

23.   *File Ref.:* 23A BC/S. 28302 and 33A, 40A, 45A, 48A, 50A, 52A (2 Group).

      Date: 21st November, 1942.

      Air Min. Ref.: C.S. 8586 A.C.A.S. Ops. and further requests of same reference 26th May, 4th June, 4th September, 1943. Also letters ref. S. 46868/IV D.C.A.S. 17th December, 1943, 14th January, 1944, 27th January, 1944.

    Alternative if

weather suitable: Schweinfurt ball-bearing factories.

      Object: To deprive the Germans of considerably more than half their requirements in ball-bearings for their production of armaments.

      Method: Attack to be made on the heaviest scale, and in conjunction with the (23A BC/S., A.Os. C.-in-C. Fighter and Coastal Command and the Commanding 28302, etc.)   General Eighth U.S. Air Force.

      Notes: Annexure B to C.S.8586, 21st November, 1942. Para. 7 stated "The complete success of this operation would warrant cessation of night bombing for two months. Attacks 23/24th February,

1944. *See also* C.S. 8586, 26th May, 4th June, 4th September, 17th December, 1943, and 14th January, 1944.

24.   *File Ref.:*   102A/IV.

        Date: 2nd December, 1942.

  Air Min. Ref.:   Cypher Signal A.M. Whitehall AX.994.

  Alternative if

weather suitable: Targets in Northern Italy *(see* Notes).

     Object: To interrupt war production with Italy.

    Method: Operation of a few aircraft with expert crews.

     Notes: Intelligence reports show recent raids on N. Italy have created serious disorganisation and affected production. Whole of Piedmont and Ligurian activities at standstill under raid warning when aircraft cross frontier.

25.   *File Ref.:*   103A and 104A.

        Date: 3rd December, 1942.

  Air Min. Ref.:   Cypher Signal A.M. Whitehall AX.44 and AX.57.
     Primary: (i) Bay of Biscay Ports. }
                (ii) Lorient Airfield } 103A

     Object: To assist Eighth U.S.A.A.F. in attacks on these ports; to attack Lorient A/F, which is used by Ju.88 fighters against our anti-U-Boat operations. *See* Notes.

     Notes: No operations involving serious risk to non-military buildings in Venice and Florence to be undertaken without reference to Air Ministry.

26.   *File Ref.:*   111A/IV and 112A/IV.

        Date: 14th January, 1943.

  Air Min. Ref.:   S.46239/11 A.C.A.S.Ops. and Cypher Message A.M. Whitehall AX.236 *(see* Method).

  Alternative if

weather suitable: Lorient, St. Nazaire, Brest, La Pallice – in that order of priority.

     Object: The effective devastation of the whole area in which are located the submarines, their maintenance facilities, and the services, power, water, light, communications and other resources on which their operations depend.

Method: Area attack. The first attack to be on Lorient. AX.236, 14th January, authorised me to select aiming-point most likely to achieve desired effect, even if resultant bombing causes complete devastation of inhabited portion of town.

Notes: War Cabinet approves area bombing of these ports owing to recent (111A and serious increase in the U-Boat menace. Attacks to have first priority, 112A/IV) but without prejudicing any planned attack against Berlin: any attack by 200 or more aircraft against important objectives in Germany.

27.   *File Ref.:*   117A/IV, Ref. 119A/111 (No. 5 above).

Date: 17th January, 1943.

Air Min. Ref.:   S.46368/111 A.C.A.S. Ops.

Alternative: Industrial Centres N. Italy – Milan, Turin, Genoa, also Spezia (without violation of Swiss neutrality).

Notes: First priority after Berlin and concentrated (200 or more aircraft) attack an important German objective.

28.   *File Ref.:*   131A and B/IV.

Date: 4th February, 1943.

Air Min. Ref.:   C.S.16536. S.46368/A.C.A.S. Ops.

Primary: Subject to exigencies of weather and of tactical feasibility *(see Object)*:— (*a*) Submarine construction yards.
(*b*) German aircraft industry.
(*c*) Transportation.
(*d*) Oil plants.
(*e*) Other targets in enemy war industry.

This order of priority may be varied in accordance with strategic situation and U-Boat bases, France.

On Demand: (i) U-Boat bases on Biscay coast.
(ii) When Allied Armies re-enter Continent, to afford all possible support in the manner most effective.
(iii) Objectives in Northern Italy in connection with amphibious operations.

Periodic: Berlin when conditions suitable for attainment of specially valuable results unfavourable to enemy morale, or favourable to

Russian morale.

Object: Primarily the progressive destruction and dislocation of the German military, industrial and economic system, and the undermining of the morale of the German people to a point where their capacity for armed resistance is fatally weakened. Every opportunity to be taken "to attack Germany by day to destroy objectives that are unsuitable for night attack, to sustain continuous pressure on German morale, to impose heavy losses on German day fighter force, and to conserve German fighter strength away from the Russian and Mediterranean theatres of war.

Notes: This directive, known as the Casablanca directive or POINTBLANK, replaces the general directive No. 5 above, S.46368/D.C.A.S., 14th February, 1942, and was issued to the appropriate British and United States Air Force Commanders to govern the operations of British and U.S. Bomber Commands in the United Kingdom (Approved by Combined Chiefs of Staff at their 65th Meeting, 21st January, 1943.)

29. *File Ref.:* 139A/IV and 111A/IV (No. 26 above).

    Date: 14th February, 1943.

Air Min. Ref.: Cypher signal A.M.AX.832.

    Primary: Lorient U-Boat base. (Attacks on U-Boat bases to be confined to this target. *See* Notes.)

    Notes: Policy of attacking U-Boat bases to be reviewed when further evidence of effect of raids available. (Heavy scale attacks on these targets were cancelled by S.46239/11/D.C.A.S. Ops. 6th April. Harassing operations to be maintained on suitable occasions.)

30. *File Ref.:* 46A and 41A – V.

    Date: 18th June, 1943. 10th June, 1943.

Air Min. Ref.: Cypher Signal A.M. AX.837.

On Demand: Targets in France *(see* Notes).

    Notes: Civilians in France having been warned by leaflets of intention to attack targets in defined areas, attacks on French targets as directed now to be made.

31   *File Ref.:*   52A – V.

      Date: 23rd June, 1943.

Air Min. Ref.:   Cypher Signal A.M. AX.2.

On Demand: Airfields and aircraft assembly plants (*see* Notes).

      Notes: List of targets reference, para. 7, S.46368/A.C.A.S. Ops., 10th June, 1943 (41A/V).

32.   *Date:*   10th June, 1943.

       Ref.:   S.46368/A.C.A.S. Ops.

   Primary: (Revision of the priorities enumerated in No. 28 above).

      First priority now the G.A.F. Fighter forces and the industry upon which they depend.

   Object: The primary object of the bomber forces remains . . . (as set out in No. 28 above). In view of factors enumerated in notes below, the following priority objectives have been assigned to the VIII U.S.A.A.F.:—

   Primary: (*a*) German Fighter strength.
             (*b*) German submarine yards and bases.
             (*c*) The remainder of German aircraft industry.
             (*d*) Ball-bearings.
             (*e*) Oil.

   Secondary: (*a*) Synthetic rubber and tyres.
              (*b*) Military motor transport vehicles.

      While the forces of R.A.F. Bomber Command will be employed in accordance with their main aim in the general disorganisation of German industry, their action will be designed as far as practicable to be complementary to the operations of the VIII U.S.A.A.F.

   Notes: The above change of priorities was made by the Combined Chiefs of Staff because the increasing scale of destruction which is being inflicted by the R.A.F. night bomber forces and the development of the day bombing offensive by the Eight Air Force have forced the enemy to deploy day and night fighters in increasing numbers on the Western front. It has therefore become essential to check the growth and to reduce the strength of the day and night fighter forces which the enemy can concentrate in the European theatre.

33. *File Ref.:* 83A.

      Date: 29th July, 1943.

Air Min. Ref.: Cypher Signal A.M.AX.678.

   On Demand: Targets in Italy *(see* Notes). Major objectives in Milan, Turin and Genoa.

     Method: Scale of attack as high as possible.

      Notes: Weather permitting to be attacked 30/31st July. Subject to cancellation at short notice owing to possibility of rapid change in political situation.

34. *File Ref.:* 87A.

      Date: 3rd September, 1943.

Air Min. Ref.: S.46368/IV/D.C.A.S.

    Primary: *See* Object.

     Object: Definition of final agreed summary of conclusions regarding Bomber Offensive by Chiefs of Staff at 204th Meeting (o), Item 8. Extracts from C.C.S.319/5, 24th August reads:—The progressive destruction and dislocation of the German military industrial and economic system, the disruption of vital elements of lines of communication and the material reduction of German air combat strength by the successful prosecution of the Combined Bomber Offensive from all convenient bases is a prerequisite to OVERLORD (barring an independent and complete Russian victory before OVERLORD can be mounted). This operation must therefore continue to have high and strategic priority.

35. *File Ref.:* 91A/V.

      Date: 10th September, 1943.

Air Min. Ref.: A.C.A.S. (Ops.)/b3.

    Primary: 3 Airfields in France. Moon period.

     Object: To reduce enemy air activity against convoys off the Spanish Coast and action by enemy fighter aircraft against Coastal Command Anti U-boat aircraft.

36. *File Ref.:* 99A/V.

Date:	10th October, 1943.
Air Min. Ref.:	S.46368/A.C.A.S. (Ops.).
On Demand:	Targets in France.
Notes:	Air Ministry emphasise the scarcity of worthwhile targets in France.

37.   *File Ref.:*   113A/V.

    Date: 26th November, 1943.

  Air Min. Ref.:   S.46368/IV/A.C.A.S.(Ops.).

  On Demand: *See* Notes.

    Notes: Electrical objectives in occupied countries in north-western Europe not to be attacked unless requested specifically by Air Ministry.

38.   *File Ref.:*   116A/V.

    Date: 4th November, 1943.

  Air Min. Ref.:   Cypher Signal A.M. AX.268.

  On Demand: *See* Notes.

    Notes: Montbeliard not to be attacked until results of S.O.E. attack are known.

39.   *File Ref.:*   125A/V.

    Date: 7th January, 1944.

  Air Min. Ref.:   S.46368/IV/A.C.A.S.(Ops.).

  On Demand: *See* Notes.

    Notes: Restrictions of attacks on targets in France in connection with S.O.E. operations.

40.   *File Ref.:*   129A/V. BC/MS.29961/C.-in-C.

    Date: 21st January, 1944.

  Primary: *See* Notes.

    Notes: Letter to D.C.A.S. explaining Bomber Command contribution in execution of POINTBLANK programme.

41. *File Ref.:* 1A/VI.

     Date: 29th January, 1944.

  Air Min. Ref.: Cypher Signal A.M. AX.3.

    Primary: German fighter aircraft and ball-bearing industries.

    Object: To ensure best possible use of short time remaining before OVERLORD. Maximum effort of strategic bomber force to be concentrated upon key installations in German fighter aircraft industry and ball bearing industries and towns associated with these key industries.

    Method: Aiming points and lines of approach to selected towns to be chosen to include best chances of destroying key installations.

42. *File Ref.:* 14A/VI, 12A/VI.

    Date: 8th February, 1944.

  Air Min. Ref.: Air Ministry Cypher Signal AX.907.

  On Demand: *See* Notes.

    Notes: Targets in France and Belgium for attack by Main Force and 617 Squadron during moon period.

43. *File Ref.:* 24A/VI.

    Date: 17th February, 1944.

  Air Min. Ref.: Air Ministry Cypher Signal AX.621.

    Object: Revised directive reading "The progressive destruction and dislocation of German military, industrial and economic systems, the disruption of vital elements of lines of communications, and material reduction of German air combat strength by successful prosecution of combined bomber offensive from all convenient bases."

    Method: Depletion of German Air Force with primary importance upon German fighter forces by all means available, including attacks against precision targets and industrial areas and facilities supporting them to create air situation favourable to OVERLORD.

    Notes: Other objectives: CROSSBOW, Berlin and other industrial areas, OVERLORD and RANKIN. Preparation and readiness should be maintained without detriment to the combined bomber offensive.

44.   *File Ref.:*   43A/VI, 60A/VI.

      Date: 4th March, 1944. 29th March, 1944.

Air Min. Ref.:   S.46368/IV/A.C.A.S. Ops.

      Primary: *See* Notes.

      Notes: A list of targets to be attacked in moonlight periods in Germany and occupied countries designed best to contribute to POINTBLANK and OVERLORD. Special mention of Friedrichshafen.

45.   *File Ref.:*   S.30716/4, 8A.

      Date: 13th April, 1944.

Air Min. Ref.:   CMS.342/D.C.A.S.

      Notes: The direction of all forces of the Royal Air Force Bomber Command assigned to POINTBLANK and OVERLORD, passed to the Supreme Commander, Allied Expeditionary Force, with effect from 14th April, 1944, Supreme Commander's authority delegated to Deputy Supreme Commander, Allied Expeditionary Force, Air Chief Marshal Sir Arthur Tedder, G.C.B.

46.   *Date:*   17th April, 1944.

Air Min. Ref.:   Directive of the Supreme Commander Allied Expeditionary Force to U.S.S.T.A.F. and Bomber Command for support of OVERLORD during the preparatory period.1

Stragetical   The particular mission of the Strategical Air Forces prior to the

Air Forces   OVERLORD assault is:—

Particular   (*a*) to destroy the German Air Force and particularly the German
Mission: Fighter Force and to destroy and disorganise the facilities supporting them,

      (*b*) to destroy and disrupt the enemy's rail communications, particularly those affecting the enemy's movement towards the OVERLORD lodgment area.

U.S.S.T.A.F.

   Primary
   Objective: (*a*) German single engined fighter airframe and airframe component production.
      (*b*) German twin engined fighter airframe and airframe component production.

(*c*) Axis controlled Ball-bearing production.

Secondary   (*d*) Installations supporting German Fighter Air Forces.

Objective: (*e*) German Bomber Air Forces and installations supporting them.

The enemy's rail transportation system.

R.A.F. Bomber Command:

In view of the tactical difficulties of destroying precise targets by night *R.A.F. Bomber Command will continue to be employed in accordance with their main aim of disorganising German industry.* Their operations will, however, be designed as far as practicable to be complementary to the operations of the U.S.S.T.A.F. in particular where tactical conditions allow their targets will be selected so as to give the maximum assistance in the aims of reducing the strength of the German Air Force and destroying and disrupting enemy rail communications.

Other Objectives: Other objectives of great or fleeting importance may present themselves and orders will be issued accordingly.

The responsibility of neutralising threats from CROSSBOW is laid with Air Commander-in-Chief A.E.A.F. Where necessary he may call for assistance from the Strategical Air Forces in the United Kingdom through the Deputy Supreme Commander.

Note: This Directive will be subject to review after OVERLORD is established on the Continent.

47.   *File Ref.:*   S.23746, 89A/VI.

      Date: 3rd June, 1944.

  Air Min. Ref.:   S.46368/IV/A.C.A.S. Ops.

     Primary: The Jaegars Ball Bearing Factory at Wuppertal.

     Object: First priority for OBOE attack.

48.   *File Ref.:*   93A/VI.

      Date: 13th June, 1944.

  Air Min. Ref.:   BC/TS.23746/Air/Ops.

     Notes: Letter to D.C.A.S. enclosing appreciation on attacks on synthetic oil plants in the Ruhr. Letter raises question of chain of command and responsibility for choosing strategic objectives.

49.   *File Ref.:*   B.C.K. 32131/8 1A.

      Date: 8th July, 1944.

Air Min. Ref.:   Air Ministry Signal AX. 170.

      Primary: Germany and Western Europe.

50.   *File Ref.:*   S.30716/4, I5A.

      Date: 29th July, 1944.

Air Min. Ref.:   TS D/O letter to me from the V.C.A.S.

      Notes: Explanation of chain of command.

51.   *File Ref.:*   S.23746/VII. 11 A.

      Date: 25th September, 1944.

Air Min. Ref.:   C.M.S./608/D.C.A.S.

First Priority: Petroleum industry with special emphasis on petrol (gasoline) including storage.

*Second
Priority:*   (i) The German rail and waterborne transportation systems.
(ii) Tank production plants and depots, ordnance depots.
(iii) M.T. production plants and depots.

Direct support: The direct support of land and naval operations remains a continuing commitment. Requirements of Supreme Commander Allied Expeditionary Force to be met promptly.

Alternative: When weather or tactical conditions are unsuitable for operations against specific primary objectives, attacks should be delivered on important industrial areas using blind bombing technique as necessary.

Note: *See* footnote to No. 46 above.

52.   *File Ref.:*   S.23746, 11A/VII, S.30716/4, 25A.

      Date: 25th September, 1944. 19th October, 1944.

Air Min. Ref.:   CMS/608/D.C.A.S.

      Notes: Executive responsibility for control of strategic bomber forces in Europe vested in C.A.S. and Commanding General U.S.A.A.F. jointly. D.C.A.S. designated to provide control and local co-ordination. As C.-in-C., Bomber Command, I was directed to meet promptly requirements of direct support for land operations by Supreme Commander. I wrote to Air Ministry questioning meaning of this directive and referring to a memorandum from S.H.A.E.F. on the same subject.

53. *File Ref.:* 12A, 13A.

     Date: 27th September, 1944. 30th September, 1944.

Air Min. Ref.: Air Ministry Cypher Signal AX.91.

    Primary: Bergen and Trondheim.

    Object: To destroy or seriously damage submarine pens before completion and virtual invulnerability to bombers.

    Notes: D/C.-in-C. wrote back to Air Ministry explaining difficulties in making effective attacks against these pens.

ADDENDUM

    File Ref.: BC/S. 32128 3A.

53A.   *Date:* 13th October, 1944.

  AirMin. Ref.: CMS/608/D.C.A.S.

    Subject: Operations "HURRICANE I" and "HURRICANE II".

    Object: (i) To concentrate bombing effort on the vital areas of the Ruhr. Outside the question of the great concentration of enemy economic and military resources in the Ruhr, the Supreme Commander has stated that our best opportunity of defeating the enemy in the West lies in striking at the Ruhr and the Saar.

           (ii) In order to demonstrate to the enemy in Germany generally the overwhelming superiority of the Allied Air Forces in this theatre. This is to be done as soon as weather and other circumstances permit.

The common object of these demonstrations is to bring home to the enemy a realisation of this overwhelming superiority and the futility of continued resistance.

    Notes: *"HURRICANE I"*

The intention is to apply within the shortest practicable period the maximum effort of the Royal Air Force, Bomber Command and VIIIth United States Bomber Command against objectives in the densely populated Ruhr. The plan is to be initiated on the first occasion when visual bombing conditions are favourable in that area but when they do not permit of visual bombing against the primary objectives (oil) elsewhere in Germany. The targets for R.A.F. Bomber Command are to be areas selected from the undamaged parts of the major industrial cities of the Ruhr. The maximum tonnage is to be concentrated on these areas in order to achieve a virtual destruction of the areas attacked.

2. Subsequent to the launching of "HURRICANE I" the effect is to be maintained and if possible increased by directing to the Ruhr the maximum night and day bombing effort which can be made available from R.A.F. and VIIIth Bomber Commands. These operations will not, however, be to the prejudice of any operations which can be delivered effectively on oil targets in Germany generally.

"HURRICANE II"

This plan provides for the maximum concentration of Allied air attacks against precise targets in Germany on the first occasion on which visual bombing conditions obtain over that country generally. Maximum effort of R.A.F. Bomber Command and the VIIIth and XVth Air Forces will be directed on the first day on which weather conditions permit against the major oil targets throughout Axis Europe. Targets are to be selected from the current priority list. R.A.F. Bomber Command is to contribute to this plan by making a maximum effort against the Ruhr-Rhineland synthetic oil plants.

54. *File Ref:* 19A/VII.

Date: 1st November, 1944.

Air Min. Ref.: CMS/608/D.C.A.S.

Primary: (i) Petroleum industry; (ii) German lines of communication.

Object: Maximum effort is to be made against enemy petroleum industry, oil supplies and storage.

Alternative: Important industrial areas when weather or tactical conditions unsuitable for primary.

55. *File Ref.:* S.30716/4, 28A, 29A, 32A.

Date: 14th November, 17th November, 15th December, 1944.

Air Min. Ref.: CS/22500/S.6.

      Notes: Letter from Air Ministry and my reply to it. Further letter from Air Ministry, to finalise question of command of strategic bomber forces. Orders to be issued to me on behalf of C.A.S., operational instructions being limited to strategic offensive. Tactical direction of operations to be my own responsibility.

56. *File Ref.:* S.23746, 27A/VII.

      Date: 28th November, 1944.

  Air Min. Ref.: CMS/340/D.C.A.S.

  On Demand: *See* Notes.

      Notes: Restrictions on attacks against targets in Norway.

57. *File Ref.:* 28A/VII.

      Date: 23rd December, 1944.

  Air Min. Ref.: CMS/608/D.C.A.S.

  On Demand: Support of Naval Operations.

      Object: Certain objectives in enemy's U-boat organisation to be attacked whenever possible without detriment to conduct of offensive in support of land battle and offensive against enemy's petroleum industry, lines of communication, industrial areas and G.A.F. Admiralty to supply priority list of appropriate targets.

58. *File Ref.:* 30A/VII.

      Date: 19th January, 1945.

  Air Min. Ref.: CMS/608/D.C.A.S.

    Primary: German Air Force and petroleum industry.

      Object: The attack on the G.A.F. and primarily its jet production, training and operational establishments has been accorded no fixed order of priority in relation to the petroleum industry, since operations against the G.A.F. are in effect security measures to be adjusted from time to time to meet the development of the threat.

      Notes: Attacks on the enemy's petroleum industry and oil supplies are to be maintained and if possible, intensified, so as to reduce production to an appreciably lower level than at present.

59. *File Ref.:* 32A/VII.

	Date:	27th January, 1945.
	:---	:---
Air Min. Ref.:	CMS/608/D.C.A.S.
Primary:	*See* Object.

Object: Subject to overriding claims of oil or other approved targets, one big attack on Berlin and related attacks on Dresden, Leipzig and Chemnitz to be undertaken in support of Russian armies and to exploit confused conditions likely to exist there.

60. *File Ref.:* 34A/VII.

Date: 7th February, 1945.

Air Min. Ref.: CMS/608/D.C.A.S.

On Demand: Enemy U-Boat offensive.

Object: To increase marginal bomber effort on U-boat assembly yards, in particular those at Hamburg and Bremen, to maintain marginal effort against U-boat bases and to increase by 100 per cent. air mining against U-boats.

61. *File Ref.:* 36A/VII.

Date: 11th February, 1945.

Air Min. Ref.: Air Ministry Cypher Signal MSW. 220.

On Demand: Tank factories. *See* Notes.

Notes: In view of the enemy's lack of tank reserves and the tank wastage likely in ensuing months, tank factories are to be attacked on equal priority to communication targets. Priority list of tank targets will be issued periodically by Combined Strategic Targets Committee.

62. *File Ref.:* 39A/VII.

Date: 30th March, 1945.

Air Min. Ref.: Air Ministry Cypher Signal MSW. 446.

On Demand: Kiel.

Object: To destroy the large amount of shipping assembled in port of Kiel.

Method: Attack to be in full force and co-ordinated with VIII U.S. Air Force.

63.   *File Ref.:*   45A/VII.

   Date: 6th April, 1945.

Air Min. Ref.:   Air Ministry Cypher Signal MSW. 480.

   Primary: *See* Notes.

   Notes: Area bombing designed solely to destroy industrial areas to be discontinued except when disintegration of enemy's ground resistance can best be served by this means.

64.   *File Ref.:*   48A/VII, 53/A/VII.

   Date: 16th April, 1945, 5th May, 1945.

Air Min. Ref.:   Air Ministry Signal A.34 and CMS/608/II/D.C.A.S.

   Notes: Henceforward main tasks of Strategic Air Force will be to afford direct support to Allied Armies in land battle and to continue offensive against enemy sea power.

65.   *File Ref.:*   50A/VII.

   Date: 3rd May, 1945.

Air Min. Ref.:   Air Ministry Cypher Signal AX. 970.

   Notes: In event of formal German surrender "Cease Fire" will be signalled. On receipt of this signal offensive against enemy to cease.

66.   *Date:*   5th May, 1945.

Air Min. Ref.:   CMS/608/11/D.C.A.S.

General Mission: The main mission of the Strategic Air Forces is now to give direct assistance to the land campaign.

   Objectives: (*a*) Against oil supplies with special emphasis on petrol.
   (*b*) Against enemy lines of communication.
   (*c*) To such other missions as may be requested by the Supreme Commander.
   (*d*) Policing attacks against the G.A.F.
   (*e*) Certain objectives in the enemy's U-Boat organisation.

67.   *File Ref.:*   55A/VII.

   Date: 7th May, 1945.

Air Min. Ref.:   Air Ministry Cypher Signal AX. 134.

    Notes: All German land and sea and air forces in Europe will cease
active operations at 0001B hours 9th May, 1945. "Cease fire"
orders being issued to Commands separately.

NOTE:

1. *There were subsequent modifications of priorities within the terms of this general directive. The
numerous executive orders, postponements and cancellations issued by A.E.A.F. have not been
listed.*

SECTION 4

COMMENTS ON THE WAR DESPATCH

by Group Captain S.O. Bufton
D.D.B. Ops: 1 November 1941-10 March 1943
D.B. Ops: 10 March 1943-27 June 1945

INTRODUCTION

The despatch is extremely well presented, comprehensive, and supported by a wealth of statistics and technical information. It is a valuable record of the work and experience of Bomber Command.

2. Written from a Bomber Command background it naturally tends to find virtue at home, and all waywardness elsewhere; but doubtless the various commentary's which have been made upon it will point the way to a striking of the right balance.

3. My own detailed and general comments are contained in the following paragraphs.

PART I.
INTRODUCTION

4. In paragraph 3 the C-in-C states that his main task, under S.46368/D.C.A.S of the 14th February 1942 was to "Focus attacks on the morale of the enemy civil population, and, in particular, of the industrial workers," through the attack of major industrial centres.

5. That interpretation was correct for the period immediately following the issue of the directive, but it does not, in my view, as the person who drafted the directive

originally, embrace the whole intention of the air staff at that time. The intention was always to return to the bombing of precise targets as quickly as tactical capabilities of the Bomber force would permit.

6. The earlier directive to Bomber Command were based on the attack of precise targets, e.g. synthetic oil plants, aircraft factories, concentration of barges and so on. Through the latter half of 1940 and the year 1941 however the development of enemy defences, particularly searchlight concentration had forced crews to operate from higher altitudes at which, with the ineffective flares and technique in use at that time, precise bombing became increasingly ineffective. This ineffectiveness was gradually demonstrated and confirmed by night photography, which was increasingly introduced through 1941.

7. The Transportation and Morale directive in July 1941 was the first positive swing away from precision night bombing; it allowed for the *precise* attack of rail centres ringing the Ruhr during the full moon period of the month, but *area* attack of Ruhr communication cities, situated on water, during the non-moon period when precision bombing was accepted as beyond the capabilities of the Bomber force, and only large targets near water were likely to lead to good results.

8. The February 1942 directive went one stage further; it recognised, on the basis of experience, that for the time being the Bomber force could not profitably be used against precise targets, even on moonlight nights, and should therefore be concentrated against the most important industrial centre of Germany. Certain cities within the range of T.R.1335 were nominated as first priority, with others *beyond* the range of T.R.1335 to which the Command could progress when the development of their raid tactics enabled them to do so.

9. In this latter connection it should be remembered that the Air Staff had been pressing Bomber Command to adopt the large scale use of flares and a target finding force from as early as November 1941 (e.g. letter and memorandum to S.A.S.O. Bomber Command, 2244/D.B.Ops. dated 30th November 1941. See D.B. Ops. Folder Operl. Pol. – Tactical Use of Flares). A rapid development of tactical ability resulting from T.R.1335 *and* a target finding force was envisaged in the framing of the directive, and implied in its wording. And with this in mind, priority lists of *specific* targets, within and beyond T.R.1335 range were also included in the directive.

10. In the event Bomber Command were reluctant to adopt the target finding force; and even afterwards the technique was not for a long time developed beyond the point required for area attack. It was not until after the intensive bombing of rail centres in occupied territory in support of the invasion that the bombing of precise targets in Germany (notably oil targets) was undertaken on a large scale by the main force. It was, furthermore, clear from many letters received subsequently from Bomber Command that the C-in-C had little faith in the value of attacking precise targets, or in the soundness of the advice offered by the Ministry of Economic Warfare in their selection.

11. In my experience, apart from invasion tasks, Bomber Command tended to attack German industrial cities whenever possible, and were reluctant to devote effort to precise targets in Germany such as Schweinfurt, for example (see correspondence

with Bomber Command). It may be a reflection of this attitude that in paragraphs 3, 4 and 5 of the despatch no mention is made of the request to attack a precise the precise targets mentioned in the Directive.

12. The point of these comments is to stress the fact that while the Air Staff had been driven to accept, temporarily, the need to concentrate effort on area targets, it hoped later, with improvement of night bombing technique, to be able to revert to the attack of precise targets.

PART II.
THE COURSE OF THE CAMPAIGN 1942-1945.

Paragraph 14

13. In this paragraph the C-in-C comments that the command was "expected" to "destroy completely" Essen and other West German industrial centres in the course of three months; despite the fact that only a small part of the bomber force was equipped with "Gee"; and that both object and general method of attack were laid down by the Air Ministry.

14. The Air Staff had naturally to state the object of the attacks on the industrial centres. As to method, they sent an estimate by the Air warfare Analysis Section, based upon damage investigation in this country, of the tons required to do effective damage to the major targets selected, as a guide to Bomber Command, and advanced the principle of concentrating that estimated tonnage on one target before proceeding to the next. At that time Bomber Command's methods and results indicated the need to concentrate more (c.f. paragraph 12). It was appreciated that only a proportion of the force would initially be equipped with "Gee," and in the directive Bomber Command was urged for this reason to develop tactical methods which would confer the benefit of the available equipment upon the force as a whole (i.e. the flare techniques and the target finding force which they had already been pressed to adopt).

Paragraph 15

15. The "Crackers" experiments, following on the Air Ministry memorandum to the S.A.S.C. Bomber Command (2244/D.B. Ops. 30th November, 1941, reply BC/S.24886/DO/T.M.W. of 6th December 1941, and further letter 2244/DO/S.O.B. dated 10th December 1941 refer. See D.D.B. Ops. Folder Operl. Pol. – Tactical use of Flares) were not to my mind sufficiently exhaustive to ensure the right solution. This then vital link in the process of finding and bombing the target sight have been more carefully explored than it was in one successful trial. The flares were dropped in long sticks on a "Gee" reading. More experiments, with concentrations rather than sticks, variations in the fuse settings to find optimum burning heights, visual dropping

after frits accurate illumination of the target etc., might have given a far better idea of the potentialities of the scheme. This opinion is substantiated by the report at Appendix 'A'. In any case it is clear, as pointed out at the time, that combinations giving good results over the Isle of Man might be entirely inadequate in the face of searchlights etc. in heavily defended areas of Germany.

16. As it is I am drawn towards the conclusion that the code name given to the experiment reflected bomber command's attitude to an Air Staff essay in the tactical field.

Paragraphs 16-19.

17. The difficulties referred to, at least apart from blind bombing could have been overcome to a considerable extent had the following action been taken:

(i) The optimum employment of flares been fully determined, as suggested above;

(ii) a target finding force formed to drop the flares on the basis of a carefully devised and developed technique relying on flares dropped on "Gee" to locate area, visually dropped flare concentrations to illuminate target for bombing, followed by the laying of an initial and substantial concentration of incendiaries on the target. This concentration of incendiaries would not have been so vulnerable to decoys or jettisoned loads.

18. As it was, the system adopted, selected crews spread throughout the command dropping long sticks of flares on "Gee" reading, failed to produce the results. It is to be noted that the principle, which has been recommended from November 1941, of finding the target with selected flare dropping crews and then maintaining an effective flare concentration over it, is referred to a "marked advance" in the technique of illumination when tried out by the pathfinders in the middle of September 1942 (paragraph 20 of Appendix "B"). This principle could and should have been thoroughly tested out and adopted at the "Crackers" stage.

Paragraph 19

19. At the end of this paragraph the C-in-C refers to his request for a marker bomb. The potentialities of such a weapon were fully appreciated in the Air Ministry at the time, but all ideas on the subject up till then had been ruled out as impracticable owing to ease of simulation or some other obvious defect. A great share of the credit for the solution to the problem should go to Wing Commander A.P. Morley, O.B.E. at that time in B.Ops.1. He flew as an observer on the first "Gee" raid on Essen on 8th/9th March 1942, and came back with the conviction that a full stick of Incendiaries, if coloured, would defy effective simulation. His enthusiasm and drive took him for many days to M.A.P. As a result of his endeavours it was decided that

the colouring of 4lb. I.B.'s was impracticable, but that 250lb. bomb cases which could tail eject pyrotechnic candles would serve the purpose equally well if dropped in sticks. Thereafter he kept up the pressure, and obtained the enthusiastic co-operation of the M.A.P. section concerned, until this important link in the P.F.F. chain had been developed to the operational stage.

Paragraph 20

20. In my view an attempt has been made in this paragraph to write down the immense improvement in bombing which followed directly from the formation of the Pathfinder Force, and to suggest a better solution would have emanated from Bomber Command if they had been given a free hand. In my opinion the argument, while plausible, is entirely misleading, neglecting, as it does, to give due weight to the time factor.

21. The Air Staff discussed the idea of forming a special target finding force with various members of the bomber Command Staff in November 1941, and the memorandum referred to earlier embracing the principle of the flare technique and a special target finding force to implement it was later to the S.A.S.O. on 30th November.

22. The arguments for and against the Target Finding Force are recorded in Air Ministry files, on I believe the C.A.S.'s folders, and in the several D.O. letters which passed between myself and the C-in-C from the middle of March 1942 to the beginning of May, copies of which are in the old D.D.B. Ops. Folders. I attended, with D.B. Ops., the C-in-C's first conference with the Group Commanders on the subject of the T.F.F., at which, as at later ones, the proposal was turned down unanimously. It was highly significant, to my mind, that I, my observer, was the only person present at the conference with experience of night bombing in the war. This major, and purely tactical problem, was discussed, and a decision made, in the absence of any person with the relevant operational experience. I am certain that if the issue had been put squarely and fairly to a conference of experienced operational personnel, the opposite decision must have been reached. When, shortly after, the scheme was outlined, separately and individually, to some 12-16 of the most experienced operational officers in Bomber Command, they were, without exception, enthusiastically in favour of it.

23. The basic principle of the scheme was to get a number of the best crews, put them *together* in the same unit, or adjacent units, so that they could discuss, develop and co-ordinate their techniques; and to give them all the special aids to navigation and bombing possible, and as soon as possible, without waiting until there were sufficient supplies for the Command as a whole. Bomber Command fought to the end against this. The C-in-C informed me in his D.O. letter of the 17th April 1942 that it was proposed that each group should designate each month as its target finding Squadron the one which produced the best photographic results over the preceding month. Such a system would clearly not enable a technique to be developed in any

one squadron, particularly as they would be operating on main force bombing up to selection, and for the following month would be operating in a T.F.F. role which would give perhaps a smaller chance of good photographic results for the squadron as a whole and thus continuance in that role. Moreover, as stated in paragraph 12 of the report, raids at that time, and indeed almost up to the invasion, involved the use of the whole force against a single target, and the method proposed would permit of no development of technique and co-ordination between the selected T.F.F. squadrons of the various Groups. Such a system of monthly selection would have precluded, too, the concentration and exploitation of the new radio aids in the T.F.F.

24. The C-in-C states that his contention that each group should find and maintain its own pathfinder Force was proved infinitely the superior method when tried out in No.5 Group. This, in my opinion, is an entirely fallacious argument. It is perhaps arguable that when, towards the end of the war, some two years after the P.F.F. controversy, the tactical situation and the increased size of the bomber force made the attack of more than one target necessary, no great harm would have come of allocating portions of the Pathfinder Force, its technique now fully developed and crystallised, to individual groups. But that is a very different thing from initiating the force in that way in 1942. Had it been adopted the rapid development of technique which was achieved, and the highly effective series of attacks of 1943/1944 would not have been possible.

25. Again No.5 Group was the only exception to the rule, and to support his argument it would be necessary for the C-in-C to show that if the Pathfinders had been scattered between 1, 3, 4, 5 and 6 Groups better results could have been achieved than through the medium of 8 Group.

26. There was unfortunately a clash of interests and of personalities between 8 and 5 Groups, the latter being given priority for the supply of certain equipment (e.g. V.H.F.) over 8 Group to implement new ideas which could have been developed just as profitably in 8 Group. I do not think 8 Group ever succeeded in obtaining the best crews from the other Groups, and at times it struggled with a deadweight of ex O.T.U. crews.

27. Thus while 5 Group did achieve excellent results, the same or better results could have been achieved through the medium of 8 Group if it had been given the best personnel and a full measure of support from all quarters.

28. The intricacy and development of the Pathfinder technique as described from paragraph 20 onwards in Appendix 'B' is in itself sufficient evidence of the need for a single P.F.F. at the outset.

29. The Commander in the field was not overruled at the dictation of junior staff officers in the Air Ministry. The idea of a Pathfinder Force (and its accompaniment of a Bomber Development Unit) was fully discussed within the Air Staff and with Bomber Command. The arguments for and against were weighed by the Air Staff, and the C.A.S., after full discussion with the C-in-C., finally decided that the scheme should be put into effect.

30. In paragraph 20 the C-in-C refers to the P.F.F. as a "Corps d'elite." The C.A.S. at the time remarked that the Corps d'elite principle was only bad when all units had the *same job*. The T.F.F. had a different job and would therefore be regarded as a

specialist force and not a "corps d'elite". This name was frequently used in the attempt to counter the formation of a P.F.F.

31. Many valuable months were lost in argument; the Pathfinder Force could and should undoubtedly have been formed at least six months before it was – on the 15th August, 1942; had it been, it would have had the advantages of unjammed "Gee", and the good weather of the summer to give it a good start. Nevertheless it is interesting to note from paragraph 20, that within a matter of some four months of its formation many points of operational importance with regard to the illumination and marking of targets were brought to light as a result of the work of the Pathfinder Force.

32. Towards the end of paragraph 20 the C-in-C states the success of the P.F.F. was limited. Presumably he means over the remainder of 1942. Some reasons for this are given in para. 23 of Appendix 'B', one of the main ones being the failure to build the force up from the best crews of the Command. Nevertheless a great improvement in concentration and an increase in accuracy was quickly noticeable, in spite of the less favourable conditions, compared with the March to August 1942 period, of deeper raids in the poorer weather of the winter season. The important factor, however, was that the P.F.F. was organised and functioning by the time Oboe, the marker bomb and H.S. were introduced. These devices could thus immediately and effectively be exploited.

33. There is no doubt in my mind that one of the major shortcomings in the Bomber Command organisation towards the end of 1941, and for a considerable time after, was the failure to ensure that operationally experienced officers were placed in positions of responsibility in which they could foster and control the development of tactics. As a result both command and Group Headquarters were unnecessarily insensitive to the full significance of such tactical ideas as were submitted to them. Until a very late stage in the war the great majority of the senior Air Staff posts in Command and Group Headquarters, and many of the Station Commander posts, were held by officers without operational experience, and the operationally experienced officers on these Staffs were either not selected for their tactical flair, or were not in positions in which they could exercise it effectively. I consider that it should be a cardinal principle, at the outset of another war, to organise and operate the staff so that the tactics of the bomber force are moulded and developed, from the earliest possible stages, by carefully selected officers of recent operational experience.

Paragraph 45

34. Towards the end of 1942, when the Admiralty were disturbed at the increased U-Boat threat, Bomber Command and the 8th Air Force were directed to do what they could by precise attack upon the Biscay Port U-Boat installations. Efforts in this direction did not achieve the desired effect on U-boat activity, and eventually the Admiralty pressed for the destruction of the port and towns, by heavy scale *area* attack, of Brest, Lorient, St. Nazaire and La Pollice. The Air Staff was strongly opposed to this plan on the grounds that such heavy destruction of French life and

property could not materially affect the U-Boat operations. For instance, the Admiralty suggestion that power supplies might be cut off was countered by the contention that one U-Boat or other vessel could itself supply the power required to keep the pens in operation. In the end the War Cabinet agreed that a controlled experiment should be made against one or two of the targets. This was done against Lorient and St. Nazaire where heavy destruction of the ports was inflicted. After examination of the results, which confirmed the Air Ministry's contention that U-Boat activity would not be affected materially, further attacks of this kind were abandoned.

Paragraphs 82-84

35. While Berlin was always an important industrial target under the Air Staff directives, I can not remember any particular emphasis being placed on its destruction in the 1942-1943 period. This must have been done mainly between the F.M., C.A.S., S. of S. & C-in-C in the signals referred to in your letter. I cannot comment usefully on this point from memory.

36. With regard to the attacks which were delivered, however, I feel strongly that the Oboe repeater systems should have been developed for, and employed against, Berlin. Development was dropped in about the autumn of 1943, when, given sufficient backing, the system could probably have been operational in the winter 43/44, and might well have made a big difference to the success of the Berlin attacks. There was considerable controversy over the question at the time.

Paragraph 135

37. The significance of this large scale operation against enemy positions South and East of Caen is somewhat obscured by the description of one of its small tactical effects. This operation was the first of a type advocated by the Air Staff (D.B. Ops. and D.A.T.) in collaboration with the War Office (D. Air) and adopted by 21 Army Group, i.e. a combined operation in which the Army plan was made dependent upon the execution of the air plan. The basis of the air plan was the concentration of a maximum scale of heavy bomber effort on a limited and dense sector of the enemy front – as opposed to the sporadic light-scale and dispersed effort which had previously been the rule. The attacks described in the preceding paragraphs, 130-134, were of the then more usual type in which the army called for heavy bomber support as and when it encountered difficulties. Subsequent attacks of the new type included the American heavy bomber attack at St. Lo which preceded the bog break-through.

Paragraph 157

38. Some special mention should be made, in passing, to Bomber Command's brilliant attacks on the more remote synthetic oil plants. These precision attacks, of

deep penetration, were undertaken initially with some reluctance on the part of the C-in-C (see relevant correspondence between C.A.S. and C-in-C). But the Pathfinder technique, which had become highly polished in the attacks on French rail centres, proved most effective. The attack on Brux for example, perhaps the best of them, was made through 10/10ths (low) cloud. The Bomber Command attacks could do far more damage to an oil plant than an American attack owing to the greater weight and concentration of attack possible with the (individual aiming) night bombing technique. The number of combat wings (of Fortresses, carrying say 4000lbs. as opposed to the Lancasters 10/12,000) which could be put on to one target was limited by tactical factors (to some 3 or 4), so that the density of bombing achieved was always low compared with a Bomber Command attack. The American attacks generally immobilised the big oil plants for 3 or 4 weeks which was alright up to September, when repeat attacks could be made within the repair period, but in few, something more was required. That was why Bomber Command were pressed into the task of reducing the more distant plants. Another reason was that Politz and Brux were out of daylight range of American bombers in the short winter days – just as targets much beyond the Ruhr were beyond Bomber Command's night range in the mid-summer months.

Paragraph 164

39. The C-in-C mentions the 57 German towns with a pre-war population of 100,000 or more. It was apparently his objective to destroy these, though I have no knowledge of any Air Staff directives to this effect. The project might of course been discussed on the P.M. C.A.S. level. The pursuit of this plan appeared at times to conflict with the wholehearted implementation of certain Air Staff directives, particularly those relating to specific targets; e.g. with the major directive, provided the towns attacked were of industrial importance, and provided its pursuit did not result in insufficient effort being devoted to higher priority commitments.

PART III.
SUMMARY OF THE BOMBING EFFORT AND RESULTS

Paragraph 186

40. Our intelligence on U-boat accumulator production was not good. As far as I know, we were unaware of the existence or importance of the Acfa factory at Hanover. We knew of the one at Hagen, but were advised by M.E.W. that the surplus capacity for accumulator production in Germany and the Occupied Countries was such as to make the attack of this target system unprofitable. This advice was probably right, except perhaps at the end of the war, when the occupied territories had been retaken (including Posen).

41. I agree that the final judgments in respect of the effects of bombing must be made in light of the British and American bombing survey reports. These will no doubt give full consideration to both the direct and indirect effects on production of the bombing of industrial areas. I hope the difficulties of assessment in this particular case will not result in an underestimate. In this connection, diversion of production should not be overlooked; paragraphs 191, 192 and 193 are relevant.

PART IV.
CONCLUSIONS

42. The last half of this paragraph should I feel be regarded with considerable reservation. The enemy's *most vulnerable* sinews of war, oil and communications, were generally outside his industrial cities.

They were the ones that were severed and most potently brought about his collapse. Nevertheless, it is probably true that the great bulk of his armament production came from the industrial cities. But this can hardly have been demonstrated, as stated, *by the experiences* of the war. Of the 70 cities attacked by Bomber Command, 46 were approximately half destroyed (paragraph 183). If this damage had been compressed into the last 2 years of the war (most of it was) this averages two cities half destroyed per month. Hamburg, probably the hardest hit city of all, progressively re-established its production to nearly 100% of pre-attack within a period of some 4 months; in other words, its production to loss was some 50% of pre-attack for four months, or say 100% for two months. Applying, generously, the same sort of loss to all the other cities half destroyed, it can be seen that very roughly speaking, the results of Bomber Command's sustained offensive against industrial cities (absorbing 417,133 tons, or 45% of the total dropped by the Command in the whole war) was each month to suppress *for two months* the output of two industrial cities. That is, the sustained bombing pressure denied to the enemy, on an average, continuously, the output of only four industrial cities (assorted in size and product), or $4/70 = 5.7\%$ of the output of the 70 cities attacked. There was, of course, considerable war production elsewhere as well. Thus it is conceivable that the enemy could have sustained city bombing at the tempo actually achieved by Bomber Command more or less indefinitely – say for another two years – as far as war production was concerned. Of course, other factors entered into the question; the accumulating administrative problems, and morale. The object of this argument is to cast doubt upon the soundness of the statement in paragraph 206 which is referred to above. It is also to show that the attack on cities failed to produce conclusive results because, *in view of the recovery factor,* its tempo was too slow. Speer was probably right when he said that if the Hamburg attack had been followed by six more "Hamburgs" in quick succession it would inevitably have crippled the will to sustain war production. A substantial increase in tempo might well have changed the picture.

43. Such an increase in tempo was not practicable however. From March 1943 to March 1944 Bomber Command's main effort was against industrial cities with few major diversions. From then on the invasion commitments took priority for practically the remainder of the war, though a big effort went on to cities from September 1944. The American Bomber Forces were committed, through 1943 up to March 1944, in winning the air battle, without which achievement the invasion could not safely have been launched, and the continued air attack of Germany might not have been possible. They were concerned with, primarily, the destruction of the G.A.F. Had they concentrated upon the attack of cities they might well have allowed the German fighter force to establish an ascendency over Germany. Had this been done, there would have been nothing to prevent its consolidation. Then, the invasion would have been impracticable or extremely costly; and even if a bridgehead had been established, its exploitation in the face of an effective fighter force would have been problematical.

44. However, for the future, new weapons may make the requisite tempo in the attack of industrial centres a practicable proposition.

45. To my mind one of the major lessons emerging from our war experience is that all target systems, oil, ball-bearings, transportation, or the industrial cities themselves, are resilient under attack; that is, each target attacked may be expected to recover its production, or have its production made good elsewhere, within a period dependent upon the effectiveness of the attack, and the "recovery factor" characteristic of the particular target system. Thus a given scale of effective attack, or "bombing pressure," against a selected system will only depress activity in that system so far, and no farther. If the scale of effective attack which can be applied by the force available, (in the light of its operational capabilities) is sufficient to depress the activity in the selected system below the critical level and to hold it there long enough, then the aim will be achieved – the enemy will be derived the products of that particular activity essential to his continuation of the war. But if the scale of effective attack is not sufficient to depress activity in the selected system as far as the critical level, then even though the bombing be continued indefinitely, no decisive effect can be anticipated.

46. Thus, of the approximately 2,000,000 tons of bombs dropped by the R.A.F. and U.S. Strategic bomber forces in the European theatre, the 9% directed against oil was decisive, while the 24% against industrial cities was not. The number of targets attacked in each system was of the same order. In the case of oil the tempo of attack was ultimately sufficient to keep practically all the plants out of production at the same time; in the case of the cities, however, as shown above, the number out of production at any one time was only a small proportion of the whole.

47. Factors governing the selection of strategic bombing targets should embrace the following:-

(a) The scale of effective attack available – a compost of total bomb lift, operational capability in placing bombs on the target, and the intrinsic destructive power of the bombs carried;

(b) The total number of targets in the target system considered and the percentage of these which must be kept simultaneously out of action to depress the activity of the system below the critical level;

(c) The proportion of the available effort which is required to put one of the targets out of action. This will react upon the number which can be attacked simultaneously, and thus upon the tempo which can be achieved. (This averaged out at about two a month for cities).

(d) The resilience of a typical target in the system; that is, the time required to make good a target's activity, after effective attack. The length of this period governs the minimum tempo of attack which must be achieved to produce a decisive result through the medium of that target system. Thus it is essential to attack effectively, within half the period, at least the proportion of the total number of targets in the system referred to in (b) above.

48. Strategic bombing is essentially a dynamic, as opposed to a static, process; a process in which time is an all pervading factor.

49. Again, in Paragraph 206, the C-in-C suggests the problem of the selection of targets was never satisfactorily solved. I think we got very near to the solution with the Combined Strategic Target Committee system. This certainly worked extremely well, but the work of selection must always depend heavily on intelligence resources. The oil offensive was one of the best examples of the working of target selection and priorities. It is significant that the Americans adopted this system lock, stock and barrel, for the air offensive against Japan. In the case of Bomber Command their reluctance to attack specific targets, born partly of operational inability and partly of their own underestimate of their ability, made it difficult to advocate for them any real target system other than industrial areas – which they wanted most to attack.

COMMENTS ON APPENDIX 'C' OF DESPATCH

50. In my view there are considerable grounds for the complaint which is registered in the opening paragraph of this Appendix.

51. I arrived at the Air Ministry in November 1941, after 14 months in Bomber Command, with a deep seated conviction that whereas the Signals and Navigation branches were always ahead of operational requirements, i.e. they produced new and better equipment while we were reasonably content with the old, the Armament branch lagged behind the minimum operational requirements. This conviction was not dispelled by my experience at the Air Ministry, in spite of the fact that vast improvements in Armament matters did take place in the latter half of the war, probably as a result of readjustments in M.A.P. and in the Air Ministry.

52. My impression is that the failings, if failings there were, were too deep-seated

to be rectified without the most far-reaching measures for which the resources were not then available. It would seem that in the inter-war period air armament development aligned itself in organisation, procedure and tempo with naval guns and artillery, and that its war organisation and establishments were framed accordingly. Thus when the air war came, with its urgent demands for new and better equipment of all kinds, made necessary by rapid changes in the tactical situation or by the widely varied demands upon the flexibility of the bomber force, the armament organisation was taxed beyond its limits, and could not expand and re-organize quickly enough to make up the lee-way.

53. Many examples can be quoted to illustrate this point. No provision had been made before the war to render the 4-lb, incendiary bomb aimable, and even by the end of the war the clustering problem had not been satisfactorily solved. Barometric fuses and hooded flares were pressed for urgently early in 1942, but it was well over a year before the fuses came into use, and much longer before hooded flares were available, and even they were not entirely satisfactory. P.F.F. pyrotechnics were on the other hand developed in a commendable manner, but primarily because a special development organisation had been set up, working on "fire-brigade" lines, with direct contact between the development personnel, the Pathfinder Force and the Air Staff, and with the highest priorities for its requirements.

GENERAL COMMENTS

The Air War

54. Little or no reference has been made in the Bomber Command despatch to the winning of the air war over Europe. It was won almost wholly by the American Strategic Bomber (including fighter) Forces, Bomber Command's contribution being small, and incidental, mainly, to city attacks. The eclipse of the G.A.F. made invasion possible, and the latter resulted, after the summer of 1944, in the disruption of the German early warning system which had previously been deployed throughout France and the Low Countries. It was this factor which made possible the subsequent night bombing of Germany at a low loss rate.

55. It is interesting to speculate upon the progress of the night bomber offensive against Germany through 1944 had the early warning system not been overrun. Our night losses over Germany had risen to serious proportions by early 1944, when the major effort was diverted to short range invasion tasks. At the end of 1943 our scientists were wracking their brains to devise some means of keeping losses down. But they admitted they had little up their sleeves, for the enemy had largely caught upon the great lead we had at first in airborne radar. No.100 Group was formed to exploit all the countermeasures we could command, including night escort fighters. But clearly the fighters could not materially reduce losses, as the relatively few casualties they inflicted on the enemy could easily be sustained. The development of radar was eliminating the advantages of darkness, and bringing day and night tactics

more and more into line. The Air Staff strove to increase the Mosquito bomber force, against which the enemy defences were not orientated, but widespread demands on limited production precluded any solution in this direction.

56. The immediate solution to these problems was provided by the diversion of Bomber Command to invasion tasks over France where the enemy night defences were operating under difficult conditions, followed after D-day by a period of short hours of darkness which in any case precluded deep penetration. Thereafter the advance of the ground forces solved the problem for the duration. But in the winter 1943/44 the situation *was* serious. These points are brought out for two reasons:-

(a) In a future war the advantages of night bombing which we enjoyed in the last, i.e. powers of evasion, are not likely to exist, for the development of radar, essential even in daylight for sub-sonic aircraft, will virtually have eliminated darkness.

(b) A sustained bombing offensive against an enemy country of comparable technical achievement will only be possible once the air war has virtually been won. As the Americans won the air war for us in 1939-1945, we, reflecting primarily on R.A.F. experience, may be in danger of over-looking the importance of this factor. For example, in the development of long range fighters.

Leaflet Dropping

57. No adequate account seems to have been included in the despatch of the large part played by Bomber Command in the propaganda campaign against enemy occupied Europe. Many millions of leaflets were dropped by the Command, and for the sake of completeness some reference to this should surely be made.

58. Conversely, the B.B.S.U. report should include some assessment of the results of this effort in order that an estimate may be made of whether it was worth while, or could better have been expended in some other direction.

Revision of Graphs and Statistics

59. Some of the information contained in the despatch, such as casualty statistics and the graph No.9 in Part V, were necessarily unconfirmed at the time it was written. If the despatch is to be circulated to staff colleges etc. for study or research purposes it would be valuable to correct such information in the light of later knowledge.

28th December, 1946.

ABBREVIATIONS

AA	Anti-Aircraft
AAO	Air Armament Officer
ACAS	Assistant Chief of the Air Staff
ACIU	Allied Central Interpretation Unit
AEAF	Allied Expeditionary Air Force
AES	Armament Experimental Section
AI	Airborne Intercept
AGL	Automatic Gun-Laying
AGS	Air Gunnery School
AM	Air Ministry
AMO	Air Ministry Orders
AOC	Air Officer Commanding
AOC-in-C	Air Officer Commanding-in-Chief
AP	Armour-Piercing
ARP	Air Raid Precautions
ASV	Airborne Surface Vessel (as in Air to Surface Vessel radar)
BAU	Bombing Analysis Unit
BBC	British Broadcasting Corporation
BBRM	British Bombing Research Mission
BBS	British Bombing Survey
BBSU	British Bombing Survey Unit
BCIS	Bomber Command Instructors School
BCDU	Bomber Command Development Unit
BDU	Bombing Development Unit
BSDU	Bomber Support Development Unit
CAS	Chief of the Air Staff
CH	Chain Home
CSBS	Course Setting Bomb Sight
DAS	Damage Assessment Section

DB Ops Directorate of Bomber Operations; Director of Bomber Operations
DCAS Deputy Chief of the Air Staff
DF Direction Finding; also D/F
DP Deep Penetration
DR Dead Reckoning
ESO Engineering Staff Officer
FCLO Flying Control Liaison Officer
FIDO Fog Investigation and Dispersal Operation
Flt Flight
Fps flashes per second
GAF German Air Force (*Luftwaffe*)
GCI Ground Control Intercept/Interception
GD General Duties
GEC General Electric Company (British-based industrial and engineering conglomerate)
GGS Gyroscopic Gun Sight
GH A type of Allied blind bombing device
GHQ General Head Quarters
GP General Purpose
GPI Ground Position Indicator
Gp Group
GPO General Post Office
HC High Capacity
HCU Heavy Conversion Unit
HE High Explosive
HTV High Terminal Velocity
HV High Velocity
IB Incendiary Bombs
ICAN International Commission/Convention for Air Navigation
IF Instrument Flying
IFF Identification Friend or Foe (electronic equipment is used to identify friendly aircraft)
IP Initial Point (easily identified point on the ground from which a ground attack run would be started)
IR Infra-red
IS Intelligence Summary

JPS Joint Planning Staff (before 1941, Joint Planning Sub-committee of the Chiefs of Staff Committee)

LD Long Delay

MAP Ministry of Aircraft Production

MC Medium Capacity

MF Medium Frequency

MG Machine-gun

MPI Mean Point of Impact

MTU Mosquito Training Unit

MU Maintenance Unit

ORS Operational Research Section

OTU Operational Training Unit

PFF Path Finder Force

PFNTU Pathfinder Force Navigation Training Unit; Under the control of No.8 Group, the PFNTU was established at Gransden Lodge on 10 April 1943. The unit's task was to train crews selected from Main Force Squadrons for Pathfinder duties

PPI Plan Position Indicator; This is a cathode ray tube on which is displayed a rotating radar trace which shows in its afterglow the location of echoes known as blips or, in more modern terminology, 'paints'

RAAF Royal Australian Air Force

Radar An object detection system which uses radio waves to determine the range, altitude, direction, or speed of objects

RAE Royal Aircraft Establishment

RAF Royal Air Force

RAFVR Royal Air Force Volunteer Reserve

RCAF Royal Canadian Air Force

RCM Radio Counter Measures

RDF Radio Direction-Finding (as in radar)

RDX Research Department Explosive, an explosive nitro-amine widely used in military and industrial applications

RNZAF Royal New Zealand Air Force

RT, R/T Radio Transmission; Radio Telegraphy

SABS Stabilised Automatic Bomb Sight

SAP Semi-Armour Piercing

SASO Senior Air Staff Officer

SBA Standard Beam Approach

SBC Strategic Bombing Campaign; Small Bomb Containers

SEO Senior Engineering Officer

SHAEF Supreme Headquarters Allied Expeditionary Force; the headquarters of the Commander of Allied forces in north-west Europe, from late 1943 until the end of the war

SIU Special Intelligence Unit

SRR Sortie Raid Reports

TI Target Indicator

TNT Trinitrotoluene; an explosive

TRE Telecommunications Research Establishment

TU Training Unit

USAAF United States Army Air Force

USSTAF United States Strategic and Tactical Air Forces

VCAS Vice-Chief of the Air Staff

VHF Very High Frequency

WRNS Women's Royal Naval Service; popularly and officially known as the Wrens, this was the women's branch of the Royal Navy

INDEX